American Legacy

Volume I
(1492 to 1877)

Douglas G. Beaudoin

Copyright © 2018 Douglas G. Beaudoin

All rights reserved.

ISBN-10: 0692049347
ISBN-13:978-0692049341

DEDICATION

In Memory of
David (Lucky) E. Beaudoin
(1940 -2017)

ACKNOWLEDGMENTS

Cover photo: Artist: Charles Marion Russell
1905 Lewis & Clark, Lower Columbia River
Public Domain Source:
http://en.wikipedia.org/wiki/
Image: Lewis, Clark and Russell

TABLE OF CONTENTS

Introduction

1	Exploration and Colonization	Pg#8
2	Colonies in America	Pg #29
3	Colonial Discontent	Pg #75
4	The American Revolution	Pg #95
5	The Continental Congress	Pg #111
6	The Constitution	Pg #127
7	American Politics	Pg #148
8	The First Industrial Revolution	Pg #191
9	The Jacksonian Era	Pg #279

TABLE OF CONTENTS

10	American Expansionism	Pg#303
11	Prelude to Civil War	Pg #329
12	American Civil War	Pg #358
13	Reconstruction Era	Pg #432
14	American Frontier	Pg #451
	Epilogue	Pg #474
	Appendix A	Pg #476
	References	Pg #482
	Author	Pg #487

DOUGLAS G. BEAUDOIN

"Sad will be the day when the American people forget their traditions and their history, and no longer remember that the country they love, the institutions they cherish, and the freedom they hope to preserve, were born from the throes of armed resistance to tyranny, and nursed in the rugged arms of fearless men."

--- Roger Sherman, Founding Father

INTRODUCTION

American Legacy begins in 1492 and chronicles the history and the lives of the men and women who created a nation from the toils and hardship of life on the American frontier. The reader revisits history and the periods in American history that follows the lives of those who have accomplished so much and in envisioned a new form of government in which the citizenry would be the ultimate power of government. This form of representative democracy would be under constant attack over the next 231 years. The American Revolution ended a period of foreign colonization that lasted 267 years.

Revolutionary patriots such as Nathan Hale stood on the gallows waiting to be hanged as a spy at the age of 22, would declare his list words heard; *"my only regret is that I only have one life to give for my country"*. Patriots and ordinary citizens of the time served their country out of a sense of duty and obligation without personal or monetary gain and with unselfish sacrifice. In this volume of American Legacy, the reader will realize that the founding fathers were not professional statesmen or politicians, but rather ordinary businessmen, frontiersmen and citizens who gathered for a common vision of how life should be in America and in a government who the ultimate authority lays with the people. Most were forced to sell their plantations and estates to pay the debts they accrued while in service to their country, but didn't lose sight of the goal they envisioned or the principals they left behind for all to aspire too.

When the founding fathers wrote the Constitution, they didn't visualize the challenges that lay ahead, nor did they envision the challenges that nearly divided a nation in a Civil War that guaranteed that all men are created equal. Their legacy was an act of devotion that was passed from generation to generation. It is an act supported by a guiding principal based on moral and religious principals of knowing the difference between right and wrong. Throughout history we have at times lost our moral compass, but in the long term, most Americans are pragmatic toward a unified nation regardless of race. Those who have sustained lasting legacies are those who have devoted themselves to the good deeds of humanity. For the politician and president who initiate tax cuts, trade tariffs, regulations and treaties; often fail to realize that these acts do not build upon legacies, but rather they are fiduciary responsibility that goes with the position and the office they hold. It is and always will be the public that determines the legacy of an individual. Historians most often do not necessarily rate one's legacy on his or her political accomplishments, but rather the accomplishment that is carried forward through time and in doing so, their accomplishments are interconnected to their ability to bring a divided nation together as one rather than dividing it in a maladroit way. On occasion, some presidents have attempted to diminish another's legacy by excoriating others accomplishments. History records the events and leaves their accomplishments to be judged by the populous to decide what accomplishments are enduring and those that are not. As political ideologies change over time; what may be politically acceptable today, are often forgotten tomorrow, since people most often remembers a person's failures and seldom remember the accomplishments. A person's legacy transcends the four or eight years in service. Most remember Washington as a General, but seldom remember his accomplishments as the first President. Jefferson wasn't known for his Presidency either, but rather his contribution in writing the Declaration of Independence, Grant wasn't known for his Presidency either, but his service as General of the Union Army during the Civil War, and so on. Poles based on popularity can be misleading and not represent the lasting accomplishments he or she has made. Those that have succeeded have shown a certain demeanor and sincere devotion to bring all people together, regardless of their ethnic and religious beliefs. Today, former presidents devote their lives to charity work long after leaving office. They have become best known for their accomplishment after leaving office than when they were in office; President Jimmy Carter is one that comes to mind. This new trend in post Presidential legacy may well define a new page in Presidential legacy.

As for those who created a lasting legacy who were not Presidents; their accomplishments are recognized in monuments that adorn public parks and public offices and home town museums and their birth places. It is the very least that we can do for those who gave so much.

The greatest legacy one can pass on to one's children and grandchildren is not money or other material things accumulated in one's life, but rather a legacy of character and faith.

-Billy Graham

DOUGLAS G. BEAUDOIN

Chapter 1
Exploration and Colonization

1490 – 1620

Christopher Columbus (Colon)
(1451 – 1506)

Christopher Columbus never set foot on the mainland of North America in October of 1492, nor did he at any time in his life, but rather on an island believed to be San Salvador in the Bermuda Islands in the West Indies. He made four separate voyages during his lifetime and establishing several colonies in the West Indies for the benefit of the Spanish Crown, who financed his exploration. Fate dictated his success and failure and Columbus experienced both. His discovery of the West Indies (Caribbean Islands) wasn't his American legacy, but rather his efforts to colonize the West Indies. European explorers sailed across the Atlantic Ocean and discovered a new Continent, for which he believed was the Island of Japan. The actual discoverer of America was discovered by Ponce de Leon, who landed in Florida, even though he isn't celebrated for his discovery.

Christopher Columbus was born in the Republic of Genoa, Italy in 1451. His real name was Cristoforo Colombo. His father was a wool weaver and owned a small cheese stand on the streets of Genoa. He had three younger brothers and one sister. Columbus was especially close to his youngest brother, Bartolomeo who would later become a cartographer. The two would move to Spain to pursue his cartography trade. Columbus left school at the age of 14 to apprentice himself on a merchant trading ship and over time learned to speak Latin, Portuguese and Castilian (Spanish). Columbus was tall and fair skinned with reddish blond hair that turned prematurely white by the age of 35. He had light blue eyes and a slightly hooked nose. Columbus was a devout Roman Catholic which played an important role in his later life. In 1470, at the age of 19, he made several voyages to Chios in the Aegean Sea, where historians believe he learned celestial navigation and dead reckoning and became among the best in dead reckoning navigation in Spain by the time he was in his mid twenties.

In 1473, Columbus began his career as an apprentice trading agent for the Centurione family of Genoa, Italy. The Centurione family was a well known trade merchant around the Mediterranean and European coastal port areas. In 1477, he moved to Lisbon and partnered with his brother in a small map and book shop and fell in love with Filipa Perestrelo, the daughter of the regional governor in Portugal. They would marry in 1478 and have son; Diego Columbus (spelt Diego Colon at the time). Historians believe that his wife, Filipa may have died in 1485 and after her death Columbus moved to Castile and later remarried and have a second son, Fernando in 1488.

During the 15th century, the Iberian Peninsula was divided into smaller ruling kingdoms; Portugal, Castile, Aragon, Navarre and Granada. The Lower Peninsula was controlled by the Moorish, called Granada. The Iberian Peninsula merged into modern day Spain and Portugal after the Spanish defeated of Granada in 1492. The Kingdom of Castile and Aragon was consolidate into a single state with the marriage of Ferdinand II of Aragon and Isabella I of Castile in 1469 and declared it a catholic state of Espana (Spain) and Portugal in 1479.

Trading between Asia and Europe was conducted using the Silk Road between Europe and China. The Silk Road route used by Marco Polo began in Venice and traveled overland through Turkey, Persia, and India and into China. This was the principal trade route for centuries and was called the Silk Road. With the fall of Constantinople to the Ottoman Turks in 1453 and the creation of the Ottoman Empire, it became difficult and hazardous to transport goods over-land without being hijacked by bandits and by the Ottoman's. It soon became obvious to traders and merchants that a sea route was the best option for importing and exporting goods to and from Cathy (china) and the East Indies.

It was well established at the time of Aristotle, that the earth was spherical rather than flat contrary to American history books. This fact was documented and recorded by Ptolemy as far back as 723 AD. In the third century BC, Eratosthenes calculated that the earth was 24,000 miles in circumference, but the distance to Cathy (China) from Europe by sea was unknown. Ptolemy estimated that China was 180 degrees longitude, rather than the actual 130 degrees west from Europe. Ptolemy surmised that China was on the opposite side of the planet, 180 degrees from Europe, even though it was just an estimate.

Columbus estimated the longitude of Japan as 225 degrees west, which equated to only 135 degrees of ocean between Europe and China. He also estimated that the Canary Islands in the Atlantic lay only 2,300 miles from Japan, when in fact is of historical importance. His miscalculation led Columbus to believe that if he sailed west from Spain it would take only a month or two to sail to Japan and China. Had he not miscalculated his distances, he may not have ever attempted to sail across the Atlantic at all. It is also worth noting that small ships at the time were only 100 feet long and were unable to carry enough food or water for long voyages lasting longer than two months. Time and distance was a critical element in planning early explorations by ship. Scurvy was common on long voyages and the loss of life of a working shipboard crew was essential to its success, since experienced crew could not be replaced. Fresh water was also a serious factor, since water was stored in oak barrels for long periods of time they became rancid and implantable. The British carried alcohol to replace water, however, Columbus being deeply religious, never allowed alcohol aboard his ships.

Columbus's major obstacle was finding a patron to finance his voyage.

In 1485, he approached Italy, Portugal, England and Spain with his proposal, but all refused based on his estimated distance to China, which was vastly different than Ptolemy's calculations centuries before. In 1488, Bartolomeu Dias of Portugal found a route around the Cape of Good Hope and the southern tip of Africa to trading ports in the East Indies in Asia. The new discovery of a sea route to Cathy circumvented the treacherous overland route through Asia Minor and rendered Columbus's proposed western route across the Atlantic too risky and unfeasible. Even worse, it minimized Columbus's sales pitch to persuade a sponsor to finance his western route to Japan and China. As years passed, in January of 1492, King Ferdinand and Queen Isabella would finally conquer Granada and control most of Iberian Peninsula. Ferdinand decided to reconsider Columbus's proposal and enter into negotiations. By January of 1492, an agreement was reached in which all lands discovered by Columbus would be governed by Columbus under the title of Admiral of the Ocean and Seas and Viceroy and Governor of all the new lands he claimed under Spain. In addition, Columbus was to receive 10 percent of all revenues from any new land discovered in perpetuity and one-eighth interest in any commercial venture from its profits. As was customary with explorers at the time, the terms and of the agreement was based on Columbus colonizing the lands he discovered and firmly taking possession of them on behalf of Spain.

His flag ship the Santa Maria, was a converted merchant ship with a length of 75 feet and a beam of 25 feet. It had three masts and 5 sails. The two other ships in his fleet were the Pinta (Pint) and the Santa Clara, nicknamed the Nina (Girl). On August 3, 1492, all three ships departed Palos de la Frontera, Spain and arrived in the Canary Islands to replenish its food and water. They departed the Canary Islands on September 6th and after five weeks of sailing; Juan Rodriguez Bermeo spotted land which was presumed to have been San Salvador Island, Bermuda   He would then sail to the northeast coast of Cuba and anchor on October 28th. He departed Cuba and sailed to the northern coast of Hispaniola, known today as Haiti/Dominican Republic, in which he would name "Dominica". On October 12th, Columbus ran Santa Maria aground and abandons it and transferred his flag to the Nina and sailed back to Spain with the news of his discovery.

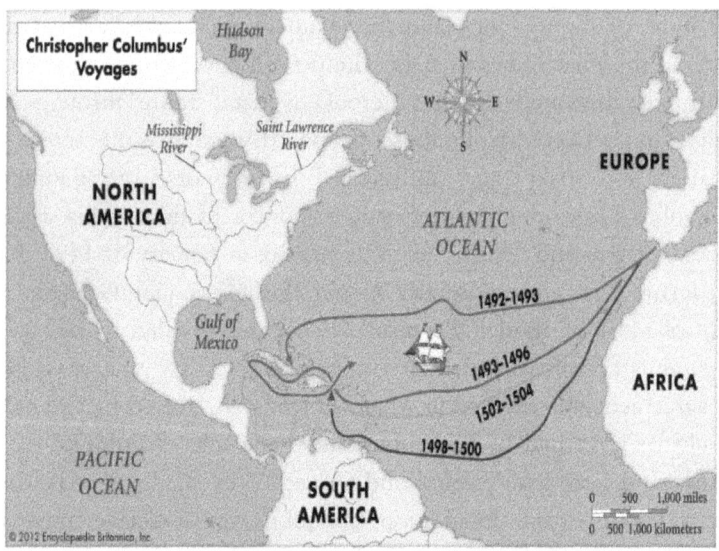

Map 1, Columbus' four routes to the West Indies

On his second voyage, 1,200 men and supplies were loaded aboard ships in an effort to establish a permanent colony on Dominica, named La Navidad. From Dominica he discovered the Greater Antilles, Puerto Rico, Jamaica and other islands in the Caribbean. On his third and fourth voyage, he continued to explore the Caribbean, Central America and the coast of South America. He served as Governor of all lands claimed for Spain. In 1500, he was accused of tyranny, brutality and torture of the Spanish colonist and was over powered by the Spanish colonist and arrested and returned to Spain to stand trial, however, his crimes were pardoned by the Crown and he was allowed to return to the colonies, but stripped of his governorship.

By the time of his fourth voyage, he was plagued by arthritis, gout and serious eye problems. His health was slowly deteriorating and he spent days and weeks in bed. On May 20, 1506, at the age of 54, Columbus died while in Spain. His legacy stands out as a person who took a risk that other explores dare not take because of the unknown certainty of his success. Most explorers view Columbus' voyage as too risky with a high probability of failure. It wasn't as much as the discovery of the West Indies, but rather his discovery opened the door for further exploration which would lead other explorers; Amerigo Vespucci in 1501 who explored South and Central America. Vespucci's maps and charts would bear the name of Amerigo for which South and North America would bare his name. **[1-1]**

Juan Ponce de Leon
(1460 – 1521)

Juan Ponce de Leon was born in 1460 in a noble family in Santervas De Campos, Spain (Aragon). He became a soldier and fought in the war between Spain and Granada as a conquistador in 1492. After the war, he heard of Columbus's exploration in the new world and volunteered for duty as a conquistador for Columbus's second voyage in 1493. During Columbus's second voyage, 200 men volunteered to remain in Dominica and establish colony. As a reward, they were given land grants to develop plantations using local slave labor.

Ponce de Leon would be one of the gentlemen plantation owners that remained behind to colonize. In 1502, Nicolas de Ovando was appointed governor of Hispaniola (Dominica). He requested Ponce de Leon to put-down a rebellion by the Tainos Indians who attacked and took over a Spanish garrison on the east side of the island. For his reward, Governor Ovando gave him a land grant and slaves to build a plantation that provided supplies to returning Spanish ships to Spain. He prospered financially and developed a portion of his land into a gold mine. He would later marry Lenora, an Inn Keepers daughter, and have three children together.

As his business prospered and his wealth grew, it was rumored that the island of Puerto Rico had large deposits of gold as well. He decided to explore the island and prospect for gold in 1508. After exploring the island and finding gold, he moved to Puerto Rico with his family and operated a large scale mining operation. He was appointed Governor of San Juan Bautista by King Ferdinand II of Aragon 1509.

In Spain, a law suit was filed in the Royal Court on behalf of Columbus's heirs to his estate by his son Diego Colon (Columbus), over the inherited rights from Columbus's original terms of the agreement granted by King Ferdinand II and Queen Isabella in 1492. Diego Colon prevailed in his law suit and Governor Ovando would be replaced by Diego Colon and named Viceroy and Governor of the Spanish colonies as a result of his father's discovery. Diego Colon and Ponce de Leon became political rivals over the next two years and their relationship would gradually deteriorate. As enemies, Ponce de Leon's plantation fell under the control of Diego Colon, the newly appointed Governor of Spanish West Indies. Ponce de Leon was proclaimed Governor of Puerto Rico by Governor Ovando, but Diego Colon stripped him of his title in Puerto Rico.

Ponce de Leon pursued other ventures beyond the reach of Diego Colon's authority. King Ferdinand II commissioned Ponce de Leon in 1512 to search for new lands northwest of Hispaniola in which slave traders claimed they saw islands northwest which the sailors called Biminis Islands. The islands they were referring to was the Bahamas off the coast of Florida or part of the Bermuda Islands.

The Crown sent Ponce de Leon a royal contract; that outlined the terms and conditions of his exploration. He was to finance, out–of–pocket; all expenses including men, ships and the cost of colonization for all new territory discovered. In exchange, the King would grant him Governorship for life for all new lands and territories discovered outside of those of Diego Colon. In addition, a formula for distribution of gold and profits from the land, including the capture of

Natives for slaves was addressed. This arrangement would free him from the reaches of Diego Colon, since Colon's contract only applied to the Spanish West Indies.

Ponce de Leon purchased and supplied three ships with 200 men and departed Puerto Rico for the Biminis Islands on March 4, 1513. Twenty-three days later they sighted an island, which historians believe may have been the Bahamas Islands since the Bermuda Islands were south of Florida. They continued due west in open water until April 2, 1513, when land was once again sighted land, believing it also was an island. He would name the island La Florida, meaning "The Flowers". They came ashore near Melbourne Beach or perhaps north near St. Augustine, the exact location is unknown. After five days, they continued south along the coast and landed at Key Biscayne and took-on fresh drinking water. They continue to sail south looking for a passage through the Florida Keys and north towards the Florida Panhandle, which would be Pensacola, the exact location is once again unknown. Some historians claim he only sailed as far as Tampa and Fort Meyers on his first voyage based on ship navigation logs.

They had several encounters with unfriendly Calusa Native Americans but would anchor in a bay near present day Fort Meyers. They were attacked from canoes by whirling arrows from their long bows as the ships were anchored, which kept them from going ashore and exploring further. Other attempts to land resulted in more skirmishes with the Calusa. After several attempts, they were able to land and capture eight Calusa Natives and took them aboard the ship as slaves. They sailed toward Puerto Rico in late June and met a Spanish slave trading ship under the command of Diego Miruelo. They encountered the ship several days later as it had run aground on a reef during a storm. His fleet arrived in Puerto Rico on December 19, 1513. Some historians suggest that Diego Colon may have ordered Diego Miruelo to follow de Leon's fleet and spy on his discoveries, however it is unlikely. Ponce de Leon arrived in Puerto Rico and immediately sailed to Spain to inform Ferdinand of his discovery before Diego

Colon had an opportunity to claim his discovery as his own. He was knighted and given a coat of arms. His discovery was added to the maps of the New World including navigation charts for future explorations. A new contract was drawn giving Ponce de Leon the right to govern Biminis and Florida, which at the time was still considered a large island rather than the North American Continent.

While in Spain, three ships were purchased for a second voyage to Florida. Ponce de Leon departed Spain in May 14, 1515 for the voyage to Puerto Rico. From his base in Puerto Rico, he sailed to Florida and around the Florida Keys to the mainland of the southwestern tip of Florida and encountered the Calusa Natives once again. A battle ensued and he was forced to return to Puerto Rico. King Ferdinand II died in 1516, so it was imperative that he establish a colony in Florida in keeping with his contract. After returning to Puerto Rico, he organized his last voyage in 1521 and boarded 50 horses, domestic livestock, tools and 200 men and set sail to Florida to establish a colony near the Caloosahatchee River; situated on the southwest coast near present day Fort Meyers. The colonists were immediately attacked by the Calusa which ended with Ponce de Leno being wounded in the thigh with a presumably poison arrow. His wounds were not life threatening however, or so they thought and they set sail back to Havana, Cuba where Ponce de Leon would die of his injuries. Contrary to historical legend, Ponce de Leon's mission to find the fountain of youth was perhaps mostly myth. No record exists of him mentioning a search for a fountain of youth and as many history books suggest. He had expressed an interest in finding a fountain of youth year prior, but it was never mentioned in his contract or ships logs.

Juan Ponce de Leon's legacy however, was over shadowed by Christopher Columbus's discovery of the Spanish West Indies. Ponce de Leon wasn't the first European to set foot in North America; the Norsemen had landed in Newfoundland and Labrador around 1000 AD, but never established a permanent colony. Ponce de Leon was a renaissance man. He was a man of many skills, known today as a renaissance man; a farmer, plantation owner, governor, miner, businessman, explorer, soldier and sea captain. He was successful in every venture he undertook except establishing a permanent Spanish colony in Florida, however it was not without trying. It is important to note, that Spain made two more attempts to colonize America after his death, all of which failed. It wasn't until the French establish a fort on the banks of the St. Johns River in 1564 that Spain renewed its interest in colonizing Florida, partly out of fear that the French would claim Florida as its own possession. [1-2]

As for Diego Colon, he was named Governor of the West Indies in August of 1508 and built a home, Alcazar de Colon in Santo Domingo (Dominican Republic). Diego's relationship with King Ferdinand's royal officials deteriorated and Diego was recalled back to Spain in 1514. After the death of King Ferdinand in 1516, he was reinstated as governor in 1520 by King Charles. King Charles would recall Diego back to Spain over an incident that involved a native revolt in 1520 and a slave revolt in 1522 in Santo Domingo. He would die in Spain in 1526, his father's estate, Christopher Columbus, would eventually be settled between his remaining heirs in 1536.

France's Quest for Florida

After Ponce de Leon's death in 1521, King Francis I of France renewed his interest in finding a trade route west, possibly a northwest passage from the Atlantic to the Pacific. Francis I commissioned the Italian explorer Geovanni Da Verrazzano to sail across the Atlantic and find a trade route to Asia and claim any new land discovered for France. Florida was considered to be an Island by the Spanish, while some speculated that it may be part of a new continent, since early fishing fleets from Europe had fished the waters off the coast of Newfoundland for cod as early as 1473, 19 years before Columbus set sail to the West Indies. Early fishing expeditions didn't map or chart the mainland or record their landings on the continent. It is conceivable that the fishermen would have landed somewhere on North America to replenish fresh water and supplies for their ships before sailing back to Europe. Ships of the period always carried long boats aboard to go ashore for loading barrels of water and provisions for long voyages.

In 1523, the Italian explorer, Verrazzano, set sail from France with four ships. He encountered a violent storm that forced them to sail south toward Spain and Portugal. Two of his ships were lost and presumed sunk while the other two, La Dauphine and La Normande, returned to France for repairs. They set sail again due south and landed at Maderia Island, 250 miles north of the Canary Islands. The La Normande was forced to return to France after having mechanical problems and the La Dauphine would set sail alone on January 24, 1524 to Florida.

On March 1st he arrived off the coast of Cape Fear, North Carolina, believing that it was the beginning of the Pacific Ocean, which in retrospect makes little sense. He continued north, skirting along the coast of New England until reaching the mouth of the Hudson River and followed along the shore of Long Island and entered Narragansett Bay. After several weeks exploring the area, he headed north and followed the coast while mapping as far north as Maine, Nova Scotia and Newfoundland. He returned to France in July of 1524. The new territory discovered would be recorded on the maps as New France.

Subsequent voyages included exploring Florida and the Bahamas and Lesser Antilles. His death remains a mystery, but it is believed he died in 1528 on the island of Guadeloupe in the Lesser Antilles. His legacy and explorations were over shadowed by Magellan's circumnavigation around the world and Hernan Cortes conquest of Mexico in 1521. Little notice was given him for charting America's eastern seaboard, which would be used by other explores in establishing colonies in the new world. Henry Hudson would use his charts to explore the eastern seaboard and the Hudson River in New York.

King Phillip II of Spain assigned Admiral Don Pedro Menendez de Aviles with the task of colonizing Florida and proclaimed him as Governor of Florida and the newly discovered islands (excluding the Spanish West Indies) near the Florida coast. He arrived at an old abandoned Native Indian village on the east coast of Florida, 40 miles south of the St. Johns River in 1565, and established a well fortified fort that was designed to protect the colony from pirates and natives. The fort was continually under attack by Native Americans Indians but remained a viable Fort and would be re-named St. Augustine. Over the next nine years, he developed a working relationship with the local native's tribes. After his death in 1574, his nephew, Pedro Menendez Marquez was appointed the Governor of Florida; however one year earlier, the French established a fort on the St. Johns River named Fort Caroline. The Spanish under the command of Aviles dispatched troops to Fort Caroline and attacked the Fort, killing all the French colonist and French troops. Over the next 35 years, the Spanish attempted to establish colonies and missions as far north as Chesapeake Bay and as far west as Pensacola, but only St. Augustine would endure. Disease, starvation and Indian attacks hampered attempts to establish a permanent colony other than St. Augustine.

The Spanish and Portuguese dominated exploration and colonization in both North and South America until 1568. Colonization was a means of accumulating wealth by colonizing new lands and developing new trade routes and territories. Plantations were established in the colonies for producing cotton and tobacco and other exports such as sugar cane. Gold and Silver was also a driving force for colonization. The European monetary trade system was called mercantilism which will be discussed in detail later in the book. France began to make attempts to establish colonies by the end of the 16th century; however, much of the West Indies, South America and Central America were claimed by Spain and Portugal. England began to colonize and explore after the French established Fort Caroline in 1564 in the Carolina's, however it began a race between the two countries to colonize new frontiers in North America. During the eight year war in

Europe, called the "Dutch Revolt" between the Netherland's and Spain in 1568, the war eventually bankrupt Spain on two different occasions and forced Spain to cease supplying their colonies with men and provisions. Spain concentrated their efforts on overland explorations in Mexico and the American southwest. Partly in search of gold and silver that would replenish their treasuries. It would open the door to France and England to colonize and claim vast territories yet to be explored in Canada and the interior of America. England seized the opportunity of Spain's misfortune by colonizing Virginia and New England. England was late in colonization, partly because of the frequent wars between rivals in Europe. But once they anchored a foot-hold in New England, they defended their acquisition with their superior military and naval force.

Roanoke Colony (1584)

Queen Elizabeth I granted Sir Walter Raleigh a charter to colonize North America in the spring of 1584. His charter specified that he was to establish a colony in America; else he would forfeit his charter and the right to colonize and reap any profits he derived from it. The original purpose for establishing a colony in America was not intended for trade alone, but rather establishing a port and a base in which privateers could operate from. Privateers were government sanctioned pirates who raided ships for a portion of the booty they captured. The Crown would pay the privateer set percentage of the proceeds. France, England, Spain, Portugal and the Netherlands were active in sanctioned high seas piracy. It was not only profitable for the Crown but it served as a means of replenishing a crown's treasuries by seizing their ships and cargo and recruiting able bodied seamen. Rogue pirates not representing any particular country were considered pirates and if caught, were hanged, but privateers were not considered pirates, at least not in the eyes of the government who sponsored them.

Raleigh's Charter to establish a colony had another motive; he was to construct a military fort against Spanish invasion in the event war between England and Spain, which appeared to be imminent at the time. By 1584, much of the eastern sea board of America was mapped and charted. A number of settlements were established in Canada by the French and in Florida by the Spanish, but most colonies failed after a few years. In 1584, Raleigh sent an expedition to sail along the east coast of America to find a suitable location for a citadel. His expedition leaders Phillip Anadas and Arthur Barlowe selected Roanoke, Virginia as a possible site. A second expedition was sent the following year with five ships commanded by Richard Grenville, but during the voyage across the Atlantic, they encountered a severe storm and two ships failed to arrive at the designated rendezvous point in Puerto Rico. Grenville departed Puerto Rico without his two ships, but gave instructions that should the two ships arrive in Puerto Rico, they were to continue to Roanoke. One ship run aground off the coast of Virginia and most of the food supplies were lost or damaged, however they elected to off-load the 107 passengers on Roanoke Island to start constructing a fort.

The plan was to return the following April of 1586 with fresh provision for the Roanoke settlers. The settlers constructed a fort, but by June of 1586, the relief ships failed to arrive due to a declared war with Spain. As a result of the war, the Spanish implemented a blockade of all shipping in and out of England. In the summer of 1586, local Powhatan Natives attacked the fort which was first repelled by the colonist. Sir Francis Drake, hearing the news of the attack, sailed north from the Caribbean to Roanoke on his way back to England and offered assistance to the colony. Several colonists elected to return to England with him, while the rest remained. In 1587, Raleigh sent another fleet with 115 colonists led by John White, to establish a colony at Chesapeake Bay. White made an attempt to send a party to Roanoke by ship, but was forced to return due to bad weather. The war with Spain further hampered any rescue efforts and was unable to send a resupply ship from England. Many ships were being pirated by privateers and any further attempt to resupply the Roanoke colony was terminated until August of 1590. When White finally returned to Roanoke, he found the colony deserted with only the name "Croatoan" carved on a tree. The island of Croatoan lay 50 miles north, which is known today as Hatteras Island. When they arrived at the island they found no evidence of a settlement or any colonist. Some speculate that the Roanoke colonist were starving and left the Roanoke Colony. Some believe they assimilated into Croatoan Native tribes. Years later, colonist reported seeing light skinned Croatoan Natives in the forest while hunting. The mystery of the lost colony has never been solved. [1-3]

By 1600, Spain and Portugal were still the major colonial powers in the Caribbean, Central America, South America and Florida. In 1600, more than 500 ships annually were fishing off the coast of Newfoundland and Nova Scotia for cod. The French established trading posts along the Saint Lawrence River for buying furs and establishing a presence in eastern Canada. At this point in time, England had only established a colony at Chesapeake Bay while Roanoke no longer existed.

The war with Spain depleted the treasuries for both Spain and England and both wanted private enterprise and investors to finance the cost of establishing colonies in North America under a charter granted by the crown.

The charters were issued by the ruling monarchs of the time; Queen Elizabeth I and after her death in 1603, by James I (1603 – 1625), Charles I (1625 – 1649) and Charles II. The Virginia Company of London was granted a charter to establish a new colony at Fort Jamestown, Virginia in May of 1607 by King James I. Other European countries were already active in establishing colonies in the West Indies, Central America, Mexico and Florida. England was concerned that they may have missed a rare opportunity to establish their own trading colony in the new world. Spain and France had already established colonies throughout the West Indies and expanded their influence on the mainland America.

Jamestown-Chesapeake Bay Colony (1609)

In 1607, English entrepreneurs' set sail on three ships under the command of Captain Christopher Newport, bound for America. They landed in America at Cape Henry, and explored along the coast to find a suitable location for a new colony. The new site was to be defensible against invasion by the Spanish and French as well as the local Native Americans in the area. The site selected was Chesapeake Bay at the confluence of the James River; however it was marsh land of tidal salt flats, unsuitable for agriculture. In the first year from 1609 and 1610, more than 80% of the colonist died of disease and starvation. It would be abandoned temporarily but later more colonists arrived and would reconstruct the colony once again further inland on higher ground. The Virginia Company also established a second colony at St. George in Bermuda in 1608. Fort James would later encompass a village outside the citadel in 1619, the village however burned down during the Bacon's Rebellion in 1676.

Bacon's Rebellion (1676)

William Berkeley was appointed governor of the Jamestown Colony in 1676 by the Virginia Company of London. As settlers pour into Virginia to establish plantations they were under constant attacks by the Native Americans who gradually encroached further west into the Virginia territory. Nathaniel Bacon was a settler and insisted that Governor Berkeley use military force to drive the American Natives further west so as the settlers were not under the constant threat of attacks. Berkeley refused to get involved and Bacon amassed nearly 1,000 settlers to march against the colonial government in Jamestown, forcing Berkeley to flee Jamestown. The settlers set fire to Jamestown and burned it to the ground. Two ships from England arrived to quell the uprising and as a result 23 colonists were hanged, however Bacon was not one of them, since he had died of dysentery in October of 1676. Eventually, the rebellion was quelled and only a few pockets remained entrenched in the wilderness. King Charles II launched an investigation and recalled Berkeley back to England. Changes in the government followed; with voting rights to land owners, reduction in taxes and a more aggressive approach toward Native American attacks upon colonist.

John Rolfe (1585 – 1622)

John Rolfe set sail aboard from England aboard a supply ships in 1610, bound for the Virginia colonies. The ship landed in the Bermuda Islands for resupply. Rolfe noticed that the Spaniards had planted tobacco years earlier that had grown wild. He harvested the seeds to take to Jamestown to grow, but the tobacco wasn't especially popular in England. A year later he acquired a much sweeter tobacco from the Orinoco River in Guiana and planted it on his farm 30 miles upstream on the James River in Virginia. It was the first introduction of tobacco to America, which became Virginia's cash crop. John Rolfe became wealthy by exporting tobacco to England. He would later marry Pocahontas, the daughter of Chief Powhatan, which led to several years of peace between the colonist and the Powhatan Natives. Pocahontas would die in 1617 while visiting England.

Investors in England funded the colonization and development of large tracks of land for tobacco using John Rolfe's seeds. The plantations were called; "hundreds", which was a plantation capable of producing and supporting enough food to support 100 colonists, most of which worked on the plantations as indentured workers or servants for a specified period of time under a contract, most often from three to seven years.

By 1617, there were dozens of "hundreds" scattered along the rivers of the Chesapeake Bay area. This was also the case in Bermuda as well. Such names as Smith's Hundred, Martin's Hundreds, Bermuda Upper Hundreds and Shirley Hundreds were scattered throughout the Chesapeake Bay region and islands.

Many from England were given passage across the Atlantic for exchange as indentured workers and servants for a negotiated period of time. At the term of their service, they were given land, often 50 acres. Europeans, such as Germans, Danes and Dutch, were called "redemptioners" in which they paid a portion of their passage and agreed to pay the remainder when they got a job in the new colony.

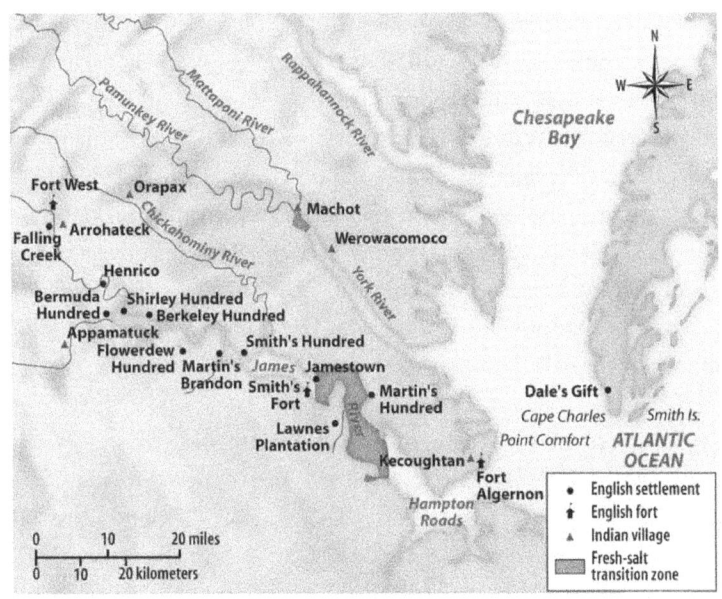

Map 2, Chesapeake Bay Colony

Few settlers realized the risk and hardship they may encounter in America and few survived the first year. The colonist arrived by ship with the vision of starting a new life, but most were ill prepared for what lay ahead. Of the 6,000 settlers that arrived at Jamestown between 1608 and 1624, only 3,400 survived.

In 1608, the Virginia Company of investors weren't happy about the colony in Jamestown. Jamestown struggled during the first few years, with starvation being a factor and unable to produce little in return on their initial investment. In 1609, in an effort to recover their investment, the Company sold shares in the company valued at 12 ½, 25 and 50 pounds per share. There dividends were promised from the sale of gold, land and commodities recovered in Virginia over a seven year period. Since their charter allowed the company to establish their own laws and punishment of the colonist, they appointed Sir Thomas Gates and Sir Thomas Dale to govern the colony with an autocratic and dictatorial hand. Because of the reputation the colonies had toward the harsh treatment of colonist, few volunteered to relocate to Jamestown. By 1618, the Virginia Company continued to lose money and Sir Edwin Sandy; the Company Treasurer implemented the "Virginia Headright System". The systems plan was to distribute 50 acres to each person who paid their own way to Jamestown and another 50 acres for each person they brought along. He gave 100 acres to each investor and changed the governing body into an elected assembly of colonist. By 1619, tobacco plantations extended throughout the Chesapeake Bay area of Virginia. Colonies were no longer called colonies but cities.

In 1734 by order of the King of England, there were four cities within the region; Charles, Elizabeth, Henrico and James. Greater Virginia was divided into eight counties called shires. There were about 15,000 native America's within the Chesapeake Bay area, mostly Powhatan, and as the settlers moved inland for better soil to plant crops, conflicts developed between the colonist and the Powhatan Native Americans. Because of the sites selected, much of the energy of the colonist was focused on building forts rather than growing food. The investors in England were becoming frustrated after several supply ships returning from Jamestown contained little trading commodities to pay for the cost of the voyage. They sent Captain John Smith to the colony with laborers and craftsmen to help make Jamestown a profitable colony, however, Smith would be injured and returned to England shortly after arriving. Governor Baron De La Warr, for which the State of Delaware was named, arrived in 1610 as his replacement.

Since tobacco was labor intensive, a Portuguese ship arrived in 1619 from the West Indies carrying 50 African men, women and children to Jamestown, which was perhaps the first introduction of slaves to America. The land around Jamestown expanded further west along the river system where the soil was better for agriculture and in particular tobacco.

While Jamestown was finally becoming a permanent settlement in America, the influx of colonist from Europe began arriving by the hundreds with each trading ship, and "back-hauling" tobacco and other trade goods to England. Williamsburg, Virginia at the time was called Middle Plantation and later became a fortified settlement between the James and York Rivers in Virginia in 1632.

In the beginning, it was a fort designed for the protection from the Powhatan Natives who conducted regular raids against the encroaching settlers in the territory. In 1699, Williamsburg later became the Capital of Virginia after the State House in Jamestown burned down in 1698.

The Plymouth Colony (1620)

Catherine of Aragon was the daughter of Queen Isabella I of Castile and Ferdinand II of Aragon. When she was 16, she married Henry VIII's Brother, Arthur in 1501, but he died five months later. Henry VIII saw the opportunity and married Catherine of Aragon in 1509. Henry VIII became romantically involved with Anne Boleyn during his marriage with Catherine. King Henry wanted to annul his marriage to Catherine and marry Ann Boleyn, but Pope Clement VII refused to annul the marriage on religious grounds, principally being Roman Catholic. In retaliation, against the Pope, King Henry banned the Roman Catholic Church from conducting religious services in England in 1534. As a religious replacement, King Henry created the Church of England and declares himself the Supreme Head of the Church and proclaimed he was to govern over all religious matters in

England.

Over the years, King Henry purged the priest and laymen who practiced Catholicism in England. Even his closest confidants such, as Sir Thomas Moore, Cardinal Thomas Wolsey and Thomas Cromwell were ordered to swear allegiance to the King and to the Church of England and denounce Catholicism. Those who refused were stripped of their title and positions and in some cases, executed, such was the case of his most trusted confidante, Sir Thomas Moore. King Henry died as a result of complications of his obesity in 1547.

After the death of Henry VIII, his half brother Edward I ascended the throne and ruled until his death in 1553. Upon Edward's death, Edward stated in his Royal Will that Lady Jane Grey become Queen Regent, however she was deposed by Mary I of Scotland shortly after becoming Queen. Mary I was a Catholic, whereas Elizabeth, the eldest daughter of Henry VIII, was a protestant in the Church of England, which became a rivalry between the two sisters. Mary I ordered the arrested of Elizabeth and placed her in prison for one year for allegedly supporting the protestant rebels. After five years under Mary's rule, Elizabeth usurped the throne from Mary with the support of Parliament at which Elizabeth imprisoned Mary I and later executed her. Elizabeth I became the Queen of England until her death in 1603.

James VI of Scotland, the great grandson of Mary of Scotland, ascends the throne as James I, who supported the protestant faith and in particular, the Church of England. Under the 1559 Act of Uniformity, parliament passed a law that made attendance in the Church of England mandatory and the use of the 1522 Book of Common Prayer compulsory. James I wasted little time to punish and impose fines and imprisonment for those who didn't attend the church, refused to sign an allegiance to the Church of England or for conducting religious services and religious meetings inside their homes. This included all forms of religions, not just Catholicism.

Chapter 2
Colonies in America

1620- 1760

Colonizing America involved being awarded by being appointed or bequeathed a Colonial Charter by the King of England. A group of investors gathered to form a company and finance an expedition and establish a single or multiple townships in the new American colony. During the early period of colonization in North America; Netherlands, Spain, France and England were eager to expand their colonies and territories in North America. Sweden had a small colony in up-state New York, but by 1620, much of the colonies along America's eastern sea board were eventually taken-over by England, either by negotiation or by force. There were two colonies that remained after the American Revolution; Florida, which was claimed by Spain and the Louisiana territory claimed by France. The western panhandle of Florida was part of the Louisiana territory. England still had forts in the Ohio River Valley and refused to give them up after the American Revolution, which would later be resolved through negotiation and eventually the war of 1812, which will be discussed later.

One of the confusing aspects of American colonial history was the frequent and broad use of the term "Colony". Trade companies made a request to the King to issue a charter for land to establish a colony for trade in a newly discovered and acquired territory in America as well as other parts of the undiscovered world. The charters would be called colonies; however, as more and more settlements "sprang-up" they too were given land grants within the colonial territory and the original colony was in essence administered as a Province, in which the term "colony" was interchangeably used. The Massachusetts Bay Colony would in fact become a Province, and of course later a State, which incorporated several other colonies and settlements that fell under the jurisdiction of the original territorial colonial Charter. Within the Massachusetts Bay Colony; Plymouth and Dorchester Companies were chartered colonies within Massachusetts, which later became incorporated into the Massachusetts Bay Colony. Some of the original thirteen colonies became known as provinces; such as North and South Carolina and Georgia. Maine was the exception, since Maine became annexed by the Massachusetts Bay Colony and later the State of Massachusetts until Maine became a State in 1820 and new boundaries were drawn in what is now New England.

During the period of exploration, colonies were established on behalf of independent countries. Ownership of new territory was recognized by the establishment as permanent colonies and settlements. Foreign governments commissioned trading companies to construct and finance new colonies at their own expense; in exchange for a trade monopoly with future profits from the colony. The Charters were issued by the Monarch that allowed them the freedom to establish their own colonial governments and laws with little or no oversight from the mother country. It was also understood that the colonial government could not make laws that supersede the laws of the mother country or violate the terms of the charter itself. The final authority rested upon the Monarch, who had complete authority to void or vacate or extend the charter at anytime and for any reason. Each of the original chartered colonies was ruled differently from one another. Once a Colony became profitable, the Monarch often proclaimed the charter void and declared it a Crown or Royal Colony of England. The Royal Charter was governed by a Lord who was appointed by Parliament and approved by the Monarch.

There were 3 basic Charters issued by the Parliament and the King of England:

1. Proprietary Charter,
2. Royal Charter
3. Joint Stock or Corporate Charter.

Proprietary Charters gave deeded land to lords, who where most often of English nobility. There could be any number of proprietary lords to a particular territory; such was the case in New Jersey and Pennsylvania who had only one Proprietary Lord; William Penn, however Carolina and Georgia had eight, of which were Earl's, Baron's, and Duke's from England, while several were knighted by the King as well for prior services rendered to the Crown. Charters allowed ownership by hereditary; such was the case in the Carolina Colony. In the Province of Maryland, George Calvert, 1st Baron of Baltimore, was a former Secretary of State to King Charles I. Upon his death in 1632, his son, Cecil Calvert, 2nd Baron of Baltimore, was named Governor of Maryland. Proprietary Lords managed the land for which they administered. For those living on the land it was expected that they pay rent, called "Quitrents" to the Land Lord. To raise money, the land lord would sell or disperse land to settlers and levy taxes based on the amount of acreage they purchased or leased.

> Royal Charters where Colonies that were taken over by the King in the event that a Proprietary Charter or Joint Stock Corporate Charter who violated the terms of the Charter. Such being the case in the Massachusetts Bay Colony when the King vacated the charter and made it a Royal Charter as a result of the "Salem Witch Hunts" in which 16 were hung under the suspicion of being witches. An action such as this was a direct violation of British law where due process was paramount in the legal system.

There were three Joint Stock Charter colonies in New England; Massachusetts, Rhode Island and Connecticut. In a charter colony, England granted more liberties and allowed them to self-govern the colony. Massachusetts Bay Colony was allowed to self-govern but had turned into a theocracy and had to be contained by appointing a

Governor authorized by King James II. Connecticut and Rhode Island colonies remained a self-governed charter even after the signing of the Declaration of Independence and after the Revolutionary War. They would adapt the original written charter as part of their State Constitution.

Joint Stock Charters where given to Companies who issued stock to investors. The thirteen original colonial boundaries had changed over the next 150 years under English colonial rule, thus the Plymouth Colony would be absorbed by the Massachusetts Bay Colony in 1691 and the Salem Colony in 1629 and the Dorchester Company Colony in 1624. The Province of Maine was granted a charter in 1622, but would be purchased by the Massachusetts Bay Colony in 1677. King James II would vacate the Massachusetts Bay Colony Charter and rename it the "Dominion of New England" in 1686 (discussed later in the Chapter). This was an example of how colonies and provinces at the time merged and became absorbed by other colonies for financial gain encouraged by trading company and their investors back in London.

The Pilgrims (1620)

The term "pilgrim" was a broad term used to represent a group of people leaving their homeland for new frontiers, not just for the sole reasons of expressing and practicing their religious theology, but for the independence and free land being offered by the colonial investors to settle in a new frontier. The actual number of religious Separatist who sailed to Plymouth aboard the "Mayflower" was only about 40 out of the 101. Sixty were either employees of the Trading Company or individual adventurers seeking to resettle in a new frontier that either paid for their own passage or entered into a contract with the investors to assist in establishing a colony for a period of time in exchange for land and free passage. Most often the term of the contract was for 3 to 7 years of indentured service.

The Separatist Pilgrims denounced the catholic views of the Church of England and wanted to form their own conservative protestant following. The original founders of the separatist movement were Richard Clyfton, Robert Brown, Henry Barrowe and John Greenwood. William Brewster was the former diplomatic assistant to the Netherlands, who held regular meetings in his manor in Scooby, England, which was in violation of the Kings edict. It would later become the impetus for the Pilgrims migration to the Netherlands and later to America. As the Separatist movement gained in popularity, King James I became more determined to punish the Separatist. England levied heavy fines on those holding religious meetings in their homes and if caught were executed. Separatist leaders; in 1593, Barrowe and Greenwood were arrested and charged with sedition and both were executed. These act prompted most Separatists to move to the Netherlands.

The Separatist Pilgrims believed that their lives were predestined by God as to who would go to heaven or who would go to hell. They believed that baptism of a child would cleanse the sins from a previous life. Their biblical inspiration came from the Geneva Bible, which was published in 1575. The Pilgrims would only read the book of psalms from the Bible. They rejected any prayer written by men and did not observe Christmas or Easter, since they were holidays created by man and not by god. They forbid working on Sunday, since it was a day devoted to god. Pilgrims rejected the worship of religious icons and relics, crosses, images, stained glass windows or statues. They were an off-shoot of Calvinism, and they considered marriage a civil matter rather than a religious ritual. Unlike Puritanism or Congregationalist, Pilgrim separatist were non-judgmental and did not force or preach their religious views on others. They allowed all religious faiths to become part of their colony and actively participated in governing the colony.

The Separatist under the leadership of William Brewster, moved to Amsterdam and later to Leiden, Netherlands. The Dutch tolerated their religious views, but it was difficult for the Separatist community to make a living, for most did not speak the Dutch language and their religious views isolated them from the general population. Most were farmers, but were forced to work for wages as craftsmen and laborers. Since their views were extremely conservative for the time, the Dutch had a more liberal view toward life and religion, thus were unable to bridge the theological gap between the two cultures.

The Separatists hoped to expand their community by recruiting and converting the Dutch into their religious belief, but it failed to materialize. After 12 years of living in the Netherlands, rumors circulated concerning a new colony being established in Virginia in 1607, and in particular, Jamestown and the Chesapeake Bay drainage. In 1617, renewed interest in leaving the Netherlands spread through the community and plans were prepared for a pilgrimage to the Hudson River near New York, far enough from the British colony of Virginia, yet close enough to benefit from the protection they needed from the Native Americans Indians.

The Separatists Pilgrims had little money and saved little while in the Netherlands and needed to borrow money from the London investors to purchase two ships for the voyage to America. They envisioned having a missionary colony of like-minded colonist in America were they could practice their religious beliefs openly. While only 40 of the younger and stronger members would make the initial voyage, more than one hundred would remain behind until the colony was established. The ship "Speedwell" was purchased and sailed to the English port of Southampton. It was to rendezvous with the ship "Mayflower" and its 60 passengers hired by the investors. After final arrangements were agreed upon, the two ships set sail from Southampton in August of 1620.

Shortly after leaving port, the "Speedwell" began taking on water as a result of a modification to the masts, which were larger and taller than the ship was designed to handle. It would be forced to divert to

Dartmouth, Devon for repairs. The two ships once again departed and once again the "Speedwell" took on water and forced to return to Dartmouth, Devon.

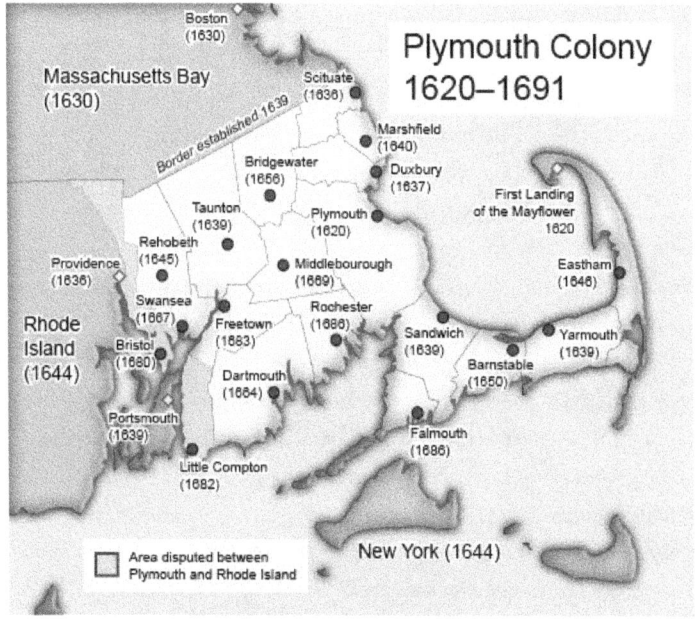

Map 3, Plymouth Colony 1620

It was decided to abandon the "Speedwell" and transfer supplies and passengers onto the "Mayflower". They once again set sail on September 16, 1620. Due to the limited space aboard the Mayflower, only 102 passengers and crew would make the voyage to America. The 28 remaining Separatist from Leiden remained behind.

While the voyage went smoothly except for a major storm, only one passenger died during the voyage across the Atlantic. Land was sighted on November 9th, which was to be named Cape Cod; however, they continued to sail south toward the Hudson River as planned, but encountered shallow shoals and strong currents and decided to anchor in Provincetown Harbor. While the ship laid anchor off the coast of Cape Cod, the Colonist leader, William Bradford, wrote the Mayflower

Compact. The Mayflower Compact was the first form of a written constitution that granted all colonist equality treatment under the laws of the colony. It also bound the colonist to obey the laws of the colony without prejudice. It was the impetus for our system of majority rule. Women were not allowed to vote or sign the Mayflower Compact however.

"In the name of God, Amen. We, whose names are underwritten, the loyal subjects of our dread Sovereign Lord King James, by the Grace of God, of Great Britain, France, and Ireland, King, defender of the Faith, etc.

Having undertaken, for the Glory of God, and advancements of the Christian faith and honor of our King and Country, a voyage to plant the first colony in the Northern parts of Virginia, do by these presents, solemnly and mutually, in the presence of God, and one another, covenant and combine ourselves together into a civil body politic; for our better ordering, and preservation and furtherance of the ends aforesaid; and by virtue hereof to enact, constitute, and frame, such just and equal laws, ordinances, acts, constitutions, and offices, from time to time, as shall be thought most meet and convenient for the general good of the colony; unto which we promise all due submission and obedience.

In witness whereof we have hereunto subscribed our names at Cape Cod the 11th of November, in the year of the reign of our Sovereign Lord King James, of England, France, and Ireland, the eighteenth, and of Scotland the fifty-fourth, 1620."

This would be the first form of government rule established by people in America, however the Mayflower Compact would not apply outside the boundaries of the Plymouth Colony and when the puritans arrived in 1629, they establish the Massachusetts Bay Colony with strict religious laws based on puritan theology, rather than the will of the majority. It would become a colony base on a theocracy form of government which would last for 75 years.

The original Charter between the colonists and the Virginia Company of London was not finalized at the time the Mayflower set sail from England. They didn't have a patent or a finalized Royal Charter to land in America, as was the standard practice at the time. John Carver who chartered the Mayflower was elected Governor of the Colony. The Mayflower Compact established the first system where laws were to be voted upon by the colonist with a majority rule. The actual landing of the Colonist took two weeks. The skiffs aboard the Mayflower, were dismantled to make space aboard the ship so new skiffs had to be built to off load supplies and passengers. A British military mercenary named Myles Standish was hired to take command of a militia for the defense of the colony. His second in command was Christopher Jones. They commanded the two skiffs to search for a suitable place to build a colony along the coast which was to be defendable from invasion from land and sea. While searching for a suitable site, they encountered Native Americans of the Patuxet and Pokanoket tribe and managed to capture several American Natives to take back to England as slaves, Years earlier, Thomas Hunt would sail to Cape Code and take twenty American Natives back to England as slaves, one of which would be Squanto who eventually escape and become a Christian and returned to New England on a supply ship. When Squanto returned, he found his tribe had died from plague.

The American Natives viewed the English settlers as land hungry exploiters, whose goals were to enslave them and send them to Europe. When the colonist arrived in 1620, the American Natives fought ferociously to defend their land and against slavery of their people.

When Myles Standish returned to the Mayflower, he selected a site twenty-five miles south on a hill which would be called Plymouth Rock. But upon his return, most were ill with scurvy and had serve respiratory ailments, perhaps due to being enclosed in tight quarters aboard ship. It was mid-winter and ice and snow formed on the ship's deck. For heat, coal and whale oil lamps were used below deck, which may have precipitated in the respiratory problems that the passengers were experiencing.

Even though many became ill, the construction continued through winter on a common house where colonist would gather and have meetings. Once the common house was constructed, most moved into the common house where fire wood was used to heat the building. Each family was given a plot of land to build their own house. Much of the colony was completed by early February of 1621.

By March of 1621, only 47 colonists survived the winter out of the original 101 that landed in Plymouth. Much of the crew of the Mayflower died, including the first appointed Governor, John Carver. William Bradford was appointed the new Governor of the colony and would serve eleven consecutive terms until his death in 1657. In 1621, a peace treaty was signed by the Wampanoag Native tribe, which brought peace between the regional Native tribes and the colonist for the first few years. In 1640, Bradford surrendered the patent to the Plymouth colony and turned over the land to the freemen with the exclusion of three tracts of land. Colonial "Freemen" were male colonist who were not member of the church, but were elected by the General Court or Council of the colony. Being a Freeman allowed them the right to vote in colonial elections. It is important to note that by 1630, Puritans and settlers of many different denomination arrived in the colonies, so it was not necessarily a separatist missionary colony envisioned by the original founding Separatist Pilgrims, and as a result, the requirement of belonging to the church was relaxed by 1640.

The term "Pilgrim" was not used to describe the colonist who landed at Plymouth until 200 years later. Daniel Webster used the term on December 22, 1820, while addressing the audience during the Plymouth's bicentennial. The term later gain popularity in historical books and writings. England referred to them as Plymouth colonist and "Separatist", since the majority of the colonist in Plymouth was considered settlers with various religious faiths, of which only 40 were radical separatist. [1-4]

As word spread about the new colony, a small group of Puritans sailed to Jamestown in 1718, two years before the Pilgrims landed at Plymouth, Massachusetts. The largest migration occurred around 1629 and 1630, when the Massachusetts Bay Colony received a Royal Charter from Charles I in 1628, and later the Connecticut Colony in 1636 and New Haven Colony in 1638. The Rhode Island and Providence Plantations were established after settlers were banished from the Massachusetts Bay Colony for expressing non-conforming religious opinions. By 1741, the number of Puritans that migrated to America slowed down, only to be replaced by the Amish Mennonites, Quakers, Anabaptist and the Pennsylvania Deutsch. Most of these religious groups took refuge in the Dutch Colony of New Netherlands, which encompassed New York, New Jersey and Pennsylvania. [1-4]

Massachusetts Bay Colony (1628)

The Massachusetts Bay Colony was made up of mostly conservative puritans with a theocracy form government. They viewed the colony as a haven for religious pilgrimage of puritans who shared the same values and heritage. Hence, their laws were written around puritan theology. Unlike the Plymouth Colony, the Massachusetts Bay Colony became a theocracy where as the Plymouth Colony started as a socialist system and would later evolve into representative democracy. It was forced to do so, because the colony was not providing enough food to feed the community and starvation was a constant threat for survival. To avoid starvation, a collective or co-op was created that supplied food to the entire colony.

The Puritans arrived in 1623 at Cape Ann, Massachusetts which was financed by the Dorchester Company. The colony failed in 1626 as did the Dorchester Company. The Massachusetts Bay Company merged with the investors of the Dorchester Company and the Massachusetts

Bay Company and received a Royal Charter in 1628 to establish colonies at Salem and Boston. The colony was successful in trade with England and the West Indies and established the first mint in 1652. Because the colony was making money for the investors in England, they left the colonial government alone to administer laws and carry-out justice, both civil and criminal in Massachusetts Bay Colony. The Puritan religious ideology was different from that of the Pilgrim Separatist. While some Puritan's believed in total separation from the Church of England, most puritans did not, and only demanded that the Church of England make changes toward a more protestant form of religion, rather than the existing catholic ritualized version. Puritans were mostly loyal to England and the Church of England; however they were unsuccessful in getting the Arch Bishop of Canterbury and the King of England to make changes to the Church of England's doctrine. Puritanism slowly morphed into a Presbyterian protestant form most common in Scotland and the Congregationalist religion from England with full communion. As a result, they elected to settle mostly in Boston and Salem, Massachusetts.

By 1629, Plymouth had a population of about 200 people, while Boston had a population of over 1,000. Many colonists who weren't Separatist or any particular religion and their goal were to established plantations and throughout much of the Massachusetts territory. The Puritans were not farmers like the Pilgrim Separatist, but rather business oriented and well educated in trade and business. Over time they became very dominant and powerful. The Separatist Pilgrims and the Puritans had different religious theology and did not get along well together. Many of the Separatist Pilgrims', known as Reformed Baptist, moved to the Rhode Island Colony and establish colonies of their own without the influence of the Puritans political system of government.

Roger Williams, a Reformed Baptist, arrived in Boston in 1631 and began to preach separatism to a Boston congregation and afterwards he was invited to preach separatism to a congregation in Salem, in which both were Puritan enclaves; however, the local political leaders forbid Williams to address the congregation. To continue his message, in 1635, he moved to Plymouth for two years and accepts a position as pastor in a church and later moved to Salem. He wrote a religious manifesto declaring the Church of England and its members as sinful and King Charles was not a Christian. He also publically declared that the citizens were required to take an oath of allegiance to the separatist Baptist faith, which was forbidden by Matthew 5:33-37, or so they claimed. It is important to clarify to avoid confusion; that the Puritan religion began to split into different factions shortly after arriving in America, some became Reformed Baptist and Congregationalist and even deists. Each faction overtime established their own colonies within the declared boundaries of the Massachusetts Bay Colony.

Williams manifesto outraged the Puritan leaders and he was soon expelled from the Massachusetts Bay Colony completely. He was the first puritan to advocate the separation of church and state and freedom of religion which eventually become part of America's Bill of Rights, a concept unacceptable to mainstream Puritan theology.

Banishment from the Colony was administered by the Massachusetts General Court, as ordered by the General Council, which was consisted of members who were devote Puritans with strong religious principals. Other religious faiths were considered fanatic, heretics, radicals and non conformist and were not allowed to vote or take-part in the governing body of the Massachusetts Bay Colony. Many non-believers were banished to Rhode Island or even sent to the West Indies on trade ships, either willingly or bound and gagged.

For the most part, especially in Maryland, Virginia and the Carolina's, the system of government worked well for England, even though it was a system ruled by the elite and wealthy land owners, however the Massachusetts Bay Colony began to become a "head ache" for the English Crown and Parliament. England tolerated the Massachusetts

Bay Colony and granted a great deal of latitude and discretion toward how they managed the colony; however news of religious indiscretion toward colonist concerned the King. In 1640, Oliver Cromwell's puritan majority took over the English government which started the Civil War of 1640, so Parliament had other pressing issues other than dealing with a rogue colony.

Due to an over-sight in the original Charter, Company meetings were held in the Massachusetts Bay Colony which was a violation of the Charter. All investor and company meetings were to be held in company headquarters in London and not in the colony itself.

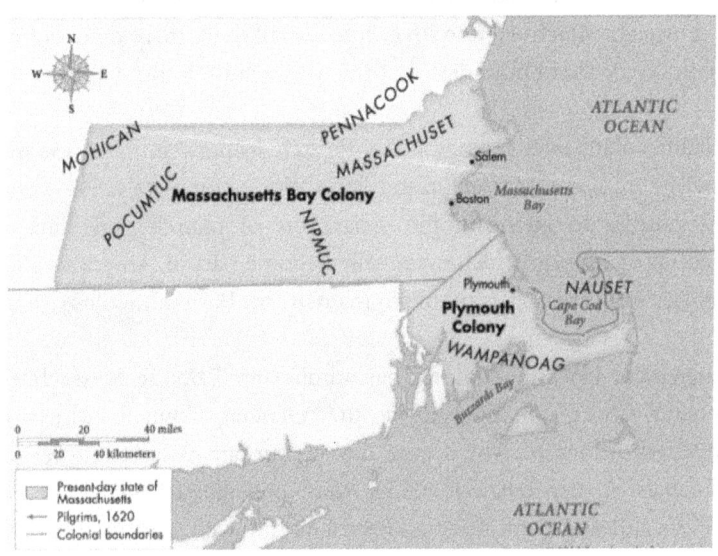

Map 4, **Massachusetts** Bay Colony 1628

In doing so, the King and Parliament had no voice or knowledge of what was occurring in the Massachusetts Bay Colony. As it were, only a select group of puritans called the General Council, made laws and enforcing them on religious grounds and violating the terms of the charter. As it would happen, the Company created a self-governing religious commonwealth that excluded those who were not of the

Puritan faith. In 1632, Boston became the capital of the Colony and King Charles II was restored to the throne after the execution of Oliver Cromwell in 1660. When news arrived in England about cruel and inhumane treatment of Quakers and other religious minorities and the violation of the Charter, King Charles voided the Massachusetts Bay Charter.

King James II sent several Royal Commissioners to Boston to confront the Puritan General Council with an edict for change. Each time the Royal Commissioners were rebuffed and the General Council refused to compromise their political position toward religious laws imposed on the citizenry. Finally in 1684, King James II became King and revoked the Massachusetts Bay Charter on a list of violations that included; establishing religious laws and operating an illegal mint. The following year, he appointed Sir Edmund Andros as governor of the colony and united all the colonies of New England into one single colony renamed "Dominion of New England". (Discussed later) The new colonial administration outlawed town meetings and establishes new taxes as punishment.

King James II was overthrown by William of Orange during the English revolution of 1688. A mob assembled in Boston and seized the Colonial seat of government and removed the royal officials in a coup. They once again installed a Puritan General Council as the ruling body and issued a new charter which united the Massachusetts Bay Colony, Plymouth and the Maine Colonies as one single colonial government. The Salem Witch Hunts began in 1692 and lasted one year. Its purpose was to purifying the population from demons and devils and the supernatural. During the Salem witch hunts and trials, 19 people were hanged, mostly women who were accused of practicing witchcraft or considered possessed by demons. It would be a turning point for the Puritans in their control over government, as the citizens felt the puritan clergy and leadership had gone too far. Shortly after the Salem Witch Trials, the Puritan movement lost their political influence in the Massachusetts Bay Colony. England establishes a Royal Governor and instituted an elected assembly. With the new charter, it would dismantle the religious control of the Puritans.

Puritan's and the Separatist Pilgrims were part of the present day Congregationalist Church. When the Irish and Scottish began their migration to America, many settled in western New York and Pennsylvania. Scottish Presbyterians and English Congregationalist would eventually merged and share separate, yet similar theologies. In the late 1700's, the Congregationalist Church would once again split to form several factions called the Unitarians and Baptist. The separatist Pilgrims didn't believe in constructing churches and most prayer meetings were held in homes. Much of this may have been the result of the persecution of open prayer and religious study in England during Henry VIII's rein when he established the Church of England.

Massachusetts Bay Colony continued to be a problem for England and remained so through the Declaration of Independence and the Revolutionary War of 1786. However, it was Britain's most profitable trade colony at the time. The Virginia Colony was a Royal Colony and most citizens were loyal to England, but Massachusetts was a colony of Puritans who expressed the desire for succession from the rest of the colonies and establish their own religious State. [1-5]

The Plymouth and Massachusetts Bay Colony were not proprietary colonies, but rather joint stock Charters granted to the Virginia Company of London, who financed both colonies and establish trade monopolies for England. During the early 1600's, Plymouth, Massachusetts Bay and Virginia Colonies were established as joint stock Royal Charters but as previously mentioned the Virginia Company failed in 1624 and the colonies were taken over as a crown colony of England.

By the mid 1600's, settlers flooding into the America's eastern seaboard from Europe and trading ports were established in the cities of Boston, New York and Philadelphia. Colonial territorial expansion was inevitable, with each colonial province competing against each other for trade.

William Penn
(1644 – 1718)

Pennsylvania and New Jersey Colonies

William Penn was born in an affluent Anglican family in 1644 in Essex, England. His father was Admiral Sir William Penn, a well respected member in the King's Court. He was known as a heroic naval leader and served most of his life as a naval officer for the crown. In 1666, at the age of 22, Young Penn joined the Religious Society of Friends, known as the Quakers. He was a close friend of George Fox, who was the founder of the Quaker religion in northern England.

Quakerism, like many religions of the time, had its beginning in 1647. George Fox's followers were called the Religious Society of Friends which included a cross-section of rural English working society, with a strong belief that god spoke directly to them directly (spoke in tongues). It was considered blasphemy to the Puritans and some protestants and carried severe punishment and imprisonment if caught holding meeting. The term "Quaker" was given because they shook and quaked when receiving communications from God during prayer. Their religious manifesto advocated not heeding to the word of clergy, (priest or pastors) and not to pay tithes or engaging in deceitful practices against mankind. It was hardly a reason for imprisonment, but the fact that they were able to communicate with god was considered blasphemy and punishment often resulted in stockades and execution. George Fox was imprisoned in England from 1650 to 1670 by refusing to take the Oath of Allegiance to the King and the Church of England. England implemented the Conventicler Act of 1664, which forbid individuals from holding service in private. When

James II of England came to power, two acts were made law; the Declaration of Indulgence in 1687 and the Toleration Act, which allowed free worship without persecution. Many of the Quakers migrated to the Netherlands in 1655 and Providence Plantations in New England, which was previously established by Roger Williams in Rhode Island. William Penn helped King Charles II draft the reform of religious persecution for Parliament which carried favor with Charles II. In 1681, Charles II gave William Penn proprietorship of the land known as Sylvania; some historians claim it was the debt that England owed to his father for a life time of naval service. The French or Latin word; "Sylvania" means woodlands or forest. When King Charles gave Penn the charter, he named it "Penn – Sylvania", after Sir William Penn and not William Penn as history books claim.

In the Massachusetts Colonies, Quakers were considered heretics and were imprisoned, tortured and banished from the Massachusetts Bay Colony. Many fled to Rhode Island and settled in the territory claimed by Netherlands called New Netherlands. Some were sent on cargo ships back to England, and many were whipped and branded as punishment. Their life in America was far worse than the life they endured in England. In 1657, Quakers arrived from England and settled in New Amsterdam, which was situated on the Island of Manhattan, which is New York City today. They thought they were able to practice their religion without persecution in the Dutch colonies, since the Dutch had a liberal tolerance toward religion, however, much of New Netherlands was colonized by other Europeans as well, most notably the Puritans, who established churches and missionaries throughout all of New England. The Dutch government in New Netherlands was tolerant of the Quakers even though they disliked the message they preached and tolerated their presence, religious persecution continued in New Netherlands as well, only on a lesser scale.

In 1677, a group of prominent Quakers, including William Penn, received a Royal Proprietary Charter for a portion of New Jersey. The charter was later expanded to include Pennsylvania. The Quaker migration to America lasted for the next 50 years, in which William Penn spent little time in America overall. From 1682 to 1684, he traveled to Pennsylvania and drew-up plans for a new City called Philadelphia.

While Penn constructed Pennsbury Manor situated on the Delaware River, his last visit to America was in 1699, where he promoted consolidating all the colonies into one single Colonial Federation, which was not well received by the other colonies. His goal was to settle in Philadelphia, however he encountered financial problems and was forced to return to London where he was arrested and placed in debtor's prison. His financial advisor, Philip Ford embezzled large sums of money from Penn over the course of many years. He spent his later years in court in an effort to recover monies from Ford. He died penniless in 1718, at his home in Ruscombe, England. [1-6]

The Quaker's contributed greatly to American society and especially in commerce and manufacturing in early colonial America. They establish the first pharmaceutical business, iron mills and were well known for their furniture making, which established colonial America as an industrial colony. Philadelphia became the first planned city in America and the first American Capital for which the Constitution and Declaration of Independence was written.

New Netherlands Colony
(1626)

In 1602, the Dutch East India Company received a charter from the Republic of the "Seven United Netherlands" to explore and establish colonies in America. As previously mentioned, Henry Hudson was commissioned by the Dutch to explore a route to the East Indies by way of a northwest passage from the Atlantic to the Pacific Ocean. Hudson sailed up the Hudson River to Nassau, which would become Albany, New York. In 1614, Adriaen Block explored the East River and Block Island Sound and named the new territory "New Netherlands". Manhattan Island would be called "New Amsterdam" after Peter Minuit arranged the purchased from the Lenape natives in 1626 for an amount equal today for $951 in goods. The goods included:

- 10 boxes of shirts
- 10 ells of red cloth
- 30 pounds of powder
- 30 pairs of socks
- 2 pieces of duffel
- some awls
- 10 muskets
- 30 kettles
- 25 adzes
- 10 bars of lead
- 50 axes and knives. [81]

Minuit was the director of the Dutch West India Company who was given a charter by the Dutch government to colonize New Netherlands. Dutch colonies sprang-up on the Connecticut, Delaware and Hudson Rivers. Towns such as Hartford, Cambridge, Albany, New York City, Bronx, Brooklyn and Long Island would be settled. These cities and landmarks had their origins from the Dutch settlements from 1624 to 1664. It was at that period of time the Pennsylvania Dutch first originated.

In 1664, Prince James, the Duke of York and Duke of Albany were the brothers of Charles II, and ordered an English naval fleet to sail into the harbor of New Amsterdam and take over the colony by force from the Dutch. The Director-General, Peter Stuyvesant, surrendered New Amsterdam to the English which was renamed New York after the Duke of York. In 1674, the Treaty of Breda was signed between England and Netherland in which Netherlands would relinquish New

Netherland and a subsequent treaty; the Treaty of Nijmegen surrenders all claims to North America by the Dutch.

Provinces of the Carolina's (North and South) (1663)

The French established the Carolina's by building Fort Carolina in 1563. It was named after King Charles IX of France and includes the territory from the 30th and 36th degree north latitude and extended to the Pacific Ocean. King Charles I of England claimed the territory by virtue of Cabot's discovery years earlier, however a charter was granted to Lord Clarendon, Sir William Berkley, Sir George Carteret and four others in 1663, with the power to settle and govern the new territory. In 1640, Lord Clarendon brought tobacco planters from Virginia to the mouth of the Chowan River in Albemarle Sound. It was managed and supervised by William Drummond. Two more plantations were settled in 1665 and 1670, located at Cape Fear River and along the Ashley River near present day Charleston. Governor Sayle was the first governor to form a government in the Carolina's. Lord Shaftesbury, under the guidance of John Locke, proposed installing a court that consisted of Lord Proprietors; one of which was to be elected President for life. In addition, the plan would institute a hereditary nobility system and a parliament, identical to England's monarchial system. The parliament would have two representatives from each district, however the plan met heavy opposition and among the settlers. The plan would later be abandoned and returned to the original proprietary form of government. The location of two of the colonial plantations were not producing well, which forced most of the settlers to move to Charleston and the Albemarle region, where the soil was better for planting cotton, rice and tobacco. Soon settlers were referring to the Carolina's as North and South, even though it was still a single Carolina Colony.

The Proprietary government continued their attempt to implement John Locke's plan for a new government in the Carolina's. When Lord Shaftesbury became Chancellor of England, he sent Seth Sothel to the

Carolina in 1683 to restore order and discipline among the dissenters. Sothel ruled under a heavy hand which created more discontent and throughout the colony. After six years of tyranny under Sothel's rule, local militia seized Sothel and gave him a brief trial and banished him from the colony. James Colleton was appointed governor in which his goal was to expel disobedient and uncontrollable members from the Proprietary Colonial Assembly. He made vigorous attempts to collect rent from land owners which only exacerbated the insurrection that led to open rebellion against the governor and his policies. The settlers seized the records and imprisoned the colonial secretary and banished Colleton from the Colony. Sir John Archdale, a Quaker, became the governor in 1695 and restored law and order to the colony. He implemented a democratic form of government which helped bring peace to both North and South Carolina. Even though they began to enjoy stability, their hardship and difficulties were far from over. As emigrants flooded into the Carolina's, the Proprietors issues generous amounts of farm land, that encroached on local Native American lands, causing discontent and unrest between the local tribes and the colonist. The local Native American population had been decimated over the years by forcing the Tuscaroras and Corees to move further inland.

On the night of October 2, 1711, one hundred and thirty settlers along the Roanoke River and Pamlico Sound were massacred. In retaliation, Colonel Barnwell and one thousand men engaged the Natives in several skirmishes that ended in a peace treaty. The Tuscaroras eventually join the Iroquois Tribe of Six Nations of the Iroquois Confederacy. There would be many more conflicts between local Native American Tribes and settlers in the coming years.

The colonists of the Carolina's have long since been unhappy with the management methods used by the Lord Proprietors in the Colony. Arbitrary rent increases and heavy taxes placed undue financial burden on the colonist. In 1719, the Assembly gathered and presented the Governor of Carolina, Robert Johnson, a proclamation that his governorship was under the oversight of the King of England and not the Lord Proprietors.

Johnson refused and the Assembly appointed Colonel James Moore as governor. The colonial militia marched into Fort Charleston and declared that Moore was governor of Carolina under his majesty's name. When news arrived in England that the issue was adjudicated by the Privy Council in the Carolina's, it was determined that the proprietors had forfeited their charter and Carolina's would become a Royal Charter of England.

Map 5, Colonizing Virginia and the Carolina's

In 1729, an agreement between the Proprietors and the Crown was reached, in which the English government would reimburse the Proprietors seventeen thousand five hundred pounds sterling for their rights and interest in the Colony of Carolina. In 1729, the colony of Carolina was divided into North and South Carolina, each having Royal appointed governors under the British Crown. **[13]**

Province of Georgia (1732)

In 1732, a corporate charter was issued to General James Oglethorpe for the Province of Georgia, which at the time, was part of the colony of South Carolina. It became a Proprietary Colony under control and management by Oglethorpe. He recruited English subjects who were incarcerated in debtors' prison in England and treated them as unpaid workers in which they agreed to work off their debt in the Georgia Province. General Oglethorpe established local laws in the colony which made it illegal to have alcohol and banned slavery. He gave 50 acres to each family and paid their passage to Georgia to establish homesteads. For those who paid their own passage to Georgia, he gave each 500 acres parcels.

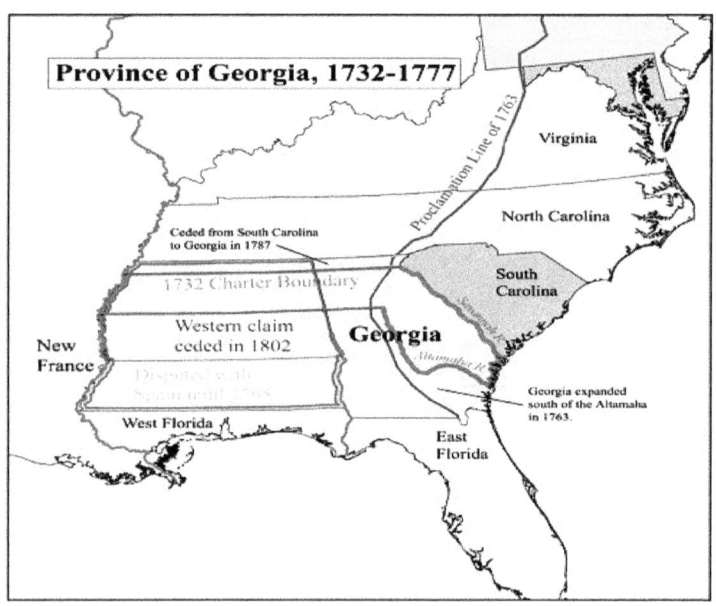

Map 6, Georgia Province 1732

King George and the Privy Council granted the charter to General Oglethorpe as a border colony for the purpose of protecting the Carolina's from encroachments by the French and Spanish in Florida and the Louisiana Territories. Oglethorpe and his selection committee selected thirty-five families from the debtor's prison in England and sailed to the Province of Carolina and traveled overland to the Savannah River. His strict colonial laws toward the colonist were an effort to create a civilian militia to defend the southern boundary of the British American colonies. Oglethorpe served as the governor of Georgia for 12 years. After his departure in 1852, the Council of Trustee's spent much of their time feuding among each and was accused of mismanagement. The Council issued a "Deed of Reconveyance" to the Crown and abolished the proprietary colony and its charter in 1755. In 1804, Georgia ceded the Mississippi Territory, which later became the States of Alabama and Mississippi. In 1788, Georgia became a State one year after the signing of the Constitution.

The Province of Maine (1607)

As other colonies in America gradually expanded into undeclared territory, Maine remained mostly unsettled even after America's independence. In 1606, King James I granted a joint stock company for two colonies in America. The first colony was Jamestown, Virginia and the second, Popham, Maine in May of 1607.

When the first ship arrived from England with 100 men, they built Fort St. George on the Kennebec River, but 55 settlers returned to England before the second winter arrived. The following winter, the remaining 45 settlers returned to England as well, partly due to dwindling food stores and the lack of leadership.

In 1613, the French established a trading post near modern day Castine, seven years before the Plymouth Colony was established. The Pilgrims established a trading post in Penobscot bay in 1620. Christopher Levett, a member of the Plymouth Council, acquired a 6,000 acre royal grant near present day Portland, Maine. He built a small settlement and called it "York", later to be named "Falmouth".

He left a small group of men in York while he sailed back to England in 1623 to gather more support for his settlement; however he died on his return trip back to York. The settlers of York were never seen again and the settlement of York would fail. Sir Ferdinand Gorges and John Mason of England were given a royal patent in 1622 by King James I for all the land laying between the 40th and 48th parallel from the Atlantic shores to the Pacific Ocean.

In 1629, Gorges and Mason agreed to split the land grant at the Piscataqua River. Mason claim all land south, calling it New Hampshire and Gorges acquire all land north of the river and called it the territory of New Somersetshire. In 1639, Gorges revised his new patent and royal charter from King Charles I, which excluded Mason's New Hampshire patent. Gorges would die in 1647 and New Somersetshire would be renamed "Maine", which had only a few established settlements at the time of his death. By 1658, the Massachusetts Bay Colony claimed all of the Somersetshire Colony as well as a portion of the New Hampshire Colony.

King James established the Dominion of New England in 1686, but the Dominion collapsed in 1689. Maine would eventually gain statehood from Massachusetts in 1820. [1-7]

The Province of New Hampshire (1691)

The Province of New Hampshire was first settled in mid 1620's which was part of the Massachusetts Bay Colony Charter originally. England's King Charles II appointed John Cutt President of New Hampshire in 1679, but England dissolved the Massachusetts Bay Colony and creates the Dominion of New England in 1686 as previously mentioned, which incorporated all the charters in New England into one single authority.

In 1691, New Hampshire and Massachusetts Bay Colony was reorganized into an English Crown Colony from 1692 to 1741, and a single Provincial Governor was appointed for both Provinces. In 1741, Benning Wentworth was appointed governor of New Hampshire which began a race to claim provincial lands west of the Connecticut and east side of the Hudson River.

New York disputed Wentworth's territorial land claims which created the Vermont Republic. Wentworth was replaced as governor of New Hampshire by his son, John Wentworth. He would remain the governor of New Hampshire until the start of the Revolutionary War in 1776. New Hampshire was one of the original thirteen colonies in January 1776. **[65]**

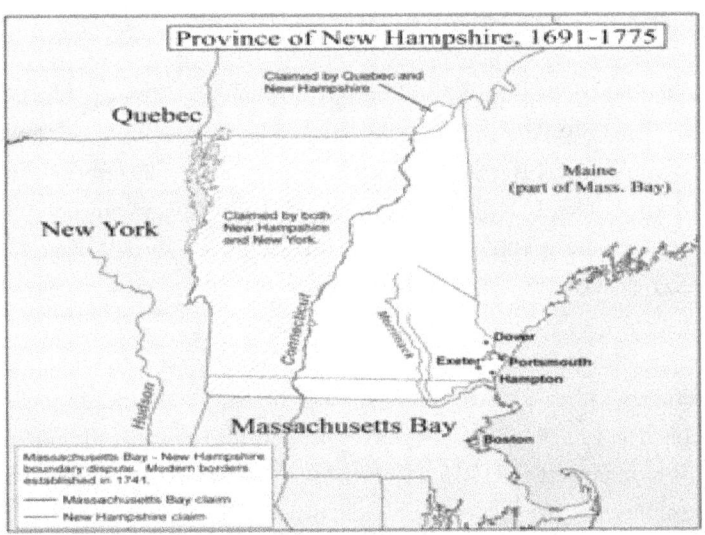

Map 7, New Hampshire Province 1691

The Province of Connecticut (1636)

The original name of the Connecticut Province was the Connecticut River Colony. It was first colonized in 1636 by Puritan Minister Thomas Hooker who led one-hundred Puritans to Connecticut with the help of John Hayes, who at the time was the Governor of the

Massachusetts Bay Colony.

Hayes' motive was to expand the Puritan influence beyond the boundary of the Massachusetts Bay colony. There were two other colonies that merged to form the Connecticut River Colony; Saybrook Colony in 1644 and the New Haven Colony in 1662. Puritans were socially connected to the Plymouth and Massachusetts Bay Colonies residents. The Massachusetts Bay Colony gradually absorbed much of the New England Colonies; Maine, New Hampshire, Vermont Connecticut and Rhode Island Colonies, until all Charters became part of the Dominion of New England in 1686 as previously mentioned. [67]

The Province of Rhode Island (1663)

The Connecticut and Rhode Island Provinces were established in 1636. Roger Williams, a Puritan, was exiled from the Massachusetts Bay Colony for his religious beliefs which were contrary to Puritan theology. Chief Sachem Canonicus of the Narragansett Native American tribe occupied Rhode Island and gave Roger Williams land, which he called Providence Plantation.

The first known settlement in Rhode Island was a trading post at Sowams. Other exiled groups moved to Rhode Island as well and establish colonies. Samuel Gorton arrived and purchased land from the Narragansett's in 1642 and called his Colony "Shawomet". Massachusetts Bay Colony claimed his land but Gorton traveled to England to appeal is case before Parliament. The 2nd Earl of Warwick, Robert Rich, was elected to intervene in the matter. The Earl of Warwick sent a letter demanding that Massachusetts Bay Colony had no claim to the land and was to cease and desist. Gorton would name his Colony after the Earl of Warwick, known today as Warwick, Rhode Island.

The smaller colonies of New Hampshire, Rhode Island and

Connecticut at the time became safe havens for religious freedom from the dominate Massachusetts Bay Colony controlled by the Puritan's. Charles II was sympathetic to those who wanted to practice their own religion without interference from the local colonial governments that ruled as a theocracy. In 1663, King Charles granted Rhode Island a Royal Charter and united four settlements in Rhode Island to form a single Province. [66]

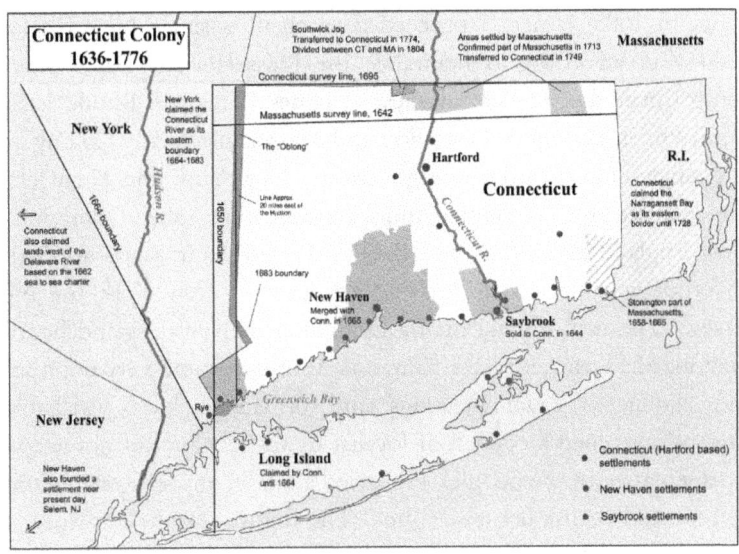

Map 8, Connecticut and Rhode Island Colony 1636

The Dominion of New England

King Charles II was concerned about the direction New England was taking toward some colonies, such as the Massachusetts Bay Colony and Pennsylvania was becoming a religious theocracy. Other colonies such as the Carolina's were belligerent toward appointed governors. Each colony enacted laws and punishment that were not uniform throughout the colonies. Colonial governments consisted of councils that were religiously biased.

The Massachusetts Bay Colony was defiant and non-compliant to the laws of England. Charles II was sympathetic toward the Catholic religion, even though England was protestant. Charles wanted New England to enforce the Navigation Act, which prohibited New England Colonies from trading with other countries, other than England. When the Massachusetts Bay Colony refused to relax its religious voting laws and mandatory biblical teachings, Charles II revoked the Massachusetts Bay Charter in 1683. Charles II, however, would die shortly after announcing his edict and James II became King. In 1685, James II proceeded to create a single New England Colony in an effort to neutralize the Massachusetts Bay Colony's control over the smaller colonies. James II merged Rhode Island, Connecticut, Plymouth Plantation and Massachusetts Bay Colony into one single colony under one governor. New York and New Jersey was acquired from the Dutch and was included into the "Dominion of New England in 1688 as well. Sir Edmund Andros was appointed governor who previously was the governor of New York and New Jersey. The new Capital of the Dominion of New England became Boston, Massachusetts. Sir Edmund Andros became very unpopular and eliminated town meetings and disbanded local legislatures. Andros convened a council of loyalist to advise him, but not act as a representative of the people. He levied a tax on imports, estates and a poll tax and even a tax on alcohol. The follow year, he informed the public that all land belonged to the King and all titles to land were void, with the exception of the land owned by close friends. This act went a little too far.

The Colonies were no longer operating under a representative legislature, even if some colonies concept of a representative democracy was narrowly interpreted as being democratic. Andros' close friends and advisors strongly suggested that he reconsider his tactics toward compliance in the new Colony. Andros had a strong dislike for the Puritan faith, and devoted much of his time antagonizing the Puritans by ordering maypoles to be erected in Boston and Charlestown. Puritan's didn't believe in Christmas or Christian holidays and Andros ordered everyone to participate in

Christian events, dancing, picnics and games, which offended the Puritans and was an attack on their religious principals.

During England's Revolution in 1688, James II was forced to abdicate his thrown. In February of 1689, his Son-in-Law, William of Orange and James' daughter, Mary became the King and Queen of England. When news was received of the overthrow, riots broke-out in Boston and throughout New England. Andros was placed on a ship bound for England.

In May, the reassembled old council of the Massachusetts Bay Colony voted to adopt and reinstate the Puritan charter as before. William and Mary had other plans. In 1691, the Massachusetts Bay Colony became a Royal Charter Colony in which the governor was appointed and the Plymouth Colony was incorporated into the Massachusetts Bay Colony. In essence, the new Royal Charter removed the Puritan political influence. One year later, 1692, the Salem Witch Trials began.

Over the next 70 years, colonial laws and tariff enforcement were relaxed and colonies enjoyed a Laissez-faire and prosperous period. It ended in 1763 during the Seven Year War with the French and Indian Wars in America. Britain had drained its treasury and believed American colonies should be held responsible in carrying the burden of debt for the war, since it was for their benefit, so they surmised. A flood of taxes and tariffs ensued upon the colonies which stoked the flames of resentment toward being colonized by a nation thousands of miles from its shores. **[64]**

By the mid 1700's, America had about 4 million people. Much of the eastern seaboard was developed yet still under the influence of Great Britain. America as a colony to Britain became a source of revenue. They allowed the colonies partial self rule but there was an underlying discontent over the taxes and tariffs that Britain imposed and the non competitiveness of trade between nations. As a result, British goods were expensive, mostly due to the tariff and taxes levied. Smugglers were common at the time, since they could purchase shipments of trade goods much cheaper from the Netherlands, France and Spain.

Trading Companies

There were dozens, if not hundreds of trading companies operating between the fourteenth through the twentieth century's. Most countries and merchants used trading companies to connect buyers with sellers. The trade company stored and ship products from the colonies and territories for which they were granted a trade monopoly by each Monarch of each respective country. Their profits were derived from commissions they received from the sale of the goods. As previously mentioned, trading companies during the colonial period were granted charters by the monarch for a particular territory of trade. The Colony could only trade with the trade company that was charted by the monarch. They were in essence, a government sanctioned trade monopoly. What the government got from the trade monopoly was tariffs and taxes on the goods imported to and from the colony. The charter was issued to incorporated companies, which offered investors limited liability, which was attractive to stock holders and investors. The companies most often were given legal title to all the land in the colony and the exclusive right to trade. In exchange, the company often provided the colonial government and military jurisdiction over the colony. If the company failed to garner profits to pay dividends to investors, they could exercise the option of selling land to speculators and real-estate investors in exchange for dividends. As previously mentioned, it is important to note that the colonial government could establish their own laws as long as the laws didn't conflict with the mother country or violate the royal charter. Some colonies were held in strict compliance to the terms, while others, such as the Massachusetts Bay Colony, was given free reign over establishing religious base laws and punishment for non compliance to Puritan law.

Mercantilism

Mercantilism was an economic system commonly used in Western Europe between the 15th and mid-18th centuries. Its goal was to generate trade between colonies without relying on importing goods from other nations. In other words, the goal was to export more than you imported, thus creating a trade balance for one nation and a trade imbalance toward a competing nation. The form of payment for trade products were precious metals; gold and silver coins or bullion. Finance Ministers believed there was only a specific amount of gold and silver available in circulation at anyone given time. They reasoned that the more bullion they acquired through trade, it would increased their wealth while depleting the amount of gold in circulation available for other nations. Of course the theory was flawed, since the act of colonization increased the amount of gold and silver being mined, especially in Mexico, South and Central America, thus putting more gold and silver into circulation. Each European nation was competing vigorously against each other in establishing more colonies in the Americas' to increase trade opportunities, thus selling more products to Europe for gold and silver in exchange.

While Spain and Portugal concentrated on colonizing Mexico, Central and South America, England and France concentrated their efforts in North America. The Spanish was successful in acquiring large amounts of silver and gold, but the region had little to offer in trade goods, other than sugar cane, corn and a healthy slave trade. England on the other hand, colonized much of the eastern seaboard of North America and was unsuccessful in acquiring precious metals, but reaped financial prosperity through the sale of trade products such as timber, fish, potatoes, corn, rice and tobacco which was in high demand in Europe.

Having a large treasury was the result of colonization; however as colonization spread, so did the feuds over territorial claims with other countries, which most often led to wars. Having a depleted treasury forced countries to sell assets, most notably Florida and Louisiana. With the shortage of cash flow, they were unable to defend their larger and more valuable territories from encroachment or take-over, especially during periods of war. The Spanish sold the Florida Territory, France the Louisiana Territory and Russia, Alaska in 1867. Eventually colonial empires gradually were reduced and confined to their own boundaries and forced to purchase on the open market without the advantages they once enjoyed.

The mercantile economic system created a colonial land "rush" between the 15th and 16th centuries. The European nations were forced to compete by searching for newer and more profitable trade routes and colonies. New territories were colonized by companies under grants and charters for profit which were controlled by monarchs who practiced absolutism to gain wealth, which was common in Europe at the time. The Pilgrims' and Pertains paid for passage and entered into labor agreements that bound the colony for seven years to supply England with cheap imported fish, corn, leather, timber and other products which could be easily sold in Europe.

Mercantilism would become a "double edge sword" however. While some aspects allowed for rapid acceleration in wealth and colonial expansion, it also created a trade monopoly in which colonies were forbidden to trade with other competing foreign trading companies. In America, it was the British East India Company mostly. As a result of the trade monopoly, it eventually evolved into a tariff system on imported products which eventually planted the seed for revolution in America that led to the Revolutionary War. England levied an import tax on tea from India that was supplied by the British East India Company. After the American Revolution, the mercantile economic system collapsed by 1789 as the first industrial revolution would change the mechanism for worldwide trade. It is worth noting that mercantilism and corporate colonization wasn't completely banished by 1789; Russia and America later engaged in colonization of Alaska well into the early late 20th century which will be discussed in volume II of "American Legacy".

The one thing America had which couldn't be exported was land. It was given away freely during the colonial period with the hope of creating farm land and products for export.

Debtors Prison and Land Speculators

The concept of debtor's prison had its origins from England. Debtor's prison in America was finally made illegal in 1833. In the mid 1700's and early 1800's, many affluent plantation owners invested heavily in land speculation. Land was a commodity that any person could make a decent return on their money, since land was abundant and cheap in America and could be acquired legally by making deals with the Native Americans and the colonial government. The colonial government gave land away if one wanted to travel to America and become a farmer. Later, land could be purchased either from the Government or from a private party for $1 per acre. By 1800, land prices rose to $2 per acre for a respectable 100 percent profit. The war debt for the Revolutionary War was huge, so the newly formed U.S. Government sold land on a payment plan for $2 an acre with a minimum purchase of 640 acres. Payments were to be made in four equal installments over a one year period. For most, the money was borrowed, thinking they could "flip" the land quickly or subdivide and sell parcels for a profit, or so they thought. State banks were established thought-out the states, especially east of the Mississippi River and were unregulated. Anyone could open a bank and accept deposits; in return the banks would issue promissory notes to the borrower, holding the land as collateral. The money the banks loaned speculators came from the depositors saving accounts, thus it was nothing more than a "Ponzi scheme". The Government continued to sell land after the War of 1812 to pay off its war debt, which would take 26 years. In the interim, the U.S. Government gave millions of acres to the railroad industry to sell as a means to raise money to build the transcontinental railroads. It takes little imagination to see that from 1776 to 1857 land had little value and everyone began selling land at a loss to keep from going into debtor's prison. Land speculation contributed to the Panic of 1819, 1837 and 1857, when depositor's fell on hard economic times and demanded their savings deposit, the banks closed its doors and went out of business, leaving the depositor's penniless. The bank would move to another town and open another bank and repeat the process. Banks were nothing more than an unregulated money store.

While many immigrants ended in debtors prison since they were unable to pay for rent and food, but surprisingly, even wealthy and affluent plantation owners were imprisoned over debts, mostly from land speculation and poor investments. Daniel Boone from Kentucky became famous as a pioneer and a respected citizen in Kentucky. In 1800, he invested in land and borrowed heavily and was unable to pay his debts. To avoid debtor's prison, he moved to Missouri, which was part of the Louisiana Territory owned by the French at the time. However as luck would have it, Thomas Jefferson purchased the Louisiana Territory from France in 1803, and Daniel Boone was once again forced to make regular payment to the debtor to avoid debtor's prison, however, he died 7 years later, leaving the bank holding the debt.

Nearly all of the Presidents of the period were on the verge of bankruptcy during and after their term as President; Washington, Jefferson, Madison and Monroe, were forced to sell their estates to provide for their family before and after their death. Two of the Founding Fathers who signed the Declaration of Independence were sent to debtor's prison as well. William Morris was sent to prison for 3 years from 1898 to 1801 and the honorable Associate Justice of the Supreme Court and Founding Father, James Wilson spent time there as well. Much of the financial problems resulted in land speculation or poor investments.

Pirates and Privateers

High sea piracies of merchant trading ships were common events during the mid 16th and late 19th centuries. European nations began colonizing the Caribbean Islands, Spanish West Indies and Latin America which required frequent trips by ships with trade goods and even Spanish pieces of eight. Pirates used the outer banks of the Carolina's, Bahamas' and Bermuda Islands as safe harbors for Pirates and Privateers. Larger ships required deep harbors for mooring ships, but smaller and faster pirate ships were able to hide in shallow water bays, coves and estuaries that were inaccessible to war ships looking for pirates.

Privateers were used by European countries to raid competing merchant ships under the guise of being pirates. Britain was especially notorious for using privateers to raid other nation's merchant fleets for cargo and hard currency. It was characterized as an undeclared naval war between nations. A privateer was a non-military sea captain who raided other nation's merchant fleet for profit on behalf of their country of origin and would share the bounty with the crown. The crown gave the ship's captain a letter of Marque, which authorized the captain to seize foreign merchant ships and trade goods for a designated percentage of the profit they seized on behalf of the crown. As long as the privateer had a letter of marquee, he would not be prosecuted as a pirate; however, the letter of marquee was of little value if captured by another nation, in which case, he would be hanged as a pirate.

During the golden age of piracy, from the 16th century to mid 18th century, there were only about 4,000 pirates, including crew. The Captain was elected by the crew and drafted a "pirate's code of conduct" that was signed by all crew members. Any crew member violating the code of conduct would receive harsh punishment. Every member of the crew received a predetermined percentage of the booty depending on their rank and position on the crew. Pirate's recruited volunteers from merchant ships they seized to join their crew. It was found that every merchant ship would have at least three or four sailor's willing to live the life of a pirate, even though the average life expectancy was only 5 to 10 years. Pirates were known to be alcoholics and heavy drinkers, and every merchant and naval ship had large stores of rum, whiskey and scotch. Confrontations among pirate crews often lead to sword fights and deaths. Pirates were known to capture slave ships and recruit black slaves as pirates as well.

Pirates of the Carolina's

While piracy was rampant throughout the world around trade routes into Asia, Mediterranean, Caribbean Islands and North Africa, I will only discuss the activity in North America and in particular, the East Coast of America and in particular outer banks of the Carolina coast. Pirates were known to take refuge as far north as Massachusetts, with its shallow estuaries and bays. But, after the Massachusetts Bay region became populated, the pirate's moved to the outer banks of the Carolina coast.

The Carolina coastal region in the 17th and 18th centuries was considered a lawless pirate frontier. The Carolina Colony under Governor, Charles Eden, divided Carolina into two provinces; Currituck and Roanoke. He offered the pirates immunity if they stopped the piracy of ships along the coast of the Carolina's. Merchant traders were reluctant to sail in or near the outer banks of the Carolina's because of the pirate activity against merchant ships. The pirates were bad for business to the southern colonies. Edward Teach, known as "Black Beard", Stede Bonnet, "The Gentleman Pirate", Charles Vane, Jack Rackham, "Callico Jack" and William Kidd, "Captain Kid", made the outer banks of the Carolina's their pirate heaven as well as Nassau in the Bahamas'. The local townships of Bath and Ocracoke and Cape Fear openly welcomed the pirates, since they provided protection and shared the bounty of the seized goods with the locals for a fraction of the price. The Governor of

Virginia, Alexander Spotswood, believed piracy was bad for business in Virginia and the Carolinas and sent Lieutenant Maynard of the British Royal Navy to the Carolina's to capture Edward Teach, alias Black Beard", who served as a British privateer during the Spanish War for Queen Anne of England. When Maynard arrived at the outer banks of the Carolina's, Black Beard opened fired on Maynard's ship, but after a skirmish, Black Beard was shot five times and stabbed with a sword 20 times. His head was severed and hung on the bowsprit of his ship.

As previously noted, there were other pirates who used Carolinas' outer banks as base of operation as well, gentleman pirate, Stede Bonnet was captured in the fall of 1718 by Colonel William Rehett and hanged in Charleston, South Carolina. Charles Vane was perhaps the most cruel and deceitful of all the pirates. He was known for his cruelty toward the crew of captured ships and for stealing booty from his own pirate crew. The Crew eventually got "fed-up" with his treachery and marooned Captain Vane on a deserted island. He was rescued by a passing ship, in which the Captain realized he was the notorious pirate, Charles Vane. He was hanged in 1721.

Jack Rackham, alias "Calico Jack" got his name because of his colorful and loud attire he graciously wore. He became famous in using the "Jolly Roger", skull and two crossed swords he raised during the seizure of a merchant ship. He had two women pirates on his crew, who became his lovers; Anne Bonny and Mary Read. In 1720, his ship and crew was captured in Jamaica and was hanged in Port Royal. Bonny said at his trial, "If he fought like a man, he need not have been hang'd like a dog". Bonny and Read were not hanged because they were pregnant. Read would die in prison and Bonny's fate is unknown.

The last of the famous pirates was William Kidd, alias "Captain Kidd". Contrary to popular belief, only Captain Kidd buried his treasure. Kidd was from Scotland and was a privateer for the British in the late 1600's. He would retire and marry a wealthy woman and settle in

New York City, he enjoyed the social life while in New York and was often a guest of Governor Richard Coote at social events, perhaps more of a novelty, however the temptation was too great for Kidd and he returned to pirating in 1699, leaving his wife and social life behind. His crew deserted him in Madagascar, but Kidd was resilient if nothing more and acquired a ship and crew and continued to raid and capture merchant ships until arriving in the Carolina's. One of Captain Kidd's supporters and backers was Massachusetts governor Richard Coote who decided that Kidd was becoming a political liability. Coote had Kidd arrested and sent to England to stand trial. Captain Kidd was hanged in 1701.

The Virginia Company

The Virginia Company was a double joint stock company from London which was organized and established for the purpose of trading and colonizing new territories for profit for England and its investors. They were given exclusive rights to govern and trade within a designated Charter authorized by the monarch. In essence, they were corporations with investors who owned stock in the company.

Trading companies established trading posts, forts and colonies in the new frontiers, which included Canada, America and the West Indies. They paid the expenses of building and purchasing ships, materials and supplies and labor for the newly established colony, of which they shared in the profits from trade with its stockholders. Of course gold and silver was the preferred cargo, but in Virginia there was no gold or silver to be found. American natives were captured and sent to Europe as slaves at first, but as colonies began to be developed, forest products, fish, spices, tobacco and rice became profitable commodities. During a return voyage from America, potatoes, corn and turkeys were sent and introduced to England. The investors in England charged passengers to help defray the cost of sea travel for those wanting to establish roots in America. For those who could not afford passage, they signed labor contracts for working on farms and plantations to pay-off their travel debt.

There were two Virginia Charters made by James I; the first Charter of 1606 granted the Plymouth Company which was a subsidiary of the Virginia Company, to establish a colony in New England between the 38th parallel and the 45th parallel and the Virginia Company between the 34th parallel and the 41st parallel. Part of the charter included a competitive clause which stated that the company that prevailed financially and did not go into bankruptcy would be entitled to the over-lapping territory between the Plymouth Company boundary and the Virginia Company boundary. The overlapping territories did not permit the establishment of colonies within 100 miles of each other by either company. The 1609 Plymouth Company Charter was abandoned, partly because the trading company of investors failed to establish a colony within the required time frame, but the charter added the Bermuda Islands, which was financed by the Somers Isles Company, a subsidiary of the Virginia Company to colonize Bermuda. The Virginia Company was granted a joint stock Royal Charter in 1620 to colonize Plymouth. Many of the Colonial Charters switched from a royal charter to joint stock charter or from proprietary charter to a royal charter depending on the wishes of monarch in power. Such was the case with the Virginia Company which became insolvent and disbanded in 1624, leaving both Plymouth and Virginia Colonies as Royal Colonies under the governorship of the King of England, rather than by self rule. The Plymouth Colony for reasons unknown, remained under self rule, even though it was a crown colony after 1624. King James appointed Sir Francis Wyatt in 1624 as the Crown Governor of Virginia.

The Governor's Council

With trial and error, the Council established system of self rule and a local government run by a select group of colonist. By late 1600's, most of the Colonies established Governor's Councils in which council members were appointed at the pleasure of the Governor, who in turn was appointed by the British Parliament and the King. Most of the Council members were appointed by virtue of their social and financial status within the colony, while the remaining members were selected on the perception that the appointee represented a typical cross-section of the people. Most appointees were selected through their connections and business dealings with government officials. The Council served as the Court for the local towns and villages. The justice of the peace was appointed to administer local justice; such as land disputes and minor misdemeanor offenses. Other duties of the Council included budgetary and finance, taxes and appointments. The Council position was not a paid position as were most appointments in colonial government at the time.

The Colonial Assembly

Each colony convened some form of an assembly. In Virginia, it was called the House of Burgesses, which originally ordained 22 assemblymen that were selected based on their wealth and station in life. Other Colonies such as Maryland had the Assembly of Freemen and other colonies called them the House of Delegates. Each colonial assembly functioned in the same manner, whereas members were elected annually and received no pay and would convene for short a sessions to address specific issues deemed important by the Governor's Council. Members were white land owners generally. All others were excluded from the assembly membership.

Colonial Education

Educational Standards varied from Colony to Colony and region to region. In the Massachusetts Bay Colony, education was primarily religiously based in which students were required to read and memorize biblical scriptures. Math and writing was also taught with strict corporal punishment for those who failed to recite scriptures properly. Corporal punishment was a standard practice throughout the 1700 and 1800's in schools. Young girls remained in the home and were taught sewing, cooking and housekeeping skills. It was required that girls were to write their name by the age of 10.

In the southern colonies, such as Virginia and the Carolina's, education had a strong British influence, both in speech and grammar. Schooling was divided among the poor and the more affluent and wealthy. Towns and villages had local schools that taught children to read and write by a teacher who conducted classes in their home. Each parent was required to pay for their child's education. Children, mostly boys, attended school from 5 to 10 years of age, after which, they were to be apprenticed in a trade for 3 to 10 years; such as Printers, blacksmiths, silversmiths, merchant and maritime naval pursuits and lawyers As part of their apprenticeship, they were often given free room and board but no pay. One school year lasted 44 weeks a year, 5 days a week, 6 am to 5 pm, with a 2 hour break in the afternoon. Fridays were reserved for examinations and punishment. For the affluent and wealthy; tutors were hired. They were taught English, religion, writing, math and Latin, Greek and French. It was required that students learn Latin in preparation for college.

College enrollment began at the age of 15. For the wealthier, it was a common practice that many were sent to live and learn in France or Britain for their education. Most of the founding Fathers were aristocrats and were well educated, while some, such as Ben Franklin, only attended school to the age of 10 and apprenticed himself as a printer with his older brother. Many of our Presidents received little primary education but apprenticed themselves as lawyers or made a career in the military.

Horn books were used as texts. Only the wealthy had access to books and libraries, since they were few and were very expensive. Horn books were shaped like a small tennis racket made of hardwood. A parchment sheet was attached to the paddle with scribed lessons in black ink. The horn was shaved in thin sheets and attached over the top of the parchment to protect the parchment from damage. Later in the early 1800's students were given slate boards with chalk to write lessons on. The use of slate boards was even common as late as the mid 1900's and gradually disappeared in schools by the early 1950's in America in some states. The slate board had a wooden oak frame that bordered the slate. One could use white chalk to write on both sides.

For the curious reader, it will become obvious later, that most of the earlier affluent colonist had a choice of many primary Colleges to attend. Most were established in the 15th to 16th centuries, such as Harvard, William and Mary, Yale and Pennsylvania colleges.

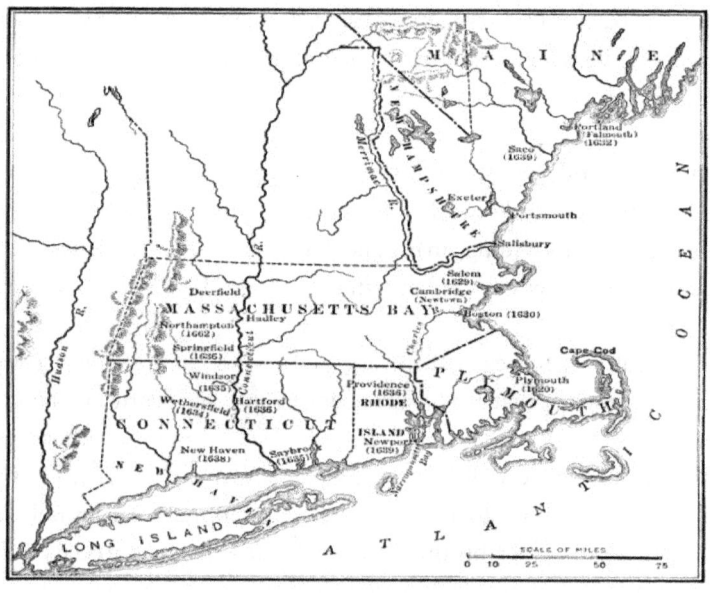

Map 9, New England Colonies (Bagley & Beard)

It is also worth noting that a greater emphasis was placed on Latin and foreign languages. John Quincy Adams was fluent in German, Dutch, French, Latin and Greek. Equally important was penmanship, vocabulary, writing style, proper grammar and public speaking and debate. Curriculum also included classes on letter writing. Writing, debates and speech were important during the colonial period, which established a person's station in life. Colonial America was a tiered system of poor and aristocrat that was derived from England for which most immigrated from,

As a result of British influence in the southern colonies of Virginia, Carolina's and Georgia, large tobacco, rice and cotton plantations were passed down from generation to generation to the eldest son. The inheritance laws originated from England and designed to maintain an Aristocratic society of Dukes, Barons and Earls. Massachusetts became a hub for imports and exports in which merchants and trading company owners became very wealthy. They passed down their businesses to the eldest son or surviving relative. As a result, inheritance laws followed closely to those of Great Britain, which over time develop a socially elite and upper class by the 17th and 18th centuries.

Children raised in an aristocratic society were schooled by private tutors and attend finishing or prep schools which led to a formal education in Harvard, Yale or William and Mary Colleges. Such colleges were beyond the normal means of the lower class. Required reading included Peacham's "The Complete Gentleman" of 1622, Allestree's "The Whole Duty of Man" and "The Friendly Instructor" of 1745.

Gentleman's demeanor was everything, especially in key positions of government, military and business. Just because a plantation owner was wealthy, didn't necessarily guarantee he or she became part of the social aristocratic elite. Undesirable behavior such as; vulgarity, crassness, displays of temper were considered socially unacceptable under any circumstance. Gratitude was also considered among the attributes of a gentleman. One who failed to demonstrate gratitude was considered low class and not worthy to be called a gentleman. A true gentleman does not raise his voice or show facial expression of joy or displeasure when communicating with others. Name calling or rants were a sign of poor breeding; however, gossip among the wives was a common pass time. The men seldom engaged in such pettiness, or at least openly. The hierarchical system was controlled by the wealthy colonial plantation owners and traders. The southern cast system gradually faded away after the Civil War. The term Southern gentleman continued in the south long after the Civil War on larger cotton plantations in Georgia, Alabama and Mississippi. In Virginia and the Carolina's, Jefferson made it a personal cause to have the inheritance laws changed. As it were, the eldest son inherited the estate, but Jefferson wanted the estates divided among all siblings of the household upon death of the owners and the spouse. Surviving widow's did not inherited the estates after their husband died, they only served as a trustee until the eldest male or surviving child became of age. The widow would receive some form of compensation for management and perhaps several slaves to care for her in her later years. Inheritance taxes became a factor in the decline of large plantations and by 1840, most large plantations in the south we subdivided and taxed out of business.

At the time of Jefferson's and Madison's death in the early 1800's, they were forced to sell their slaves to pay their debts. Both former presidents died poor and left their heirs penniless. This example was not an exception for politicians of the day; it was common in Virginia and the Carolina's during the 1830's and 1840's as Britain no longer depended on imports of cotton, rice and tobacco from the south, partly because it was over-priced. Britain realized that civil war was imminent and developed cotton plantations in India and other temperate colonies. Southern cotton became expensive and Britain had colonized India and planted cotton, rice and tobacco in Asia for markets in England. The embargo with Great Britain during Jefferson and Madison presidencies caused economic problems in New England but had little effect on British imports. The southern farmer and plantation owners were unable to sell their harvest to England and had only a small European market. The age of the lavish plantations were soon becoming obsolete and with the Civil War looming in the distant future, foreign nations found other willing nations to trade with.

Chapter 3
Colonial Discontent

1760 - 1774

It shouldn't be a surprise that those who were most active in rebelling against British occupation, taxes and tariffs would later become delegates to the Constitutional Convention and signatory's to the Constitution and Declaration of Independence. Some participated in the drafting of the Declaration of Independence, while others became Senators and Representatives in Congress after the ratification of the Constitution. Many immersed themselves into the political system in many different ways. The line between being a patriot and a politician became one of the same thing and business men, farmers and tradesmen participated in many aspects of the revolution. However, not all immersed themselves into politics before, after and during the revolution. Most would return to their farms and shops and continued to make a living as if nothing had happened. Some were immortalized for their bravery in books, songs and poems, while others would fade away into oblivion without mention. James Otis, Paul Revere and Thomas Paine would be a few that accomplished so much in which their only reward was to have a voice in deciding their nation's future. History books often embellish on their accomplishment while neglecting the contribution and sacrifice others have made. It must be remembered that not all of the patriots and founding fathers were scholars or wealthy plantation owners and businessmen. Many were ordinary citizens with a unified goal for independence and a goal of choosing their own destiny as a nation.

It is further noted that many of the early patriots and revolutionary leaders had personal experiences with British revenue agents over taxation, tariffs and search and seizure laws that were imposed by the British Parliament. It would be of little surprised that colonial patriots later include remedies into Bill of Rights, such as the right to bear arms, freedom of speech, double jeopardy, search and seizure and quartering of troops without compensation in the Bill of Rights.

Over the year's small impositions such as tariffs and taxes became more frequent, partly due to Great Britain's involvement in numerous conflicts that were rapidly drained its treasuries, which lead to growing insurrection within the colonies and required firm and sometimes punitive retaliation to bring opposition into compliance. Like the American Civil War, nearly one hundred years after the American Revolutionary, discontent in the colonies grew over time, efforts on both sides failed to reach a compromise, and any compromise only served to delayed the inevitable. So history essentially repeated itself. The only difference was the British had a country to return to, whereas, the colonial confederacy did not.

Many of the revolutionaries during the period didn't want a war with Britain; in fact many practiced dual patriotism. James Otis didn't object to the taxes that were being levied, he objected to the right to debate the fairness of the taxes being levied upon the citizens and the methods being used to collect the taxes by allowing tax collector to invade homes in search of contraband products. While the Revolutionary War could have been completely avoided temporarily, in contrast the Civil War, one hundred years later could not.

America was no longer a child of Great Britain, and most American's wanted to try their own wings, without malice toward England, they wanted more input in government decisions and the right to debate the fairness of the taxes being levied upon them. James Otis was one such person who became vocal toward revenue agents and demanded to have representation in parliament.

James Otis
(1725 - 1783)

"It is a clear truth that those who everyday barter away other men's liberty will soon care little for their own." - James Otis

Tensions between the American colonies and Britain began as a result of James Otis and his personal declaration in 1764; announcing publicly that Britain's tax on imports amounted to taxation without representation. Along with others, he felt it to be an injustice. The idea of taxing American colonies by England without the option of debating the issues in Parliament was a basic right. Boston merchants began boycotting luxury goods from Britain under the guidance of James Otis, who repeatedly confronted the local authorities over taxes and search warrants issued by British customs officials. Britain made attempts to "crack-down" on smugglers who were not paying duty on imported goods.

James Otis Jr. was from a prominent family in Cape Cod, Massachusetts. He attended Harvard College and practiced law in Plymouth, Massachusetts. He later opened a law practice in Boston. In 1756, he was appointed as Advocate General in the Vice Admiralty Court, in which his primary duty was to prosecute smugglers. Britain used a new legal instrument called a writ of assistance that allowed custom officials and prosecutors to enter homes and businesses in search of contraband. He resigned his commission as Advocate General and continued his law practice in Boston defending aggrieved persons. In 1761, he represented local Boston merchants in a legal battle over Britain's use of the Writ of Assistance. His case was heard in February in which he gave a five hour argument. His argument began with;

"A man's house is his castle; and whilst he is quiet, he is as well guarded as a prince in his castle."

Even though Otis lost his case in court, he continued to represent the people of Boston in adversarial legal challenges against British colonial laws that were imposed on the American Colonies. Over the next three years, he continued his advocacy of American rights and was elected to the speakership of the General Court in 1766, but the governor (who was appointed by England) vetoed his acceptance to the position because of his ideology toward British overreach. Otis joined his fight with Samuel Adams, the cousin of John Adams, to stop the enforcement of the Townshend Act of 1767. John Hancock would later join his cause, which will be discussed later.

In 1769, he made a vicious attack in the Boston newspaper concerning a particular Boston custom-house official. Late one evening while walking down a street in Boston he was confronted by the very same Boston Custom-house official he berated in the newspaper. An argument ensued in which the custom-house official severely beat him about the head with his cane, causing severe brain damage. He spent the remainder of his life walking the streets aimlessly. In May of 1783, he was struck by lightning and killed while walking down the streets in Boston. Samuel Adams would take-up his cause and continued where James Otis left off.

The relationship between Samuel Adams and James Otis has taken little notice in history, but both fought for the repeal of taxes imposed by Britain upon the colonies. James Otis was the original and principal leader of insurrection against taxation without representation. It would become the foundation for the Constitution long after his untimely death. Otis would be the torch of justice carried forward by Samuel Adams, John Hancock and others. Otis did not fight to oppose taxes; he fought for the right to debate publicly about the need for taxes and the importance of equal representation in parliament toward rebuttal. He confronted the British over the search and seizure laws called the Writ of Assistance" which would be part of the Fourth Amendment of the Bill of Rights in the Constitution. [79]

Samuel Adams
(1722 – 1803)

"No people will tamely surrender their Liberties, nor can any be easily subdued, when knowledge is diffused and Virtue is preserved. On the Contrary, when People are universally ignorant, and debauched in their Manners, they will sink under their own weight without the Aid of foreign Invaders."
- Samuel Adams

While most people think of Samuel Adams today as a popular brand of beer, his endeavored at making beer was a complete failure. He disliked being a brewer and thus gave it up shortly after beginning. While his business sense was poor, he gravitated toward politics, which was more to his liking.

Samuel Adams was born in Boston in 1722. His father, Samuel Adams Sr., was a successful businessman and a politically activist in Boston. Adams Sr. became actively involved in a number of organizations, such as the Boston Caucus and Boston Town Meeting. He was a member of the Massachusetts House and a Justice of the Peace. The Adams family was of puritan heritage in which his father became the deacon in the Old South Congregational Church.

He was a member of the "popular party", also known as the "Whigs", that advocated strict enforcement of the Massachusetts Charter of 1691, which protected the rights of citizens in colonial America from the over-reach of British authority. Samuel Adams Jr. was well educated and attended Harvard College and graduated with a master's degree. His father attempted to set him up in business on several occasions but his lack of money management was the result of numerous business failures.

In 1739, Massachusetts was suffering from a severe shortage of currency and Samuel Adams Sr. and the Boston Caucus created the "Land Bank", which provide loans to farmers and issued currency notes secured by the farmers land as collateral. The "Court Party" was political party that opposed the Land Bank and had ties and influence with the Royal Governor of Massachusetts and the Governor's Council and the upper chamber of the General Court, all of which had connections and appointments from the British Government. In 1741, the British Parliament dissolved the Land Bank and the Directors of the bank became personally liable for the currency notes in circulation from the loans. Since Samuel Adams Sr. was a Director, he became personally liable for the debt, for which he was ordered by the court to pay the debt in gold or silver. It wasn't long before the Government came to seize the family estate. Samuel Adams Sr. died seven years later. **(1)**

Samuel Adams Jr. put his communications skills to work in the fight against the British Colonial system. After his father's death, he realized the injustice of the British system and the laws they imposed and enforced upon the colonies under the auspices of self rule.

He was later appointed as a tax collector, but couldn't bring upon himself to collect taxes from those who couldn't afford to pay. He would be sued and forced to pay the uncollected taxes. The uncollected taxes of 8,000 British pounds would eventually be paid by the Boston Town Meeting members for whom he and his father was active member.

Great Britain was involved in the seven years war, also known as the French and Indian Wars, from 1756 to 1763. The war had drained the British treasury and they became desperate to raise revenue to pay off the war debt. The American colonies were the most likely source of revenue, so the Parliament enacted the Sugar Act which was a tax on sugar and molasses imported into the colonies from the British held colonies in the Caribbean.

Footnote (1): The Court Party wasn't a political party per se, but rather a club of judicial administrators who were patriotic toward England's colonial rule. Their appointments were based on their loyalty to the King and England.

The Town Meeting was responsible for selecting representatives to the Massachusetts House and became a perfect forum for Adams to give speeches denouncing the British taxation without representations in Parliament, which was a violation of previous colonial charters signed by the British Parliament.

The original colonial charter between Great Britain and the colonies gave the colonies the authority to tax its citizens for the purpose of paying the Judiciary, Governor and their staff, even though they were appointed by the positions were held by British appointees. Adam's speech was published in the media in May of 1764, which drew the attention of James Otis Jr. (previously mentioned), who became closely associated with Adams and John Hancock. The two would confront the British Parliament over taxation by writing letters and giving public speeches.

In 1765, an act of defiance against the colonies was issued by the British Parliament, in which they passed the Stamp Act, which was a tax on all printed media. The Stamp Act created a tremendous backlash throughout the Colonies. The House of Burgess in Virginia sent the King and Parliament a "Set of Resolves" against the Stamp Act, but neither authority responded. Colonial discontent began in Boston and spread throughout the colonies. Riots began to erupted and as a result, nine men in Boston formed the "Sons of Liberty" who would later be the principal's involved in the Boston Tea Party.

When Adams was elected as the clerk of the Massachusetts House, he convinced the Mayor of Boston, John Hancock, to join the tax rebellion. The Stamp Act was repealed by Parliament but in its stead, Parliament passed the Townsend Act of 1767, which imposed duties on goods imported into the colonies. The taxes collected were to be used to pay the Royal Governors and Judges, which was once the responsibility of the Colonies. To enforce the Townsend Act, Britain created a customs agency in the colonies which forced Adams to call a meeting of the Boston Town Meeting and demanded a boycott of all British goods. Adams and Otis drafted a letter which was known as the "Massachusetts Circular Letter" which was to be circulated to all colonies condemning the Townsend Act as being unconstitutional and requested that all colonies unite to fight the Act.

Lord Hillsborough was the British Colonial Secretary and the highest Administrator in the colonies at the time. He decreed that all colonial governments would be dissolved if they responded to the Massachusetts Circular Letter, demanding a boycott of British goods. The British Ship, HMS Romney, arrived in Boston Harbor and seized the sloop "Liberty" which was owned by John Hancock, under the suspicion that the "Liberty" was importing goods from the Netherlands illegally without paying the tariff. Lord Hillsborough ordered four army regiments into Boston which precipitated in riots around Boston. A confrontation between British troops and rioter in Boston led to the Boston massacre in 1770, in which 5 civilians were killed. Eventually the riots subsided and the Parliament repealed the Townsend Act in exchange for New York, Philadelphia and Boston abandoning the boycott of British goods. Samuel Adams was devastated in losing the fight over his tax revolt. He would later was re-elected in the Massachusetts House in 1772 and confronting Parliament once more over the Sugar Act, thus the Townsend Act was repealed as part of a negotiated agreement between the two.

In 1773, the Tea Act was passed by Parliament, which was the impetus for Boston Tea Party. Some historians claim that Adams was not involved directly in the tea party and this maybe true. In retaliation, the Parliament enacted a series of Acts; one of which one was the Boston Port Act, which forbid ships into the Boston Harbor until the East India Company got paid for the loss of the tea that was dumped into the Boston Harbor. The Massachusetts Government Act canceled the election of government officials and the Administration of Justice Act, which wouldn't allow criminals to stand trial in the colony for which the crime was committed. Adams and four other members of the Massachusetts House were selected to attend the First Continental Congress in Philadelphia in September of 1774. When Adams returned to Boston, he served on the Massachusetts Provincial Congress where they established a militia army of volunteers called the "minutemen". He would later be selected to attend the Second Continental Congress in Philadelphia. In June of 1776, Richard Henry Lee introduced a three part resolution in the Continental Congress calling for a declaration of Independence from Great Britain. Samuel Adams and John Hancock were among the two delegates to sign the Declaration of Independence on or about July 4, 1776.

During the revolutionary War, Samuel Adams remained active by serving on the Board of War and was appointed to the committee to draft the Articles of Confederation, which was ratified by the colonies in 1781. He retired from the Continental Congress the same year due to health issues. He had developed tremors and was unable to write legibly, however he remained active in the Boston Town Meeting and was elected to the Massachusetts State Senate. He served as Lt. Governor under John Hancock who served as Governor of Massachusetts, and after Hancock's death; he became the Governor of Massachusetts as well. One of his greatest accomplishments was his ability to convince delegates to incorporate the Bill of Rights into the Constitution. Because of tenacity he and John Hancock were able to convince others the importance of a bill of rights within the Constitution as a right for all future states under a unified federal government. The "Father of the Revolution", Samuel Adams, the cousin of John Adams, died on October 2, 1803 in Boston.

Samuel Adams Legacy

Samuel Adams devoted his entire life for the cause of self rule. From his puritan heritage, he held a strong belief in what he perceived as morally right and justified. When he attended the First Continental Congress in Philadelphia, they took donations to help him purchase nice clothes to wear at the Constitutional Convention, since he wore tattered clothing and always looked like a vagrant. His cause was not about money or power, but a strong belief in a republic, where issues are debated and compromises made. Samuel Adams is a perfect example of the principles of democracy where the people are the ultimate power over government and that one person can effect change over the possible overreach of government.

When the Articles of Confederation were drawn-up and sent to each State for ratification, many States had their own State Bill of Rights, and many delegates believed it wasn't necessary to incorporate them into the U.S. Constitution. Samuel Adams was adamant about including the Bill of Rights as the first Ten Amendments to the Constitution, and having a provision in which future Amendments could be added or removed. He lobbied relentlessly to accomplish the rights we enjoy today, however his legacy as been relegated to the back pages of American history. For those who have studied American history, he will always be remembered as the father of the revolution and his relationship with James Otis and John Hancock. His legacy goes undisputed yet today he most remembered for the popular brand; "Samuel Adams Beer".

John Hancock
(1737 – 1793)

There! His Majesty can now read my name without glasses. And he can double the reward on my head! - John Hancock

John Hancock was one of the mostly forgotten figures in American history. He is most remembered as the delegate with the largest and most flamboyant signature on the Declaration of Independence, which has over-shadowed his real legacy. He was born on January 23, 1737 in Braintree, Massachusetts (now called Quincy). His father was a Pastor who lived in the same town as Samuel Adams. As a child, they would become acquainted even though Samuel Adams was 15 years his senior. In 1744, his father died and he was sent to live with his Uncle and Aunt, Thomas and Lydia Hancock. Thomas Hancock was the proprietor of the House of Hancock which imported goods and liquor from Britain and its colonies. The business was very successful and Thomas Hancock became the wealthiest man in Massachusetts. At a young age he learned the business from his Uncle and would later become a partner. He attended Harvard and graduated in 1754 and continued to work in his Uncle's business until his death in 1764. Under the terms of Thomas's will, he freed all of his slaves. John would take over the business and expand the business into smuggling products from the Dutch East Indies Company, which was forbidden by the British law, which only allowed trade to be conducted through the British East India Company.

He would continue his relationship with his childhood mentor, Samuel Adams in protesting tariff and taxes imposed upon the colonies. The Molasses Act of 1733 and the Sugar Act of 1764 were of particular importance in that he joined Samuel Adams and John Otis in their protests.

Hancock's sloop, the "Liberty" arrived in Boston Harbor with a shipment of Madeira Wine from Spain. Custom officials boarded the ship and found only 25 bottles of wine on board. The custom official suspected that Hancock had unloaded the wine during the night at another port before entering the harbor. A month later a similar situation occurred in which custom officials found 20 barrels of tar and 200 barrels of oil for which there were no bill of laden or permit of loading.

The "Liberty" was seized by custom officials who precipitated into a riot in Boston over the seizure. Hancock had to appear before the court concerning the seizer of the "Liberty", in which he lost his court case, only to have the ship burned in Rhode Island by rioters or revenue agents. The charges against Hancock for smuggling were dropped.

John Hancock didn't take part in the Boston Tea Party; however he gave a speech at the town meeting that same evening of the Boston Tea Party. In retaliation for the Boston Tea Party, the British Parliament enacted the Boston Port Act which created a blockade of the Harbor until the cost of the tea was repaid. To enforce the Act, British troops were sent to Boston to restore control of the mobs that had gathered. Later in the spring of 1775, the first shots were fired in Lexington and Concord which began the Revolutionary War. During the War, Hancock was selected as a Massachusetts delegate to the Continental Congress in Philadelphia and unanimously elected President of the Continental Congress, for which he served two years.

In August of 1775, he wed Dorothy Quincy and would have two children. Their daughter would die 10 months after birth and their son would die as a result of an ice skating accident at the age of nine.

Hancock was voted President of the Continental Congress when the Declaration of Independence was adopted and signed. In October of 1777, he returned to Boston and was re-elected to the House of Representatives and a delegate to the Continental Congress. When he returned to Philadelphia, he voted for the Articles of Confederation, which was ratified in 1781. He was elected Governor of Massachusetts from 1780 to 1785.

When the U.S. Constitution was drafted and sent to the States for ratification, he first opposed the ratification of the Constitution unless it included a Bill of Rights, which was later added to the Constitution as ten separate amendments in 1791. During his later years as governor of Massachusetts, his health began to fail. On October 8, 1793, with his wife at his side, he died at the age of 56.

During the later part of his political career, his relationship with Samuel Adams became strained and they seldom associated, partly because of his flamboyant style, which Adams felt was not in keeping to the principals of the revolution of the common man. Samuel Adams became the Governor of Massachusetts after his death declared a State Holiday in honor of Hancock. The funeral was the largest and most lavish funeral procession in American history at the time.

John Hancock was a flamboyant patriot and always dressed elegantly. Because of his wealth and the image he wanted to project, it drew criticism from other delegates who believed Hancock wanting notoriety and a position in society and politics, however much of his physical demeanor was "window dressing" and far from reality.

He was very generous with his money and spent most of his wealth supporting the revolution at the expense of his own personal wealth. He fought vigorously against British rule in the colonies and because of his foreign business connections; he was able to garner financial support to continue the revolution when it appeared all was hopeless. But, contrary to some historian's view of John Hancock, he did not seek notoriety selfishly; and was selected as a candidate for President, but did not campaign. He requested Washington for a commission in the colonial army but was turned down, as Washington felt his contribution was much more valuable in the Continental Congress, than on the battle field. John Adams wrote of Hancock, "he was almost buried in oblivion". Because of John Hancock's ship "Liberty" being seized, on suspicion of smuggling goods, Hancock wanted Amendments IV and V made part of the Bill of Rights concerning the search and seizure provision as a basic right of the people.

It would be difficult to imagine not having John Hancock as one of our founding fathers. His contributions and sacrifices he made both financially and his unselfishly. He was dedicated to his principals that have endured for more than 230 years.

Patrick Henry
(1736 – 1799)

> *"Is life so dear or peace so sweet as to be purchased at the price of chains and slavery Forbid it, Almighty God I know not what course others may take, but as for me, give me liberty, or give me death"* -Patrick Henry

Patrick Henry was born in 1736 in Studley, Virginia. His father, John Henry, was an immigrant from Scotland who was well educated and attended King's College prior to moving to Virginia in 1732. John would marry a wealthy widow in Virginia and have 10 children, of which, Patrick would be the second oldest.

Patrick Henry married Sarah Shelton, whose father gave the couple 300 aces and 6 slaves upon their marriage; however it was an old tobacco farm which had been over cultivated over the years and Patrick was unable to sustain a suitable living from the farm. The main house burned down in 1757, and he and his family moved into a small cottage on their land and would have six children together. In 1771, they moved to Hanover Tavern owned by Sarah's father where they lived upstairs. He opened a small mercantile store in Hanover, but it failed after a few years. After moving back to his farm, Sarah suffered from mental illness and would die in 1775. After the death of Sarah he apprenticed himself with a local lawyer and later was admitted to the bar.

In 1777, Henry married Dorothea Dandridge and would move to Williamsburg. He went into politics and was elected regional governor in which he remained in office for two years. Henry and Dorothea would have eleven children together.

Henry was elected as a delegate to the first Continental Congress in 1774 and the following year was elected as a delegate for Louisa County in the House of Burgesses. While in the House of Burgesses, he proclaimed that Britain had no right to impose the Stamp Act, since under British law, only the Colonies could tax its own citizenry. "Caesar had his Brutus; Charles the First his Cromwell; and George the Third...may he profit by their example. If this be treason, make the most of it." He would later apologize to the House of Burgesses and the King and for his treason against the King.

In March of 1775, he gave a speech in the Saint John's Church in Richmond, Virginia while the House of Burgesses was pondering the possibility of mobilizing a militia against the British military. Patrick Henry gave the following speech to the members:

"Is life so dear, or peace so sweet, as to be purchased at the price of chains and slavery? Forbid it, Almighty God! I know not what course others may take; but as for me, give me liberty, or give me death!"

In August of 1775, Henry was commissioned as a colonel in the 1st Virginia Regiment and in 1779, and jointly partnered the purchase of 10,000 acre known as Leatherwood Plantation in Henry County, Virginia. He would own 64 slaves along with his son-in-law who owned 18. Henry felt slavery was morally wrong and believed that someday slavery would be abolished in America.

He was elected governor of Virginia two times and was active in debating issues during the Articles of Confederation; however he declined to attend the Constitutional Convention in 1787. He was opposed to ratifying the Constitution for Virginia because it did not originally include the Bill of Rights and felt the Articles of the Constitution gave too much power to the Federal government. He steadfastly opposed James Madison's Virginia plan, which diminished Stats Rights and reinforced the Federalist view of a strong central government.

In 1794, Henry and Dorothea retired to Red Hill Plantation, which encompassed 520 acres of farm land in the county of Charlotte, Virginia. Washington offered him several key positions in his administration, but he refused. John Adams offered him a position as emissary to France and also refused. He was elected to the Virginia House of Delegates as a Federalist, but died of stomach cancer in 1799, just prior to taking a seat as a delegate.

Patrick Henry's Legacy

Unlike many of the founding fathers during the Revolution; no other person in history devoted so much of his effort to Virginia and Virginian politics. He refused all the national positions offered him, but most always devoted his time and energy to Virginia, even after retirement and during his last days.

He was a self taught by his father and became one of America's greatest orators. Like so many Virginians' and Southerners' he advocated states rights and feared that the United States as a Federalist nation would become a monarchy over time. He predicted that the South would cede from the Union and slavery would be abolished nationwide in the near future. It was later recognized that many of his premonitions would come true.

In his last will and testament, he gave his slaves to his relatives with the stipulation that they free those who were no longer needed. The single word or phrase that best describes Patrick Henry's life is; he inspired those around him and devoted his life to Virginia and the cause of liberty and the nation. He is considered one of the greatest orators in American history.

Thomas Paine
(1737 – 1809)

"Independence is my happiness, and I view things as they are, without regard to place or person; my country is the world, and my religion is to do good."
— Thomas Paine's " Rights of Man"

Thomas Paine was born in 1737 in Thetford, England and raised as Quaker. Benjamin Franklin and Thomas Paine met in London and with the help Franklin; he immigrated to Philadelphia in 1774. While on his transatlantic voyage, he became ill and remained in his cabin during the entire voyage.

Typhoid fever swept through the ship that killed 5 passengers during the voyage. When he arrived in Philadelphia after recovering from his illness, he began writing a brief article in the "Pennsylvania Journal and Weekly Advertiser:" titled "African Slavery in America". The article was critical of slavery and demanded the abolishment of slavery in America.

In January, 1776, he wrote and published a pamphlet called "Common Sense", which advocated American's independence and became an instant success, selling more than 100,000 copies the first 3 months of publication. Washington ordered his troops to read the pamphlet prior to Washington crossing the Delaware River to help inspire his troops and help them to understand what they were fight for. Two years later he published a second pamphlet titled "The American Crisis", which bolstered a surge in revolutionary recruitment, which was greatly need at the time. With Paine's literary success, he became more critical and less tolerant toward what he perceived as inequities in government which led to personal attacks against him.

Paine got involved in a personal attack against passage of the Jay Treaty with France and the Silas Deane Affair, where Deane was sent to France as a secret diplomat to encourage the French governments to help finance the colonist in the war against England. Paine publicly attacked Deane as a war profiteer while being employed by a wealthy Virginian, Robert Morris, who was a delegate at the Constitutional Convention in Philadelphia. Paine's criticism of the Jay Treaty and his alleged profiteering allegations was published in the "Pennsylvania Packet", which embarrassed the French government and nearly derailed efforts to secure financing from France. John Jay was the

President of Congress and was the chief negotiator with France in the Jay Treaty which he denounced Paine as being unpatriotic toward America's efforts toward independence. His credibility was severely damaged and forced his resignation as Secretary of the Committee on Foreign Affairs in 1779, for which he was appointed. He had even suffered personal attacks on the street as a result of his criticism and personal attacks accusing Silas Deane of war profiteering.

In 1787, Paine returned to England and wrote his third pamphlet called, "Rights of Man", which encourage the English people to rise-up and revolt against the monarchy. His pamphlet advocated social welfare, progressive taxation, retirement benefits and public employment. He would be charged with seditious and libel in England and tried in absentia as he fled to France to escaped imprisonment. He was elected to the French National Convention for which he could not speak French, yet advocated and voted against the execution of King Louis XVI, during the Reign of Terror and the French Revolution. Robespierre considered him an enemy of the State when the Jacobins came to power in France. He was arrested in December 1793 and sent to the Luxembourg Prison in Paris.

While Paine was in Prison, he began writing his next pamphlet, "The Age of Reason". Paine was slated for execution by the French, but for a minor stroke of good luck he was spared. Guards roamed the cells each day and placed an "X" on the doors of the prison cells to indicate who were to be executed the following day. A guard arrived at Paine's cell and found Paine sick and ordered the cell door opened to get fresh air. As the markers strolled past Paine's cell they placed the chalk mark "X" on the door, but since it was open, the "X" appeared on the inside of the door not the outside. When the door was closed the following day, the chalked "X" was not visible.

James Monroe made a deal with the French for his release from prison in 1794, but he elected to remain in France until 1802. While he was in France, Paine publicly accused George Washington of conspiring with the French to have him imprisoned. His criticism of Washington became personal, in which he convinced a well known Anti-Federalist, Benjamin Bache, to publish his letter in the Philadelphia newspaper, criticizing Washington. In his published letter he stated,

"....the world will be puzzled to decide whether you are a apostate or an impostor, whether you have abandoned good principles or whether you ever had any". 1796

He published his fourth pamphlet titled, "The Age of Reason" which defended deism and attacked the principals of Christianity and the agrarian justice system and demanded land reform for the farmers. When he returned to America in 1802, he came under attack by the evangelical Christians for his writing about deist principals, in which he was called an atheist. He would die in 1809, in which only 6 people attended his funeral.

Thomas Paine's Legacy

There was no other person in American history more controversial than Thomas Paine. He did much for America during the most critical time during the deliberation and debates over America's independence. Even though he had a disdain toward George Washington as a General and President, it was Washington that recommended to Congress that he be compensated in retirement for his contribution to the revolution when he returned to America. Washington held no malice toward Paine, even during his vicious attacks and never defended nor responded.

While at great cost to his honor and patriotism, he did not waiver in his philosophical views toward religion, independence and revolution against monarchial governments. He was the voice of common man rather those of the elite and wealthy. He was an inventor and it wasn't until Thomas Edison; 100 years later, acknowledged that Thomas Paine's inventions were 100 years before their time. Thomas Paine was also credited in giving the name to America, "United State of America", which appeared first in his pamphlets, and later used during the Constitutional Convention in 1787.

Paine advocated retirement for the elderly, a minimum wage for workers, land reform for farmers, free medical and abolishment of slavery. While he was consider a radical liberal at the time and even by today's standards, all of what he espoused eventually came to volition, which makes him a visionary among other things. He was a 21st century man born in the 18th century.

Thomas Paine was credited with writing "African Slavery in America", which proposed the emancipation of Slaves in America and the abolition of Slavery. As was common during the period in America, many authors such as Benjamin Franklin, would use "pen" names to conceal their identity from readers, since sedition was not tolerated in England or the Colonies and could lead to imprisonment or possible execution by hanging. However, it is widely believed that Thomas Paine was the true author.

Thomas Paine was said to be a "deist", in which many notable founding fathers were at the time. Jefferson, Adams, Washington were also said to be deist.

Deist believes there is a god, but they don't believe in his supernatural spiritual intervention with man. They believe in the "Laws of Nature" and not the doctrine of the Trinity or divine revelation.

Chapter 4

The American Revolution

1775 -1783

The American Revolution could be characterized as a civil war between two foreign counties. The American Revolution was different from other revolutions in history with perhaps the exception of the French Revolution. Ho Chi Minh organized a revolution to remove France as a colonial power in Vietnam and Indochina and install a political ideology called communism, which already existed in China and the Soviet Union at the time. The same was true with Mao Zedong; who wanted to do away with the capitalistic system and military style government and replace it with socialism. The American Revolution was different, in that the revolution didn't have a sole leader and an existing form of government it wanted to immolate, but rather create its own form of government that would become a republic run by the people rather than a ruling party or monarch. While Democracy was not new in history, most would eventually fail, but those who created the new style of representative republic had learned from the failures of other governments of similar structure.

America at the time was a British colony but not all colonists were loyal to the British crown. Parts of America fell under the control of Spain and France and certain enclaves in New York were of Dutch ancestry. In Virginia, a large population of British immigrants had established roots in the colonies decades before and as a whole, 80 percent were of British linage. There were many immigrants from all over Europe and especially from Scotland, Ireland, Poland and Prussia. They establish their own life styles and traditions brought over from the "old country" which made them feel comfortable in a new land. Many if not most immigrates to America participated in the American Revolution against British colonization and became soldiers of fortune. The colonial government recruited experienced soldiers from Europe for duty in exchange for land and citizenship for military services rendered.

It would have been very difficult for the colonial militia to win the war against Britain had it not been for France and Spain's intervention. General Washington openly admitted that he had little military training and knew very little about military strategy and tactics, however he welcomed those in his army that help provide the skills he lacked and the training the colonials needed. The continental congress sent ambassador's to Europe for the purpose of recruiting experienced military officers to help train militia and the continental army. One such person was Gilbert du Motier, also known as Marquis de Lafayette.

In January 1774, after the Boston Tea Party, the British Parliament met to discuss military action against the Colonies for insurrection. Prime Minister Frederick North headed the meeting in which the ministers maintained that the colonial militia would suffer an early defeat under the well organized and discipline British Army. Britain had the largest and most powerful Navy in the world, and may ministers felt it was a war soon won shortly after it began. As debates continued for several months, Britain's military leaders raised concerns over military logistics that went unheeded during the meetings. How could the British Navy blockade 1,000 miles of coastline? How far could the British troops advance into the interior without supplies that was situated on the coast? How is it possible to supply an army 3,000 miles from home? Would the cost of the war bankrupt England? Would other countries come to aid of colonies? **[9]**

After months of deliberation, Lord North's government agreed that America posed little challenge in the event of war, since they had no Army, Navy or military leadership. When the Continental Congress convened in America, King George III told the Ministers that "blows must decide" if America "submits or triumph." **[9]**

Great Brittan's decision to go to war with America was predicated on the fact that the colonial militia was ineffectual as a fighting force. The British considered them a "rag tag" group of farmers using shovels and pitch forks as weapons and fighting a war against a well disciplined and organized military with unlimited resources. General Washington's strength as a military commander was his ability to assess the strength and weakness of his men and select the battles he felt he could win or at least incur the most damage to the enemy, a tactic known today as "guerrilla warfare". His most valuable asset was his leadership and the ability to lead men into battle. Washington organized a militia as a backup force that consisting of the elderly and young men and women as support for the continental army. Many served as spies, messengers in guerrilla warfare of hit and run and sabotage. They were used as a second line of defense in the towns and villages for skirmishes against British patrols that would eventually weakened their desire to fight and die for little cause. George Washington had another characteristic that made him a great leader; his ability to realize that he needed other professionals who had skills that his army needed to defeat a superior force. Franklin went on a recruiting campaign in Europe to find such men.

Friedrich Wilhelm von Steuben
(1730 – 1794)

The Washington's regular army fell under the training of the Prussian General, Friedrich Wilhelm von Steuben. He was recruited under the advice of Benjamin Franklin. Steuben was appointed by Congress as a Lieutenant General in February 1778. He arrived in Portsmouth, New Hampshire with his aide de camp and his military secretary and two other men, who followed him everywhere. He was assigned to Valley Forge with Washington and was appointed temporary Inspector General with the rank of Major General. Washington was pleased with his performance, since he saved the military thousands in lost and stolen muskets. He was later appointed to train 120 men from various regiments in military discipline, dress, honor guards and military tactics. The 120 men would return to their respective regiments and train others. He would arrive during training classes in full military dress, without a wrinkle in his uniform. He trained them on the proper use of fighting using bayonets and bayonet charges. As a result, von Steuben's men engaged the British in the Battle of Stony Point with unloaded muskets and defeated the enemy using only bayonets taught by Steuben in his training program. He would write the book; "Regulations for the Order and Discipline of the Troops of the United States" which remained in use in the U.S. Military until 1814, after the War of 12, against the British.

It was assumed by many that von Steuben was gay when he met a young American officer whom he made his aide de camp. However, it did not influence his ability as an excellent military leader. He became ill and was taken leave after the Battle of Blandford. His command was given to Lafayette, but he returned to active duty to fight in the Battle of Yorktown. During his commission, he fought in 4 battles in which Congress awarded him full citizenship for his bravery and service to America.

Steuben was one of four high command European military leaders to serve in the Revolutionary War. In 1788, the New Jersey Legislature gave Baron von Steuben title to the Zabriskie Estate with 40 acres. Steuben was in heavy debt and sold the estate and moved to upstate New York on land granted him by the military for his duty during the war. A portion of his upstate New York estate became part of the University of the State of New York. Steuben never married and had no children. Upon his death, in November of 1794, he left his estate to his male companions, Captain Benjamin Walker and William North.
[9]

Marquis De Lafayette
(1757 – 1834)

"When the government violates the people's rights, insurrection is, for the people and for each portion of the people, the most sacred of the rights and the most indispensible of duties." — Marquis De Lafayette

Lafayette was born in 1757 in which his family was a wealthy land baron in Chavaniac, France with an ancestral background of famous French military leaders. He was commissioned as a military officer in the Musketeers at the Age of 14 in Paris and later attended the Military Academy of Versailles and commissioned as a lieutenant in Dragoons in 1773. American Diplomat, Silas Deane, had meetings with Louis XVI and requested aid to America and military officers to serve under George Washington. Lafayette eagerly accepted, even though he met resistance from his father-in-law, de Noailles and his family. However, he decided to pursue his convictions and sailed for Georgetown, South Carolina in June of 1777. Washington commissioned him as a Major General at the age of 19.

The Continental Congress was overwhelmed by the number of French officers that Deane had recruited while in France. Most could not speak English and had little military training and experience, however, Lafayette offered to serve without pay. Benjamin Franklin was well acquainted with Lafayette's family and their military history and encouraged Congress to accept him. He would become a member of Washington's staff and later given his own command.

The French officially enter the war when the French Naval fleet arrived in New Port, Rhode Island in July of 1778, under the command of Navy Admiral d'Estaing. This would be the turning point of the war. Over the next 3 years it became increasingly difficult for the British to maintain supplies to their troops. Local towns and villages were eager to supply the continental army with food and lodging but would not British troops. In addition, it would take 2 months for ships to arrive from England and bring military orders to field commanders. Once they orders arrived, the battle plans had drastically changed and could not be implemented in most cases, else the battles were over before commands arrived.

The final major battle of the revolutionary war culminated in the Battle of Yorktown, Virginia in June of 1781, and the surrender of Cornwallis and his army on October 19, 1781. The British still had control of several port cities; however, the Treaty of Paris between Britain and America would end the struggle for independence and the war.

When Lafayette returned to France in 1781, he received a hero's welcome. He would later fight in the French Revolution and became the leader of the King's National Guard. During the French Revolution the King was executed and Austria declared war on France. Lafayette was taken prisoner by the Austrians and spent 5 years in solitary confinement. General Napoleon Bonaparte released Lafayette's family from prison, where they fled to Prague and was turned over to the U.S. Consul in Hamburg, Germany. The US Government wanted to remain neutral in the war, but after his wife and children were released, the U.S. Minister to France, James Monroe, obtained passports for her and his daughters to immigrate to Connecticut and granted the entire family citizenship, but they refused and remained with Lafayette during his incarceration. Napoleon released Lafayette after 5 years in prison, but refused to allow Lafayette to return to France. All his money and land was seized which left him and his family penniless. The U.S. Government, with the help of Thomas Jefferson, provided Lafayette an income for his services while serving under Washington. He and his family managed to sneak across the border using false passports under the name of Motier. Bonaparte found out, but allowed them to remain in Le Grange, France as long as he did not engage in politics.

Over the years he kept in contact with Jefferson, in which they exchanged letters and gifts. He was not allowed to attend Washington's memorial held in Paris, in which he became close friends with during the war. Bonaparte restored Lafayette's citizenship in 1800.

After Napoleon was deposed in June of 1815, President James Monroe and Congress invited Lafayette to visit the United States in 1824, to celebrate America's 50th anniversary of its independence, which he gladly accepted. He was accompanied by his son, George Washington, whom he named after President George Washington. He received a hero's welcome in America in every city and State he visited. He would be a guest of Thomas Jefferson at Monticello during his visit.

In January 1834, Lafayette would contract pneumonia, but would briefly recover but several months later would once again catch pneumonia and remain bedridden. He would die on May 20, 1834 at the age of 76 in France. He was buried next to his wife a Picpus Cemetery in France. His son, George Washington, placed soil from Bunker Hill under his coffin. When news reached America of his death, President Jackson ordered a funeral honor only given to Presidents, with both Houses of Congress draped in black bunting for 30 days with members of Congress wearing mourning badges. John Quincy Adams gave a three hour eulogy, in which he said:

"high on the list of the pure and disintested benefactors of mankind" **[94]**

Lafayette's Legacy

Lafayette played an important role in defeating the British during the Revolutionary War and being wounded in the leg during the Battle of Brandywine, he and Washington both spent the winter at Valley Forge. He became an American icon before and after his death. The French considered him a mediocre commander, since being a commander of the Kings Guard to protect King Louis from the mobs and the reign of terror during the French Revolution and failed. He wanted France to become a Republic like America, and was imprisoned for his beliefs, but stood firm on his convictions. While not popular in France, in the 1790's, he became an icon in France long after his death. In America, he has always been considered a hero. He was one of the most patriotic Generals of the American Revolution. Historian Marc Leepson concluded in his study of Lafayette: "his legacy that few military leaders, politicians or statesmen can match" [10]

He has always been considered a patriotic American from France. During Lafayette's interview with the Continental Congress concerning his commission as General, he volunteered not to accept pay while in the service of the Continental Army, however Thomas Jefferson and James Monroe requested from Congress a bill which would restore his pay with interest for his service to America.

The Declaration of Independence

The Declaration of Independence was the first stage toward cutting ties with Great Britain and its mercantile system imposed by protected trade, taxes and tariffs. It was a declaration in which the American colonies wanted to publicly inform the rest of the world that America was no longer dependent on the British Common Wealth for imports and exports on trade and further opened the door for all nations to trade. To resist efforts against British authority, it carried a punishment of treason and sedition punishable by death. The five men who drafted the Declaration of Independence were considered traitors and were well aware of the punishment they faced should they not succeed.

England wanted an imbalance in trade, in which they would export more products than they imported into England. This system was called mercantilism and was common practice by many European nations at the time, as it is today. The thought of losing America as a colony could have severe financial implications to England, and they were not eager to lose one of their biggest colonial assets without a fight.

The Second Continental Congress convened on May 10, 1775 and over the next year, little progress was made toward mediating a resolution with King George and the British Parliament. In the interim, King George commissioned German mercenaries to quell the rebellions against the crown. John Adams gave Thomas Jefferson the task of drafting the Declaration of Independence, which would be edited and voted upon by the Continental Congress committee. The Second Continental Congress continued to meet at various locations while the Revolutionary War continued under the leadership and command of George Washington and his newly established Continental Army.

Thomas Jefferson stayed at a boarding house at Market Street and South 7th Street in Philadelphia when he drafted the copy of the Declaration of Independence, which was called, "A Declaration by the Representatives of the United States of America In General Congress Assembled". On June 28, 1776, Thomas Jefferson presented the draft to the Continental Congress committee for final editing and eventual acceptance by the entire Congress.

A committee of five were selected to edit the draft; John Adams of Massachusetts, Benjamin Franklin of Pennsylvania, Thomas Jefferson of Virginia, Robert Livingston of New York and Roger Sherman of Connecticut. Once edited, it would be voted upon on the floor of Congress after an open floor debate on July 1, 1776. Each State had one vote in Committee, regardless how many delegates were present. Pennsylvania and South Carolina voted against independence and New York abstained. Delaware cast no vote since they only had two delegates and each split their vote. Nine States voted for independence which cleared the way for a floor vote in Congress. On July 2, 1776, the Continental Congress voted with twelve affirmative and one abstention. On July 4, 1776, the edited version of the Declaration of Independence was approved and sent out for publication and distribution.

It wasn't necessary to have the delegates sign the document to make it official; however, fifty-six delegates signed the document but not necessarily on July 4th. It has been said that John Adams after signing the Declaration of Independence told Benjamin Franklin, "…we must hang together on this" and Franklin replied, "Or hang separately."

The Declaration of Independence was a document that expressed international sovereignty and independence of the United States. The original draft listed the grievances' the American colonies had against England, but would later be removed and edited as to not inflame Britain with specific issues of discontent. America still wanted friendly relations with Britain and not wanted to fan the flames of war.

It was not a legal document per se, but rather a philosophical document that represented the feeling of the majority of Americans. Its purpose was to allow American's to vote on their own destiny and serve notice to other nations that America was independent and not part of the Common Wealth of Great Britain and open for trade.

The Slave Trade

Boston was a major sea port on the eastern seaboard of America during the colonial period, which traded in goods and products that arrived from England and other British colonies. The tax acts imposed by Parliament directly affected merchants and traders in New England.

Slaves were loaded aboard ships in the African British colonies of Gambia, Ivory Coast, Nigeria and Ghana; bound for the East Coast of American and the Caribbean. Slaves were shipped to the Caribbean to work in coffee and sugar plantations that were owned by wealthy British plantation owners. British ships loaded sugar, coffee and rum bound for America after off-loading slaves from Africa. It would be called the British trade triangle. The Portuguese were also slave traders and would ship slaves to its colonies in South America and the Caribbean. The slave trade continued until the early 1800's, even though England ended slavery decades before and abolished slave trade in the Slave Trade Act of 1807, however it did not apply to the British Colonies or to the British East India Company, who were the major transporters of Slaves to America and the Caribbean Islands. England had between 10 to 14 thousand slaves in residence, but most were household servants. In America, there were 700 hundred-thousand slaves prior to the Revolutionary War. In 1772 the legal case, Somersett Case of 1772, held that no slave could be forcibly removed from Britain, even though it did not apply to the British Colonies. Slavery was completely abolished in the British Empire in 1833, but didn't apply to the British East India Trading Company until 1843.

America's Strategy of Wining the Revolution

General Washington knew the American militia alone could not defeat the British Army in open battle, but he elected to use hit and run tactics to reduce casualties of his army and prolong the war with Britain. His tactic was to stall and engage the British while Washington was able to recruit assemble and train a regular army. This would require military help from Europe. To everyone's surprise, including Washington, America did have some outstanding military leaders to draw from. One such person was Nathanael Greene. Even though he didn't have prior military training, he had natural leadership ability and a remarkable military sense, even though being raised as a Quaker and a pacifist. After Greene's sudden death in 1786, his wife, Catharine "Caty", hired an inventor named Eli Whitney, to build a machine that would help her remove seeds from cotton, which would provide for her family of six children. It would be known as the "Cotton Gin", which would make Eli Whitney famous and wealthy, and "Caty" being able to sell seedless cotton to support her family.

Nathanael Greene
(1742 – 1786)

Nathanael Greene was raised as a Quaker and pacifist as mentioned. He was born in Warwick, Rhode Island in 1742, where his father worked as a metal smith and owned a small foundry. His father belonged to a sect of Quakerism that didn't believe in literature or the arts, so his primary education was centered on mathematics and law. However, he was self-taught by Reverend Ezra Stiles who would later become the President of Yale University in New Jersey.

At the age of 32, he joined the militia, known as the Kentish Guards in Rhode Island and became active on a full time basis. His choice to enlist into the militia prompted the Pacifist Quaker sect to expel him. A year later, he was promoted from private to major general of the Rhode Island Army of Observation. Later in the same year he was appointed brigadier general of the Continental Army in which Washington assigned him to Boston in 1776. He would fight numerous battles with brilliant results and was revered as among the best military tactician of the revolutionary war. It was expected by the Continental Congress as well as George Washington that Greene would be Washington's replacement in the event Washington was wounded in battle. His most famous battle was in South and North Carolina and the Dan River skirmish and the Battle of Guilford Court House in 1781. Eventually controlling 90 percent of the South from a superior British force commanded by General Cornwallis.

After the war, the Carolina and Georgia gave General Greene large land grants as a gift for his service, which he would sell to pay for the rations he purchased from his own pocket during his campaign in the South. He would retire on his land grant estate in Georgia, called Mulberry Grove Plantation in 1785 after refusing a position as Secretary of War. He died of sunstroke one year later at the age of 43 on his plantation in Georgia. Upon hearing of Greene's death, George Washington volunteered to raise his children as a sign of respect for his most trusted and gallant officer of the America Revolution.

John Paul Jones
(1747 – 1792)

Most American's today know little of John Paul Jones' legacy and his contribution to American history His real name is John Paul and was born in Scotland in 1747. At the age of 13, he began his naval career aboard numerous British naval merchant ships and slave ships.

As he rose to the rank of Captain, he was embroiled in controversy over the flogging of a carpenter aboard a ship he commanded in which the sailor died of his wounds. His reputation was tarnished when it was learned that the sailor was from an influential family in Scotland.

His leadership problems continued when he killed a mutineer named "Blackton" with his sword over a wage dispute while sailing in the West Indies and commanding the ship "Betsy". He was due to report to the Admiral's Court in Scotland but fled to Fredericksburg, Virginia to handle the affairs of his brother's will, who had recently died. He added the name of "Jones" to his name and never returned to England to answer the charges against him. In 1775, as war with England was imminent, he offered his services to the Continental Navy with an endorsement from Richard Henry Lee and was appointed 1st Lieutenant on the 24-gun frigate.

Commodore of the Continental Navy; Esek Hopkins assigned Jones to several supply voyages to the West Indies, where he captured a British military supply ship. The Continental Navy commissioned 13 frigates in the anticipation of war. Nova Scotia, Canada was under firm control of the British as a coal mining facility and port. Jones was commissioned to command the "Providence", where he captured 16

British supply ships off the coast of Nova Scotia. His success did not go unnoticed by Commodore Hopkins. He was given the assignment to liberate hundreds of Americans imprisoned in Nova Scotia who were forced to work in the coal mines. He was unable to free the prisoners; however he captured the British ship "Mellish" which was carrying General Burgoyne's winter clothing for his troops.

John Paul Jones was a masterful ship commander; however he lacked the tactful skills of accepting orders from his superiors and was frequently accused of insubordination. He entered into a feud with Commodore Hopkins over naval tactics and strategy, in which he was reassigned to command a smaller ship "USS Ranger" in 1777 and ordered to France to wait for Benjamin Franklin, Silas Deane and Arthur Lee to complete their work in Paris. His naval career appeared to be stalled as a result of his insubordination with Commodore Hopkins.

France entered the American Revolutionary War on February 6, 1778 with the signing of the Treaty of Alliance with America, Jones' attention was diverted to the coast of Ireland and Scotland in an attempt to attack coal supply ships anchored in Carrickfergus, Ireland. The first attempt resulted in a failed attempt and he diverted his ship to Whitehaven, Scotland where his sailors resorted to pillage of the town for booty rather than as a military tactic. He would later once again return to Ireland and confront the British war ship "Drake" by defeating it in a gun battle and capturing it. While his defeat of the "Drake" exonerated Jones as a "privateer", it proved he was an exceptional naval commander.

In 1779, Jones commanded the USS Bonhomme Richard, which was a modified merchant ship owned and built by the French. It was joined by a fleet of French and Spanish war ships bound for England, Jones was to sail toward the coast of Ireland as a diversion, while the remainder of the armada continued toward England. The British fleet intercepted the Bonhomme Richard and its small fleet off the coast of

Ireland and Scotland.

Jones would eventually engage the British in the Battle of Flamborough Head on September 23, 1779. Being over gunned by the British ships "HMS Serapis", "HMS Alliance" and "HMS Countess Scarborough", the Bonhomme Richard and "Pallas" was unable to over-come the bombardment of its 50 guns. When asked to surrender, as the Bonhomme Richard was burning and slowly sinking, Jones replied, "I have not yet begun to fight". The "Pallas" engaged the HMS Scarborough and after an hour battle, it was captured. The British was unable to board the Richard, since Jones had snipers stationed on the long arms of the ship firing volleys on to the ship as it approached for boarding. The Richard was beyond repair and it was decided to sink the ship rather than attempt to repair. Jones took command of the HMS Serpis, in which he captured and headed for Holland for repairs.

King Louis XVI of France bestowed the honor as "Chevalier" on Jones and would receive the Merit of Honor and Sword. The Continental Congress would give him a Gold Medal of Honor for his heroism in battle. From 1782 to 1787, Jones would not receive a command or a ship. He would take a commission with the Catherine II of Russia. (7) His first assignment as Rear Admiral in the Russian Navy was in command of the flag ship "Vladimir" in the Black Sea, fighting against the Ottoman's. He would fall out of favor with Prince Potemkin of Russia and 1 other Admirals and called back to St. Petersburg. In 1789 he was accused of having sex with a 12 year old girl, who was a prostitute.

He would be acquitted of charges but his navel career in Russia was over. His reputation followed him to other countries in Europe as well, where he would fail to get another commission. Jones returned to Paris in 1790. He applied for another commission in the Russian Navy, but was turned down. In 1792 he was appointed as U.S. Consul acting on behalf of America in an effort to negotiate the release of

American captives in Algiers.

In June of 1792, John Paul Jones was found dead at the age of 45 of interstitial nephritis, in his Paris apartment. He would be buried in the St. Louis Cemetery in Paris. The Property was later sold and his burial plot has long been lost and forgotten. In 1905, with the help of Ambassador to France, General Horace Porter, they searched for 6 years in an effort to find his burial plot by searching though old burial records. His body was exhumed and returned to the United States under a flotilla of U.S. Naval Battleships that arrived in 1906. His remains was interred in a bronze and marble sarcophagus at the U.S. Naval Academy in Annapolis, Maryland.

In 1999, the Port of England, gave Jones a posthumous pardon for the raid of the town. The U.S. Navy was given the "Freedom of the Port of Whitehaven", which was the only time in 400 years that such an honor has been granted.

Chapter 5
The Continental Congress

1773 - 1787

The Continental Congress was established in 1774 as a result of Britain enacting the Intolerable Acts against the American Colonies. In Boston, protests against the Acts resulted in Britain declaring martial law and closing the Boston Harbor for shipping. It would lead to the Boston Tea Party and a series of uprisings throughout Massachusetts that spread throughout the colonies. Benjamin Franklin proposed a Continental Congress to formally protest the Intolerable Acts with little resolve from King George III. The first Congress was held in Philadelphia in the fall of 1774 and as a result the Tolerable Acts were repealed by Britain on December of 1774. In October 1775, Congress prepared a list of grievances to be addressed by King George III and the Parliament, the Parliament refused to discuss the grievances. The colonies instituted a boycott on British goods, which further exacerbated the problem the between the colonies and Great Britain and would lead to war in 1783.

The First Continental Congress met at Carpenter's Hall in Philadelphia in 1774; a year after Benjamin Franklin proposed that the Colonies establish a Continental Congress when Britain instituted a British blockade of the port of Boston as a result leading to the events of the Boston Tea Party. The attitudes of the colonist would change in 1774 when the British Parliament and King George the III enacted the Coercive and Intolerable Acts of 1774.

It would begin in May of 1773, when the British Parliament passed the Tea Act. The British East India Company was having financial difficulty thus requiring that all tea imports bound for America be received at the port of London to be assessed duty and tax, before being shipped to America. To save money, the East India Company wanted to ship tea directly into Boston to avoid having to handle the product twice and having to pay taxes in England and in America. Britain enacted the Townshend Act which levied duty on products imported to America. Colonist became in sensed over the duty and not having representation in parliament to rebuke the law. The Colonist elected a boycott of purchasing British goods and commodities such as tea. Colonist began growing tea in retaliation. *

*Author's note: The British East India Company was a trading company chartered by the British Government to export and import trade goods from the British colonies. This was a common practice during the period

In November of 1773, three ships arrived in Boston Harbor with tea and other goods. A local group known as the "Sons of Liberty" dressed in Mohawk Indian dress, they tossed 342 crates of tea overboard while being careful not to damage other products. In retaliation, the British Parliament enacted the Coercive/Tolerable Acts in the spring of 1774.

The colonies felt it necessary to convene the First Continental Congress to protest their grievances to King George III. There were fifty-six delegates representing the thirteen colonies, in which Peyton Randolph of Virginia was elected the first Continental Congress President. Revolutionary War with England had already begun by 1773, with skirmishes occurring randomly throughout New England.

The first Continental Congress was split between those who wanted to remain under the British Crown and those who wanted independence from Great Britain. The delegates of the Continental Congress made a list of grievances and presented it to the British Parliament and King George, which was not warmly received.

On November 30, 1774, King George III gave his address to the British Parliament, in which he condemned Massachusetts over the embargo of British products and defended the blockade of Boston that effectively blocked American Ships from entering and leave the Port. The list of colonial grievances was ignored by Parliament which prompted a second Continental Congress adjourn to deal with the On going issues between the British Parliament and King George III.

In drafting the Articles to the constitution, James Madison, of Virginia assumed the role as a sponsor in drafting and presenting to the Continental Congress and outline for debate. Perhaps the most volatile issue was State sovereignty and slavery. The division between delegates followed closely to geographical boundaries of North and South. It was well known at the time, that most delegates in the South were wealthy aristocrats who own large land holding and plantations with slaves, hence the issue of slavery was carefully averted in debates of abolishment and only addressed when it came necessary to determining how to proportion the population when selecting members to the House of Representatives in regards to the number of slaves within an election district.

The Second Continental Congress met shortly after the War began. As a result the British government in the colonies collapsed and the Second Continental Congress initiated a Declaration of Independence in 1776 and drafted the articles of confederation. The Continental Congress would meet again on March 1, 1781, after which the Congress of the Confederation was established, and created the Bank of America, Land Ordinance of 1784 and 1785 and the Northwest Ordinance of 1787. The 10th and last Congress of the Confederation was held in New York in November 1788; at which the Congress of the United States was adjourned in Philadelphia for the purpose of establishing the Constitutional Convention of the United States a year before.

The Articles of Confederation

The Articles of Confederation was essentially the first Constitution of America. It was drafted hastily as a result of the Revolutionary War that began in April 1775. It was important for the Colonies to unite to confront the superior forces of the British Army and Navy. The Articles of Confederation had to be written in a manner that accommodated all the colonies equally, and in doing so, most colonies didn't want a strong central government. They enjoyed the autonomy of being an independent province within the colonies as a whole.

When drafting the Articles, it stressed state sovereignty and gave little authority and power to a central government. Six drafts were prepared and presented to the Continental Congress, in which a final draft was accepted in 1777. After considerable debate the final Articles of Confederation was passed by the delegates from each colonial state.

The Articles that were ratified provided an interim unicameral government of Congressmen, each state having one delegate in Congress. The delegates were elected by the State Legislature as they existed at the time. Each State would retain their sovereignty and independence. The new government could not levy taxes or regulate commerce. However, the new Congress was given the following jurisdiction:

1. The government was to be financed by each state in accordance to the value of the privately owned land within the boundaries of each State.
2. Entering into foreign relations, treaties with other nations.
3. Jurisdiction in declaring war and maintaining militia a standing army and navy.
4. Regulate currency and minting currency.
5. Establish and Maintain a Postal system.

6. Establish and maintain a Judicial and court system.
7. Mediate disputes and grievances between States.

One of the failings of the Articles of Confederation was its ability to tax, negotiate treaties and organize a standing army or navy. Some states didn't want to provide revenue to pay for the new interim government or even the war debt that accrued during the war. The Articles didn't address a remedy for collection from the states. By 1784, one year after the Treaty of Paris with Britain, America's war debt was $40 million. $8 million was owed to the Dutch and French and the remainder being government bonds, certificates of indebtedness and such. Most of the soldiers fighting in the Revolution were not paid nor were merchants that supplied goods and materials to the Continental Army on credit.

As a footnote in history, Colonial America at the time didn't realize that having an interim Constitution during the war would ultimately clarify the major issues that were necessary in maintaining a new and better Constitution. Most felt that the Articles of Confederation would be the only Constitution needed. Had America accepted the Articles of Confederation and limited and restricted power of the federal government, eventually serious issues would occur as they were beginning to surface during the war. As a result, many of the Articles were deleted during the drafting the Articles of the Constitution, most notably the means and method of revenue collection and the budgetary process and a standing army. For many colonies, especially Virginia, they felt it gave too much power for a central government, which they opposed strongly.

America was in heavy debt, in which a new crisis developed that changed American history and how the U.S. Constitution would be re-drafted as a result of the Shay's Rebellion. The Shay Rebellion was important in many ways; it reaffirmed the right of all Americans to engage in a peaceful demonstration against a government for the inequity of a tax system imposed by Britain, yet only to be replaced by a new government that carried forward the same policy they fought against.

The Shay's Rebellion

Before the Constitution Convention was held in 1786, a small group of farmers returned from the war and found themselves in heavy debt over taxes imposed upon their land and farms in western Massachusetts. In some cases, their land was seized to pay the debt on loans and taxes owed the colony. Since many soldiers fought for years in the Revolution without pay, they were unable to pay the loan or the taxes when they were discharged from service. A revolt began to develop among the farmers in rural Massachusetts, led by Daniel Shay and a group of like farmers. What began as a peaceful assembly would later escalate into a much more serious rebellion. To make matters worse, European business partners who maintained a line of credit to Massachusetts merchants demanded hard currency for goods and refused further lines of credit. John Hancock was the Governor of Massachusetts and a merchant did not demand hard currency and refused to prosecute for delinquent taxes, but his predecessor, Governor Bowdoin, was less sympathetic to the farmer and demanded payment in hard currency and no credit. Bowdoin had ulterior motives; he was a wealthy merchant who held 3,000 British pounds in Massachusetts notes and had little sympathy for the merchants. As discontent swelled into other states, the rebellion expanded into a raid on the Springfield Armory where 1,500 protesters were fired upon by state militia, which left 4 dead and 20 wounded. Violence erupted throughout New England and as far south as North Carolina. Governor Bowdoin ordered the army to round-up the leaders of the rebellion. More than 4,000 were captured, 700 were indicted, 18 were sentenced to death, but later pardoned and 2 were hanged for looting on December 6, 1787, all others were given amnesty. As a result of the Shay's Rebellion, the Massachusetts Legislature cut taxes in December of 1787 and issued a moratorium on debts. Governor Bowdoin would lose the election in an overwhelming defeat to John

Hancock.

The Rebellion occurred while the Constitutional Convention was taking place in Philadelphia. The delegates were split between state sovereignty and a stronger central government. The Shay's Rebellion became a topic of debates concerning the rights of ordinary citizens to protest and have grievances heard. Some historians agree that the Shay's Rebellion painted a different picture of America's future when deciding issues of the Articles of the Constitution. It certainly became an issue when deciding the Bill of Rights toward the issue of the right to protest and the right for peaceful assembly and the right to bear arms.

During the colonial period, verbal communication and eloquent writing skills established a person's education and station in life. Many founding fathers were self-taught or taught by a tutor. Most were apprenticed to a local law firm or served as an aid to a local Politician who tutored them and recommended them to the bar. Wealthy plantation owner provided education and room and board to close friends who were unable to provide for their family or in the case of death of one or both parents and raise and educate their surviving children. It was how Thomas Jefferson, James Madison and James Monroe were educated.

In some cases, such as John C. Calhoun; his two older brothers worked and earned money to send Calhoun to Yale College. This act of generosity was common at the time, since families were large and the cost of education was beyond most people's financial means. In the colonial period, the most valued asset was a person's word and his honor, in which duels were fought to protect them.

The delegates to the Continental Congress were not elected by the people, but rather by their wealth or standing in the community. Most aristocrats occupied positions of authority, such as Judges, colonial legislators, delegates, governors, justice of the peace and such. The politics during colonial America was a "carry-over" from the aristocratic system used in Britain where Dukes, Barons and Earls represented the aristocratic elite in which their income was derived from the land they owned and passed down from generation to generation.

The Articles of Confederation and later the Articles of the Constitution were debated on the floor by the delegates. James Madison was active in drafting the Articles of Confederation and the Constitution. It would be Madison, Jefferson, Franklin and Washington who insisted the Articles of Confederation be voided and a new set of Articles be drafted in Philadelphia in 1787. The Constitutional Convention lasted 100 days, and James Madison insisted on voiding the entire Articles of Confederation and re-drafting a new set of Articles for the Constitution. With his persuasion and elegant style of logic and reasoning, he was able to convince other delegates to re-draft a new set of Articles and incorporating the ideas of the previous articles of Confederation.

Various plans were presented for the new Government such as Hamilton's proposal of a monarchial system of a King with a Parliament, while others wanted a system in which each state would be a sovereign state and a central government that dealt with foreign affairs and a standing military. But James Madison's Virginia Plan would be the system the majority of delegates would incorporate. Madison had drafted an outline for the delegates to debate its merits. Committees were organized to work on the details of the new government.

The Constitution Convention was held on May 25, 1787 at the Pennsylvania State House in Philadelphia for the purpose of drafting the Articles of the Constitution. The final draft was completed on September 17, 1787 and signed by 39 delegates from twelve states. Three delegates abstained. The next step was ratification by the 12 states, Vermont would be the thirteenth State admitted into the Union at the same time it ratified the Constitution. It is important to note that Vermont was not a State or recognized as a colony during the drafting of the Constitution and had no delegates represented during the drafting of the Constitution. On September 13, 1788, Congress certified the Constitution when 3 quarters of all states ratified the document. The Amendments; one through ten would become the Bill of Rights, which was not included in the original Constitution until December 15, 1791. The US Constitution has 7 Articles and the original 10 Amendments were called the bill of rights. Over time, 17 additional Amendments would be added to the Articles of the Constitution by Amendment and ratification of 3 quarters of the States.

During the first and second colonial congress, most laws were enacted by the individual states or colonies. Each state organized their own government, militia and State Bill of Rights, tax structure and would elect their own governors and appointed their own delegates to the Continental Congress in Philadelphia in order to draft the Articles of Confederation. The federal government really had no power over the states during the formation and creation of the Constitution. The federal government (colonial government) had no militia, no constitution or judiciary or authority. Since they had no real authority, most delegates wouldn't bother showing up to vote on issues, but only participated at the State legislature level, since it was more convenient for travel. The larger states; New York, Virginia and Pennsylvania dominated over smaller states due to having more delegates. George Washington and others saw the potential for problems when designing the Constitution and decided that a nation needed a strong central government and judiciary when negotiating treaties with foreign countries and domestic policies that would protect everyone equally under a single Constitution. Delegates and framers of the Constitution purposely avoided mentioning slavery as an issue while declaring that all people should have equal rights under the law, while most of the founding fathers owned slaves.

George Mason
(1725 – 1792)

George Mason was called the "Reluctant Founder" and played a significant role in the formulation of the Constitution and voiced his personal views toward abolishing slavery.
To my chagrin, history books seldom mention George Mason, but he was an important figure in the drafting of the Constitution and the Bill of Rights. Mason was a member of the Virginia Constitutional Convention which drafted the original Virginia Constitution and Virginia Bill of Rights. Washington later asks him to become a Virginia delegate and assist in drafting the U.S. Constitutional in Philadelphia in 1787. His father drowned when he was 10 years old and was left to his mother to manage his late father's large estate. Mason didn't have a formal education and was self taught. After his mother's death, he became among the wealthiest men in Virginia and a self taught scholar.

Each colony or State had their own Constitution and a Bill of Rights and many delegates were opposed of including a Bill of Rights in the U.S. Constitution. Many believed that each state would write their own Bill of Rights that applied specifically to each State's social condition. Mason believed that the federal government had too much power over the states and that the Constitution, as written, treated the south unfairly. He supported Article 1, Section 9, which outlawed the importation of slaves after 1808, even though he was a slave owner himself he refused to sign the Constitution during the Constitutional Convention. His legacy became not as a major contributor as other founding fathers, but rather the delegate who refused to sign the Constitution after assisting in drafting of it. Washington was elected President in 1789 and he became resentful of Mason for his uncompromising position against the constitution as written, which drove a wedge in their friendship.

George Mason was well known in Virginia, but much of his diaries and personal documents were lost, stolen or misplaced after his death. Little documentation of his service during the Constitutional Convention exists today, other than comments made by other delegates, such as Jefferson, which was recorded. Mason returned to his business and estate in Virginia and never entered politics again.

He was among the strongest supporters toward the abolishment of slavery, especially during his later years. It was his skill in writing the Virginia Constitution and Bill of Rights that provided the delegates at the Constitutional Convention a guideline on how it should be written. Most states used the Virginia Constitution as a guideline for their own state Constitutions, as well as the French Constitution which also was adopted from the Virginian Constitution as a template.

James Wilson
(1742 – 1798)

"Government, in my humble opinion, should be formed to secure and to enlarge the exercise of the natural rights of its members; and every government, which has not this in view, as its principal object, is not a government of the legitimate kind." – James Wilson 1790

James Wilson was born in Scotland in 1742 and came to America around 1765, the actual date is not known for sure. Samuel Adams, John Otis were already actively denouncing British authority over the Sugar and Stamp Acts when Wilson arrived in America, however, he became a strong supporter of the revolution by denouncing British authority to tax the colonies. He attended Philadelphia College and graduated with a law degree and gained notoriety by publishing his thesis; "Considerations on the Nature and Extent of the Legislative Authority of the British Parliament" which became widely read in the colonies. In 1775, he was commissioned as a Colonel in the Cumberland County Battalion and later became a Brigadier General of the Pennsylvania State Militia. The following year he became a member of the Continental Congress which last only one year, and served on the Committee on Spies along with John Adams, Thomas Jefferson, John Rutledge and Robert Livingston.

He became very wealthy after acquiring large tracks of land, along with other partners and share holders during the war for independence. He became President of the Illinois-Wasbash Company and continued to acquire more land in Pennsylvania, Virginia and the Ohio Valley and became one of the largest land holders in the United States. He aliened himself closely with aristocratic and conservative republican groups at the time.

He became a delegate to the Constitutional Convention of 1787 in Philadelphia in which his contribution to the Convention was his intellect as a political theorist, in which he studied the causes and effects of every revolution and political institutions in the world since Grecian Commonwealth to present time. He advocated the 3/5 compromise for apportionment and wanted members of Congress and the President to be elected by popular vote. He also advocated the theory of dual sovereignty, in which the United States would operate as both a central government and by state governments. He was an avid Federalist as well.

 Wilson was a driving force behind the ratification of the Constitution, even though he did not agree with all elements of the document, but actively pushed states to ratify the Constitution.

He later was appointed Associate Supreme Court Judge in 1789, under President Washington and became the first law professor of the College of Philadelphia in 1790, which later became the University of Pennsylvania. James Wilson would die at the age of 55 in 1798. He was most notable as founding fathers, comparable to James Madison and Thomas Jefferson. He spoke 168 times at the Convention in which most of his views followed closely to that of Madison and Jefferson. He was a member of the Committee of Detail, which produced the first draft of the United States Constitution. He and

Madison were the scholars at the Convention and understood the problems of dual sovereignty and the issues that needed to be addressed in drafting the Constitution. He believed the Constitution as written, would make America the greatest nation on earth. He seldom dwelled on insignificant details of the Constitution, but believed that great men would fine tune and resolve the issues over time, such as slavery, Bill of Rights and state Sovereignty, which divided most delegates at the Convention of 1787 and threatened the adjournment of the Constitutional Convention before the Constitution could be finalized and voted on.

Richard Henry Lee
(1732 – 1794)

Richard Henry Lee was born in Virginia in 1732. His father was Colonel Thomas Lee, who was a prominent figure in Virginian political circles. During his early years he was tutored and received a formal education in England at the Queen Elizabeth Grammar School in Wakefield, England. After returning to Virginia, he was appointed Justice of the Peace in 1757. In 1758, he was elected to the Virginia House of Burgess and later established the Committees of Correspondence, which advocated Independence for America. In 1774, he was chosen as a delegate to the First Continental Congress in Philadelphia and the Second Continental Congress. He filed a motion during the Second Continental Congress that read;

"... That these United Colonies are, and of right ought to be, free and independent States, that they are absolved from all allegiance to the British Crown, and that all political connection between them and the State of Great Britain is, and ought to be, totally dissolved."

He became President of the Continental Congress in 1784 that was held at the French Arms Tavern in Trenton, New Jersey. He was elected President of the Continental Congress and served one year, which was customary at the time. During his administration, he established the United States dollar, which was based on the value of the Spanish dollar as a national currency. He insisted that the government be funded by the sale of land ($1.00 per acre) rather than levy federal taxes on its citizens. Along with Thomas Jefferson's surveying skills and support by William Grayson and James Monroe, the current US Survey System was establish based on the 6 mile square, divided into proportional plots. The Land Ordinance of 1785 was passed in May of 1785. This system of land surveying continues today.

His method of selling land to fund the government eventually failed as a result of the "glut" of territorial land available. Most of the government land was occupied by Native American's who refused to acknowledge government ownership of the land. White settlers who squatted on Native lands were met with hostility. The government didn't have the resources to enforce land laws and ownership.

Lee was a signatory on the Articles of Confederation and the Declaration of Independence. After the Revolutionary War, Lee served as a US Senator pro tempore from Virginia from 1789 to 1792. He would die on his estate in Virginia in 1794. Lee was the Great Uncle of another famous man in American history, Robert E. Lee.

Gouverneur Morris
(1752 – 1816)

Gouveneur Morris was a Pennsylvania Delegate during the Constitutional Convention of 1787. For more than 100 days during the adjournment of the convention, Morris scribed the Articles of the Constitution with ink and quill on parchment. Even though it was a rough draft, it was given to Jacob Shallus, for emboss on parchment, with three original copies that was later signed by most but not all of the delegates.

Morris was raised in a family of wealthy land owners in New York. He attended Columbia University and studied under Judge William Smith. He would was later be admitted to the New York Bar and elected to the New York Provincial Congress and in January of 1778. He moved to Philadelphia to serve as a delegate in the Continental Congress and elected as a delegate from Pennsylvania during the Constitutional Convention of 1787. He would serve on the committee that wrote the final draft of the U.S Constitution.

Morris was outspoken and well known for his wit and wisdom. He was vocal on his political views on how a new government should be structured and his out-spoken views toward religion alienated several pious delegates. He was a strong advocate for the Constitution and opposed revolution and believed it could have been negotiated without the bloodshed. He believed only those with significant land holdings should be allowed to vote and the President should be elected by the elite rather by the citizenry. He advocated no term limits for Senators and Legislators and felt that the qualifications for holding congressional office should be based on the amount of taxes one paid. He was the most vocal of all the delegates at the Constitutional Convention, in which he spoke 173 times during the Convention. He was appointed to the Committee of Style that drafted the "wording" in the Constitution. Morris became a United States Senator from 1800 thru 1803 and was appointed US Ambassador to England and France. In later life he became Chairman of the Erie Canal Commission.

Morris was one of the few delegates to raised concern over slavery. He felt strongly that slavery should be e addressed in drafting the Constitution and was a vocal critic of slavery, which he raise the issue often during the convention.

In 1780 he was involved in a carriage accident that resulted in his right leg being amputated below the knee. He received many messages of sympathy from friends and delegates; however one letter in particular explained how fortunate he was to lose only one leg. Gouverneur Morris replied back;

"My dear Sir, your reason so convincingly and you show me so clearly the advantage of being without legs, that I am almost tempted to get rid of the other one."

Roger Sherman criticized Morris as a man of "few religious principals and sacrilegious in his speeches". But most misconstrued Morris' cynical comments and failed to appreciate his wit and wisdom from his dry satiric humor, which became his personal legacy. [2]

Morris was one of the founding fathers who served on the committee that wrote the final draft of the United States Constitutions. He was a Federalist and believed in a strong central government. He served in the Continental Congress and worked closely with George Washington to establish the method and the means for training troops and improved conditions for the Continental Army. In addition to his many accomplishments during the revolution, he became a signatory of the Articles of Confederation in 1778.

His greatest legacy was the tie-breaking vote in Congress that retained George Washington as General of the Continental Army, when many in the Continental Congress lost confidence in Washington as a military leader and wanted him replaced. His single vote and a strong belief in Washington's ability would change the entire history of America, and certainly American Revolution. He is worthy of being called one of the most influential founding fathers in American history.

Chapter 6
The Constitution

1787

"An elective despotism was not the government we fought for; but one in which the powers of government should be so divided and balanced among the several bodies of magistracy as that no one could transcend their legal limits without being effectually checked and restrained by the others."

February 20, 1788   James Madison, the Federalist Papers #58

I believe no better delegate exemplifies the American spirit more than Roger Sherman. He was not an aristocrat, scholar or a wealthy land baron, but rather a delegate who represented the common man. He was self taught and didn't attend school. He worked on his family farm and immersed himself into the cause of independence as he felt it was his duty to become part of an effort to determine his destiny and the destiny of others.

Roger Sherman
(1721 – 1793)

Roger Sherman was born in Newton Massachusetts in 1721. His father was a cobbler and shopkeeper until his death in 1741. Roger and his older brother moved to New Milford, Connecticut where they the two purchased a small store and worked part time as the county surveyor. In 1754, he was admitted to the Connecticut bar, even though he had no formal education in law and became the Justice of the Peace and county Judge in Connecticut. In 1761, he moved to New Haven, Connecticut and managed two stores and was later appointed to the Connecticut Superior Court and served as a representative in both houses of the colonial assembly.

Roger Sherman became a delegate from Connecticut during the Continental Congress of 1774 and serve for eight years. In Connecticut he served in the legislative, executive and judicial branches of government. Historians claim that he was not necessarily a good speaker, but he spoke 138 times at the Constitutional Convention. Thomas Jefferson once replied, "There is Mr. Sherman of Connecticut, who has never said a foolish thing in his life." He worked as a shoe maker, Surveyor, lawyer and a judge during his career.

Sherman was married two times and had 15 children. He was the second oldest delegate at the Constitutional Convention of 1787 in Philadelphia and was known as a very hard working, pious and well respected delegate at the Convention. He had a strong religious conviction and was well versed in the biblical scriptures. He advocated that the President be elected by the Legislature for a single 3 year term. His ability and legacy was his extraordinary ability to compromise and get delegates to compromise and advocated revolution and colonial boycotts.

He is most remembered in history for mediating a "dead lock" at the Constitutional Convention between the small states and the large states. The stalemate nearly caused the Northern and Southern colonies to walk out of the Convention, but Sherman was able to remind the delegates of what was at stake.

He was opposed the Bill of Rights being added to the constitution and followed the Federalist ideologies in supporting a national bank and enacting a tariff to provide economic stability in government and assuming State debts that accumulated during the revolution.

He was credited in saying;

"The question is, not what rights naturally belong to man, but how they may be most equally and effectually guarded in society."

His position on slavery was less clear. Even though he dislike the idea of slavery on a personal and moral level, he aligned himself on issues with delegates from Virginia that voted against abolishing slavery in an Articles in the Constitution in exchange for compromising on issues he favored.

Roger Sherman was one of only two delegates who signed all three historical documents; the Declaration of Independence, Articles of Confederation and the U.S. Constitution. He was among the most devoted and respected delegates at the Constitutional Convention. He received an Honorary MA Degree from Yale College in 1768. His most notable legacy was the Connecticut Compromise, which became the compromise between the Virginia Plan and the New Jersey Plan that offered a bicameral legislative branch of government that we have today.

The Virginia Plan

The Virginia Plan was a plan designed by James Madison and sponsored by Edmund Randolph, who was the Virginia Governor and delegate at the time. Randolph presented the plan to the convention floor on May 29, 1787. It proposed 15 resolutions that outlined the powers of the national government. Among the resolutions was a proposal that established three homogenous yet separate branches of government; the legislative, executive and judicial. Each branch of government provided a checks and balance on each other. The one flaw of the Virginia Plan was it favored larger states in congress and allowed larger states to have more delegates than smaller states.

The Virginia Plan proposed a legislative branch that consisted of a bicameral legislature. Each house had a upper and lower legislative branch in which the delegates were to be elected by the people, based on a population-weighted representation. The lower house delegates would be elected by the members of the upper house based on apportionment. One could see that this system could easily be dominated with crony capitalism and lend itself to corruption, nepotism and business favoritism.

Virginia vs. New Jersey

Virginia Plan	New Jersey Plan
Legislative branch with two houses	Legislative Branch with one house
Representation determined by population (proportional representation)	Each state would have one vote (equal representation)
Strong national government	Weak national government

The Virginia Plan also favored larger states with larger populations. Virginia and New York were the largest States during the colonial period, thus they benefit from the Virginia Plan, having a majority of representatives in Congress. The southern states also favored the Plan, such as North and South Carolina and Georgia. The single smaller State of Massachusetts also favored the Virginia Plan since it was among one of the most populous states.

The New Jersey Plan

The New Jersey Plan was introduced by William Paterson of New Jersey. It dealt little with the issue of the legislative branch of government other than to recommend a unicameral legislature in which each state would receive one vote (legislative delegate). The plan had nine elements. The New Jersey Plan was not universally accepted by most Convention members, partly because the plan left the Articles of Confederation in place. Some aspects of the plan would be incorporated into a compromised plan that became acceptable to both the large state and small state delegates.

Connecticut Compromise

After nearly two months of debate over how the legislative branch was to be organized that gave equal representation to small states and large states and populations disparities, Roger Sherman presented a plan that would take the best elements of both plans and propose a compromise plan that would be agreeable to both sides. It would be called the "Great Compromise" by some and the "Connecticut Compromise" by others.

Sherman and Ellsworth of Connecticut proposed a bicameral legislature in which the upper house, called the Senate would consist of two elected representatives from each State. In the lower house, called the House of Representatives, a representative would be based on proportionate population of 40,000 free citizens within each State. Benjamin Franklin proposed that revenue bills would originate in the House of Representatives, which satisfied the larger states concern of losing power and giving too much power to the smaller states. Final adjustments were made that allowed Senator's a six year term and House Representatives a two year term in office.

On February 4, 1789, George Washington was elected by Electoral College as the nation's first President, and one month later the United States Congress and the US Senate convenes. On February 2, 1790 the US Supreme Court convenes with Chief Justice John Jay presiding. On January 10, 1791, with Vermont's ratification of the Constitution and the application for admission to the Union the US Constitution becomes the law of the land. Even though the constitution and the government was operating as intended, there was a split among delegates as to ideology on how the government and the states would function together and coalesce into a single form of government. It would be the beginning of the American political party system that divided the founding fathers into two distinct political ideologies; a strong central federal government or a strong State government.

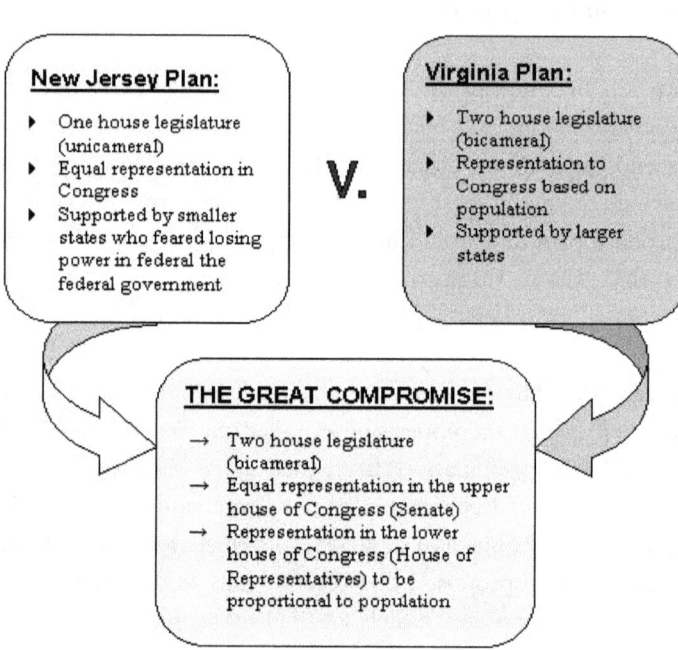

During the Constitutional Convention, many delegates refused to vote on the Constitution as it was written. One such person was George Mason who would leave the Convention out of protest, however thirty-nine delegates eventually accepted the Constitution as written and passed to each state for ratification. Many realized the Constitution was not a perfect document, regardless of how many debates and writes it would take, there would always be someone who would not accept the document. State Sovereignty issue was perhaps the biggest issue that could not be mediated or slavery. It would be difficult to reach a balance between too much power in the central government and not enough power for state governments.

State Sovereignty

"But as the plan of the [Constitutional] convention aims only at a partial union or consolidation, the State governments would clearly retain all the rights of sovereignty which they before had, and which were not, by that act, exclusively delegated to the United States." -Alexander Hamilton

The Tenth Amendment

Powers not granted to the federal government are granted either to the states or the people (the basis of federalism).

The Tenth Amendment of the Constitution was not specific about the powers granted to the States, other than the powers not specifically stated in the Constitution were powers reserved for the States. Under Article I, Section 1 of the Constitution, the U.S. Congress granted certain powers; such as coining money, regulating interstate commerce, declaring war, raising an army and navy and establishing laws and policy on immigration were specifically given to the Federal Government. Section 9 forbids states to coin money, entering into treaties, charging duties on imports and exports and declaring war. During the Colonial period, those who favored a strong central government were called "Federalist" and those who favored a strong state government were "Anti-Federalist" which gradually morphed into to Jefferson and Madison's Republican-Democrat coalition. These two groups should not to be confused with the Federalist Party, which had a different political platform, and came into existence under John Adams in 1797, which is discussed later. George Washington was elected as an independent, since he didn't belong to any political party, even though he believed in a strong central government and was considered a Federalist, he personally disliked political parties, which he made clear in his Farewell Address to Congress and other writings.

DOUGLAS G. BEAUDOIN

Alexander Hamilton was George Washington's Treasury Secretary and close confident. Hamilton was disliked by both John Adams and Thomas Jefferson. When Washington called his first Cabinet meeting in 1793, he excluded John Adams from most of the meetings, partly because he felt the Vice President's role was to be on standby in the event of his death or unable to carry-out the office of President and be available as a tie breaker in the Senate. But perhaps most importantly, Washington did not get along well with Adams. Washington and Adams had contrasting points of view on how the government should function and perhaps didn't want Adams present during cabinet meetings. His cabinet was most often headed by his Treasury Secretary, Alexander Hamilton, who controlled most of the agenda at the meetings, which created resentment among other cabinet members. John Adams personality was uncompromising and obstinate at times however; Jefferson admired Adams even though politically they did not communicate much while Adams and Jefferson were both Presidents. This information about Alexander Hamilton is important in understanding the issue of State Sovereignty, since Hamilton bitterly debated and advocated the necessity of having a strong federal or central government when drafting the Articles of the Constitution.

Alexander Hamilton as Treasury Secretary wanted a Federal Bank which he called The First Bank of the United States. Jefferson, Madison and Attorney General Edmund Randolph strongly protested to Washington on Hamilton's efforts to create a National Bank. Washington asks Hamilton to defend his argument for a First National Bank based on Constitutional grounds.

Hamilton's argument was based on the premise that Washington had the right to establish the First Bank of the United States based on implied powers given to the federal government by the Constitution, in the best interest and general welfare of the nation as a whole. Washington accepted Hamilton's argument and established the First Federal Bank charter lasting for 20 year.

During the Constitutional Convention, delegates did not directly addressing the definition of "Implied Powers" and realized it gave the Federal Government more power than they imagined. The term "Implied Powers" was left for interpretation in the General Welfare clause, Necessary and Proper clause and the Commerce clause which allowed Congress to have unlimited authority to use implied power, thus giving the Constitution more flexibility to Congress than the founding fathers originally intended. This may have been the reason Madison, Jefferson and Randolph objected strongly to Hamilton's assertion that "Implied Powers" can be used when ever Congress deems necessary. "Implied Powers" could easily be abused by any political party that is in power in both the Legislative and Executive branches of government.

The Federalist Papers

After the Constitution was written and accepted by the Constitutional Convention in early September of 1787, the remaining task was to have it ratified by the 12 colonies and acceptance by the people. A campaign was launched in support of the ratification of the Constitution which involved a number of articles published in the "Independent Journal", "The New York Packet" and the "Daily Advertiser" in which the contributing authors used "pen" names so as to keep their identity private in presenting the merits of the proposed Constitution. There were a total of 75 articles published between October 1787 and August of 1788. Eight more articles were written between 1788 and 1790. .

For reasons unknown, the unanimity of the authors were kept secret until after the death of Alexander Hamilton in 1804, at which time it was revealed that Alexander Hamilton, James Madison, John Jay and William Duer wrote the articles in defense for the ratification of the proposed Constitution. Even though the authors supported the Constitution as written, Alexander Hamilton himself opposed the inclusion of the Bill of Rights thus made his position known in the

Federalist Paper No. 84.   The Federalist Papers are important in history because much of the Constitutional interpretations used by the Supreme Court Cases were based on the opinions stated in the Federalist Papers by the founding fathers and in particular James Madison, known as the "Father of the Constitution". The Federalist Papers have been in the news even recently over the issue of "Executive Privilege" and the question: "Is the President above the law". Ultimately, the answer is contained in the Federalist Papers and in particular Alexander Hamilton's papers where it is discussed in detail.

Even though the Federalist Papers have become a key element in Constitutional intent, the opposition to the Constitution presented sixteen anti-Federalist Papers that offered a rebuttal to the opinions to the Federalist Papers. They appeared in the "New York Journal" from September of 1787 to the early 1790's. It is not known exactly who the author's were that contributed; but Patrick Henry being one, George Clinton, John Dewitt and perhaps Richard Henry Lee and Robert Yates to name only a few. It appears that most who opposed the ratification of the Constitution were those from Virginia and the Carolina's, since they were the founding fathers that refused to sign the document in 1787 and walked out of the Convention. As a final note about the Anti-Federalist Papers; the sixteen papers were not used as a legal precedence in law as it was for the Federalist Papers. The papers were mostly relegated to the back pages in history, even though some of their predictions were accurate.

Benjamin Franklin
(1706 – 1790)

"A wise man will desire no more than what he may get justly, use soberly, distribute cheerfully, and leave contently." -Benjamin Franklin

Perhaps no other person in American history captures the imagination and patriotism more than Benjamin Franklin. It is difficult to place

Franklin in any particular category in history, since he was active prior and during the revolution. He contributed in all aspects during the creation of the Articles of Confederation and the Constitution.

Ben Franklin was born in Boston in 1706, his father; Josiah was born in England in 1657. His first wife died and he married Abiah Folger from Nantucket, Massachusetts. Between his two wives, they had seventeen children of which only 13 survived to adulthood.

His father was a candle and soap maker in Boston. Abiah, Franklin's mother was raised a Puritan and was among the first pilgrim's to migrate from England in 1635. His father wanted Ben to become a clergyman, but was unable to pay for school. He only attended school until he was 10 years old and at the age of 12 he became an apprentice in his brother's printing business. When he was 15, his brother founded the first independent newspaper in the colonies. His brother was jailed for printing subversive commentary about American independence and Ben resume the business. A warrant was issued for arrest for subversive commentary and he would flee to Philadelphia to avoid capture and while in Philadelphia he worked in several printer shops.

In 1727, at the age of 21, he created the "Junto", which was the equivalent to the English Tea and Coffee Shops, were people gathered to discuss new books and various literary topics of the day. It became very popular and prompted him to establish a subscription library where members would pool their money and purchase books for the members to read known as the Library Company of Philadelphia that exists today.

In 1728, Franklin went into partnership with Hugh Meredith and opened a newspaper called "Pennsylvania Gazette" and began publishing the "Poor Richard's Almanack" (Almanac in new English) in 1733. He published the Almanack using the pseudonym Richard Saunders. It was common for Franklin to use pseudonyms when writing articles, perhaps of the times when editorials were often censored. In 1741, he published a monthly magazine, "The General Magazine and Historical Chronicle for all the British Plantations in America". It would be the first monthly magazine published in America.

Franklin began to experiment with electricity in 1746, when he attended Archibald Spencer's lectures on static electricity (called electrical fluids). The demonstrations intrigued Franklin. Franklin went on to discover that that electricity involved positive and negative charges and conservation of charge. In 1748, he constructed a multiple plate capacitor to store the electrical charge, which is known today as a "battery". In 1750, he proceeded to prove that lightning from a storm is also electricity by flying a kite into an electrical storm to prove his theory. French scientist, Thomas Francois Dalibard installed a 40 foot iron rod on a building and induced an electrical spark from a thunder cloud, proving that Franklin's theory was correct.

Franklin commented in his writings:

"When rain has wet the kite twine so that it can conduct the electric fire freely, you will find it streams out plentifully from the key at the approach of your knuckle and with this key a Leyden jar, and all other electric experiments maybe performed which are usually done by the help of a rubber glass globe or tube; and therefore the sameness of the electrical matter with that of lightening completely demonstrated"

From his experiment, he invented the lightning rod in which he would receive an honorary degree from Harvard and Yale Universities in 1753. This is one of many inventions Ben Franklin pioneered over his life time.

In the 1730's and 1740's, Franklin was taking notes on the science of demography. Population studies of America, which included slaves and whites. He estimated that America's population was doubling every 20 years and would surpass England in 100 years. His study appeared in a Boston newspaper under an assumed name. Soon economist Adam Smith of England would use his facts to estimate Britain's economic outlook in the future. It would create a stir in the Parliament which led Britain to impose tighter regulatory restrictions on America's economy. However, Britain's restrictions only delayed the inevitable. As restrictions increased, more discontent in the colonies increased as well.

Franklin's and Politics

By 1747, Franklin was already wealthy and did little to devote himself to printing. In 1757, he was appointed by the Pennsylvania Assembly to go to London and protest William Penn's heir's authority to control the colony as proprietors. The Pennsylvania Assembly wanted to change the present Proprietary charter of the Penn heirs to a Royal Charter. However, his effort would backfire, and Franklin was removed as a member of the Pennsylvania Assembly. He would return to London to oppose the 1765 Stamp Act. He would remain in London and travel throughout Europe throughout the 1760's and when Franklin returned to Philadelphia in May of 1775, the American Revolution had already begun. He returned to Pennsylvania where he was appointed as a member of the Committee of Five that drafted the Declaration of Independence. Physically he was not well; he suffered from gout and had difficulty walking and unable to attend all of the meetings. In July of 1775, the Second Continental Congress established the United States Post Office and appointed Franklin as the first U.S. Postmaster General.

He was appointed Ambassador to France from 1776 to 1785 and the American Minister to Sweden. When he returned to America in 1785, he became a delegate to the Constitutional Convention. He was the only Founding Father to be a signatory of all four important documents; Declaration of Independence, Treaty of Alliance, Treaty of Paris and the United States Constitution.

Franklin disliked the idea of slavery, even though he had two house slaves and five that worked in his shop. He would free them in 1770 and wrote several pamphlets condemning slavery and the slave trade, even though he was cautious in raising the issue of slavery during the Constitution Convention for fear that the Constitution would never become ratified.

Benjamin Franklin died on April 17, 1790 at his home in Philadelphia at the age of 84. Twenty thousand people attended his funeral.

When Franklin was 22, he wrote his epitaph:

"The body of B. Franklin Printer: Like the Cover of an old Book, Its Contents torn out, and stript of its Lettering and Gilding, Lies here, Food for Worms. But the Work shall not be wholly lost: For it will, as he believ'd, appear once more, in a new & more perfect Edition, Corrected and Amended by the Author." Library of Congress

Peyton Randolph
(1721 – 1775)

Peyton Randolph was born in August of 1721 in one of America's most influential political families in Virginia. The Randolph linage dates back to Warwickshire, England and Henry Randolph, who immigrated to America in 1643. William Randolph, the nephew of Henry Randolph, moved to Virginia in 1669 and established a homestead on Turkey Island, James River, Virginia and would marry Mary Isham Randolph. John Randolph was the son of William Randolph and the father of Edmund Randolph. Peyton Randolph was John Randolph's brother and Edmund's uncle. Peyton graduated from William and Mary College as a lawyer and admitted to the bar in 1743. He was appointed Attorney General of the Colony of Virginia in 1744. He would resign as Attorney General in 1766 and be appointed Speaker of the House of Burgesses. He became a delegate to the first and second Continental Congress and elected President. Peyton Randolph would die while traveling to Virginia. John Hancock succeeds him as President of the Continental Congress. His legacy endures as many claim he was the first President of the United States, even though the Declaration was not signed.

Edmund Randolph
(1753 – 1813)

Edmund Randolph was the nephew of Peyton Randolph. He was selected as one of seven Virginia delegates to the Continental Congress in 1779 and in 1786 he was elected governor of Virginia and later the second Secretary of State and the first United States Attorney General. Even though Edmund was one of seventy delegates at the constitutional convention, he refused to sign the Constitution, as did all seven of the delegates from Virginia. He did not sign the Constitution because he believed it did not have enough checks and balances. He would later reverse his decision to ratify the Constitution, but he did not sign the Declaration of Independence.

Randolph while serving as Washington's Secretary of State in 1795, he was involved in an embarrassing scandal involving a letter that the British Navy intercepted from a captured French naval ship that was addressed from Edmund Randolph to the French Minister, Joseph Fauchet. Britain gave the letter to President Washington, who would recall Randolph from France and hold a cabinet meeting and confront Randolph about the contents of the letter. The letter discussed details to the French Minister that Washington's administration was hostile to the French. The letter mentioned internal conflicts within Washington's Cabinet concerning France. Randolph immediately resigned. For the entire Randolph Virginia dynasty, it would damage their political influence, for which they would never recover from.

Some of the more well known descendants of the Randolph family include: Payton Randolph (1721 – 1775), son of Sir John Randolph, the first and third President of the Continental Congress.

John Marshall (1755 – 1835), was the great grandson of Thomas Randolph of Tuckahoe, Virginia. He was the fourth Chief Justice of the United States Supreme Court and a member of the US House of Representatives. He served as Secretary of State under President John Adams from 1800 to 1801.

Thomas Jefferson (1743 – 1826), was the great-grandson of William Randolph. He was the principal author of the Declaration of Independence and a delegate to the Continental Congress. He served as Governor of Virginia during the American Revolution, Minister to France and U.S. Secretary of State from 1790 to 1793. He served as Vice President under John Adams and the Third President of the United States.

Robert E. Lee was a third great grandson of William Randolph. He was the General of the Confederate States of America.

George W. Randolph was a third great grandson of William Randolph who served as a general in the Civil War in the Confederate States of America. He was the first Secretary of War in the Confederacy.

Other decedents include Pocahontas, Davy Crockett, actor Lee Marvin.

Alexander Hamilton
(1755 – 1801)

Constitutions should consist only of general provisions; the reason is that they must necessarily be permanent, and that they cannot calculate for the possible change of things. -Alexander Hamilton

Perhaps one of the most controversial figures in American history was

Alexander Hamilton. He had a close relationship with George Washington during the revolution, which continued until Washington's death in 1799. Historians believe that a portion of Washington's Farewell Address was written or drafted in part by Hamilton; it has not been historically confirmed for certain.

Alexander Hamilton was born in 1755 on the Island of Nevis in the British West Indies. In 1772, he traveled to New York and attended school in New Jersey and later enrolled in King's College in New York, but never finished with a degree. In 1776, he became a Captain in the Army, and a year later became a Lieutenant Colonel in the Continental Army as General Washington's aide-de-camp. He resigned his commission and returned to New York in 1780, where he met and married the daughter of Philip Schuyler, who was one of New York's privileged and prestige's families. He returned to military service and fought in the Battle of Yorkton and passed his New York Bar exam in 1782.

During his tour of duty in the military, he became disgruntled over the Continental Congresses ineffectual and indecisive decisions due to the constant bickering and political rivalry between Congress, in particular, the State and local governments. Hamilton and Washington both wanted a strong central government to unify the new nation called Federalism, which would become Hamilton's lifelong advocacy. He became a New York delegate to the Continental Congress and became vocal in the local newspapers advocating the ratification of the new Constitution in New York. These articles and papers would be known as the Federalist Papers, in which Hamilton would write 51 of the 85 essays.

Hamilton was a respected New York attorney and delegate to the Continental Congress and Constitutional Convention. Alexander Hamilton had a spiteful side to his personality. He frequently used newspapers to express disdain for his enemies which became slanderous.

DOUGLAS G. BEAUDOIN

When the Articles of Confederation was being debated, two proposals were presented; The New Jersey Plan which was sponsored by William Paterson who advocated a unicameral legislation in which congress elects the federal executive (President). Each state would get one vote in the legislature. The other Plan was the Virginia Plan which was sponsored by James Madison. Madison's plan was to have a bi-cameral government with a legislative, executive and judicial branch of government. All members of the legislative and executive branches would be elected by the people, with term limits. Hamilton was not satisfied with either plan and on June 18, 1787, he introduced the Hamilton Plan to the Convention. He gave a speech in which he said that there were five principals necessary for the support of government:

"1. An active and constant interest in supporting it."
"2. The love of power. Men love power"
"3. An habitual attachment of the people"
"4. Force by which may be understood, a coercion of laws or coercion of arms."
"5. Influence."

His basic plan was to introduce an authoritarian form of government in which the Executive, Legislative and Judicial members would be appointed for life. Instead of a King, President or General Secretary would be called the Federal Governor. State governors would be appointed by the national legislature and the Federal Legislature would have veto power over all state legislatures. His goal was to take all power and control from the States. What Hamilton proposed was essentially a dictatorship or authoritarian form of government with a capitalist economic system run by a politburo and central committee. Fortunately the members of the Constitutional Convention saw through his proposal and elected to use the Virginia Plan instead.

While serving under General Washington during the Revolutionary

War, Hamilton voiced his opinion about the creation of a central banking system that would be operated by civilian bankers but financed by the government that would give business loans and capital for manufacturing and industry. It would also be a Federal Bank, where revenues would be deposited and coinage and currency for budget appropriations. It would be called the First National Bank of the United States. While the concept and feasibility appeared plausible, many were fascinated by the prospects, including George Washington and bankers in New York. When George Washington became President in 1789, he appointed Alexander Hamilton to be his Treasury Secretary. After considerable debate by his cabinet, Washington and Thomas Jefferson, James Madison and Attorney General Edmund Randolph protested the constitutionality of the Government operating the United States First National Bank. Hamilton claimed the authority came from "Implied Power", which powers were given to Congress that were implied and not directly written in the Constitution, but considered necessary in executing the powers for the better good of the nation. James Madison argued that the bank was really for businesses and not for common people who would not benefit directly. Hamilton argued that it was for business and industry and manufacturing which was for the greater good of the nation which would have a favorable impact on all people. President Washington accepted Hamilton's argument and authorized 10 million dollars as start-up capital for the First Bank of the United States in Philadelphia, which would be chartered for 20 years. The federal government would have a minority stake in the Bank, but the board of directors would be private citizens. In July 1791, the Bank became publicly available which immediately drove up stock share prices. When the Charter expired in 1811, the Senate did not renew the Charter. When James Madison became President he needed the Bank to fund the war of 1812 and renewed the Charter in 1816, but once Andrew Jackson became President he and his Secretary of State opposed the United States Bank and closed it for good. The Secretary of State during Jackson's Administration was James Alexander Hamilton, the son of Alexander Hamilton. The Federal Reserve

System would eventually be passed into law in 1914 under President Woodrow Wilson.

Elections were held in 1800 in which John Adams represented the Federalist Party against Thomas Jefferson's Democratic-Republican Party and Aaron Burr who was running as an Independent from the State of New York. Even though Hamilton and Adams was both Federalist, Hamilton published sarcastic criticism of Adams and promoted Thomas Jefferson and his Democratic-Republican Party publicly.

In the election of 1800, Thomas Jefferson defeated Adams in the Presidential elections; however there was a tie between Thomas Jefferson and Aaron Burr for President, which was ultimately decided by a vote in the House of Representatives. Hamilton campaigned vigorously to swaying congressional leaders to vote for Jefferson over Burr, since he disliked Jefferson for his political views but disliked Burr for personal reasons. Hamilton was successful and Jefferson became President and Aaron Burr his Vice President. In retaliation, Burr obtained a copy of a manuscript written by Alexander Hamilton meant for private circulation only, titled; "The Public Conduct and Character of John Adams, Esq., President of the United States." Aaron Burr made public his personal opinions of Adams, which purportedly humiliated Hamilton. In retaliation, Hamilton published his criticism of Burr in the New York Post. Burr finally had enough and in 1804, challenged Hamilton to a duel. This wasn't Hamilton's first duel, since he had nearly a dozen challenges in the past; however he was able to talk his way out of most of them. This time however, was different and Burr was determined to settle the issue for the last time.

On July 11, 1804 in Weehawken, New Jersey, Aaron Burr and Alexander Hamilton stood face to face as two shots rang-out from their .58 caliber muzzle loaded pistols and Hamilton fell to the ground, mortally wounded. He was taken to his home in New York where he died the following day. Hamilton's eldest son died in a duel in 1801 at the very same location as Alexander Hamilton. Burr was charged with two counts of murder while serving as Vice President under Thomas Jefferson. Later the murder charges were dropped and Burr completed his term as Vice President. Three years later, in 1807, Burr was charged with conspiracy in an alleged attempt of leading a charge against a Spanish territory to take it over. Chief Justice John Marshall acquitted Burr of all charges. However, he would never be involved in politics after the trial. He died in 1836 in Port Richmond, New York.

Hamilton served with General Washington as his Aide de camp during the Revolutionary War. Washington spoke highly of him as an officer. Many claim his legacy was his establishment of the first Federal Bank System, however the National Bank would only lasted 20 years. Congress felt the Federal Bank didn't live up to the expectations promised and Thomas Jefferson as President would not renew the charter. Perhaps his greatest legacy was the duel between the Vice President, Aaron Burr, in which Hamilton would die from his wounds. Hamilton was the first Secretary Treasurer and one of the founding fathers' of the Constitution. He played a pivotal role in the development and creation and ratification of the document. In reality Hamilton was articulate and intelligent but had a vindictive side to his personality. For those who disagreed with him, he wasted little time seeking revenge through the media. Often times his attacks were brutal and since he had been challenged often to duels, he would use an alias when attacking others in the media. Ultimately, he attempted fate one too many times.

DOUGLAS G. BEAUDOIN

Chapter 7
Early American Politics

1776 – 1877

"There is nothing which I dread so much as a division of the republic into two great parties, each arranged under its leader, and concerting measures in opposition to each other. This, in my humble apprehension, is to be dreaded as the greatest political evil under our Constitution." — John Adams

Political Parties

The Constitutional delegates intentionally avoided mentioning political parties when drafting the Articles of Confederation and later the Constitution and its Amendments. George Washington, Thomas Jefferson and James Madison believed political parties were the bane to the democratic process by allowing political party leaders to dictate who should run for office rather than have the people select the candidates. It was common during the early years of America's political process to have multiple political parties running for office. The founding fathers believed organized political parties would diminish the principals of a representative democracy or at the very least, dilute the effects of a representative democracy. It would lead to cronyism and political influence as George Washington espoused in his Farewell Address to Congress. He made reference specifically that political parties could be a potential problem in American politics if left uncontrolled.

The Federalist coalition came into power under John Adams, who became the only Federalist President elected to office. The entire coalition dissolved in 1824. The platform under John Adams was based on a strong central government that promoted economic growth through business and industry. Federalist supported a Central national bank for the purpose of financing business and manufacturing as well as wars, should it become necessary and advocated trade relations with Great Britain. There platform was based on "Implied Powers", which was not explicitly mentioned in the constitution for instituting a Central Bank. For the Federalist it meant that Congress could exercise implied powers for the greater good of the nation, which overall would benefit big business rather than those of an agrarian society. This became one of the problems for the Federalist, since 80 percent of the populations at the time were farmers.

Up until 1817, America didn't operate as a party system. The Federalist and Democrat-Republican platform was not a political party as we know today, since it didn't have an organized political convention where candidates were selected by party members. It was an ideologically based system of general issues as previously mentioned. After James Monroe was elected President in 1817, America gradually became a two party system. Prior to that time, the political parties were not organized.

The Republican-Democrat's coalition came into power under the election of Thomas Jefferson in 1801. The coalition was active up until John Quincy Adams's Presidency in 1825. Quincy Adams ran for President under the National Republican Party, which began as a coalition but later held its first convention in 1831. Adams lost the election to Andrew Jackson, who became the first Democrat President. John Quincy Adams was the first and last President to be elected as a National Republican; however, the supporters would become the Whig Party for which Abraham Lincoln was a strong supporter. After the Whig's dissolved in early 1850's, the Republican Party replaced the Whig party and its members became the Republican Party of 1854.

DOUGLAS G. BEAUDOIN

The Democrat-Republican's supported protection of the working class and an agrarian and rural working man's party; they were against a central banking system and believed in protective tariffs on imports. They favored trade relations with France rather than Great Britain for which they didn't trust in business, but above all, they believed in a strong state government and state sovereignty which was contrary to the Federalist.

To be placed on a ticket as a candidate, the politician was bound to support its agenda, else during the next election, he would not be allowed on the ticket. During the election there could be as many as six running under separate political ideologies.

Candidates were either pro central government or pro States Rights. Other issues would come into play later, such as anti-slavery, tariffs and taxes. Political parties of today were "off-shoots" of the Federalist or the Republican-Democrat coalitions, however, both platforms failed to last after the election of James Madison. Other parties were formed that incorporated various platforms from the original two coalitions. The Democrat Party became the first and oldest political party in the United States, followed by the Republican Party in 1854. Both incorporated the political party convention of selecting candidates to run for office by party members.

America's first President, George Washington, was elected President for two terms as an independent, even though he was a supporter of federalist cause. He was not elected by popular vote, but rather by Electoral College, in which he received 100% of the Electoral votes. President John Tyler was elected as a Whig but after a year in office announced he was an independent with no party affiliation. As to be expected, he only served one term.

The Constitution didn't address term limits for the President at that time. It was George Washington who refused to run for a third term, thus allowing others the opportunity to serve their country, which establish a non-written agreement gentleman's agreement of only serving two terms (8 years). Ulysses S. Grant, Grover Cleveland and Theodore Roosevelt made bids to run for a third term, but were unsuccessful. Franklin D. Roosevelt was the only President to serve three terms as President by popular vote, but died in office during his third term, in which Vice President Harry S. Truman would succeed him. In February of 1951, the twenty-second amendment to the constitution was ratified by three-quarters of the States. It limited the President to two terms (8 years) in office, however, he could serve as much as 12 years in the unfortunate event of the death of a President or was unable to fulfill his duties as President, providing he was the Vice President at the time.

In 1854, the Republican Party was formed in Buffalo, New York and appointed its first presidential candidate, John C. Fremont in 1856; however, he would lose the election to James Buchanan. By 1860, the voters had a choice of four parties on the ballot; Northern Democrat Party, Southern Democrat Party, Republican Party and the Constitutional-Union Party. There were a few fringe parties as well. In 1861, Abraham Lincoln would be the first Republican elected President, in which his political platform was pro central government and Anti-slavery and civil rights. His first Vice President was a Democrat from Maine, Hannibal Hamin and in his second term Andrew Johnson, a Southern Democrat from Kentucky. The Republican Party of 1861 was aligned more closely toward today's Democrat Party or perhaps a moderate Republican, but keep in mind, party ideologies changed over time with the mood of the people and voters. It wasn't uncommon to have a President and Vice President with differing political ideologies, which would be completely unacceptable today. Today's Republican and Democrat parties are shaped in our current political ideologies after the election of William Howard Taft in 1813, when Woodrow Wilson, a Democrat, was elected. The Republican Party split between different factions within the Republican Party, which diluted the Republican votes, and allowing Wilson to win an easy election. This became a point in history that political strategists would not allow a three party system. The dual political systems today was a result of the Wilson election of 1913 of divide and conquer. The thought of having a three party system sends both Democrat and Republican Parties in a panic. Having a moderate or independent party would rob votes from both parties. One solution is to have 4 parties for which the voters could choose from.

There have been political parties that have faded into obscurity over time. Many gradually emerged into other parties. The Republican Party and Democrat Parties of 1861 were much different from the parties of today. The only similarity is in their name and not their political ideology. If Lincoln was running for President today he would more than likely run as a conservative or moderate Democrat as well as Grant and Hayes and many other of the period after reconstruction.

Federalist Party

The Federalist Coalition was the first political ideology in the United States, shortly after George Washington became President. Even Washington disliked political parties, his views aligned closely to that of the Federalist Party. He advocated a strong central government, a central banking system and individual taxes and tariffs to fund the government. Tariffs were used by both Britain and later America as a source of revenue for government operation. Later in history, most advocated tariffs for protectionist trade for selected manufactures, especially after individual income taxes were levied on the citizens to fund federal, state and municipal governments. When John Adams became Vice President and later President, he implemented the first political party with the help of Alexander Hamilton, called the Federalist Party. John Adams would be the only President elected as a Federalist and the party would eventually fade away by 1816. The War of 1812 would spawn a new political group called the "war hawks" who favored war with Britain, Spain and Mexico and advocated protective tariffs to finance public private industry such as subsidies to industry to build canals, railroads, roads and such. If Washington and Adams were to run for election today they would more than likely be a moderate Republican.

The Republican-Democrat Party
(Jeffersonian Party)

When Thomas Jefferson ran for President in 1800, he and James Madison formed the Republican-Democrat Party, also known as the Jeffersonian Party. Following Jefferson's two terms, James Madison was elected president from 1816 to 1820. Its platform was opposite that of the Federalist Party; which advocated strong states rights, no central banking, no taxes and the principals of egalitarianism. Egalitarian means; believing in the principal that all people are equal and deserve equal rights and opportunities. If Jefferson, Madison and Monroe were running for office today, they would run as a Libertarian or Conservative Democrat.

The National Republican Party

The National Republican Party shouldn't be confused with the Republican Party of today. John Quincy Adams was President from 1825 to 1829. Like his father, John Adams, only served a single term in office. While in office, a political strategist named Martin Van Buren would form another political party in an effort to have Andrew Jackson run against Adams in the 1828 election under the new Democrat Party. The Democrat Party is the oldest Political Party in the United States, even though the platform has changed from conservative to liberal multiple times over time.

Anti-Masonic Party

The Anti-Masonic Party was a short lived political party formed in up-state New York in 1820's. Its platform was based on conspiracy theories rather than political issues. It was the first political party to hold a national convention in America. Its only candidate was William Wirth who lost the Presidency in 1832. By 1836, the members eventually became Whigs.

The Whig Party

The Whig Party was formed in 1834, by Henry Clay, in opposition to Andrew Jackson's policies of 'sovereignty of the people'. The Whig Party consisted of various failed political parties, such as the Anti-Masonic Party and National Republican Party with roots from the Federalist Party. Its basic tenants were; modernization, central banking, protectionism of manufacturing and industry through tariffs. It was popular among industrialist of the Northeast, businessmen, entrepreneurs, and upper middle class. The Whig Party was non committal over Slavery, even though Millard Fillmore was a Whig and signed into Law the Compromise of 1850. Most of the Northern Whigs had little interest in resolving or dealing with the Slavery issue. There were four Presidents who were Whigs; William Henry Harrison (1841), John Tyler (1841-1845), Zachary Taylor (1849-1850) and Millard Fillmore (1850-1853).

John Quincy Adams was a Federalist turned Whig in 1831 when he was elected to the House of Representatives. Four other Presidents were Whigs before joining the Republican Party; Abraham Lincoln, Rutherford Hayes, Chester A. Arthur and Benjamin Harrison. The Whig Party would dissolve after the death of Henry Clay in 1852. The Whigs would eventually move to the other political parties, but most joined the Republican Party or became Bourbon Democrats from the south.

The Liberty Party

The Liberty Party's primary political platform was anti-slavery. While most political parties "skirted" around slavery issues for fear of losing votes and support, the Liberty Party was a small group of abolitionist that made anti-slavery a political issue in the 1840 and 1844 elections. However, it only garnered 2% of the votes, which split the Whig Party and cost Henry Clay the Presidential election.

Free Soil Party

In 1848, the Free Soil Party was organized under the platform of opposing the spread of Slavery into new territories and tariff for revenues only to support the government, rather than as protectionist trade. They were for a homestead act that gave federal land to those to build farms and live off the land. The Free Soil motto was "Free soil, Free Speech, Free Labor and Free Men". Martin Van Buren would run as President in 1848 as a Free Soil Candidate, but would lose to Zachary Taylor, who was a Whig, but garnered 10% of the vote. Even though they opposed the spread of slavery into new territories, they avoided abolitionism completely. The Free Soil Party would dissolve and merge into the Republican Party after the Compromise of 1850.

The Know-Nothing Party
(American Party)

The Know-Nothing Party got its name from a semi-secret social organization that became the American Party. It got its name from members who were asked about activities within the society in which members would reply, "I know nothing". It was patterned after the Free Masons and other social groups common in the day.

The Know-Nothing Party came into power from 1830 to 1860, shortly after the decline of the Whig Party. It was based on a conspiracy theory that immigrant Irish, Scottish and German Catholics were taking jobs away from the working class Americans and undermining the Protestants faith by injecting Catholicism into the Protestant religion. As members grew to over 1 million, they establish a Chapter in San Francisco and were able to persuade the California Supreme

Court to up hold a law that Chinese immigrants could not testify against White men in court. There political platform was hostile toward the wealthy, elites and immigrants. It was Protestant based party in which their popularity was primarily Protestants, working class and wealthy merchants and factory owners. It would eventually fade when Abraham Lincoln was elected in 1860 as a Republican. American Party members would lose popularity and many would join the newly formed Republican Part and Democrat Party.

The Greenback Party

The Greenback Party was formed in 1875. Its single platform was the issuance of paper money not backed by gold. Its members consisted of mostly farmers and workers. It sponsored Presidential Candidates in three elections, however none were unsuccessful. The interesting aspect of this party is that Richard Nixon, 96 years later took America off the gold and silver standard.

The Democrat Party
(Jacksonian Party)

The Democrat Party slowly began to form around the Democrat – Republican coalition formed by Thomas Jefferson in the 1790's in response to John Adams and Alexander Hamilton's Federalist Coalition. The Democrat Party would be the oldest political party in the United States, which was established in 1828 when Andrew Jackson became President. In the beginning, the party followed closely to the Jeffersonian ideology of an agrarian society of farmers, poor and middle working class citizens. The Democrat party of 1830's does not resemble the party today, in which over time the Republican and Democrat platforms would switch back and forth.

The Jacksonian's faction of the Democrat party believed in a Laissez-faire federal government, stronger states rights, agrarian and farming support, adherence to the Constitution and opening land for farming and agriculture. The problem with opening up more land to farming and agriculture involved displacing Native Americans. They opposed a central banking system and paper currency. The Democrat Party was well organized and well financed; Martin Van Buren would become the first President to establish a nationwide party coalition in each state. The Democrat Party of old opposed educational reform by opposing a public school system. They advocated individual liberty to choose home schooling or church operated schools for their children's education.

The Democrat Party was split between two regional factions; the South, below the Mason-Dixon Line, called the Bourbon Democrats, who were pro-business and represented railroad and business interests; banking, manufacturers and a gold standard, but strongly opposed overseas expansionism and high taxes and tariffs. Overtime, the Bourbon Democrats dominated the Democratic Party for the next 50 years, starting with the election of James Buchanan in 1857 and ending with William McKinley in 1898, however the Party remained a coalition of two separate regional parties; north and south, until the 1960's with the Civil Rights Act of 1964. The act was bitterly opposed by the Bourbon Democrats and divide southern democrats into a separate far right conservative faction that opposed civil rights legislation. The South voted predominantly conservative Republican from then on, while the northern Democrat gained popularity in the Northeast, Coastal West, upper mid-west and the major cities in the north.

Democratic Ideology

Basically there are four subgroups within the Democrat Party.

The Centrist Democrats were known as the New Democrats. They were fiscally conservative and supported; free trade, reducing government welfare and tax cuts. They were considered war hawks in general and supported military action over mediation.

The Conservative Democrats morphed from the Bourbon Democrats in the Southern States. Many switched parties from the Democrat to the Republican Party after LBJ's Civil Rights Act of 1964. In recent years the Conservative Democrats voted for democratic candidates in local elections but voted Republican during the Presidential elections and Congressional seat elections.

The Liberal Democrats consist of the largest voting sector of the Democrat Party. They advocated universal health care, a single payer system for health care, gun control, same-sex marriage, stem cell research, abortions and diplomatic solutions rather than military action. Many delegates believed in the separation of church and state and reduction in military spending. They advocated oversight of the America's military industrial complex and supported labor Unions as well. .

The Progressive Democrats were a far left faction of the Democrat Party. They advocate pro-labor unions and the right for employees to organize and collective bargaining, strong regulation on business and banking and stock market oversight, social welfare programs for the poor, Immigration reform, network neutrality, and the increase in minimum wages, electoral reform, elections by popular vote rather than electoral college, environmental measures and global warming policy.

The Republican Party

The Republican Party was formed in New Hampshire in 1853 by Amos Tuck. The first statewide convention was held in Jackson, Michigan in 1854, in which John C. Freemont would be nominated as the Republican candidate for President against Democrat opponent, James Buchanan. Fremont lost the election, however the Republican Party rose to influence as a result of the Kansas-Nebraska Act of 1850. Many felt that Kansas and Nebraska should decide the fate of Slavery by popular vote, while the South wanted Kansas and Nebraska to become slave states along with all new territories America acquired. The Republican platform opposed the expansion of slavery into new territories and Kansas and Nebraska became a political battle ground. Their membership was confined to the Midwest and Northeast but with the Whig Party dissolving, many Whigs shifted their allegiances to the Republican Party while the Southern Whigs became Bourbon Democrats. In 1860, Abraham Lincoln would receive the nomination for President. The Republican Party was one of five running for President. With the votes being split among the parties, the Republicans captured the Presidency. The party platform was expanded by 1861 to include a national banking system, high tariffs, income tax, excise tax, paper money that was not backed by gold or silver and the homestead laws, railroad aid, aid to education and agriculture, anti-slavery and abolition of slavery and a national debt to finance government through a US Central Bank. Much of the party's platform resembled the Federalist, only expanded to include more current issues of the time.

With the election of William McKinley and Theodore Roosevelt in 1896 and 1901 respectively, it began an era of Corporate Trust Busting. McKinley built his support around business, industry, manufacturing and transportation, but when Theodore Roosevelt became President in 1901, he and his successor, President Howard Taft, went on a campaign to divide corporate monopolies, such as Standard Oil, that was owned by John D. Rockefeller. Between Theodore Roosevelt and Howard Taft, more than 134 monopolies were dissolved in trust busting law suits.

The Republican Party has fewer factions than the Democrat Party of the time and their political platform was defined by issues of the Era. Lincoln won the election on an anti-slavery platform which was based exclusively on a single political issue, civil rights. Today however, issues range from anti-gay rights, pro big business, protective tariffs, immigration reform, chartered school education, anti-welfare and de-regulation of business. The GOP's voter base became pietistic during the Reagan years and heavily supported by Protestants religious groups.

The Republican Party platform changed many times over the next 150 years. They gradually became a strong supporter of big business and corporations with the impetus of reduced government regulation that hindered big business growth. Most staunch Republican's believe in "trickle down" economic theory that was based on the principal that if a business was financially successful, they would hire more workers and pay higher wages and build more plants, thus reduce unemployment allowing more people to spend more money and buying more products, thus feeding the economy. In theory this approach could work if businesses invested their profits back into the U.S. economy rather than moving facilities off shore to avoid paying higher taxes and higher employee wages. While in early industrial America, few business went abroad and built factories overseas, which made the theory practical, however today, with a global trade economy and cheap labor abroad, "trickle down" economics may have becomes a thing of the past.

Radical Republicans

The Radical Republicans of old were not the same as the as the radical Republicans in modern history. They were considered radical by the southern democrats for their political ideology toward slavery and civil rights, which was at time a radical concept. Today it would be more of a moderate political ideology.

The Radical Republicans were a political faction of the first Republican Party of 1854. It remained until the end of Ulysses S. Grant's Presidency in 1877, who was considered a radical Republican. Radical's were the anti-slavery faction of the Republican Party, in which northern republicans wanted to abolish slavery entirely in America and implement a strong reconstruction policy in the south. They advocated Constitutional Amendment to enforce civil rights for former slaves. Shellby Cullom was the Illinois Representative who gave the following speech to the U.S. House of Representatives in January, 28, 1867, in which he defined Radical Republicans:

"The word Radical as applied to political parties and politicians... means one who is in favor of going to the root of things; who is thoroughly in earnest; who desires that slavery should be abolished; that every disability connected therewith should be obliterated."

Many former "Whigs" became Radicals after the collapse of the party in the early 1850's. Lincoln was a Whig until that time but he was not considered a Radical Republican. He did not advocate the abolition of slavery in the South, but rather preferred not to extend slavery beyond the boundaries of the Confederacy. Grant on the other side, wanted slavery completely abolished in America and the act of slave trade made illegal.

The Liberal Republican Party

Ulysses S. Grant was a Radical Republican but shortly before the Election of 1872 and the beginning of Grant's second term in office, the Liberal Republican Party was formed as a result of the scandals occurring during Grant's Presidency. Lincoln was a Moderate Republican, but the Liberal Republican's consisted of Businessmen, professionals, reformers and intellectuals who disliked big government. They preferred less government spending and did not support manhood suffrage and enfranchisement of blacks. They believed that corruption in American businesses were the result of government interference and too much democracy. During the election of 1872, Horace Greely, the editor of the New York Times, became the Liberal Republican candidate for President. Of course he lost to Grant in his second term in office. Greely was also nominated on the Democrat ticket as well, since he opposed reconstruction in the south and the presence of the Army stationed in the south. Horace

Greely would be considered a "doughface" and had sympathetic leanings toward the Bourbon Democrat's political ideology.

Presidential Campaigning

It is difficult, especially now days, to imagine that Presidential Campaigning was once a dignified process where Presidential candidates were expected to conduct themselves in a dignified and sanctified manner, worthy of the position as President. Presidents during the first fifty years considered campaigning directly as un-Presidential act and only appeared in public to allow the public to see him as a elegant and soft spoken figure worthy to be President. It was considered shameful to lower oneself to the point of being considered a "snake oil salesman" or overly aggressive in public espousing his political views. The public and the Presidency was considered a position of authority and his role in democracy was not to politicize his position, but rather allow Congress to perform the task of presenting bills to the President, in which he would either sign or veto. The debating process was left to Congress. The President was considered the judge without malice toward any particular political party whose purpose was to represent the people in the best interest of the nation. That was the intent of the original demeanor of the Presidency and as viewed as the intent of the Constitution.

It gradually changed over time. William Henry Harrison in 1836 was the first Presidential candidate to actively campaign and engaged in several campaign tours. It must be noted that in the early years after Harrison's tours, the presidential candidate did not actively campaign, but rather had campaign manager embellished on the presidents attributes to hold office. Local Mayors, Senator or Governors gave speeches and presented the Presidential candidate for viewing on the stage. When asked to speak, he would not discuss political issues, but rather gave brief speech about antidotes about his childhood being careful not to criticize or politicize his opponent, since it was considered unbecoming of a president. The purpose of the tour was to demonstrate to the public his demeanor and elegance to be President. Often, the purpose was to show the candidates health since most died in their 50's at the time. His speeches most often were brief and involved only his personal life. Not many Presidential candidates were good public speakers. Many wrote well, but had difficulty in large audiences. Lincoln was somewhat of the exception at the time, since he was a great debater, writer and orator.

The Presidential campaign was conducted in the backrooms, where posters, buttons, flyers were prepared for distribution by supporters and volunteers. The candidates were never involved in the task of promoting himself. When Henry Clay, a Whig, ran for President in 1844 against James Polk, Clay aggressively campaigned while touring the South, however, as was customary at the time, he avoided campaigning on particular issues or at least extremely vague. Clay lost the election due to an overly aggressive style of campaigning, which many believed was undignified and un-Presidential. While Clay was perhaps the best orator at the time, it was his presidential demeanor that cost him the election and not his qualifications and oratory skill.

Steven A. Douglas was a ranking Congressman from Illinois, who like Henry Clay, was aggressive in his approach to campaigning. He toured the South under the auspicious of visiting his mother, but during his speeches, he included political issues that encouraged the voters in the South not to secede from the union should Lincoln be elected President. It was a subtle political tactic meaning if Lincoln were elected, the South would secede from the Union over the issue of slavery. It was a "backdoor" political maneuver to convince southerners to vote for Douglas to avoid Civil War. However, his campaign tactic backfired and it cost him the election. The Lincoln-Douglas debates would be Douglas's downfall as well. Douglas decided to debate the greatest debater in American history, Abraham Lincoln, which would become the standard used today to present political issues to the public in a subtle, yet dignified manner through the debate process, rather than by campaigning directly on issues and criticizing or demeaning his opponent which was considered unpresidential.

During the election of 1868, between General Ulysses S. Grant and Haration Seymour of New York, Grant only made one campaign tour to Denver, along with Generals William Sherman and Philip Sheridan. Grant never spoke during his campaign rally and eagerly waved to the crowds during his campaign train stops. When he arrived at his home in Galena, Illinois, he remained on the front porch to greet well wishers and supporters. Seymour in contrast, went on a frequent campaign tours and delivered the same partisan speech to all cities he toured from New York to Chicago. He would lose the election however. In 1872, Horace Greely run against Grant but as before, Grants' "front porch" campaign would win the election. In 1880, Republican James Garfield applied Grants method of campaigning as well, using the "front porch" campaign and would win, even though his opponent toured America for six weeks, while Garfield drank tea from his front porch and chatted with the local media and curious "on lookers".

William Jennings Bryan, a Democrat, was the first Presidential candidate that spent much of his entire campaign touring America and addressing political issues during the 1896 campaign against William McKinley. He would lose the election but later nominated in 1900 again to run against Theodore Roosevelt and William Howard Taft in 1908. However, he lost all three of his election attempts. William McKinley's approach toward campaigning was a carry-over from the early campaign strategy of a front porch campaign made famous by U.S. Grant. McKinley was the first President that used mail-outs and the media during his campaign; however, he didn't use it as a means to defaming or criticizing his opponent, rather to inform the voter of events and decisions he made while President. The modern day campaigning style on political issues began during the Bryan and Taft election of 1908, where both candidates campaigned on issues exclusively. Woodrow Wilson in 1916 was the first sitting President to campaign while holding office during his second term, which was considered inappropriate to campaign while holding office, but it worked well for him, however, he would have won the election anyway because of his popularity.

Elections and Voting in Early America

Voting in America hadn't changed much in 230 years, however, during the birth of America in 1788, the balloting and voting has changed over time due to the addition of more voting locations and precincts. The Electoral College existed from the very first election of George Washington in 1789, however only 10 states from the original 13 colonies participated in the first election. Of the 10 states casting electoral votes, only 6 chose electors based on popular vote.

The first election was held on February 4, 1789, in which Washington was elected unanimously with 69 Electoral College votes. John Adams would be elected as Vice President since he garnered the second highest electoral votes of 34. There were a total of 12 Presidential candidates running for office in 1788. The balance (69) for Vice President would split among the 11 candidates.

It is worth noting that there were only 43,782 popular votes cast in the election of 1789, in which the Federalist received 90 percent of the popular vote, even though there were more than 3 million in America at the time. The low voter turn-out was due for several reasons; each State had different qualifications for voting. Only white men were allowed to vote. None of the States had laws barring non-English speaking immigrants from voting; however they used other tactics to keep them from going to the poles. One practice didn't allow non property owners to vote or by using coercion tactics at the poles. Ordinary citizens were barred from voting by the "forty pound rule" which was an English rule that a person must have 40 pounds (British currency) of land and yield 5 percent return from the land in order to vote.

Some States used the "Gentlemen rule" where they must own a substantial amount of land and must prove they were morally adept and fit to vote. It was strictly an arbitrary system designed to exclude the poor, yet reward the elite gentleman farmer. Some States, such as Rhode Island and Virginia allowed only protestant religious citizens to vote and excluded Catholics, Jews, and Quakers. In Massachusetts only Congregationalists were allowed to vote. There were a few states like Pennsylvania that allowed all citizens the right to vote, except women. Women were not allowed to vote nor were African Americans; however that changed with the ratification of the 15th Amendment which removed the racial and gender barriers to voting and the 19th Amendment in 1920, which allowed women to vote 132 years later.

The issue of who was allowed to vote was not addressed specifically during the drafting of the Constitution. It was assumed that only men could vote. The founding fathers believed the Electoral College should provide a more uniform voting method without the necessity of having voting precincts. So the Electoral College was as much about the economics of voting as voting itself. During this period in history, traveling hundreds of mile on horseback to vote wasn't a viable option for most rural citizens. The founding fathers were certain the Electoral College system would work if the delegates were selected or appointed by each State that represented the popular vote, if not the wishes of the populous within each state. Now days, the political parties elect the delegates that is to represent the populous. The only stipulation in the Constitution was the person holding office as Senator or Representative in Congress could not be a delegate in the Electoral College and the Electoral votes from the home state of the President and Vice President could not be counted toward the Electoral College.

When Washington became President in 1789, political parties weren't established yet. In several States, they had not designed a system of balloting or established voting precincts. It wasn't until nearly twenty years later that all thirteen original colonies had open elections.

Presidents and Vice Presidents were elected by the Electoral College. Few states were able to organize election balloting during Washington's bid for the Presidency, so the Electoral College elected Presidents and Vice Presidents, as outlined in Article II, Section 1 of the Constitution. Some states such as North Carolina, Rhode Island were not eligible to vote, since they didn't ratify the Constitution at the time of the Presidential election of 1788. The system used during Washington's election has changed over time, but the principal remains the same. The 12th Amendment was amended in 1804 in which the President and Vice President was placed on the same ballot ticket as the Presidential candidate. The political party would select the Presidents and their Vice Presidential running mate later in history. In modern elections, the Vice President is selected from the same political party as the Presidential candidate. However, it was not always the case. Lincoln selected Andrew Johnson because he felt it best to have a Vice President that represented the South which helped him to sway votes from the south, even though he doubted his competency as a Vice President.

In 1975, House Joint Resolution 681 was introduced that proposed direct elections of the President and Vice President, but the bill failed in the Senate. There has been five times in history that a candidate won the popular vote but lost the Electoral College and the Presidency. Most always the loss was within 100,000 or less, but in a most recent election between Hillary Clinton and Donald Trump, a gap of nearly 3 million popular votes separating the loser from the Electoral College winner, Donald Trump. The voting system in America is flawed, but it still functions reasonably well.

The principal of the Electoral College was designed by the Founding Fathers for the purpose of representing each state as well as those states with large populations that have more electoral delegates. The founding fathers were skeptical about the citizenry electing the two highest offices in the land, partly because the less populated states wouldn't necessarily have an equal say in selecting a President and

Vice President. To level the playing field, each state would have two delegates (Senators) and the number of Representatives was based on a 10 year population census. The Electors were selected by each respective political party, such as 538 Republican electors and 538 Democrat electors and remain on standby until the votes were tallied. Every State except two, (Maine and Nebraska), assigns their electors to the candidate that wins the popular vote within each respective State, but not bound legally to do so. Maine and Nebraska appoints electors by those who win election districts within the state. The President and the Vice President is selected by the political party within the party caucus.

The Primary is either an open or closed primary that allows the voter a chance to choose only a party candidate from a list of candidates from the same party; called a closed primary. An open Primary allows voters to vote for any candidate regardless of political party affiliation. This system lends itself to "cross-over" voting in which during the primary a voter selects a candidate who is likely to lose in the election and then selects the candidate he wants to win in the general election. While the system is slightly flawed, it may be the most equitable system for voters, since the largest voting majority are often independents are not affiliated with any particular party and vote for those they believe qualified for office. For those who were strict loyalist, a closed primary is preferred, however if you were an independent voter, an open primary most often best. Some states incorporate all three. If you register as an independent, the voter would receive a ballot that contained all parties listed in the primary.

Often election controversy erupted over inequities in the Electoral College. The Electoral College was hastily conceived when drafting the Constitution, thus careful thought was not given to the effects and potential problems that may occur. Its purpose was to give smaller States equal leverage as larger states. Many criticize the Electoral College as it may allow candidates to campaign regional issues only in swing states that do not vote along traditional political party lines. It becomes easy to manipulate electoral votes if swing states can be identified early in the campaign. There have been five elections in U.S. history where Presidents were elected by Electoral College but lost by popular vote; however it has only occurred once before 1877 and four times after:

1. Grover Cleveland (D) defeated by Benjamin Harrison (R)
2. John Quincy Adams (*) defeated by Andrew Jackson (D)
3. Hayes (R) defeated Tilden (D)
4. George W. Bush (R) defeated Al Gore (D)
5. Donald Trump (R) defeated Hillary Clinton (D)

Note: During John Quincy Adams second term as a candidate for president, he campaigned as a National Republican. His loss would begin the era of America's two-party system.

Elbridge Gerry
(1744 – 1814)

Gerrymandering was the "brain child" of Elbridge Gerry, who was one of the founding fathers and delegates to all three Continental Congresses representing Massachusetts. Gerry signed the Declaration of Independence; however, he was one of 3 who refused to sign the proposed Constitution on the grounds that it did not contain a provision for the Bill of Rights and other specific concerns. He became James Madison's Vice President in 1813 to 1814, which led him to devise a plan called "Gerrymandering" that allowed election districts in Massachusetts to be re-drawn for the purpose of getting James Madison elected President and himself elected as Vice President. Gerry served in the US House of Representatives and at the time was Governor of Massachusetts. He was well educated, with a Masters Degree from Harvard College and was among the wealthiest American's at the time.

Gerry was not without controversy throughout his political career. He accepted positions with the British colonial government while attending the Continental Congress which drew considerable criticism from other delegates in which some questioned his loyalty. He had switched party loyalties between the Federalist and the Republican Democrat Party in his later years, while supporting Alexander Hamilton and John Adams in their Federalist beliefs. Many found it difficult to understand what his real political position was. What is known is that he favored a centralized government and a Central Bank System, which was to his financial benefit, since he held large quantities of IOU's issued to merchants by the Continental Congress for goods and services to the Revolutionary Army, and as a result, Gerry became even wealthier as a result.

He was a major partner in the Ohio Company that purchased large tracks of land in Ohio on speculation that a transcontinental railroad would be built, and his real estate holdings in Connecticut and Massachusetts also involved political wrangling. He was one of three delegates involved in the negotiations with France when Talleyrand wanted a bribe in exchange for signing a trade agreement between the US and France, known as the XYZ Affair. The XYZ Affair started a brief Naval War between France and America who refused to pay a bribe for a trade agreement. The Naval war with France lasted almost two years. As news broke-out about the XYZ Affair in America, crowds were burning effigies of Gerry in the streets, since Gerry remained in France to broker a deal with Talleyrand after the other delegates returned to America, it was never divulged what concessions Gerry may have negotiated with Talleyrand. He would be blamed for the XYZ Affair however, but later he pleaded his case in Congress and was exonerated, but doubt always existed in the mind of his constituents and the public. Hamilton had high regard for Gerry as well as John Adams. Gerry's closest friend was James Madison who considered him a great patriot. It is my understanding that few really knew Gerry well. He despised war profiteers, yet he took advantage of it as well. He maintained he never increased his prices or took advantage of the situation as a war profiteer as many did. He was certainly devoted to democracy; however, he wasn't shy about taking advantage of a political situation should the opportunity presented itself.

Throughout his political career, he was constantly defending himself over quasi-legal ventures he was involved in and possible conflicts of interest. Even if he had honest intensions during the XYX Affair, his history of dubious business ventures made it difficult for the public to accept his explanation at face value.

The term "Gerrymandering" came about in 1812 when Gerry was Governor of Massachusetts. The Republican-Democrats controlled the Massachusetts's legislature and mandated that new electoral districts be re-drawn. The re-drawn districts were odd shapes and one in particular looked like a dragon or Salamander. The Republican-Democrat's re-drew the districts in a manner in which the boundaries enhanced the party's control of the Electorates. Gerry as Governor signed the legislation. When the newspaper saw the configuration of a particular district that resembled a curved Salamander, it was published in the newspaper and labeled; "Gerry-mander".

Gerrymandering was intended for political advantage in manipulating district boundaries. Two methods were used and are still used today; "Cracking" and "Packing". Cracking diluted the voting power of the opponent by spreading his voters over multiple districts. Packing concentrated the opponent's voters in a single district. The term "Malapportionment" is when the number of eligible voters is widely distributed throughout an election district.

Gerrymandering favors the incumbent. The boundaries for districts can be established by "pack" a particular party or group in an election district or "cracking" voters into a particular demographic area. These political groups can include; political, racial, religious, and ethnic voters who typically vote for a particular political party. They are most often placed in a packed boundary via gerrymandering or dispersed and spread over multiple boundaries so that their vote is deluded. It is often referred to as the "wasted vote effect".

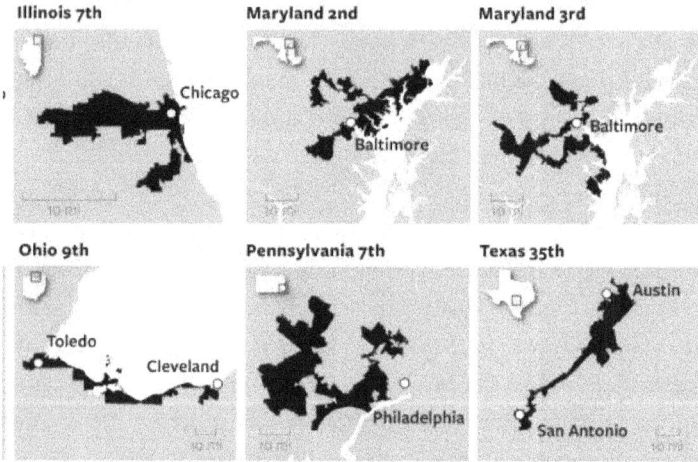

Map 10, common examples of Gerrymandering

The Electoral College can be part and parcel to gerrymandering as well. The Constitution is silent about how the States may elect their electors and how districts are drawn. It was to be left to the States to decide. In 1792, State legislatures selected the delegates for President, but by 1800, Virginia decided to use statewide popular vote to select the President, while the other States were mixed between the legislature and States using election districts. When John Adams from Massachusetts was running for President, Massachusetts used "winner takes all", a system most common today. It wasn't until 1820 when James Madison was running for President that legislatures played a dominant role in selecting electors. The last state to abandon using the state legislature as electors was Colorado. In states where a political party is in the majority, they were given free rein to redistrict seven states, it was found that the popular vote was 50% for each party, but the political party power was responsible for drafting the boundaries by gerrymandering and received 68% of the congressional districts. [22]

Political parties differ in America from those in other countries, such as England and Australia, which has a parliamentary system of government. The United States is the only country with our form of dual representative democracy. Most countries use a Parliamentary form or variations of it. In most parliamentary governments, the people elect their representatives and the ruling party with the most seats in parliament selects the Prime Minister. Most nations prefer a parliamentary form of government but this system lacks a three way checks and balance system. The people of the United States elects their Congressional representatives by popular vote, however, the President and Vice President are elected by Electoral College vote. In reality, American citizens do not vote directly for the President or Vice President, nor do the people vote for the electoral delegates. This system is flawed since candidate's focuses their campaigns in swing states which influence the balance of electorates and avoid the more populated states they consider traditionally favor the opposing candidate.

Capitalism and America's Economic System
(1492 – 1880)

"I wish it were possible to obtain a single amendment to our Constitution. I would be willing to depend on that alone for the reduction of the administration of our government to the genuine principles of its Constitution; I mean an additional article, taking from the federal government the power of borrowing." – Thomas Jefferson

The U.S. Constitution makes no reference to the type of economic system America was ordained to have. The term "capitalism" as it is used today, didn't appear until the mid 1800's and the term wasn't commonly used until Karl Marx published his pamphlet; "The Communist Manifesto" in 1848. However, the term "Capitalism" was mentioned in the mid 1700's by Adam Smith, in his book, "Wealth of Nations", which may have been the inspiration of Karl Marx and Fredrick Engels who used the term in their pamphlet. Marx and Engels were regular contributors to the Chicago Tribune and the New York Tribune as well as other newspaper in Europe. He published a regular article in the newspapers in the 1860's, called "Capital". They later publish a three volume set of books called "Capital" between 1861 and 1894. It is perhaps where the term "capitalism" became popular among the general population.

The Rise of Corporate America

In early American history the term "capitalism" and "free market economy" was not a common term used during the colonial period. To reiterate from previous discussions, mercantilism was the most common system used by traders and merchants during the colonial period. Chartered companies were granted a charter by the Monarch to establish a stock ownership company known today as a corporation or limited liability company. Since they were government charters, the terms of the charter and the enforcement in the colonies were left to the corporate management. The first known corporate entity began in Rome during the Roman Empire, but with the expansion of world trade and colonization, Britain used stockholders as a means to raise investment money and establish colonies with the promise of vast profits with limited liability in the event of failure. It is of little wonder that the colonies that were established by British stock holding charters were managed and controlled by corporate managers, known today as CEO's and a Board of Trustees, called Governors. The British influence was an old technique of enforcement and it became a symbiotic relationship between government and the corporation that continues today.   Should a rebellion break-out in the colonies, the corporation could always rely on the British military to thwart any up-rising.

After the Revolutionary War and the drafting of the Constitution in

1787, American's didn't have a need for the British corporate structure that operated in each colony or province at the time. The American public became suspicious of all business corporations that were administered by British stock holding companies for 267 years; however the founding fathers realized the importance of corporations in large projects that required large amount of investment money. The early corporations were tightly controlled in America after its independence and only a few companies were give approval to incorporate by Congress and were over-seen by state government. Most incorporations were to demonstrate public need, such as public works projects; roads, canals and railroads and such. In addition, individual states attached terms and conditions to incorporation as well. The following conditions were applied toward being incorporated during the 100 years after 1787:

- ✓ Corporate charters were granted for limited time and could be revoked for violating the charter and the laws;
- ✓ Corporations could engage only in activities necessary to fulfill the terms of their charter.
- ✓ Corporations could not own stock or property in other corporations which was not essential in their charter.
- ✓ Owners and managers were held liable for criminal acts committed on the job.
- ✓ Corporations could not make political or charitable contributions nor spend money to influence law.

Today, most, if not all, do not apply to corporations or enforced. During the early creation of charters in America, directors and even stock holders were not protected from wrong doing, abuse or criminal acts to defraud the public or its investors. A single violation resulted in dissolution of the charter and sometimes imprisonment of its managers and board of directors. Corporations in early America were viewed as a charter that was granted by the people for public need and not just to the stockholders soul benefit to secure profit. The reason the rules toward corporations were strict was the result of a carry-over of prior colonial rule, in which the public viewed chartered stock companies as the judicial, administrative and executive branches of colonial government and without government or public oversight of their fiduciary responsibility and moral and ethical obligation.

As our nation expanded, the number and size of the corporations grew as well. The original laws were not enforced and with frequent public out-cry for a more competitive system and oversight, led to anti-trust laws. Politician's who supported railroads, coal, iron, oil and other industries wanted corporate regulations relaxed and with their money and political influence were able to sway congressmen and judges to relax regulations over-time. By 1864, a year before Abraham Lincoln assassination, Lincoln gave a speech concerning the rapid acceleration of corporations and corporate power in America:

"I see in the near future a crisis approaching that unnerves me and causes me to tremble for the safety of my country. As the result of the War, corporations have been enthroned. An era of corruption in high places will follow, and the money power of the country will endeavor to prolong its reign by working upon the prejudices of the people. Until wealth is aggregated in a few hands, and the Republic is destroyed."

In 1886, President Rutherford B. Hayes stated:

"This is a government of the people, by the people, and for the people no longer. It is a government of corporations, by corporations, and for corporations" 1886 Rutherford B. Hayes

In 1886, the court case of Santa Clara County v. Southern Pacific Railroad declared that corporations were "natural persons" and the ruling was upheld by the U.S. Supreme Court which declared that the Fourteenth Amendment gave corporations individual and equal and free rights as an individual person, even though the Fourteenth Amendment was enacted for the protection of the African American.

However, with the need came the abuse and monopolies and corporate corruption became common during the second industrial revolution. **[95] [96]**

The American Economic System

There are 4 types of Economic Systems in use today;

1. Traditional Economic System
2. Command Economic System
3. Market Economic System
4. Mixed Economic System

Much of rural America in the 1700's enjoyed a traditional economic system in which the rural residents relied on bartering for goods, since money and hard currency was in short supply in rural communities. Products such as agricultural products, lumber, leather, furs and manual labor were commodities readily available and could be easily bartered and traded locally. Most of the population were farmers in early America, in fact during Jefferson's presidency, 80% of America were rural farmers and lived off the land. In cities, a market economic system was in place, but controlled by England's trade monopolies, such as the East India Company, which levied heavy tariffs on imported products from British colonies. I assume that once America gained its independence from England, the mercantilist economy gradually disappeared and a free market economy replaced it. The founding fathers had little need to consider which type of economic system America should have, since it already establish a localized free market system during the colonization of America. America during the colonial period didn't have a merchant fleet to compete with European colonial mercantilism. In addition, many delegates at the Constitutional Convention, such as John Hancock, were merchants traders themselves, if not smugglers, and were well aware of the short-comings of the mercantile system that limited free trade with other nations.

James Madison and Alexander Hamilton were well acquainted with Adam Smith's book "Wealth of Nations" that was written in 1776. Adam Smith believed that free trade and competition would build more wealth than depending on high tariffs and protectionist trade policies used in the Mercantilism system. The founding fathers were also well aware of its pit-falls and made assurances that the Constitution was written in a manner as to foster free trade between nations and discouraged monopolies and a free flowing mercantilism system common at the time.

Even though America enjoyed a market economic system, a true free market economy may not exist in the world, even today. There will always be government regulations to protect and regulate fair trade, monopolies, banks and stock market improprieties and corporate greed and Corporate take-overs. But, even with a regulated controlled economy, the system is relatively safe, and will always need to be regulated to protect the system from devouring itself over the greed of others. As businesses become larger and begin devoured smaller businesses, monopolies will occur that are counter-productive to the free market system. Panics were common in America in the 1800's, most of which lasted from 3 to 6 years and occurred about every decade on the average.

The early panics were caused by businesses and land speculators borrowing money from local banks, since the government offered land for sale for 1 dollar an acre with a minimum purchase of 180 acres. Additionally, currency manipulation between the gold and silver standard and paper notes generated and issued by the local banks contributed to economic instability and the lack of public confidence, since there wasn't enough hard currency to cover the amount of loans outstanding. The lack of a Federal Reserve Banking system was not necessarily the cause of the panic, but rather a failure in the regulatory judiciary responsibility of banking system that was to insure that local banks had adequate reserves in their bank vaults to cover depositor's withdrawals. In the 1800's there were no government bail-outs; banks just failed and by the hundreds during each panic. This meant that the banks didn't lose the banks money, they lost the depositor's money. The Bank would close, but reopen in a different town under a different name and continued to issue worthless paper bank notes.

Free Trade

Mercantilism was the theory that advocated exporting more goods than it imported, thus causing a trade imbalance. The imbalance would be offset in the form of bullion (gold or silver). It was once believed that to increase a nation's wealth, it required bullion in its treasury, and the more bullion a nation acquired, the wealthier the nation became. It was believed than an inverse effect would occur if there were only so many units of bullion and England acquired 60 units, then the remainder (40 units) would be distributed between the remaining European nations in varying proportions. This may be logical only if no more gold or silver was added to the market. In addition, they would monopolize the shipping and trading in their colonies and not allow the colonies to trade with other countries. England would then impose taxes and tariffs on products imported to the colonies. In 1750 to 1780, more than 70 percent of Britain's income was derived from trade with their colonies. Slavery was their biggest market and the most profitable, since slaves cost nothing, all that was required was kidnapping them.

Because of mercantilism, it led to a land rush by European nations to acquire as many colonies as possible, also known as imperialism. As a result it led to territorial disputes and trade wars between European nations. The wars required large amounts of bullion in their treasuries to support and pay for the wars and the operation of the government. As the treasury ran out of bullion they relied on taxes and tariffs from their colonies to finance their trade wars. England's French Indian War and Trade Wars with France and the Netherlands were prime examples. Many wars were fought over the mercantile system, in particular the Spanish American War around 1900 which is discussed in Volume 2.   Tariffs have also caused wars such as the War of 1812 and the Revolutionary War.

Slavery was very profitable for Britain and British merchants. In 1672, the Royal African Company was given a royal charter and a monopoly to the Port of London, Bristol and Liverpool, which lasted until 1698. It is estimated that Britain imported 3.4 million African slaves to the West Indies and America, which was about 11,150 voyages. After the British abolished the transportation of slaves in 1807, the Portuguese continued the slave trade in America for another 45 years, thus importing 5 million African slaves into America and West Indies. The US Census in 1800 stated that 4 million slaves in the South. Less than half that number was in the north, most of which were freedmen after 1800 in the North but nearly zero in the south.

In Adam Smith's book "Wealth of Nations" (1776), he maintained that the wealth of a nation was not based on how much bullion a nation had in its treasury, but rather allowing an open market of competition in producing goods which would lead to more wealth through all levels of society and government. He also advocated that tariffs thwarts international trade and the reverse effect would result in less wealth for the people and the nation as a whole. [11]

Today we call tariff and trade agreements between nations as "protectionist trade agreements". Many countries today use a form of mercantilism and government-imposed monopolies on specific trade items. By the mid 1800's most of the European countries gradually moved away from mercantilism as an economic system when colonies gradually became independent. Mercantilism caused the tax and tariff revolt and slavery issues that led to the American Civil War seventy years later and nearly divide America.

The Origin of Slavery in America

THE AMERICAN LEGACY

Not only do I pray for it, on the score of human dignity, but I can clearly foresee that nothing but the rooting out of slavery can perpetuate the existence of our union, by consolidating it in a common bond of principle. -George Washington

It wasn't a matter of who is right and who is wrong, it was a situation brought on by necessity. European trader's used slavery as a means of making money. Colonial plantation owner who settled America had land but didn't have a work force to work the fields. Slaves were first used in the West Indies even during Columbus' time to make money for Spain and of course his percentage of the profits. When colonies were established on the mainland of America, European traders moved slaves from the West Indies and sold them to the plantations in Virginia and the Carolina's. As more settlers moved in and built more plantations slave traders provided slaves directly from Africa to the American colonies.

When Britain colonized America, there were vast expanses of land for agricultural, endless forests and natural resources that could bring unimaginable wealth to the British crown. Farm land produced large quantities of cash crops that generated income to the British economy and treasury as well as the farmer who grew them. It also raised the standard of living of the colonist and the two would enjoy a symbiotic relationship. They were interested in New England as an industrial region and the south for its temperate zone of agricultural products such as cotton, rice, corn and tobacco, which were valuable commodities in Europe and England. New England provided trade goods in fish, timber and an active whaling industry on Nantucket Island for whale oil. Britain's cash crops required large parcels of farm land for cotton and tobacco which the two crops depleted the nutrients in the soil, so other crops couldn't be grown. The land that was void of nutrients were considered worthless, and was subdivided and sold or given to share croppers to work, thus few made money from much of the land, especially the poor who worked as share croppers. In the Caribbean, sugar cane was the dominate crop, but land in the islands were in short supply, thus British-American's resorted to using slaves from Africa to harvest sugar cane. The Constitution banned the importation of slaves into America by 1808, however it was seldom enforced. Britain ceased the importation of slaves after 1808, but it didn't apply to British colonies. The Portuguese and Dutch continued the importation of thousands of slaves into America between 1808 and 1840. By 1860, there were nearly 4 million slaves in America, most of which was in Carolina's, Virginia, Georgia and Alabama. There were slaves in the North but most were house servants and gardeners and became freemen after the northern state banned slavery by 1804.

Many plantation owners in the Caribbean moved to Virginia and the Carolina's and brought their slaves with them. The first generation British-American's plantation owners relied exclusively on slave labor to harvest their crops, since there was not enough Anglo-American farm labor in Colonial America at the time. Slaves filled the billets in agricultural labor, much as the Latin American laborers do in America today. Even after Lincoln's emancipation of slaves during and after the Civil War, "back-door" slavery continued. The Freed Negro signed contracts for labor for a certain monthly wage, but discovered that the plantation owner charged room and board that exceeded the labor wages they earned and found themselves as indentured servants' or share croppers. It remained a feudal system for a century or more.

In New England, the Puritan's used slaves as well, however, because of their religious belief; they treated them much better than those working on the southern plantations. It was common for slaves in the north to work side by side in the fields with their owners, which was rarely, if ever done in the south. Rhode Island became the first state to abolish slavery in 1774, followed by Vermont in 1777, nine more New England states followed by 1804.

As a result of slave labor, the southern states had little reason to industrialize. In the north it was different, since dozens of mills were processing cotton into yarn and fabric, thus increasing the quantity, quality and profits of the mill. The textile mill was designed and built in England. Once Samuel Slater memorized the design, he brought it with him to America and built dozens of fabric mills in and around Rhode Island. Water wheels propelled the mills at first, and were later replaced with steam engines which became the first industrial revolution in America, but not in the south. Southerner's paid good money for their slaves and felt it not necessary to industrialize and make slavery obsolete. The northern states became wealthy while the southern states stagnated economically. The south was relegated to growing the raw products while the north to processing into marketable products. Slavery would become the south's human industrialization which was slow and costly, since it required feeding and housing slaves even during periods before harvesting.

The thought of abolishing slavery in the south would result in the collapse of the southern plantations and the agricultural based economy. Southern slave owners invested large sums of money in purchasing slaves on the auction block. The average slave sold for $250 and as much as $400, which would be about $11,000 today. Many had 100 to 300 slaves working on a single plantation at any given time. This was one reason the Fugitive Slave Laws were passed in Congress, to recover runaway slaves which represented a large investment to the plantation owner and without slaves the plantations couldn't survive. In the north having slaves or not made little difference economically. It was perhaps cheaper to pay them $1 per day in wages than to pay $400 for the initial investment plus room and board for life. The slavery was about economics and had little to do about moral principal toward the act of slavery. As it was with Washington and Jefferson and many others; when they retired, most were sold as assets for their retirement income or "farmed-out" to other plantation owners for a contract monthly income.

Slavery and the Constitution

Slavery was a subject carefully avoided during the Constitutional Convention; however it was clearly on everyone's mind. A few delegates wanted to address the "slavery" issue; however it would be "shelved" by a vast majority of the delegates. Many of whom were founding fathers and or wealthy plantation owners who owned large tracks of land and a large number of slaves to work the fields. George Washington had over a 300 slaves at one time at Mount Vernon and Martha Custis' Plantations, as did Thomas Jefferson, James Madison and George Mason. Even some of the delegates from the north had slaves, including John Hancock from Boston; however they were mostly housekeepers or gardener's rather than farm hands. The casual suggestion of including an amendment in the constitution to abolished slavery would bring outrage among the delegates and the possibility that a Constitution would never be ratified was a real possibility. When George Washington was president, he elected not to press the issue of slavery during his presidency; however, in his last will and testament, he freed all of his slaves except a few he kept as housekeepers at Mount Vernon. Many plantation owners followed Washington's que by freeing their slaves upon their death, however many did not. More than 35% of the slaves were freed following Washington's death in 1799. Washington was not the first to free his slaves, but with his popularity, it had a great impact on others to follow his example. John Adams campaigned vigorously against slavery, as did his son, John Quincy Adams, even though neither owned slaves. Perhaps two of the most influential abolitionists were John Jay and Thomas Paine. Jay became the first Supreme Court Justice under Washington's Presidency and later served in the New York Legislature. Jay sponsored several bills to abolish slavery in New York, which failed to pass into law, even though he owned 8 slaves himself.

Gouverneur Morris insisted that slavery be abolished and wanted it included as part of the Articles of Confederation, however, his speeches fell on deaf ears. Years later John Jay was elected Governor of New York and would pass into law the gradual emancipation that later abolish slavery in the State of New York, which became among the first states to do so, next to Rhode Island. These actions gradually led to other northern states to follow suit as well.

While the Articles to the Constitution were being debated in Congress, the Enumeration Clause, Article 1, Section 2, formulated a procedure for apportionment of members of the House Representatives based on population. It was unclear how the slaves should be represented in Congress, since most were not considered citizens and considered personal property. America at the time had a population of 3.8 million people, but 700,000 were slaves, most of which lived in the South. Overall, slaves represented about 18% of the population in America, but in the Southern States, such as North Carolina, 43% of their populations were slaves.

During the debates in Congress, if states excluded slaves in their apportionment, the number of delegates in the House of Representatives would be halved, since slaves were considered property and not allowed to vote. This would be the case in Maryland, Virginia and South Carolina. The Northern States didn't want the slaves included in the apportionment plan. After considerable debate, it was agreed that slaves would be counted as three-fifths of a number and considered not a voting resident but listed as "other" in the census form. [3]   Article 1, Section 9 prohibited the importation of slaves after 1808, which was called the 20 year clause. In 1865 the 13th Amendment was added to the Constitution which abolished slavery entirely in all states. The Republican platform wanted to abolish slavery, whereas the Democrats favored restoration of states' rights and wanted each state to decide on the slavery issue independently. Surprisingly, it was Georgia that ratified the Amendment that allowed the 3/4 ratification necessary to become law.

The issue of slavery would gradually become a national issue that festered and grew in the anti-slavery north and the pro-slavery south. As states were admitted into the Union, the Southern states wanted territories admitted to the Union as pro slavery states, while the north wanted territories admitted as anti slavery states. With the Missouri Compromise of 1850 and the Kansas-Nebraska Act of 1854, it was just a matter of time before Civil War between the North and the South would erupt.

There were three Amendments which addressed the issues of slavery but were not incorporated in the Constitution. On January 31, 1865, the 14th Amendment to the Constitution was ratified that prohibiting slavery in America and the 15th Amendment in 1869, giving Black's citizenship and Black men the right to vote, however by 1896 only 44 percent of the Black's registered to vote. In 1920 the 19th Amendment allowed women to vote and in 1971, the 24th Amendment outlawed poll taxes and literacy tests as a prerequisite to voting or registering to vote.

Religion

"The purpose of the separation of church and state was to keep forever from these shores the ceaseless strife that has soaked the soil of Europe in blood for centuries." [*Letter objecting to the use of government land for churches, 1803*] — James Madison

Religion was another issue that the founding fathers confronted while drafting the Constitution. As mentioned previously, the Pilgrim's arrived from England and Europe and settled in Massachusetts in 1620 and followed shortly after by the Puritan's 1627-28 and the Quakers ten years later. The immigration of religious sects was the result of King James I (1603-1625) and his policies toward protestant and Catholic religions. King Henry VIII declared that only the Church of England was recognized as the official religion in England. **(11)**

It was forbidden to practice Catholicism and certain protestant religious services in England during King James I rein and the Parliament enacted the Popish Recusant Act, which required all citizens to take an oath of allegiance, denying the pope's authority, and as a result many different denominations fled England and moved to the Netherlands and eventually settled in New England.

Pilgrims and Puritans didn't get along well together causing most Pilgrims to move to Rhode Island and later Pennsylvania. The Pilgrims' established their own communities in an effort to disfranchise them from the Puritan's stronghold in the Massachusetts Bay Colony. The Puritans on the other hand, were well educated and business oriented and accepted progressiveness and change. Harvard College was established as a Puritan religious college and later became known as Harvard Law and Business College. Often overlooked in history was the Puritans' belief in the separation of church and state and their ideology that forbid members from holding political office in government, however, as time passed, more and more became involved in American politics, such as Samuel Adams, who was to be known as the last Puritan, figuratively speaking of course.

King James I believed strongly in witchcraft and became obsessed with "witch hunting", in contrast, most Puritans disliked witchcraft and condoned the practice, and however there were a few Puritans sects that believed strongly in the power of witch craft, such was the case in the Salem, Massachusetts. After the death of King James I in 1625, King Charles came to the throne and continued the religious policies of banning worship of Quakerism and Puritanism.

Most of those who settled in America were farmers and wanted to start a new life, since most of the land in England was owned by local Lords who taxed those living on their land or within estate boundaries, thus the term "land lord" got its origin. The founding fathers realized the inequity and addressed it in the Bill of Rights as the First Amendment to the Constitution.

"Congress shall make no law respecting an establishment of religion or prohibiting the free exercise thereof ......"

America wasn't necessarily founded on religious principal alone, but it certainly played an important part in colonial American and the moral attitude of the people at the time. It was clear to the Puritans and the founding fathers that it was important enough to be included it in the Bill of Rights. While most founding fathers were raised in a ridged religious family background, many became deist and non-practicing Christians in later life, but they were still believers in the Christian faith or at least in some degree. Franklin, Jefferson and Madison are said to have been deist later in life, yet were raised as Anglican and or Puritans. John Adams was raised a Congregationalist (Puritan), but became a Unitarian later in his life. He remarked that his work came before the church. There were few Puritan's in politics at the time, even though Franklin's parents were Puritans, he wasn't active in any particular secular religion and is said to have attended many different churches of different faiths mostly to just learn a little about each and often slept in the back pew. John Adams and Hamilton were deeply religious, and it is said that Hamilton prayed two times a day, yet seldom attended Church. What is agreed upon by historians is that the founding fathers were very private about their religious beliefs and seldom discussed it openly or publicly. The founding fathers wanted the newly formed government not to legislate and pass laws about morality and religious belief, but left it to the church to teach the virtues of morality and religious faith to the individual.

While the debate continues by scholars concerning the question; "Did America have a Christian founding?" Delegates to the Constitutional Convention were certainly Congregationalist, Presbyterian, Anglican, Baptist and even Deist, but it is not known how active they were within their church. Historian, Robert T. Handy stated, "No more than 10% -probably less- Americans in 1800 were members of congregations." [12]

Before the Constitution was ratified, each state had its own Constitution. Some states even financed the construction of state sponsored churches, such as Virginia. Nine of Thirteen States supported a state sanctioned church and religion. It would all end after the signing of the U.S. Constitution on September 17, 1787, and the Bill of Rights ratified in 1791. It demonstrates clearly that a federal Constitution was unifying the States under one common rule of law and one common Bill of Rights which supersedes those written by the individual States. Of the 55 delegates who participated in the Constitutional Convention in 1787, 39 signed the document and 16 did not. Of the 16 who did not sign, 6 left the convention for personal reasons such as business or health and 10 refused to sign for various personal reasons such as no bill of rights, insufficient checks and balances and lack of adequate protection of States rights by a central government. One delegate gave the reason for not voting: "wanted the Legislature to select the President rather than the Electoral College". His reasoning may be sound since we don't elect the President or Vice President, since the Electoral College represents the members in Congress. But for all the reasons, religion was not one of them. It is perhaps why God is not mentioned anywhere in the Constitution.

The official motto of the United States is "In God We Trust" which replaced the unofficial motto of "E pluribus unum", which was adopted in 1782. "In God We Trust" first appeared on coins in 1864, but in 1956, the US Congress and President Eisenhower declared that "In God We Trust" appear on US paper currency, which appeared first on the one-dollar silver certificate in 1957.

The Pledge of Allegiance was originally composed by Colonel George Balch in 1887, but was later revised by Edward Bellamy in 1892. Bellamy was a Baptist minister and Christian Socialist. It was adopted by the US Congress in 1942, during World War II. The words; "under God" was added in 1954 during the Joseph McCarthy period, which could have been the results of the red fear that swept America at the time. The U.S. Constitution's Preamble was written by Gouverneur Morris, a New York delegate who signed the Articles of Confederation. He was a member of the Constitutional Conventions of 1777, 1778 and 1787. Morris was the Assistant Ambassador to France and a delegate to the Continental Congress from 1781 to 1785.

Chapter 8
The First Industrial Revolution

1789 - 1850

James Madison is known as the father of the Constitution, but he didn't actually write the Constitution by ink and quill; that honor goes to Gourvenor Morris, the delegate from Pennsylvania. The actual Constitution was scribed on parchment by Jacob Shallus, who was a paid scriber who wrote the final copy for signature by the delegates at the Constitutional Convention of 1787.

Many Founding Fathers later become active into American politics after the Constitution was ratified in 1791 with its Amendments. The last Founding Father to hold the office of President was James Monroe in 1825, and he would die in 1831. Supreme Court Justice, John Marshall was the last founding father to hold office until his death in 1835, while still serving on the Supreme Court Bench. The last living founding father was James Madison, who died in 1836.

In 1788, State legislatures decided how Electors were to be chosen. The method involved each state choosing their Electors or convention delegates. Some southern states went years without having any elections by popular vote.

Many historian claims there were eleven founding fathers, but in fact there were 55 delegates who attended the Constitutional Convention of February 21, 1787, even though some contributed little to the debate, they could still be considered founding fathers. When the constitution was drafted, each state sent delegates to Philadelphia to draft and vote on a Constitution; however, of the 55 delegates who attended, only 39 delegates signed the document. Of the 55 delegates, 34 were lawyers. The crafting of the Articles of Confederation took years to be formulated and many delegates became wary of the lengthy debates over the wording. Many founding fathers were not present during the final vote on the Articles of the Constitution, such as Thomas Jefferson, Samuel Adams, John Adams, John Hancock and Patrick Henry and Richard Henry Lee. Virginia had seven delegates at the Convention but only three signed the document; George Washington, James Madison and John Blair. It is important to note that many did not attend the final signing of the Constitution and the Declaration of Independence due to the hardship of traveling long distances on horseback or carriage. In addition to the travel, many delegates had crops to sow and harvesting to do. Others were ill and unable to travel.

It must also be further noted that many patriots of the revolution were also considered founding fathers. Some founding fathers played an active role in leadership during the revolution and as delegates to the Constitutional Convention of 1787, while others were active in the signing and drafting of the Declaration of Independence and the Articles of Confederation during the Continental Congress. Franklin inspired many to the cause of American independence, as did Thomas Paine, whom Franklin met in London and sponsored Paine to publish his ideas in his Philadelphia newspaper. It must also be remembered that some founding fathers did not attend all of the Conventions, but inspired others to become active in the cause of independence through books, pamphlets and speeches. They risk the threat of treason and sedition which carried the punishment of death by hanging. So the stakes were high which history books often neglect to mention. Most founding fathers would die in obscurity while others were canonized into history, but not one delegate did it for notoriety or financial gain, but because they felt it was the right thing to do.

George Washington
(1732 – 1799)

"I hope I shall possess firmness and virtue enough to maintain what I consider the most enviable of all titles, the character of an honest man."
George Washington

George Washington was born in Virginia in 1732 to an upper middle class farming family who owned a great deal of land. In his early years he worked as a surveyor and fought in the French Indian War from 1754 to 1759 and rose to the rank of Colonel in the Virginia Militia. After the war, he resigned his commission due to his half-brother illness. Lawrence Washington was 14 years his senior and was diagnosed with tuberculosis. To help relieve his suffering, the two traveled to Barbados to see if the warmer climate would help, however, he would die one year later.

He returned to his home at Mount Vernon and married Martha Dandridge Custis, a widow with four teenage children, of which two would die of illness. She became very wealthy after the death of her husband who owned several large tobacco plantations with more than 100 slaves. Shortly after his marriage to Martha, he was elected to the Virginia House of Burgesses and served until 1774, at which time he became a delegate to the first Constitutional Congress in Philadelphia. One year later, in 1775, he was given the command of the Continental Army as Commander and Chief. Washington was not a great military strategist, however his skill lay in his ability to lead men into battle and give them hope when there was little hope to give. He was able to get his men to do the near impossible because of their respect and for leadership. General Washington won few battles during the eight years of war with England, but with the French as allies in October of 1781, he captured General Charles Cornwallis's troops, which resulted in the surrender of Cornwallis and became the pivotal point in ending the Revolutionary War. As one French General said when introduced to

General Washington, "I finally meet the most famous General who never won a battle".

In 1783, Great Britain and the Continental Congress signed the Paris Peace Treaty which officially ended the Revolutionary War. General Washington retired to his home in Mount Vernon after the war. In 1787, he was asked to attend the Constitutional Convention in Philadelphia to help draft the Constitution. On January 7, 1789 the first presidential election was held and George Washington easy won the electoral vote over John Adams who would receive the second largest votes and become Washington's Vice President.

Washington's Personality

Washington was not a perfect person as most history books may portray, but rather a normal yet intelligent person with impeccable honor and loyalty. Washington in his early years inherited Mount Vernon from his eldest brother, Lawrence who died early in life from tuberculosis. The plantation struggled for many years to make a profit, as did most plantations of the period. Washington became obsessed in becoming a Virginian gentleman and being considered an aristocrat.

To accomplish his goal, he purchased a copy of Peachman's "The Complete Gentleman" book, which he carried with him during the Revolutionary War. This Peachman's book was taught as part of the curriculum for those attending college and finishing school for the wealthy prodigy of the upper Virginian elite. Washington would leave school at the age of 10 to help on the family farm as was customary for those of less than noble heritage. With the marriage of Martha, his station in life would change dramatically.

Washington battled with his temper throughout his life. He was often criticized for being overly frugal and demanding every penny due him, which was considered low class. He had been called ungrateful by his military superiors during the French Indian Wars while commanding a squad of British troops in the Ohio River Valley campaign. He was characterized as being defiant and ridged in his beliefs. He criticized his superior's often in letters and sometimes circumventing the chain of command. As he became older and more experienced in protocol, he was able to maintain self control over his temper and criticism of his superiors. Since he had poor oratory skills, he befriended Alexander Hamilton who was well educated and considered a great oratory with impeccable writing skills. Their alliance would carry both of them to the Presidency. Hamilton would assist in composing Washington's Farewell Address to Congress in 1797, even though he posted the Farewell Address in the newspaper, rather than present the address in person to Congress. Washington spent most of his later retirement at his plantation in Mount Vernon. Historians have noted that Washington received few visitors at Mount Vernon during his retirement.

Washington's Presidency
(1789 – 1797)

On April 30, 1789 in New York, George Washington was inaugurated as the America's first president. When Washington became President, he was saddled with huge debt, land that was considered worthless and forced to sell one quarter of his slaves to pay his debts. In fact, he borrowed 100 pounds at 6 percent interest from a friend to make the trip to New York for his inauguration. One of his favorite sayings: "Worry is the interest paid by those who borrow trouble." He wrote in his daily journal of his trip to New York:

"About 10 o'clock I bade adieu to Mount Vernon, to private life, and to domestic felicity, and with a mind oppressed with more anxious and painful sensations than I have words to express, set out for New York in company with Mr. Thompson, and Colonel Humphries, with the best dispositions to render service to my country in obedience to its call, but with less hope of answering its expectations." [80]

John Adams would be elected his Vice President and Washington appointed Thomas Jefferson as his Secretary of State and Alexander Hamilton as Treasury Secretary. John Jay was appointed the first U.S. Supreme Court Justice.

Washington disliked political parties and political partisanship. He refused to belong to a political party, however much of his cabinet was divided ideologically as Federalist or Anti-Federalist. Washington, Hamilton and John Jay were Federalist, and advocated a strong central government, while Jefferson on the other hand, he was an ardent supporter of anti-federalist principals that advocated states rights over federal control over states. Washington's Vice President, John Adams was a staunch Federalist and later organized the Federalist for which he would run as President in 1797. This was contrary to Washington's ideals, but Presidents and the Vice Presidents of the day were elected by Electoral College and the two top electoral votes determined who would be President and who would be Vice President, regardless of their political affiliation or ideology.

Thomas Jefferson and Alexander Hamilton frequently disagreed about the role of government, which created tension among cabinet members. Washington was a diplomat and hosted foreign dignitaries and preferred a position of neutrality toward foreign nations and devoted much of his effort in foreign policy. He seldom discussed foreign policy issues with members of congress and believed that foreign policy issues were the duties of the Executive Branch and not the legislative branch.

After the Revolutionary War, the Continental Congress and most states had accumulated a large war debt. The Treasury Secretary, Alexander Hamilton, recommended that the Federal Government assume the States war debts. To help pay for the war debt, he suggested levying an excise tax on Whiskey. They had previously levied a heavy tax on imports and believed it to be less burdensome on the citizens. It was voted by Congress and passed in 1791, but farmers in Pennsylvania became outraged and rebelled against the tax. Many farmers had whiskey stills that supplemented their income after the harvest season. Most of the rural farmers had little disposable income to pay the tax and much of the whiskey was used as barter and self consumption. The tax was a reverse progressive tax, which meant the more you produced the less tax per volume you paid. Large commercial distilleries benefited from the tax, since it made the rural distillers of whiskey more expensive to the consumers, thus reducing competition from local rural distillers.

The Whiskey Rebellion gathered more and more rural supporters until 1794, when western farmers and distillers began to attacking revenue collectors and set fire to their homes. Some tax collectors were tarred and feathered, which was a means of keeping revenue agents from inspecting their distillery. On August 7, 1794, Washington led a militia of 13,000 to quell the rebellion in western Pennsylvania under the command of General Harry Lee, the father of Robert E. Lee. Some arrests were made but all were later pardoned by President Washington and the Whiskey Rebellion gradually ended. The Whiskey Rebellion consumed a great deal of Washington's time while President but he was able to get some domestic laws and policies through Congress. In 1795, two states were admitted to the Union, Vermont and Kentucky, and in 1793, the Fugitive Slave Act and the Judiciary Act of 1789 was passed into law.

The John Jay Treaty

The Jay Treaty was perhaps the most controversial treaty in America history. Even though it narrowly passed the Senate for approval, it eventually cost Washington his friendship with Jefferson, Madison and Monroe. It would also be the major factor in the War of 1812, whose purpose was to correct the issues not addressed in the Treaty of Paris that were to be a major issue in the treaty. At issue was the enforcement of the Paris Treaty, ending the Revolutionary War with Britain. It is interesting to note, that sometimes treaties only delay war rather than avoid them, such was the case in the Jay Treaty and perhaps to some extent the Paris Treaty as well.

Washington sent John Jay to London to negotiate a treaty with Britain. The terms of the treaty was designed by Secretary of the Treasury, Alexander Hamilton. Hamilton was known as a staunch supporter of Great Britain. During the Constitutional Convention, Hamilton proposed that the America government be designed after the English parliamentary system with a King as the head of State and a upper and lower house in parliament. While the treaty dealt with boundary disputes and compensation for ships seized on the high seas by the British Navy, it was to include a demand for Britain to cease the practice of impressments of American merchant sailors and the seizure of merchant ships and cargo during the war with France. Britain had impressed more than 10,000 American sailors during the Napoleonic Wars of 1797.

In addition, American demanded that Britain abandon its forts along the Great Lakes region, Ohio River, Pennsylvania and New York, which was fortified by British troops. Most of America's concessions were lost during the negotiations, in which the British refused to abandon impressments of American merchant sailors and compensation for the 250 merchant ships it seized. In exchange, Britain offered to vacate eight (8) forts and give America favored nation status, with the stipulation that American could not trade in the Caribbean or India. Perhaps one of the more important aspects of the Treaty that exists today is the Native American's, Canadian and American citizen's use of an open border to freely pass between countries and use inland water ways (Great Lakes) for trade between Canada and the U.S.. Britain would pay America $11.6 million for damages to American shipping, but in return, America would compensate Britain 600,000 pounds for pre-1775 debt.

While the Jay Treaty addressed most of the issues, it failed to address the most pressing issue; the seizure of the 250 merchant ships and

10,000 impressed sailors who were forced into battle under the Royal Navy. This issue alone drew considerable criticism from the general public and in particular Thomas Jefferson and James Madison. American became divided between two groups as a result; the Federalist-pro treaty and the Federalist-anti treaty. In addition, a raising wave of Anti-Federalist led by Jefferson controlled American politics at the time, after John Adams became President, which they called the Republican-Democrat's.

Most Senators and Congressmen demanded that Washington turn over to Congress all documents and notes of the negotiations during the Jay Treaty, hence, Washington refused, claiming executive privilege. It would be the first time a President would claim executive privilege and would set a precedence lasting to this day, however today much more broadly claimed. Washington insisted that the President had the authority to negotiate treaties, and Congress had the authority to vote to accept or reject, but nothing more. Jefferson resigned his post as secretary of State after two years in office as a result of Washington and Hamilton's Jay Treaty incident. Jefferson, after leaving office continued his quest to dismantle the Jay Treaty. Along with Madison, they continued to find legal and constitutional ways to void the Treaty, but with no effect. All efforts were in vane, the Jay Treaty was due to expire in 1805. Jefferson was elected President in 1801 and did not extend the Jay Treaty in the Monroe-Pickney Treaty of 1806, which will be discussed later. After the War of 1812, the Treaty of Ghent Treaty supersedes the Jay Treaty, rendering it invalidated.

Washington Retires to Mount Vernon

At the completion of his second term as President in 1797, he declined to run for a third term. He returned to Mount Vernon and with the assistance of Alexander Hamilton, wrote Washington's Farewell Address to congress.

While George Washington was well respect and honored by most, however, he had made some enemies during his Presidency. Benjamin Franklin's newspaper published articles criticizing Washington's foreign and domestic policies during the first year of his presidency. Franklin would die one year after Washington became President, but the media continued to attack Washington's policies. When he returned to Mount Vernon, many of his friends no longer visited him. Thomas Jefferson had completely alienated himself from Washington as well as Thomas Paine, to mention only a few. He and Martha remained alone much of the time until his death three years later in 1799. He was considered a hero during the Revolutionary War, but during his Presidency he was constantly criticized for being weak and ineffective as a President. He delegated much of the domestic decisions to his Cabinet and in particular Alexander Hamilton who served as his chief advisor. Hamilton had a strong and dominant personality who had little difficulty controlling the agenda during the cabinet meetings, much to everyone's dismay. His cabinet was first convened in February of 1793.

But after Washington's death, even his enemies publically announced his greatness as a leader and statesmen of the time. People purchase paintings of Washington and hung them in their homes and businesses after his death. His Farewell Address was republished in the newspapers in remembrance and he became canonized by most every citizen in America.

During Washington's Presidency, Congress passed the Residency Act of 1790 that gave the President the authority to select the site for the new Capital of the United States. President Washington took an active interest in selecting the site on the Potomac River and having surveyed the site, and named it the Territory of Columbia, later changed to District of Columbia. The new capital site became a small city that housed construction crews for the capital construction of roads and buildings. The workers called it the City of Washington. Much of the capital was built by slaves; however, they were given a good wage and decent housing and were treated very well.

The name would later be changed Washington D.C. The first President to occupy the White House was John Adams in 1800; however he spent much of his time on his farm in Braintree, Massachusetts. President Washington would not live to see his Capital completed, however being the first President, he would establish the first Presidential Cabinet meetings, Postal Service, Attorney General's office and Judiciary and Marshal Service. He created the first Department of Defense and military and the National Bank of the United States.

President Washington's legacy was not about establishing departments and cabinets or building the capital or entering into treaties with foreign countries; his legacy was his vision of a democracy and a free nation, in which he carried those ideals into the office of the Presidency.

He believed in a strong central government, whose primary function was to negotiate with foreign governments; resolve foreign issues and entering into treaties and trade agreements for the greater good of the nation. He felt strongly in the rule of law and the literal interpretation of the Constitution and Bill of Rights. He was a man of principal and upon his death, in his final Will and Testament, he freed his 100 slaves. He was unable to get Congress to consider an anti-slavery bill during his Presidency. President Washington served two terms as president, a French diplomat once said, "If George Washington resigns after two terms as President; he will be the greatest man in the world". Some historian's claim that Washington's Presidency wasn't exceptional and it wasn't, it was riddled with power struggles and bickering throughout his tenure mostly among his cabinet members, however most historians agree that George Washington created a presidential standard and demeanor for all future Presidents aspire to. He represents honesty and dignity, respect for the Office he held, even though he had among the most difficult presidency in the history, he never faltered from his principals. **[78]**

DOUGLAS G. BEAUDOIN

Martha Washington (Custis)
(1731 – 1802)

Martha Dandridge Custis was widowed at the age of 25. Her husband, Daniel Parke Custis died in 1757. Daniel Custis was a wealthy plantation owner who had several large tobacco plantations in Virginia that covered over 17,500 acres and owned nearly 300 slaves. They were among the wealthiest Plantation owners in Virginia. When George and Martha Washington married in 1759, Mount Vernon had 2,650 acres. After the death of Daniel Custis, Virginia inheritance laws were such that the estate was to be inherited by the eldest son, John "Jacky" Parke Custis. Martha would receive a dower share of one-third of the income for her life time from the estate and one-third of the slaves. She could not sell any part of the estate and managed the entire estate until her eldest son reached the age of majority. Martha's dower share included 80 of the 285 slaves in the Custis estate. The remaining two-thirds of the estate and the income it generated were held in trust for Jacky Custis.

Washington's plantation, Mount Vernon, didn't generate much income, if any over the years. Washington's wealth was accrued through land speculation, however during his life time; he only acquired real estate and seldom sold or made any profit from the land he purchased. He leased and rented land, but seldom was able to collect rent from squatters. He had dozens of squatters on his land in Pennsylvania, and after the war he was forced to take many to court to evict them.

By 1787, Mount Vernon had grown from 2,650 acres to 8,251 acres. During the Revolutionary War, Jacky Custis died of typhoid fever and the estate passed to Jacky Custis's eldest son; George Washington Parke Custis, who was a minor at the time. Martha continued to manage the estate for nearly 40 years, in which much of their household income was derived from the one-third of the profits from the income from the Custis estate. The remaining two-third was placed in a trust account for the eldest son as was required by law.

During the Revolutionary War, Britain didn't buy tobacco, flax, hemp, corn, rice or cotton from America, thus most plantations were forced to sell their slaves and land holdings. Farm land was plentiful and nearly worthless, as many plantations were forced to grow less profitable crops such as Hay, wheat and corn to feed their slaves and livestock. The Continental Congress purchased grain and produce from local farmers, but were paid in IOU's or worthless continental paper currency that British traders refused to accept.

Washington was on the battle fields for nearly eight years during their marriage, leaving Martha to manage Mt. Vernon and the Custis Plantations. Martha followed Washington to the battle fields at times during the Revolutionary War, including Valley Forge. Even though Washington was not paid for the years he served as Commanding General until after the war, he provided and paid for food for his 11 officers at Valley Forge. He eventually was paid by Congress after the war, 100,000 pounds of Continental paper currency which was considered nearly worthless. The fact that Washington was wealthy was a fallacy. Martha was forced to sell Mount Vernon and her slaves after Washington's death, since she did not legally own the Custis Estate which at one time provided a modest stream of income while he was General.

Martha Washington died in 1802, only three years after George Washington's death in 1799. She is still revered as among the most revered First Ladies in American history.

John Jay
(1745 -1829)

John Jay was an important figure during and after the Revolution. He was born in New York in 1745 into a wealthy family who owned a merchant trading company in New York City. His grandfather moved from France to New York City in 1685. Jay's parents had 10 children, all of which moved to Rye, New York, when John was only 3 months old. He attended King's College (Columbia) in 1760 and graduated in 1764. He passed the New York Bar and opened a law office in New York City in 1771. His father died in 1774, in which he inherited the 400 acre Jay Estate in Rye, New York. With the death of his father, he was financially responsible for two of his siblings who were blind from a small pox epidemic and a brother who suffered from mental disabilities.

Jay was selected to represent New York in the first and second Continental Congresses. He originally wanted to negotiate with Britain to find a common ground between Britain and America and resolve their differences that separated them. However, as negotiations continued between the Continental Congress and the British Government, it became obvious that there was an impasse. In 1774, he would assist in drafting New York's Constitution. Jay would be elected President to the Continental Congress in 1778 to 1779 and appointed Minister to Spain in 1779 for the purpose of influencing Spain in providing financial aid, however Spain refused, but agreed to loan the Continental Congress $170,000.

Jay was a firm believer in a strong central government and along with Madison and Hamilton they all three pressed for a new set of Articles of Confederation to be replaced by the Articles to the Constitution. He didn't attend the Constitutional Convention in 1787, but became active in the Federalist Papers in which he contributed 5 of the 85 papers published under an assumed alias "Publius" in favor of ratification of the Amendments and the Constitution.

The Treaty of Paris

In June of 1782, at the conclusion of the Revolutionary War, John Jay, John Adams and Benjamin Franklin negotiated a treaty on behalf of America. The Earl of Sheilburne was acting on behalf of Britain. One of the main issues with Britain was to accept America's independence, which he refused. Negotiation was halted for 3 months until Britain accepted America's independence. The term of the Treaty included withdraws all British troops in exchange for the return of the seizure of loyalist property and private debts. This aspect of the Treaty of Paris was of historical importance, since it would be one element that led to the War of 1812 under Madison's Presidency.

Jay served as Secretary of Foreign Affairs form 1784 to 1789 and acting Secretary of State until 1790. In 1790, Washington offered John Jay the position as Chief Justice of the United States, which he accepted. John Jay only served on the Court six years and only heard 4 cases. Much of the duties at the time involved establishing the rules and procedures of the circuit court and lower court review. John Jay became America's first Chief Justice and returned to New York to campaign for Governor, but would lose the election to George Clinton.

John Adams
(1735 – 1826)

"We have no government armed with power capable of contending with human passions unbridled by morality and religion. Avarice, ambition, revenge or gallantry would break the strongest cords of our Constitution as a whale goes through a net. Our Constitution is designed only for a moral and religious people. It is wholly inadequate for any other."
-John Adams

After George Washington retired from politics, his Vice President, John Adams ran for President in 1796 as a candidate for his newly formed Federalist. His opponent was Thomas Jefferson, who was a candidate under the new Republican-Democrat platform. The leaders of the Federalist were Alexander Hamilton, John Jay and Charles Pinckney. The party platform was centered on a strong central government and a central national bank. The Federalist supported neutrality in the war between France and Great Britain, partly because it was good for the economy and business and allowed trade between both France and Britain and supported import tariffs to support the operation of the government. In contrast was the Republican-Democrat's who appealed to the rural agrarian farmer, who wanted a strong state government and state rights rather than a strong federal government. Even though Hamilton and John Adams were in the same political coalition, neither seemed too trust each other. Thomas Jefferson disliked both Adams and Hamilton for their political views, but Hamilton for his demeanor.

John Adams won the election in 1797 and became the second President of the United States. He would remain in office four years until 1801, but because of his curmudgeon temperament and his unwillingness to compromise with Congress, he created many political enemies. As a result, he confined himself to the White House and spent much of his time at his farm in Braintree, Massachusetts for much of his four years while in office.

One of the more controversial legislations during his administration was the Alien and Sedition Act of 1798. The Federalist became popular in both Congress. Popular opinion had turned against the French in 1787 over failed negotiations with France, in particular the XYZ Affair. As a result, an undeclared Naval Shipping war began between France and American that lasted two years. The Administration built a navy and a large army, which was financed by raising taxes on land, houses and slaves. The Alien and Sedition Act in 1798 made it a crime to print false, scandalous and malicious criticisms of the Government. Several Republican-Democrat members were arrested and sent to prison as a result of their public criticism of the government and three Republican-Democrat newspapers were closed.

By 1799, Adams realized Alexander Hamilton was becoming a political liability and was turning public opinion against his administration. Even though he was not part of his Administration, Hamilton was offering advice to Adam's cabinet members behind his back. President Adams decided to disband the Army in which Adams reluctantly appointed Hamilton as the Inspector General in retaliation. Adams also fired several Hamilton's supporters in his Cabinet. In retaliation, Hamilton used the newspaper to discredit Adams with name calling and criticism of his performance as a President. In the end, he lost the presidential election of 1801 to Thomas Jefferson, a Republican-Democrat.

John Adams was a close friend to Benjamin Franklin and a cousin of Samuel Adams. Washington didn't get along well with Adams during his Vice Presidency, because of his stubbornness and obstinate nature. During his Presidency, his cabinet lost confidence in his foreign and domestic policies. Congress censured Adams for the passage of the Alien and Sedition Acts; even though he didn't introduce the Bill himself in Congress, he certainly had some input else he would not have signed the bill into law.

John Adams' Legacy

His legacy as President and two terms as Vice President wasn't considered exceptional and riddled with controversy. His legacy will always be his contribution and leadership in the framing the Constitution and his participation in the Continental Congress and Declaration of Independence. He played a pivotal role in the drafting and editing the Declaration of Independence. He served as Ambassadors to Holland, Great Britain and Commissioner to France. Along with Benjamin Franklin; John Adams was perhaps America's greatest statesman. Historians agree that his first year of his presidency may not have been a true representation of his potential leadership abilities, since his contribution in early years was exemplary.

The First Industrial Revolution in England

About the time of John Adam's presidency, the first industrial revolution in England was accelerating, with new invention and manufacturing techniques being developed at an astounding rate. It began around 1733 and by 1760 it had peaked in Britain. It started out as a necessity, since England had an abundance of iron and coal, but relied on unprocessed products from its many colonies. With the growing demand for cotton and other manufactured products from its colonies, emphasis was placed upon mechanical means to produce more textiles for consumers. England pioneered the corporate and investment atmosphere in which individuals could invest in stock holding companies for future dividends yet shielded investors from corporate bankruptcy, law suits with limited liability to the investor.

The British government created the patent office system we have today that protects and encouraged inventors to design and build new ways of manufacturing and increase productivity. After the revolutionary war in 1787, 80% of the American population were either directly or indirectly descendants from England or its common wealth nations and relatively well educated. Even though England pioneered such notable inventions as James Kay's "flying shuttle" in 1733, and James Hargreave's "spinning jenny", both inventions would be the building block to Samuel Crompton's textile machine that combined the spinning and weaving process into a single machine called the "spinning mule" in 1774. To go another step further, Edmund Cartwright built the "power loom" which used a steam engine as a power source in 1785. James Watt, a Scottish instrument maker, designed and built the first steam engine in 1765. With the invention of the steam engine, manufactures need not depend on the water wheel to provide energy to operate mills and industrial plants. The rest of course is history, no pun intended. Along with the steam engine came the steam powered trains and Fulton's steam ship. It wasn't but 35 to 40 years later that inventors such as Ben Franklin and Thomas Paine returned from Europe and brought their new ideas and concepts they learned in England back to America which began the industrial revolution in America as well.

America's First Industrial Revolution

Since Britain invented the method of spinning cotton into fabric, it began a new textile manufacture industry that was copied and built in Rhode Island. America needed a machine that would separate the cotton seed from the cotton plant. Nathanael Greene's widow hired Eli Whitney to invent such a machine in 1793, with interchangeable parts, that was called the "cotton gin". It would produce 55 pounds of seedless cotton in a day. However, he would sell his cotton gin to plantation owners for 1/3 of the harvest profits. It wasn't long, before the plantation owners copied the gin to avoid paying Whitney the 1/3 royalty. He patented his gin in 1794, but in 1807, the court ruled his patent was void, since he had sold his cotton gin prior to acquiring a patent, which makes little sense.

America had an advantage during the industrial period. Capital was readily available, the abundance of natural resources, navigable rivers and coastal waterways that made transportation of raw products easy to supply the industrial region of the Northeast. The Embargo Act of 1807 and the War of 1812 with Britain and the Napoleonic Wars of 1803 to 1815 in Europe, forced American manufactures to build industrial facilities that supplied American made products to foreign nations. Gradually, the American agrarian economy was becoming an industrial economy, as more and more rural farmers moved to the northeast to find work in the industrial plants and eventually became entrepreneur's themselves.

In 1785, Oliver Evens invented the flour mill that included a grain elevator and hopper that became the basis for the "gristmill" known today. The first and wealthiest industrialist in America in the early 18th and 19th century was Samuel Slater. Samuel Slater was born in Belper, Derbyshire, England in 1768 and worked in a cotton mill in England before moving to Rhode Island in 1789. He entered into an agreement with Moses Brown to assist in setting-up the mill. Brown purchased 32 spindle frames for making fabric from cotton; however he was unable to figure-out how to connect them all together. Brown offered Slater a contract to get the system operating. Since it was illegal in Britain to copy and export mechanical designs and apparatus,

Slater committed to memory the machinery design while employed by the Cromford Mill in England. Slater sailed to Pawtucket Falls, Rhode Island to help set-up browns mill. In 1793, Brown and Slater opened their first mill and began producing yarn. It would be the first water-powered textile mill in America.

At the time of his death in 1835 at the age of 66, Slater owned 13 mills. His management style was patterned after the English system. He constructed entire towns with banks, stores, churches and schools, situated on property owned by the mill. Historically, it would be known as the "Rhode Island System". By 1800, there were more than 50 mills in New England and by 1815, 140; all of which were near Providence, Rhode Island.

Steamboats, canals and interstates were constructed during the early part of the industrial revolution. Railroads soon followed and by 1840, 2,808 miles of track was laid. By 1850, 9,012 miles of railroad track was laid, which greatly expanded transportation in America. The Civil War in 1860 halted the first industrial revolution but it gained a rebirth 1870 as the second industrial revolution began which lasted until 1914.

Thomas Jefferson
(1743 - 1826)

I consider trial by jury as the only anchor yet imagined by man by which a government can be held to the principles of its constitution.

— *Thomas Jefferson*

Thomas Jefferson was truly a renaissance man; a lawyer, surveyor, architect, philosopher, inventor, horticulturalist and statesman. Most Americans are taught in school that Jefferson was the primary author of the Declaration of Independence and delegate to the Second Continental Congress, and later the third President of the United States, however few realize he was also a Legislator in the House of

Burgesses in Virginia, Governor of Virginia, Minister (Ambassador) to France, the first Secretary of State and Vice President under John Adams in the election of 1796. But Thomas Jefferson did not have an easy life, if was filled with tragedy and disappointments as well.

Thomas Jefferson was of Scottish decent. He was born in April of 1743 in Shadwell Virginia, the third child in a family of ten siblings. His father, Peter, was a surveyor and his mother, Jane Randolph was from the prominent Randolph family in Virginia. His father died in 1757 and divided his entire estate between his two sons, Thomas and Randolph, of which Thomas would inherit 5,000 acres known as Monticello. Thomas was a minor of 14, and would take possession of Monticello on his 21st birthday. In the interim, while boarding with the Randolph family, he would be educated by a private tutor hired by the Randolph's, Reverend James Maury. At the age of 16, he attended the College of William and Mary and graduated as a lawyer. Thomas was a voracious reader and accumulated more than 6,000 volumes of books by 1814. During the War of 1812, the British marched into Washington DC and burned the capital and the Library of Congress and Jefferson would sell part of his collection to the Library of Congress in his later years because of being in heavy debt.

Virginia House of Burgesses
(1769-1775)

After Jefferson graduated from William and Mary College, he was admitted to the Virginia bar in 1767 and became a delegate to the Virginia House of Burgesses in 1769.

As I had mentioned in Chapter 2, the House of Burgesses was the first legislative assembly established in North America that elected representatives that represent the citizenry in government. The House of Burgesses was established in 1619 and lasted until the Virginia's House of Delegates superseded it in 1776. The House was made up of 22 elected representatives from the community in which the representatives were most often land owners of large estate owners or those of wealth and influence. The representatives only served as advisors to the Virginia Governor's Council, which was made up of British appointees that represented the Virginia Company and British political interests. The Governor was appointed by the parliament and approved by the Monarch.

Virginia's Governor Council and the House of Burgesses would be called the Virginia General Assembly. Counties or Parishes were created and called shires, in which commissioners, judges, sheriffs and clerks were appointed by the Governor's Council. The only elected body in government was the House of Burgesses, however women still weren't allowed to vote. By 1670, only property owners were allowed to vote, which was a common practice in England at the time and was a carry-over from British law.

Thomas Jefferson represented Albemarle County in the House of Burgesses. John Murray, the 4th Earl of Dunmore served as the Virginia Colonial Governor. In 1774, the House of Burgesses adopted a resolution in support of the Boston colonist objecting to British troops quartering in Boston. When John Murray heard of the resolution, he dissolved the Assembly; however the assembly would meet privately. During the unauthorized meetings, Peyton Randolph was elected President of the Convention, and delegates were elected as part of the newly formed Continental Congress.

The House of Burgesses was reconvened by John Murray in 1775; however, the gesture may have been too late. Patrick Henry would deliver his speech; *"Give me liberty or give me death"*, or words to that affect. On May 6, 1776, the House of Burgesses held meetings under a new name, "the Commonwealth of Virginia", with a Senate and a House of Delegates.

Jefferson pressed for reforms in the slavery laws and defended seven slaves during his tenure in the House of Burgesses. The slaves wanted emancipation from slavery, but he had little success convincing the court and the Governor's Council. All was not lost in his efforts, since it would help serve him later in the drafting the Declaration of Independence; *"....we hold these truths to be self evident, that all men are created equal..."* Some historians claim his intention to treat slaves as equal and deserving equal rights was "double speak", since he himself owned more than 135 slaves at one point, but Jefferson was a much different slave owner than most slave owners of the period. He considered his slaves part of his extended family and treated them well. He encouraged them to marry and offered incentives for those who married within Monticello Plantation.

In 1768, Jefferson began construction of Monticello. Monticello in Italian means "little house". In 1770, he moved into the south pavilion, while continuing to design and build the main body of Monticello. In 1772, he married Martha Wayles Skelton, his third cousin, who was the widow of Bathurst Skelton. They would have six children together. When Martha's father, John died in 1773, she inherited 135 slaves and 11,000 acres. John was in heavy debt when he died and Thomas took on the debt, which took him years to pay off. After the birth of the 6th child and 10 years of marriage, Martha would die in September of 1782 at the age of 33, which left him grief stricken for more than three months, in which he seldom left his room.

Jefferson's Political Career

In 1775, at the age of 33, he was appointed as a delegate to the Second Continental Congress. The American Revolution had just begun and his close friend, John Adams and a committee of five wanted him to draft the Declaration of Independence. He would also draft the Virginia Constitution along with George Mason's draft of the Virginia Declaration of Rights. Most of the thirteen colonies (states) included a Bill of Rights within their State Constitutions as well.

Jefferson was commissioned as a colonel in the Albermarle County Militia at the beginning of the Revolution and elected to the Virginia House of Delegates. His passion was to pass a law that established religious freedom, independent of state sponsored religious institutions which was becoming common at the time; however his effort failed to pass the Virginia House. Virginia declared the Anglican Church a state sponsored religion, however it was eventually overruled with the support of both Jefferson and James Madison years later, declaring the separation of state and religion.

Another issue Jefferson felt strongly about was inheritance laws in Virginia. Virginia's inheritance laws were patterned after British inheritance law, whereas the eldest surviving son inherited the bulk of the estate, which over centuries created a tiered system called "hereditary aristocracy", patterned after Europe's feudal system of Earls, Dukes, Lords and Barons. The "entail" law was a system in which the eldest son inherited the estate and was not allowed to sell it. The estate was to be passed-down through inheritance to the eldest surviving son, from generation to generation. The "primogeniture" law only allowed the eldest son to inherit the estate.

As a result of the restrictive inheritance laws of the time, the plantations could only be owned by white aristocrats, expanded in size as each generation purchased more land from local farmers. The small rural farm land decrease in size and eventually was consumed by the larger plantation estates. Eventually, the poor rural farmer would be forced to leased or rented land from the estate owner as share croppers. It was in essence a traditional feudal system governed by an oligarchy. As previously mentioned in Chapter 8, "Martha Washington"; George Washington acquired 17,500 acres of land over a 40 year period. It was believed at the time that aristocrats were those who owned large plantations. Both George Washington and Thomas Jefferson acquired land (which sold for 1 dollar an acre at the time) to help elevate their status as an aristocrat. However, both had large land holdings and slaves, they were cash poor. Both would die poor and after their death would be sold to pay their debts. Politics at the time was not a profitable occupation, most political positions were unpaid positions and only the wealthy could afford to devote their time.

Jefferson was elected Governor of Virginia for a one year term of office from 1779 to 1780. He moved the State capital from Williamsburg to Richmond and during his tenure as governor, he repealed the inheritance laws and State sanctioned religious laws.

After the Revolutionary War he was appointed as a Virginia delegate to the US Congress of Confederation in 1783. He proposed that the America's monetary system use a decimal system and authored the Land Ordinance of 1784, where Virginia would cede land to the federal government; the Ohio River territory and subdivide territories which later became nine separate States. He drafted a map which encompassed nine new states in the new Ohio Territory. He campaigned vigorously for banning slavery in the newly formed Ohio Territory which became known as the "Jefferson Proviso". It would be modified 3 years later and passed as the "Northwest Ordinance of 1787".

In 1786, he was appointed Minister to France, after Benjamin Franklin stepped down due to health. John Adams was Minister to Britain at the time. His youngest surviving child, Polly, who was 9 years old, accompanied Jefferson to France, along with several of his slaves, including Sally Henings, who was 16 years old at the time. She was half English and African American with a light complexion in which he would have an affair with Sally Henings while in Paris. It was not uncommon, at the time for slave owners to have sexual relations with slaves, however, it would create a black mark on his legacy two hundred years later.

Washington was elected President in 1789 and established a cabinet of appointees. John Adams was elected Vice President, since receiving the second highest electoral votes. Washington appointed Jefferson as

Secretary of State and Alexander Hamilton as his Secretary Treasurer. As previously mentioned, the turmoil during the cabinet meetings was followed by personal attacks between Jefferson and Hamilton on political ideology. The differences involved other cabinet members in heated debates over Federalist views on banking, debt and the location of the capital. Washington allowed Hamilton to chair the meetings in his absence and as a result, the tension between Jefferson and Hamilton increased. Jefferson opposed national debt and wanted each state to finance and pay their own debt, while Hamilton wanted a national credit line through a national bank that would pay each states war debts. Hamilton wanted the new capital to be located in the Northeast while Jefferson wanted it in the South. After a year of in-house fighting, Washington was considering relieving Jefferson of his position as Secretary of State. It was clear that Washington and Hamilton was Federalist where as Jefferson favored states rights. Jefferson and Madison preferred an agrarian culture of farmers and free land holders to establish homesteads for everyone to work the land. But most importantly, Jefferson wanted more State sovereignty and less federal involvement in state issues. He wanted to confined governments role to foreign affairs, foreign policy and defense of the nation. Jefferson and Madison later establish their own coalition called the Republican-Democrat coalition several years later.

Washington was reluctant to run for President a second term, however, Jefferson wrote Washington pleading with him to run for a second term for unity of the nation. He urged Washington to unify America and fight for democracy against the political influence of banks and greedy capitalist. Washington reluctantly accepted the Presidency. I suspect that Jefferson's letter to Washington was out of fear that Hamilton may decide to run for President or at the very least, form a collision of Federalist to control the Presidency and Congress.

In 1783, Jefferson resigned his cabinet post as Secretary of State, after 2 years and returned to Monticello. His resignation was over the Jay Treaty that was approved by the Senate and his differing opinions of

Washington and Hamilton as Federalist. Washington's cabinet was divided between pro Britain and Pro France factions in Washington's Administration. Many of the cabinet members were pro British, including Hamilton. Jefferson was pro France, especially since being the Minister of France and spent years in Paris. His resignation was mostly due to the divide in the Administration and felt he could accomplish more as a Statesman on the sidelines than being in the inner circle and confined by political restraints as a cabinet member. The "Jay Treaty" with Great Britain in 1794, authored by John Jay and Hamilton, only widened the discourse between Hamilton and Jefferson. The Jay Treaty allowed America and Britain to normalize relations and increase trade between the two countries. Jefferson wasted little time criticizing the treaty publicly. However, the Jay Treaty narrowly passed Congress, a "rider" was attached that would expire the treaty in 1805, unless it were extended. The bitter disagreement over the Jay Treaty and Washington and Hamilton would sever his division in their relationship with Washington for the remainder of his life.

Thomas Jefferson was elected Vice President in 1796 during John Adams presidency. Even though John Adams was a Federalist and Jefferson a Republican-Democrat, the two got along well. Jefferson was a long time mentor of Adams ever since the drafting of the Declaration of Independence, however, when Adams enacted the Alien and Sedition Act, their relationship suffered over political issues. Jefferson felt the Alien and Sedition Acts were unconstitutional, which certainly was. He also felt the Act targeted members of the newly formed Republican–Democrat Party that he and Madison formed. Washington voiced his opinion and disdain for the Alien and Sedition Acts as well, and felt the Act would drive the states to dissolve the union.

Jefferson wanted to nullify the law on the basis that it violated the Constitution. His relationship with John Adams and Washington dissolve their relationships in which Jefferson refused to attend

Washington's funeral in 1799 and would not communicate with Adams until his last years of his life.

Thomas Jefferson's Presidency
(1801 -1809)

During the election of 1800, between Thomas Jefferson, a Republican-Democrat and John Adams, a Federalist, became one of the most acrimonious campaigns in American history. Adams brutally attacked Jefferson and Jefferson returned the criticism against Adams. Madison and Jefferson founded the National Gazette in Philadelphia to wage a political media war against the Federalist and in particular Hamilton; however the publisher would take the liberty to criticize Washington as well. Jefferson and Madison did not want to involve Washington into the fray, but the publisher took the liberty upon himself to include Washington. In retaliation, Hamilton used the Federalist newspaper the "Gazette of the United States" to attack Jefferson and the Republican-Democrat Party. However, Hamilton and Adams' efforts were in vain and Jefferson would win the Presidency over John Adams, thus denying him a second term in office. Aaron Burr was on the Republican-Democrat ticket as Vice President, in which Jefferson appointed James Madison his Secretary of State.

When Jefferson took office in March of 1801, the US debt was $83 million and after eight years in office, he reduced the debt by $36 million. To cut cost, rather than build a fleet of naval ships, he ordered a fleet of gunboats as a coastal defense to save cost. He appointed three Supreme Court Justices and repealed the Judiciary Act of 1801, which was one of Adams' acts before leaving office.

The Barbary War

Jefferson was in office less than one year when the first military crisis developed. Prior to the Revolutionary War, British war ships escorted

American merchant ships through the Mediterranean Sea near North Africa and Tripoli. The area was known as the Barbary Coast, where Barbary Pirates raided and seized merchant ships while holding the crew hostage for ransom. After the Revolutionary War, American merchant ships were unescorted through the Mediterranean Sea and became vulnerable to Barbary Pirates. When John Adams became President, he requested Congress to declare war on the Barbary Pirates of which most operated out of Tripoli. It would be the first declared war in the United States.

When the USS Philadelphia was captured, Jefferson sent an envoy to Tripoli to negotiate a peace settlement, but when negotiations failed, US Naval ships bombarded Tripoli forcing them to resumed talks and a peace settlement. The peace agreement didn't last long; it allowed American merchant ships to trade temporarily without interference from the pirates.

One of Jefferson's legacies would be establishing the Military Peace Act of 1802, which established the United States Military Academy at West Point, New York and provided free primary school education for children.

The Louisiana Purchase

Perhaps Jefferson's biggest accomplishment as President was the purchase of the Louisiana Territory in 1803, which doubled the size of the United States. He purchased New Orleans and 40,000 square miles of Mississippi River delta from France for $10 million and 827,000 square miles of French territory for $15 million. With the purchase of the Louisiana Territory, it was the last vestiges of European control in the United States which opened the door for westward expansion into the West and on to the Pacific Ocean.

Jefferson always had his sights on acquiring Florida from the Spanish. In Jefferson's second term in office in 1804, he entered into negotiations with Napoleon for the purchase of Florida from Spain for a price of 2 million dollars. Congress appropriated the money however; the sale of Florida fell through. It was a disappointment to him; however, he began an aggressive campaign on exploration west of the Mississippi River.

While Jefferson was popular during his first term in office, his second term beginning in 1804, saw his popularity waning, especially among his own party loyalist. His relationship with his Vice President, Aaron Burr had deteriorated as a result of Burr requesting Jefferson to appoint his political cronies from New York to key positions in his administration, in which Jefferson refused. It would cause a rift between Jefferson and Burr and the two rarely spoke to each other after that. During Jefferson second run for President, Burr was not nominated by the Republican-Democrat party to be on the ticket for Vice President, which ended Burr's political career. In the same year, Burr challenged Alexander Hamilton to a dual for slander and Hamilton would die from wounds resulting from the dual as previously mentioned. An arrest warrant was issued on Burr, but he fled to Georgia to escape prosecution, however the warrant was vacated and all charges were eventually dropped.

In 1805, Burr moved to Louisiana and met General James Wilkinson who was Jefferson's appointed Governor of the Louisiana Territory. Burr would meet with Andrew Jackson in Tennessee in an effort to recruit military support for the seizer of Texas, Louisiana and Florida in a military style coup. His motive is unclear but it is assumed he wanted to form a separate nation with the possibly of including Britain in some form or another.

Burr contacted the British Minister, Anthony Merry, for whom Jefferson disliked, and purposed a meeting. The proposal was to "take-over" the western territories and returns them to Great Britain in exchange for an undisclosed amount of money and British ships. When Jefferson heard of the plot from Andrew Jackson, he ordered the arrest of Aaron Burr and his co-conspirators for conspiracy and treason. In his trial, he would be acquitted of all charges. The acquittal of Burr infuriated Jefferson and created distrust with Andrew Jackson as well, thinking he was also a co-conspirator as well.

In 1807, Congress passed an Act Prohibiting the Importation of Slaves. Europe was engaged in war with Napoleon and relations with Britain were strained, Congress passed the Embargo Act of 1807 that backfired on America businesses, as other European nations would retaliate with their own embargo against America. This act caused an economic down-turn in the American economy, that most blame Jefferson and his administration.

Prelude to the War of 1812

Relations between Great Britain and America were stained throughout much of Jefferson's Presidency. During the later part of his second term in office, Britain was engaged in the Napoleonic wars in Europe. British war ships began raiding and seizing American merchant ships and kidnapping seamen for impressed service into the British Navy. America could do little to stop them, since the American Navy was reduced to mostly gunboats equipped with only two 20 pound cannons. In 1806, Jefferson asked Congress to pass the Non-Importation Acts against Britain, but it was not fully enforced as intended. The Monroe-Pinkney Treaty between Britain and America was signed between Britain and America, but the terms of the agreement did not address the impressments of American seamen, ships and cargo that were seized while supplying France during a British embargo.

The British ship HMS Leopard fired upon the USS Chesapeake off the coast of Virginia in June of 1807. Jefferson immediately armed the American militia for war. America wanted to avoid war with Britain, for which America was ill prepared for war; Congress passed the Embargo Act against England, while Napoleon extended the Berlin

Decree, banning British Imports into Europe.

The embargo was nearly impossible to enforce, since America did not have an adequate navy to enforce it. Smugglers were taking advantage of the embargo and making large profits as a result. As much as Jefferson tried to curtail the smuggling, the embargo against Britain became a dismal failure. Jefferson felt that the embargo failed as a result of greedy merchants wanting to "cash in" rather than honoring the spirit of the law. Shortly after the failure of the embargo in 1807, Jefferson announced he would not seek a third term. He would repeal the embargo in 1809, before leaving office.

Jefferson Retires to Monticello

After his Presidency in 1809, he retired to Monticello where he became active in establishing the University of Virginia. He sold part of his library collection to the Library of Congress and donates the remainder to the University of Virginia. He wrote an Autobiography of his life that covered his life during the Revolutionary War and the Continental Congress, but remained aloof about his personal and private life.

After his Presidency, in 1812, John Adams sent a New Years greeting to Jefferson in which Jefferson returned a warm letter of thank you. It would begin a fourteen year correspondence between two of the greatest men in American history. Even though they had political differences, they were now wise enough to talk about their political differences without offending each other. Over a fourteen year period, 158 letters were exchanged between them. In 1825, Jefferson's health began to deteriorate. By June of 1826, he remained bedridden. He would die on July 4, 1826 at 12:50 P.M. After his death, a gold chain was found around his neck with a lock of hair wrapped in a blue ribbon, which was Martha's brown hair.

As John Adams lay in bed waiting death, on July 4, 1826, he muttered his last few words, "Jefferson Survives" however; little did Adams realize that Thomas Jefferson died two hours before him. Both would die on Independence Day of 1826, two hours apart. Even though they were bitter enemies in the beginning, they became kindred spirits in the end. It was considered somewhat unusual for Jefferson to rekindle a relationship with Adams, since Jefferson was well known to hold deep resentment and animosity with those he had a falling-out with but remained close friends with James Madison and James Monroe.

The Lewis and Clark Expedition
(1804 – 1806)

Once the purchase of the Louisiana Territory was finalized between France and America in 1803, Jefferson focused his energy toward exploring a route to the Pacific Ocean. His goal was to find the most direct route, by water if necessary, from New England to the Pacific Ocean. Most believed there was a waterway connecting the Atlantic to the Pacific Ocean through North America, which could be used as a shipping and transportation corridor through the continent rather than by sea around Cape Horn on the southern tip of South America. Based on Captain Cook's diaries and his published book, "A Voyage to the Pacific Ocean" (London 1784), and Le Page du Pratz explorations (1763) of the Louisiana Territory, Jefferson wanted to claim all territory between the Louisiana Territory to the Pacific Ocean.

British explorer, Alexander Mackenzie had already explored and charted a route from Mexico to the Pacific Ocean and north through Canada to the Arctic Ocean in 1789. Mackenzie published his diary of exploration in a book titled, "Voyages from Montreal" in 1801. Jefferson was an avaricious reader acquired both books and decided that an overland exploration route was needed for the purpose of mapping and documenting the geologic, flora and fauna and the Native American tribes of the western frontier.

Jefferson commissioned U.S Army Captain Meriwether Lewis to lead the exploration and lieutenant William Clark as his second in command in 1803. The expedition lasted between May of 1804 to 1806. Jefferson commissioned three more expeditions during the same time; William Dunbar and George Hunter's expedition of the Ouachita River in 1804, Thomas Freeman and Peter Custis' expedition of the Red River in 1806 and Zebulon Pike expedition of the Rocky Mountains in 1806. The Lewis and Clark Expedition was his most ambitious expedition. When Lewis and Clark arrived at the mouth of the Columbia River and established Fort Clatsop on the shores of the Pacific Ocean and the mouth of the Great Columbia River, they claimed the Oregon Territory on behalf of the United States, however, Britain also claimed the territory as well, since Alexander Mackenzie had already passed though the region twelve years before. The Lewis and Clark expedition spent the winter of 1805 at Fort Clatsop before returning to St. Louis. Upon their return while traveling to Washington to give their report to Jefferson, news had already appeared in the newspapers of their expedition and they would receive a hero's welcome in every city they passed through.

Meriwether Lewis
(1774 – 1809)

Lewis was born in Albemarle County, Virginia in 1774. He was of Welsh ancestry. His father would die of pneumonia in 1779 and his mother and siblings moved to Georgia to work a plantation. Lewis did not have a formal education but devoted his early life in Georgia hunting and trapping. He became interested in natural history and the outdoors at an early age. At the age of thirteen, his mother sent him to Virginia to acquire a more formal education. He was tutored by his late father's older brother, Nicholas Lewis and would later graduate from Liberty Hall, now called Washington and Lee University. He joined the Virginia militia in 1794 and joined Washington's campaign during the Whiskey Rebellion in Pennsylvania. Lewis joined the U.S. Army as an Ensign and six years later promoted to Captain. One of his commanding officers was William Clark. He resigned his commission in 1801 and became an aide to President Jefferson. Jefferson was preparing a series of expeditions and offered Lewis to command an expedition west to the Pacific Ocean and the Oregon Territory. Lewis appointed his former commanding officer, William Clark as his joint commander of the expedition.

William Clark
(1770 – 1838)

William Clark was born in 1770 in Caroline County, Virginia. He was the ninth child of ten of John and Ann Rogers Clark. They were of English and Scottish ancestry. His family owned several small estates and had several slaves. Clark did not have a formal education and as customary at the time, was tutored at home. His English grammar was poor and often misspelled words and throughout his life, he always had others edit his journals prior to publishing them.

Clark joined the volunteer militia in Kentucky and later the Indiana militia in 1789. He was commissioned as an ensign in 1791 and a Lieutenant in 1792. He was active in the Battle of Fallen Timbers and the Northwest Indian Wars of 1794. In 1803, at the age of 33, Lewis recruited him in the newly formed military "Corps of Discovery" as a joint commander of the expedition to the Oregon Territory in 1804.

During the Lewis and Clark Expedition, Clark brought his trusted slaves "York". Jefferson would give Clark equal rank as Lewis during the expedition; even though he insisted that he didn't want more pay and was doing it out of honor. The purpose of the expedition was to map, manage supplies, record flora and fauna and hunt for food.

Jefferson kept the expedition secret from until his timing was right to present his proposal and budget to Congress. He requested Lewis to prepare an estimate of expenses for the expedition that included one officer and 10 enlisted men. The arms were secured at the Harpers Ferry Armory and a flat bottom boat was to be built in at St, Charles,

Missouri. The largest expense was $696 for gifts to the local Indians. The total cost of the expedition was $2,500. Jefferson did not want to have a large expedition party for several reasons; he was fearful that the native tribes might think that the U.S. Military was preparing to invade Indian Territory and secondly, he needed to keep the cost low in order to get funding from Congress.

Prior to the departure, Jefferson gave his final instruction to Lewis and Clark:

"The object of your mission is to explore the Missouri River, and such principle steam of it, as, by its course and communication with the waters of the Pacific Ocean, whether the Columbia, Oregon, Colorado or any other river may offer the most direct and practicable water communication across this continent for the purpose of commerce". **[86]**

It is worth noting; the Lewis and Clark Expedition never or seldom appeared in history books until after 1905, when Portland, Oregon held a Lewis and Clark Centennial Exposition. Even then, it wasn't until the mid 20th century when the Lewis and Clark Journals became public and historians were able to study and evaluate and write historical references to them.

Sacagawea
(1788 – 1812)

Sacagawea was born in 1788 in the Agaidika/Lemhi Shoshone Tribe, near present day Salmon, Idaho. When she was 12, she was kidnapped during a battle with the Hidatsa Sioux Tribe and taken to the Hidatsa/Sioux village in North Dakota. At the age of 13, she was sold to a Quebec fur trapper, Toussaint Charbonneau. Charbonneau was also married to "Otter Women" as well, but she didn't accompany Charbonneau and Sacagawea on the Lewis and Clark Expedition. Lewis and Clark built Fort Mandan on the bank of the Missouri River near Washburn, North Dakota. The Lewis and Clark Expedition

spent the winter of 1804-1805 at Fort Mandan where Charbonneau and Sacagawea offered to join the expedition west as guides and Shoshone interpreters. Sacagawea was 16 and pregnant with her first child and gave birth to a boy she would name Jean Baptieste. In April of 1805, the expedition began their trip up the Missouri River in piroques, which was a double ended small boat about 18 feet long.
The expedition poled the boats up river and portaged over waterfalls and rapids. When they arrived near present day Great Falls, Montana, they were met by Shoshone Indians and began to negotiate a trade for horses to cross the Rocky Mountains. The Chief of the Shoshone was Cameahwait, which as it turned- out to be Sacagawea's brother. They successfully negotiated a trade for horses and offered safe passage to the head waters of the Columbia River. As starvation threatened the party, they were forced to eat tallow candles for food. Sacagawea was able to find camas roots for the expedition to eat which saved them from starvation and possible scurvy. When they arrived at the mouth of the Columbia River and built Fort Clatsop, Sacagawea offered Lewis and Clark her blue beaded belt to use as an object for trading for a fur robe made of otter and seal to give to President Thomas Jefferson. [87]

On their return trip in 1806, William Clark offered to take the boy to St. Louis and educate him at the Saint Louis Academy boarding school. Charbonneau and Sacagawea remained in North Dakota but decided to allow Clark guardianship of Jean Baptieste. Three years later, Charbonneau and Sacagawea moved to St. Louis. They would have a baby girl named Lizette in 1811. Sacagawea would die in 1812 of typhus in St. Louis. William Clark file court documents of adoption of both children, however, it is believed that Lizette may have died shortly after, since no records were found.

In 1807, Meriwether Lewis was appointed the 2nd Governor of the Louisiana Territory. He hired a free African-American as his valet named John Pernia. In 1809, Lewis and Pernia traveled to Washington D.C. to meet with the President. His plans were to take a boat to New Orleans and a ship to Washington D.C., however, at the last minute; he elected to travel overland on the Natchez Trace road between Natchez, Mississippi and Nashville, Tennessee. The route was notoriously known for highway robbers and bandits. They stopped for the night at the Grinder's Stand Inn on October 18, 1809. That evening, the innkeeper's wife heard two gunshots coming from Lewis' room and found Lewis shot two times, once in the head and once in the stomach. He would die the following morning. His money pouch was missing and it is believed he may have been robbed or possibly committed suicide. Lewis owned his valet $240 in back pay as well. His valet traveled to Washington D.C. and asks Jefferson for his $240 in back pay, but he refused. John Pernia, his valet, committed suicide shortly after.

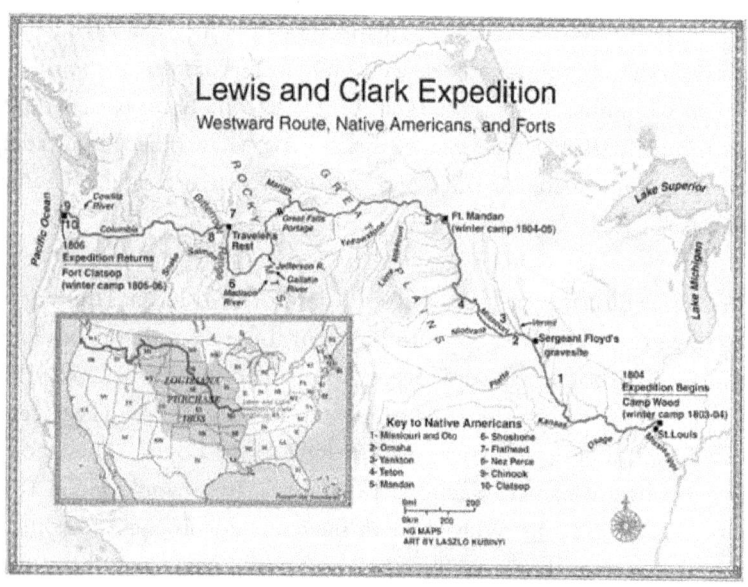

President James Madison appointed William Clark the 4th Governor of the Missouri Territory. He would marry Julia Hancock in 1808 and have five children. He named his first son Meriwether Lewis Clark. Julia would die in 1820 and he married Harriet Kennerly Radford, they would have three children together. William Clark died on September

1, 1838 at the age of 68. In 2001, President Bill Clinton promoted William Clark to the rank of full Captain in the U.S. Army, posthumously.

His adopted son, Jean Baptiste Charbonneau lived a long life of 68. In 1971 at Malheur County, Oregon, The Daughters of the American Revolution placed a marker at the ranch where he died. In 1973 the Oregon Historical Society installed a permanent marker, reading:
Jean Baptiste Charbonneau
(1805 – 1866)

"This site marks the final resting place of the youngest member of the Lewis and Clark Expedition. Born to Sacagawea and Toussaint Charbonneau at Fort Mandan (North Dakota), on February 11, 1805, Baptiste and his mother symbolized the peaceful nature of the "Corps of Discovery." Educated by Captain William Clark at St. Louis, Baptiste at 18 traveled to Europe where he spent six years becoming fluent in English, German, French and Spanish. Returning to American in 1829, he ranged the far west for nearly four decades as mountain man, guide, interpreter, magistrate, and forty-niner. In 1866, he left the California gold fields for a new strike in Montana, contracted pneumonia en route, reached "Inskips Ranche" here, and died on May 16, 1866."

John Marshall
(1755 – 1835)

John Marshall was born in 1755 in a log cabin in Germantown, Virginia. His parents, Thomas Marshall and Mary Isham Keith were the granddaughter of Thomas Randolph a well known politician from Tuchahoe, Virginia. John was the oldest of fifteen siblings, eight sisters and six brothers. His youngest brother served as a Judge on the Circuit Court of the District of Columbia from 1801 to 1803. Three other brothers became lawyers.

During the Revolutionary War he served as a Lieutenant in the Culpeper Minutemen between 1775 and 1776 and went on to serve as a Captain in the Eleventh Virginia Continental Regiment from 1776 to 1780. He would serve with Washington at Valley Forge during the winter of 1777 and 1778.

After the Revolutionary War, he became an understudy of Chancellor George Wythe of the College of William and Mary. He was admitted to the Virginia bar in 1780. In 1782 he was elected into the Virginia House of Delegates, in which he served until 1796. He would serve as one of the Virginia delegates to vote on the ratification of the Constitution in 1788 as well. It was during this period in his life that he became a staunch Federalist and opposed Jefferson's Republican-Democrat political ideology. Marshall opened his law practice during this time. He appeared before the United States Supreme Court in 1796 in the case of Ware v. Hylton. The case involved the legal right of Virginia law to supersede in the confiscation of debts owed to British subjects. Marshall argued on behalf of the State of Virginia, whom he felt had the right to make laws blocking confiscation of property to satisfy debts owed another country. The U.S. Supreme Court, John Jay as Supreme Court Justice, ruled against him, claiming that the Treaty of Paris and the Supremacy Clause of the Constitution allowed the collection of such debts.

George Washington offered Marshall the position of Attorney General of the United States, but he declined. He also declined an appointment to serve as Minister to France. In 1798, President Adams appointed Marshall as an Associate Supreme Court Justice but he declined, but accepted the position as Secretary of State under Adam's Administration.

Chief Justice of the Supreme Court

John Adams lost his second term as President to Thomas Jefferson in November of 1800. Jefferson was to be inaugurated on March 4,

1801. Adams, a Federalist and Jefferson a Republican-Democrat, engaged in a personal feud over judicial appointments. The third Chief Justice of the U.S. Supreme Court was Oliver Ellsworth, who was suffering from poor health. Adams convinced Ellsworth to retire so he could appoint John Marshall as Chief Justice before Jefferson took office in March. Marshall officially became Chief Justice on February 4th while still serving as Secretary of State under Adams, until March 4, 1801. John Adams was criticized for his "Midnight" judicial appointments partly due by Congresses passing the Judicial Act of 1801, which created 16 new judgeships on the circuit court and reduced the Supreme Court Judges from six to five. Ten District Court Judgeships were also added under the Act. John Adams signed the Act into law on February 13, 1801, 22 days prior to Jefferson becoming president. The Act reorganized the circuit courts prior to the passage of the Act. Supreme Court Justices were serving on the circuit court benches when the Supreme Court was not in session. The circuit court heard cases involving criminal and possible constitutional cases. Congress felt there may not be a clear separation between decisions being heard in the Circuit Court and those in the Supreme Court, since Supreme Court Judges served on both courts. While Adams still President, he made about 30 judicial appoints within 19 day of leaving office. Jefferson was outraged and called it a political ploy by the Federalist to stack the judicial benches with judges of similar political ideology. Jefferson being a Republican-Democrat repealed the Judicial Act of 1801 in his first year in office, in which the Supreme Court Judges would resume "riding" the circuit courts and hearing cases on the Supreme Court until 1879.

John Marshall became the fourth United States Supreme Court Justice. He served during six Presidential administrations; Adams, Jefferson, Madison, Monroe, John Quincy Adams and Jackson. He participated in 1000 decisions and wrote 519 opinions himself.

Marshall changed how the Supreme Court issue decisions. Prior to his tenure, each Associate Justice issued a separate opinion called a seriatim opinion, however under Marshall's Court, a single opinion was handed down. Today a single dissenting opinion is issued as well. Marshall most always wrote the opinion, or at least 519 of them. He was only in the dissenting minority eight times during his tenure as Chief Justice in 34 years. The Supreme Court would adjourn two months a year in Washington D.C. The Justices boarded together while in Washington and avoided outside socializing. The Justices didn't have clerks, cases brought before the court was presented to the Justices as oral arguments. Marshall didn't accept written briefs.

When Marshall was appointed Chief Justice, he had limited legal background; in fact he was Secretary of State under Adams when appointed as Chief Justice. Most of his experience was political, even though he was a practicing lawyer; his strength was his oral arguments and his ability to convince. He listens intently of each oral argument presented before the court. Associate Justice Joseph Story was a legal scholar and new case law better than any of the justices. After hearing the oral arguments, in chambers he would tell Justice Story his opinion of the case and instruct him to find the authorities to support his opinion.

Marbury v. Madison (1803)
(The Doctrine of Judicial Review)

The Marbury v. Madison case was significant in that it was the first Supreme Court Case in which an Act passed by Congress was invalidated on the grounds that it violated the Constitution which established the doctrine of judicial review. Jefferson disagreed with the decision, claiming that the Supreme Court did not have jurisdiction to give the President or the U.S. Congress an order. Marshall and the Supreme Court maintain that the court has the right of judicial review, even if it does not specifically states so in the Constitution. The Constitution is the Supreme law of the land, and as such, the Supreme Court has the authority to judge whether the actions of the President or Congress violates the law of the land and upholds the Constitution.

Marshall presented the following opinion during Marbury v. Madison: *"…..Certainly all those who have framed written constitutions contemplate them as forming the fundamental and paramount law of the nation, and consequently the theory of every such government must be, that an act of the legislature repugnant to the Constitution is void."* Chief Justice Marshall [68]

Over the 34 years serving on the bench, there have been many important cases decided that influenced how people view the Supreme Court as the protector of the principals the doctrine of judicial review of the Constitution. John Marshall made the Supreme Court an equal entity along with the Legislative and Executive Branches of Government. Prior to his tenure it closely resembled a political arm of government. Marshall gave the Supreme Court dignity and a clear focus on direction. [69]

John Marshall died in June of 1835 at the age of 79 in Philadelphia. He was buried next to his wife in Richmond, Virginia.

Tecumseh, Shawnee Chief
(1768 – 1813)

Tecumseh was a Shawnee Native American born in 1768 near the tributary of the Scioto River in the Indiana Territory, known today as Ohio. Tecumseh's parents lived in Alabama among the Pekowi Tribe and migrated northwest into Ohio. His father was killed by during the Battle of Point Pleasant in 1774 and Tecumseh would be raised by his eldest brother, Chiksika.

During the Revolutionary War, the Shawnee were allies with the British. Tecumseh and his family were forced to move many times after their villages were destroyed and burned by the Kentucky Militia fighting the British. After the Revolutionary War, Tecumseh joined a raiding party attacking flat-boats drifting down the Ohio River from Pennsylvania transporting settlers west. In 1791, Tecumseh would join his brother, Chiksika in Tennessee in a raiding party in which Chiksika was killed.

He took part in the Battle of Fallen Timbers in 1794. They would be defeated and forced to sign the Treaty of Greenville in 1795. As part of the treaty, the Shawnee give up most of the land in Ohio in exchange of $20,000 in goods and materials.

Tecumseh's younger brother, Tenskwatawa was known as the "Shawnee prophet". In 1805, Tenskwatawa began prophesying that European-American settlers would be destroyed by and apocalyptic event. His prophesies attracted a large Native American following, in which Indian Tribes traveled hundreds of miles to hear his prophecies. He urged the Indian Tribes to reject American way of life, customs, firearms, alcohol, and clothing and not cede anymore Native land to the U.S. Government.

In 1808, Tecumseh and Tenskwataswa (Prophet) decided to move west into what is now Indiana along the Tippecanoe and Wabash Rivers. This region was home to the Miami Indians. They established a village named "Prophets town". The population would expand to 3,000 Native Indian inhabitants that included 14 different tribes groups. Local American settlers became concerned that the leader of Prophets Town, Tecumseh may be planning an attack to take back the land that was part of the Greenville Treaty that Tecumseh refused to sign. In 1810, Tecumseh traveled throughout the mid west recruiting warriors for training in Prophets Town. The British provided materials, food and guns and ammo to Tecumseh as a gesture of good faith. The British had build forts along the Great Lakes in Canada expecting an invasion from America. They wanted Tecumseh to wage war on the American side of the border and take the pressure off a possible American invasion into Canada.

The Battle of Tippecanoe

When General William Henry Harrison heard that Tecumseh received war materials from the British, he marched 1,200 troops toward Prophets Town with the hope of confronting Tecumseh about his intentions, however Tecumseh was not in Prophets Town when Harrison arrived, and Harrison decided to camp across the Wabash River. Tenskwataswa ordered a surprise attack on Harrison's encampment the following morning of November 6, 1811. Harrison in retaliation attacked Prophets Town. Tenskwataswa was in command of the warriors, who had little or no knowledge of war tactics. Prophets Town was soon captured by Harrison and burned to the ground.

Tenskwataswa lost his honor among his people and migrated to Canada. Tecumseh lost his support of the other tribes and was unable to build an alliance among the other Native Americans nations. His vision of reclaiming Native Indian Lands from the government was never realized.

The Siege of Detroit

Tecumseh lost most of his support from other tribes as a result of the defeat at Prophets Town, but he would join forces with the British during the War of 1812. He marched 400 warriors north to rendezvous with Major General Isaac Brock of the British Army, near the American Fort of Detroit. Since he only had 400 warriors, he devised a plan where he used the same 400 warriors to skirt around the fort multiple times to give the impression that Tecumseh had 10 times as many warriors as he had. The British forces remained out of reach of the canon fire that lined Fort Detroit. Brigadier General William Hull, Commander of Fort Detroit, elected to surrender; thinking that they were out-numbered would be massacred. When General Hull learned of the ploy, he felt humiliated. General Brock appointed Tecumseh a brigadier general.

The following year, Detroit was once again under siege but not by Tecumseh or the British, but by Commodore Perry in 1813, who sailed his armada of war ships to Detroit. The British were forced to abandon Detroit and burned much of the city while fleeing north into Canada.

Siege of Fort Meigs

Fort Meigs lay in the northwest corner of Ohio. The British was certain that American forces would attempt to attack Fort Detroit and create a diversion by using an offensive attack against Fort Meigs, which would divert American military forces away from Fort Detroit. Tecumeseh had 1,250 warriors, while the British had 1,000 men for the siege of Fort Meigs. The American forces numbered 1,000 but the British and Tecumseh were unable to capture Fort Meigs after numerous assaults.

The battle remained a stalemate. Both sides agreed o exchange prisoners; however British Major General Proctor gave order to kill the American prisoners. When Tecumseh heard of the massacre, in which 14 were massacred, he rebuked General Proctor publicly as a man with little honor and unfit to lead men into battle. His relationship with General Proctor during the remainder of the war was strained. As a result of the confrontation, public perception of Tecumseh changed drastically and Tecumseh would be revered as an honorable and unselfish leader.

Tecumseh and General Proctor's relationship began to work against each other's goal. For Tecumseh; the British promised Native American's their own land along the Canadian-American border as a separate Indian nation for which they could travel freely across borders. The British wanted to maintain their forts along the Ohio Valley and allow an open trade route down the Mississippi River. However, Americans wanted British forts removed completely from the Ohio River Valley and in Florida and the Louisiana Territories. Americans didn't want to allocate land to the Native Americans; in fact wanted the complete removal of all Native Americans east of the Mississippi and placed on reservations.

There is little doubt that greed played an important part in the War of 1812 on both sides. For the Shawnee and other Native American Tribes, they wanted to maintain their ancestral lands or at least restore some of the land they once occupied. They were pushed further west as Anglo-Americans began their manifest destiny west and homesteaded frontiers.

During the Battle of the Thames, General Proctor and Tecumseh would make a last stand in northern Canada against General William Henry Harrison's army. On October 5, 1813, the Battle of the Thames began and ended with the death of Tecumseh and the defeat of General Proctor's army.

Tecumseh's Legacy

The War of 1812 ended with the signing of the Treaty of Ghent in 1814. The British insisted that America return the land to the Shawnee. The U.S. Government paid the Native American's $20,000 in goods in exchange for their lands covering Ohio, Indiana and Michigan. The U.S. Government refused to provide an independent nation for Native Americans. Tecumseh and the Shawnee would never realize their vision of a separate nation. Later in history, the Indian Reservation Act was signed into law. President Grant would sign more than 60 treaties with the Native Americans; unfortunately most would not be honored by later administrations.

James Madison
(1751 – 1836)

We are free today substantially, but the day will come when our Republic will be impossibility. It will be impossibility because wealth will be concentrated in the hands of a few. A Republic cannot stand upon bayonets, and when the day comes when the wealth of the nation will be in the hands of a few, then we must rely upon the wisdom of the best elements in the country to readjust the laws of the nations to the changed conditions.

Modern historians are taking a second look at James Madison and his presidency by delving deeper into his diaries and memoirs. Madison was the Father of the Constitution although he did not write the Constitution or the Articles of Confederation per se, but is best known as the architect and the most acknowledgeable on issues of the Constitution and considered a Constitutional scholar. George Washington as President often conferred with Madison when he created his cabinet and assigned duties and responsibilities to the members to ensure he was in compliance with the Constitution. Other Presidents considered Madison a Constitutional scholar, in which John Jay became his mentor and later first Chief Justice of the Supreme Court during Washington's tenure as President.

James Madison Jr. was born in 1751 in Belle Grove Plantation, Virginia. He was the eldest of twelve children for which three of his siblings would die of dysentery during the epidemic of 1775. James Madison Sr. owned a tobacco plantation with 5,000 acres of land and 108 slaves. He inherits Montpelier upon his father's death in 1801 and became one of the largest plantation owners in Virginia at the time.

Madison was only 5 foot 4 inches tall and weighed 100 pounds. He was considered good looking, shy, and soft spoken and non confrontational person. He was born with a form of epilepsy, in which he would occasionally pass-out. He addressed the Constitution Convention more than 200 times; however, most of his speeches were nearly inaudible in the back rows. He was raised as a Virginian gentleman and displayed little emotion or anger when communicating or giving public speeches. Madison was self conscious of his short stature and rarely engaged in small talk with delegates and members of Congress. People's first impression of Madison was that he had a certain air of superiority and confidence, since he picked his words carefully and deliberately before speaking. Many felt he hung on every word they spoke. Thomas Jefferson would become Madison's closest friend and political ally and a lifelong friendship would develop.

In 1769, he enrolled into Princeton University, New Jersey and graduated from College in 1771, but never practiced law after college. He devoted himself into politics and toward a political career.

He became active in Virginia politics shortly after graduation; he advocated freedom of religion during the Virginia Convention that drafted the Virginia Declaration of Rights, which failed to get enough support for passage during the convention. His views toward freedom of religion would alienate him from many Virginian delegates at the Convention. Virginia implemented a state sponsored religion and churches that were paid by the Virginia Colonial government. In fact, he was not invited back the following year as a result of advocacy toward the separation of Church and State. His debates and speeches on freedom of religion would be noticed by Thomas Jefferson who later would use Madison's arguments and wording in the Declaration of Independence. Jefferson and Madison would cross paths in later years when Jefferson appointed him Secretary of State during Jefferson's presidency in 1801. Madison was raised and tutored by Presbyterian clergymen and later became interested in a variety of different religious theologies. He later accepted deism in his later life, as did many of the founding fathers had. He would hold several key positions in Virginian politics from 1777 to 1786.

The Father of the Constitution

The Articles of Confederation was intended to be an interim Constitution that lacked the power to tax or raise money for the war and the debt that accrued during the American Revolution. In addition, the Articles placed emphasis on State Sovereignty and the issue of raising a militia by each Province or State to fight the revolution.

Financing the war and establishing laws relied mostly on state constitutions and their delegates who represented each State in the Continental Congress. The national government, known as the Continental Congress, had little power to regulate or coordinate a revolution without the unanimous consensus of each state. Some states contributed to the cost of the war while other did not. The basic premise of the Articles was to insure States Rights and share the burden of war through taxes levied by each state, however some states refused to contribute or was unable to meet there financial commitment under the Articles of Confederation. The Continental Congress had no legal authority to enforce the terms of the Articles upon a state. To further complicate the issue, the Articles could only be amended by a unanimous vote of all states, rather than a simple or super majority.

During the war, the continental congress met at various locations; Philadelphia, Princeton, Trenton, New Jersey, New York City and Annapolis, Maryland. The Annapolis Convention was held in November of 1783. It would be the 5th Confederation of Congress whose purpose was to finalize the Articles of Confederation into a final drafted designed to be the U.S. Constitution, however, fate would intervene. Madison realized during the revolutionary war that it would be impossible to have a sovereign state system where each state operated completely independent to a central government. He pressured the delegates to void the Articles of Confederation entirely and redraft a new set of Articles. This process involved additional conventions to be held in Philadelphia to finalize what would be one single U.S. Constitution, rather than 13 separate Constitutions.

Madison wanted one more chance to convince delegates to void the original Articles of Confederation and write a new set of articles specifically suited for the US Constitution. The purpose of rewriting the new Articles was to diminish the States authority in passing laws that supersedes Federal laws. Madison wanted the Federal government to have more authority to tax and make laws that would supersede State and local laws. State laws would supersede county, municipal and local laws as well. It would be a tiered legal system starting at the village or town level and end at the Federal level. Each state would have a Constitution in which all state and local laws must abide but could not violate the laws outlined in the U.S. Constitution. The U.S. Constitution would be the law of the land, in which all states and people must abide. While the system seemed practical, many southern states strongly objected, claiming they wanted states rights without government involvement of any sort.

Madison noticed a serious flaw in the Articles of Confederation when he was appointed to a committee during the Continental Congress to oversee the financing of the Revolutionary War. He realized that the present Articles of Confederation was flawed and allowed states to enacted laws that were counter to those passed by the Confederation. In addition, troops suffered unnecessarily by not being provided food, ammunition and clothing to fight battles as some states refused to tax its citizens or provide financial assistance to the Continental Congress as agreed upon in the Articles. The Continental Congress was a quasi central government, with no means to enforce its authority. Madison surmised that if the States were unable to cooperate during a Revolutionary War, how could it function during peace time?

Madison needed support to convince the delegates during the Annapolis Convention that the Articles of Confederation gave too much sovereignty to the States with virtually no authority to the Central Government. With the help of Thomas Jefferson, George Washington, Randolph and Franklin; Madison was able to persuade members to hold six more meetings to formulate a new set of Articles that would become the US Constitution.

DOUGLAS G. BEAUDOIN

In 1787, a convention was held in Philadelphia, in which Madison invited George Washington to attend. Washington's attendance would lend credence to his Virginia Plan for a new Constitution and government, thus abandoning the Articles of Confederation altogether.

Benjamin Franklin, James Madison and Washington and several delegates went upstairs to a room in what is known today as Independence Hall and held a secret meeting to decide an outline of a draft of the new articles for the Constitution. It was mutually agreed that a new set of articles be drafted specifically for the new Constitution and abandoning the old articles of confederation in its entirety. Each article was debated on the floor by all of the delegates and a vote would be taken.

There were five or six plans proposed, but only two were considered viable. One of which was Madison's Virginia plan that was introduced by Edmund Randolph of Virginia and accepted by the delegates. (Chapter 6, Constitutional Convention).

Madison's argument was a shared sovereignty plan between State and the central government. He felt strongly that the federal government should have veto power over state laws. At the age of 36, he was able to design a system acceptable to the majority of delegates. Even though he was not part of the drafting of the Constitution, it was his outline of the Virginia Plan that established our bicameral legislature. However, it must be noted that Edmund Randolph was the creator of the Virginia Plan and Madison was the conduit for its implementation and debate.

Madison opposed the Bill of Rights in the Constitution originally, partly because he felt the Constitution was in fact a bill of rights in itself; however he was insistent on having the judicial provision of citizens having a trial by jury incorporated into the Constitution, but failed to get enough support from the delegates for its inclusion into

Constitution. Madison was never a person to give-up on a principal and the trial by jury provision would later be included in the Bill of Rights which he favored. Thomas Jefferson was eight years his senior and was impressed with Madison's intellect and common sense and dedication. The two would have a lifelong friendship as a result.

James Madison's Presidency
(1809 – 1817)

In 1808, Charles Pinckney, a Federalist, ran against James Madison for the presidency. Madison, like Jefferson was a Republican-Democrat and easily defeated Pinckney in the elections to become the 4th President of the United States. Jefferson had completed his second term as President and retired to Monticello. Madison kept most of Jefferson's cabinet which became the most experienced Presidential cabinet in American history. He recruited members for his cabinet from both the Federalist and the Republican-Democrat Parties, making his administration a bi-partisan consortium of great leaders.

His first order of business as President was not to re-new Hamilton's First National Bank of the United States charter. The Charter was due to expire in 1811. Congress passed a Bill in 1814 to establish the Second National Bank of the United States for the purpose of financing the War of 1812; however, Madison would veto the Bill. In 1816, Congress once again introduced an Act to establish a Second National Bank of the United States under the encouragement of his Treasury Secretary, Albert Gallatin. Madison would sign the Act into law authorizing the Second National Bank for the purpose of funding the war.

Madison's War of 1812

The War of 1812 began during James Madison's presidency. Among the issues were the unjust treatment and perceived influence by Great Britain in North America affairs and the impressments of American merchant sailors and ships into the Royal British Navy. In addition, trade embargos that were imposed on America was viewed as unfair, since America declared itself a neutral nation, even though Britain's seizure of American merchant ships during the Napoleonic war (1793 violated its neutrality. More than 10 thousand American merchant sailors were impressed into the British Royal Navy along with their ships and cargo. In addition, Britain partnered with the Native American's to rebel against America's expansionism west. Britain on the other hand viewed America expansionist plans included the invasion of Canada while Britain was involved in the war in Europe against Napoleon. Great Britain was surprised when President James Madison declared war on Great Britain in 1812. Much of Monroe's consternation over Great Britain was over the Jay Treaty during Washington's Presidency that only provided America favored nation status in trading, but did not resolved the fore mentioned grievances such as impressments and the return of five merchant ships with cargo.

James Madison's decision was mostly influenced by the "war hawk" movement that was gaining popularity in Congress and led by the Speaker of the House, John C. Calhoun of South Carolina and Henry Clay of Kentucky. In June of 1812, Congress declared war on Britain.

U.S. military forces immediately invaded Canada as Britain had expected. Madison strongly believed the war would only last two months as a result of the invasion of Canada by American forces, which was soon recognized as a military miscalculation. By mid August, the US military suffered a resounding defeat by the British and Native American forces in Canada, thus pushing American forces into Detroit Michigan and beyond. The British now controlled most of the Great Lakes region. Eventually the army of William Henry Harrison would re-take Detroit and much of Michigan, but he was unable to advance beyond the border into Canada. In the interim, the British defeated Napoleon in April of 1814 and was able to commit more British troops to the war. British Naval ships landed in Chesapeake

Bay and advanced to Washington District of Columbia (D.C) and burned the U.S. Capital and the White House. In Baltimore, the British Royal Navy bombarded Fort McHenry for twenty-five hours, prompting the American's to hoist a very large American Flag over the fort, which inspired Francis Scott Key to write the poem; "Star Spangled Banner" in which the poem was set to an old English drinking song and later became America's National Anthem which may have been somewhat fitting at the time.

American forces under the command of Andrew Jackson attacked New Orleans and defeated the British in the Battle of New Orleans, even though an armistice was already signed between America and Britain months before. The war of 1812 was a disaster for America, since it didn't achieve its pre-war objectives. On December 24, 1814, the Treaty of Ghent was signed and ratified in January of 1815. Both sides maintained the boundaries prior to the war. It is estimated that there were 6,700 American casualties and 4,700 British casualties during the war, excluding disease and other causes. Madison was the only US President to lead an army into battle while President. The Battle of Bladensburg in 1814, when British troops advanced toward Washington, even though the battle went badly, Madison's wife, Dolly, rescued documents and valuables from the White House before the British arrived and burned the capital. One of the cherished items was purported to be a painted portrait of George Washington which currently hangs proudly on the wall in the White House today. Dolly Madison's act of bravery would not go unnoticed by the press and she would become one of the most loved respected first ladies in America.

The Era of Good Feeling

After the War of 1812, in 1815 the Federalist Party began losing their political influence. The Republican-Democrat Party occupied the White House and President Madison began implementing policies pushed by Henry Clay, John Calhoun and their "American System". Most of Madison's Presidency was consumed by the war with Britain that began with a financial surplus of nearly $10 million in 1809, but ended in 1814, that nearly bankrupt America. The US Treasury defaulted on two of its treasury notes in 1814. America had no hard currency (specie) in its vaults and was essentially bankrupt. Soldier's pay was six to twelve months in the arrears, which forced the closure of the Springfield Armory. When word circulated that the military had no money to pay its soldiers, military recruiting ceased. However, as bleak as America's financially picture was, the general public was not aware of the dire consequences that lay ahead. They remained supportive of Madison's efforts during the War, yet unaware of the financial cliff America faced. The War of 1812 cost $158 million and had a war time debt of $127 million. The Era of Good Feeling continued through James Monroe's Presidency. He became one of America's most popular Presidents; however the War debt wouldn't be paid for another 23 years. Martin Van Buren's Presidency in 1837 would finally enjoy a debt free administration.

The American System

The American System was an economic plan engineered and theorized by Henry Clay, John C. Calhoun, Daniel Webster and John Quincy Adams. The original theory of federal government sponsored subsidies for industry was the "brain child" of Alexander Hamilton's financial theory, who advocated a protective tariff system that protected American manufactures and industry from foreign competition. He created a national bank, primarily for the purpose of providing federal subsidies for railroads, roads and canals to help businesses and manufactures to get their products to market cheaply, and public works projects financed by tariffs and the sale of public land.

While the system appeared to be plausible, it failed to factor in greed. Madison wasn't a Federalist, however before leaving office, he enacted a Second National Bank of the United States which was a poorly regulated and based on the original First National Bank. Madison implemented a tariff tax system and a standing professional military.

To the surprise of many Congressmen, Madison vetoed the Bonus Bill of 1812. This Bill was intended to satisfy the American Economic Systems key feature of Federal financing of Railroads, Roads, Bridges and canals. Madison's rationale for vetoing the bill, he felt, violated the Constitution. During this period in American history, roads and bridges were built by communities, counties and State governments and not Federal government in which the Constitution only gave the Federal government the authority on international issues.

Madison's policy toward Native American's had been overly simplistic and perhaps lacked a true understanding of Native American culture. He felt they should be farmers rather than hunter-gathers. Madison was sympathetic to the plight of the American Indians and rather sending the US Army to move them off Native American land, he ordered the Army to keep white settlers from encroaching on Native lands. His view was not shared by many military generals, especially Andrew Jackson, a hawk, who often disobeyed direct orders from Madison not to harass the Native Americans. As settlers continued to move west into the Ohio Valley and beyond, the Native land treaties were not enforced, which led to increased tensions between the government and the Native American Tribes.

Madison retired from office in 1817 and returned to Montpelier in Virginia. He had accumulated heavy debt while serving as President, mostly as a result of falling tobacco prices and mismanagement of his Plantation. Madison kept detailed diaries and notes of discussions while serving as a delegate at the Constitutional Convention and while in office. He wanted to sell his notes and diaries for $100,000, to insure that his wife and First Lady, Dolley Madison, would have a retirement income after his death. Throughout his life, Madison suffered from occasional bouts of epilepsy. He was plagued with chronic arthritis that starting in his late 30's and lasted until his death in 1836.

Perhaps the most interesting aspect of Madison's personality was his later years while he was mostly bedridden in 1831 and 1832. He became obsessed with maintain his Constitutional Legacy. After retirement, he began organizing his notes and journals and refused to turn them over to the US Government to be archived. He spent countless hours and months editing notes, written conversations and opinions in his journals and diaries. He lined-through entries that illustrated errors in his judgment while serving as President.

Both Jefferson and Adams died on the 4th of July of 1826; the 50th Anniversary of the Declaration of Independence. He would die quietly on June 28, 1836, however, the actual date of his death is not known exactly. On June 28, 1836, he was found dead sitting in front of his untouched breakfast tray. It's believed his death may have been on July 2, 1826, since several housekeepers claim he was sitting in the same position for several day and noticed he hadn't touch his food. Madison's lasts words were said on June 28, 1836; *"I always talk better lying down."* Dolly Madison sold Montpellier to Henry Moncure, along with half of their slaves to pay his debts.

Madison's Legacy

James Madison was a second cousin of Zachary Taylor. He is known as the father of the Constitution, even though he may not have physically wrote the Constitution with Quill and paper, it was Madison who developed and outlined the Virginia Plan, which is the Constitution we have today. Even though Madison and Jefferson were active opponents to the Jay Treaty, they maintained a certain element of civility and respect toward John Jay. During the Constitutional Convention, William Pierce wrote;

"...every person seems to acknowledge his greatness (Madison). In the management of every great question he evidently took the lead in the Convention.....he always came forward as the best informed man of any point in debate." [20]

Even though be originally opposed incorporating the Bill of Rights into the Constitution, he realized that to get enough state delegates to ratify the constitution required incorporating a federal Bill of Rights as the first ten amendments. He was adamant about the Constitution containing provisions that all Americans have the right to a civil jury trial. It would fail to get support during the drafting of the Constitutional, but it gave Madison another opportunity to incorporate his provision into the Bill of Rights, which became the seventh Amendments to the Constitution.

"Trial by Jury in civil cases is as essential to secure the liberty of the people as any one of the pre-existing rights of nature" James Madison 1787 **[21]**

Madison was not a polished or dynamic speaker in the presence of a large assembly, but like Jefferson, his logic and reasoning always prevailed upon reasoning. He was beyond a doubt the most important founding father of America. One thing that stands out about James Madison was his keen ability as a listener and his bipartisan view and politics which an attribute seldom seen today. This was evident when he realized that America needed a strong Federal Government to enforce compliance to Constitutional law, which was counter to the belief within his own Republican–Democrat political party. He also authorized a Second National Bank which was counter to the Republican-Democrat platform and rigidly defended yet opposed by his mentor, Thomas Jefferson.

In his last months as President, he approved a tariff system, that passed Congress that authorized a professional standing army, a pension system for orphans and widows from the War of 1812 and federal financial support for roads and canals. He maintained several passions after retiring as President and as an elder Statesman. He was appointed to the Virginia Constitutional Convention in 1829, in which Virginia was in the process of revising its State Constitution. Madison was concerned about slavery in America, even though being a slave owner himself. He proposed that Black Slaves should be returned to

Africa or to the Caribbean Islands if they wish. Madison wasn't the only founding father who believed that blacks should be transported to either the Dominican Republic or Africa; George Washington had expressed resettlement plan during his Presidency as well, but never gained the support in Congress. However, most slaves were born in America by 1816, and had raised families. Most refused to leave America, Madison gave them a choice. Madison remained active in political issues, in which he argued against having chaplains in the armed forces and in Congress, however, he did feel that chaplains in the Navy should be considered, since sailors would not have an opportunity for worship otherwise.

It an interesting side note; after he retired as President, he became a forgotten senior statesman. Like Washington, Jefferson and Adams, few visit their homes and engaged in political discussions or solicit advice. Washington, Jefferson and John Adams died ten years prior to Madison; however John Quincy Adams visited him three months prior to his death and noted that Madison was a shell of person and frail and bedridden. While his Presidency was not especially note worthy, his contribution prior to office is undisputed.

Henry Clay
(1777 - 1852)

Henry Clay was born in Hanover County, Virginia in 1777 and moved to Lexington, Kentucky in 1797. His father owned a small plantation in Virginia with 20 slaves and 464 acre plantation. His family had nine children of which Henry would be the second eldest. His father died when he was 4 years old and the estate was divided among his siblings and his mother, Elizabeth.

His family moved to Kentucky while Henry Clay remained in Hanover to continue his education under the guidance of Peter Deacon. George Wythe, who was one of the signatory of the Declaration of Independence, and serving as a judge on the Virginia's High Court of Chancery, hired him as his personal secretary. He remained in that position for 4 years. Wythe arranged a position with Robert Brooke in the Virginia Attorney General's office and continued his education in the field of law. In 1806, at the age of 28, he was elected to the Kentucky Senate to fill the seat of John Breckinridge, who resigned 2 months before his term expired. In 1807, he was elected to the House of Representatives and was voted Speaker of the House.

In January of 1809, Clay and Humphrey Marshall got into a heated argument that nearly came to blows on the floor of the Assembly. Clay challenged Marshall to a duel and they would meet at Shipping Port, Kentucky on January 19, 1809. Both exchanged shots and Clay was hit in the thigh and Marshall a glancing shot below his chest. Both recovered from their wounds and both would be censured for their conduct in the Kentucky Legislature. In 1810, he was elected to the U.S. House of Representatives and one year later, elected Speaker of the House.

He was a leader of the "War Hawk" movement that advocated war with Britain over the seizure and impressments of merchant sailors into the British Navy and the seizure of merchant ships supplying goods to France during the Napoleonic War in Europe, which led to the War of 1812 under James Madison's presidency.

He helped negotiate the Treaty of Ghent, which ended the War of 1812 and developed the "American System".

Clay's American System

Clay's American System was an economic plan that had 4 points whose purpose was to strengthen and unify the nation.

1. Implementing an economic system of protective tariffs to protect American industry from foreign competition.
2. A central bank (U. S. Bank of America) that would stabilize the currency and provide control over state and local banks.
3. Infrastructure improvements of public works projects for

roads, railroads and canals.
4. The maintenance of public lands for future sale as revenue to the Federal government.

Some of the items of his plan were passed by Congress; such as the Tariff of 1816 and the re-charter of the Second Bank of America in 1816 for a 20 year period, other items failed to gain support which drew criticism from the southern states, claiming it was an economic plan for the Northern industrialist.
Henry Clay's American System became a platform for the Whig Party. Clay's three part system involved protective tariffs that promoted American industry and a national bank to encourage commerce and improve infrastructure to get goods to market faster and cheaper at the expense of the tax payer.

John C. Calhoun
(1782 – 1850)

John C. Calhoun was a major political figure in U.S. Politics. He is best remembered as supporter of sectionalism and was avid advocate of slavery.

John Caldwell Calhoun was born in Abbeville District, South Carolina in 1782. He attended Yale College in Connecticut in 1802 and graduate in 1804. He was admitted to the South Carolina Bar in 1807. Much of his political theory was shaped during his years at Yale College under his mentor, Timothy Dwight, who was the President of Yale College. Dwight challenged Jeffersonian democracy. Dwight influenced and shaped Calhoun's political and legal justification for secession and States Rights which became political rather than intellectual and educational. Those views would be passed to Calhoun throughout his political career.

He won the election for the House of Representatives in 1810, which began his career into politics. He became the leader of the "War Hawk" movement in Congress that advocated war with Britain to resolve issues of impressments, American Shipping Rights and control of Mississippi River and Ohio Valley. Speaker of the House, Henry Clay of Kentucky was also a "War Hawk" and the two created a formable alliance advocating war and maintaining America's right as a sovereign nation.

After the Treaty of Ghent, ending the War of 1812, Calhoun realized that America needed a well organized standing army and powerful navy to protect its maritime trade. He proposed the Second Bank of the United States which was approved by President Madison (previously mentioned) and internal taxation to pay the War debt.

Calhoun's gift was his ability in public speaking. Some historians maintain he may very well have been among the finest public speakers ever to walk the halls of Congress. One observer best described Calhoun's oratory skill best;

"The most elegant speaker that sits in the house…His gestures are easy and graceful, his manner forcible, and language elegant; but above all, he confines himself closely to the subject, which he always understands, and enlightens everyone within hearing." Ref: [23]

In 1817, America had accumulated a serious war debt and the Panic of 1819 looming, President Monroe was desperate to fill the position as Secretary of War. Four others declined his offer, but Calhoun he accepted the position. He remained in the position until December of 1825, but found it difficult to maintain a suitable military for defense when in 1821; Congress passed the Reduction Act, which reduced the military enlistment from 12,000 to 6,000 men.
The Division of Indian Affairs fell under the control of the Secretary of Defense. Monroe created the Bureau of Indian Affairs in 1824, and as a result Calhoun negotiated more than 40 treaties with Indian tribes and created Indian reservations in the West.

The First Seminole War of 1816 created a permanent rife between Andrew Jackson and Calhoun when Jackson, invaded Florida and killed many of the Seminole Indians in an effort to take control of Florida from Spain. Congress made an effort to censor Jackson for his actions, but public opinion viewed Jackson as a hero rather than an insubordinate General who disliked Native Americans.

During the 1824 election for President, Calhoun faced four other contenders for President; Andrew Jackson, John Quincy Adams, William Crawford and Henry Clay. The South Carolina legislature didn't support Calhoun for President, but rather preferred he run as Vice President. He won the electoral votes for Vice President easily but the candidates running for President failed to win a majority as was required by the Constitution at the time. The Presidential election was to be resolved in the House of Representatives. John Quincy Adams was declared the winner over Jackson, Crawford and Clay. Adams offered Clay the Office of Secretary of State in exchange for his support and votes in the House. Calhoun being a pro slavery advocate didn't agree with Adams policies toward slavery. Adams, like his father, was a Federalist (he became the last Federalist to be elected), while Calhoun was a proponent of States' rights and nullification of laws deemed unconstitutional and opposed protective tariffs and slavery and nullification of laws. Quincy Adams and Calhoun had a great respect for each other, even though they had opposites politically views.

In the election 1828, Jackson once again ran for President against Quincy Adams for his second term. Jackson selected Calhoun as his Vice President running mate, while Quincy Adams selected Richard Rush as his Vice President. Adams lost the Presidency to the popular Andrew Jackson, who campaigned as a man for the common people and against big business.

The Petticoat Affair

When Jackson appointed his cabinet, the Vice President's wife; Florida Calhoun organized the wives of the Cabinet members for luncheons and tea parties, which was called by the media, the Petticoat's. Florida refused to include the wife of Secretary of War, Peggy Eaton into the Petticoat's social functions. Florida Calhoun alleged that Peggy Eaton was having an adulterous affair. Jackson sided with the Eaton's while John Calhoun sided with his wife Florida. It became major headlines in the newspaper and gossip columns. To resolve the issue, Secretary of State, Martin Van Buren, suggested that Jackson replace all his cabinet members, including himself, thus dissolving the "Petticoats". Jackson couldn't terminate the Vice President since it was elected. Jackson wanted to appoint Martin Van Buren as Minister to Great Britain; however the Senate voted 50 yas and 50 nays. Vice President Calhoun cast the deciding tie breaking vote. Calhoun voted "Nay" not to confirm Van Buren as Minister to Great Britain. As fate would have it, Van Buren became Jackson's Vice President when Calhoun resigned as Vice President during Jackson's Presidency. Calhoun only had 3 months remaining in his term of office. He would run as a U.S. Senator from his home State of South Carolina. Jackson and Van Buren won the Presidential second term election for the Democrat Party.

The Nullification Crisis

Calhoun opposed protective tariffs. He believed they favored the northern industrialist and not the south. During John Quincy Adams administration, the Tariff of 1828 passed and signed by Quincy Adams. Calhoun believed as many did, that the Tariff Act of 1828 was unconstitutional and the States had a right of nullification. Calhoun supported nullification as long as it was supported by a concurrent majority. While the issue of nullification has been raised often during the John Adams presidency, the Alien and Sedition Acts, was vigorously opposed by Madison and Jefferson, both advocated nullification. The theory of nullification is based on a legal premise that a State has a right to nullify any Federal law it deems unconstitutional. The basic concept seems reasonable; however the purpose of the US Supreme Court is to pass judgment on the Constitutionality of a law and not left up to the States to determine the constitutionality. In Madison's later years as a senior statesman, he vacated his original thoughts on nullification and stated that no state had the right to nullify federal law.

Jackson would sign into law the Tariff of 1832 for the purpose of lower tariff rates to placate the Nullification theorist. However, South Carolina's legislature nullified both the Tariffs of 1828 and 1832. Jackson dispatched several naval warships to Charleston harbor with the threat of arresting Calhoun and any nullification and secessionist supporters. As a result of the confrontation, both sides agreed on the Tariff Compromise of 1833. Congress wanted the last word on the issue of nullification by passing the "Force Bill", which gave the President the authority to use military force to enforce compliance of Federal law. Of course, South Carolina nullified the "Force Bill" as well. Calhoun along with Henry Clay formed the Whig Party in opposition to Jackson and Van Buren's Democrat Party; however he would later align himself closely to the Democrat platform. Martin Van Buren became President in 1837 and William Henry Harrison, a Whig, was elected President in 1840, but would die in 1841 in which his Vice President, John Tyler became President. Calhoun resigned from the Senate in 1843 and return to his Plantation at Fort Hill, South Carolina.

Calhoun was in favor of protecting minority rights but not in the same sense as we interpret minority rights today. He felt that minorities (slaves) were property. He advocated fugitive slave laws for the benefit of the plantation owner. Calhoun was pro slavery and didn't support economic, social and political leveling of classes by giving equal rights and responsibilities to all people. [24]

Calhoun was a strong believer in "Concurrent Majority". The theory of concurrent majority was based on a system in which a specific minority group could exercise veto power over actions of the majority that they believe infringes upon the minority's rights. Calhoun viewed minority groups differently from what we view them today. Calhoun characterized minority groups as aristocrats and elites, but believed that slaves were not considered minorities since they could not vote and were considered property belonging to the American Bourgeoisie in the south. Numerical Majority was the will of the populace that makes laws based on the will of the majority, which is one of the founding principles of our form of a representative democracy.

The Calhoun Doctrine

During the 1840's, Calhoun debated the issue of the Federal Government's role in its territories, in which he maintained its role was to be a trustee to the territory. He maintained the Federal Government had no legal right to forbid a territory to engage in slavery. In 1840, there were several divided territories wanting admission into the Union. One conditions imposed by the Government was; they were to be a free slave territory in order to be a free slave state. In 1857, the Supreme Court case Dred Scott V. Sanford, Chief Justice Roger B. Taney's decision that the government could not prohibit slavery in its territories, since slaves were considered property and were not citizens. The Dred Scott decision will be discussed in more detail under James Buchanan's Presidency from 1857 to 1861. . Calhoun would die 10 years before the Civil War and his efforts toward nationalizing slavery would become among the reasons why Abraham Lincoln issued the Emancipation Proclamation and the ratification of the 13th and 14th Amendment to the Constitution that freed all slaves.

John C. Calhoun's Legacy

John C. Calhoun was a controversial figure in American politics. As the years passed, he became more and more pro secessionist and outspoken toward expanding slavery throughout America and its territories.

He will always be remembered for his defense of white southern interest, in particular the rights of slave owners and his efforts to expand slavery into western territories. His advocacy for state sovereignty, especially for the southern states is well known historically.

He strongly believed America should not be involved in foreign affairs. He disliked protective tariffs, even though they had negative effects on southern economy and business. He was a firm believer in Nullification of Federal Laws and considered them unconstitutional. In modern time, much of his historical reputation has been under attack. Many claim his southern secessionist theories lead to the Civil War and for that reason, his greatness and his contribution to American history has been over-looked. Regardless of his racial and political views, he was considered a good Vice President and Secretary of War while serving his country.

James Monroe
(1758 – 1831)

The principles and passions of men are always the same and lead to the same result, varying only according to the circumstances in which they are placed. - James Monroe

James Monroe was the 5th President of the United States. He was six feet tall, dark hair that turned gray at an early age. He had blue-gray eyes and was the last American President to wear a powdered wig tied into a queue. He was well liked and respected by all those whom he met. He was adored by the public and made frequent speaking tours and addressed audience with up-beat news on the welfare of America.

He was born in 1758 in Monroe Hall, Virginia. His father, Spence Monroe, owned a small farmer and worked as a carpenter to make ends meet. He married Elizabeth Jones in 1752 and had five children, in which James would be the second oldest. The Monroe's were of Scottish descent and arrived in America in the mid 1600's. James attended the county school; however he only attended school eleven weeks of the year, to help his father on the farm. While at school he became friends with John Marshall and would become lifelong friends. John Marshall later becomes the most famous Supreme Court Justice in American history. He would be forced to leave school at the age of 16 to help his younger brothers on the farm. His Uncle, Joseph Jones was a member of the Virginia House of Burgesses and enrolled James into the College of William and Mary in Williamsburg, Virginia. Since his Uncle had political influence, he introduced young James to Thomas Jefferson, Patrick Henry and George Washington, which had a great influence in his career as a politician.

After attending College, he dropped-out after a year and a half and joins the 3rd Virginia Regiment in the Continental Army. He was commissioned as a lieutenant and served under William Washington. Over the next two and a half years, he became involved in numerous military campaigns, including spending the winter in Valley Forge with George Washington. He returned to Williamsburg to complete his education in law and marry Elizabeth Kortright in New York in 1786. They would have 3 children, in which his son, James Spence Monroe would die at 16 months old. They purchased the Ash-Lawn-Highland estate in Charlottesville in 1799. Over the years he would acquire several plantations with slaves. He spent little time at the plantations and hired managers to oversee the work. The Oak Hill Plantation never turned a profit and reports were circulated that his slaves were frequently abused by his manager and employees. His plantations incurred large debt, as well as maintaining an expensive life style.
Gradually sold land to pay bill and pay off debt. He was active in politics after college and was elected to the House of Delegates in 1782 and elected to the Congress of the Confederation in 1788. He became a Virginia a delegate to the Virginia Ratifying Convention as well.

DOUGLAS G. BEAUDOIN

During Washington's Presidency, Monroe, Madison and Jefferson became disenfranchised with Hamilton's and Adam's Federalist ideals and policies that advocated a strong Central government. He became part of the Jefferson and Madison's Republican-Democrat Party. President Washington appointed Monroe as Ambassador to France and John Jay as Ambassador to Britain, with the hope of keeping America neutral during the French Revolution, however after only serving two months as Ambassador to France, John Jay, et al; signed the Jay Treaty with Britain, which infuriated France and the Republican-Democrats. Monroe would be recalled back to America in 1796 after writing a 400 page manuscript condemning the Jay Treaty.

He became Governor of Virginia in 1799. When Thomas Jefferson was elected President in 1801, he appointed Madison as his Ambassador to France. His primary focus was to negotiate the purchase of the Louisiana Territory with France and negotiate the purchase of Florida from Spain. In 1803, he was appointed Ambassador to Great Britain and held that position until 1807.

Madison became Secretary of State under President Jefferson; however his relationship with James Monroe became strained as a result of differing opinions toward the signing of the Jay Treaty. Monroe believed Jefferson and Madison could have avoided war with Britain and stabilized the American economy if Jefferson extended the Jay Treaty another 10 years. Both Jefferson and Madison held firm in their conviction that the Jay Treaty was an attempt by Britain to gradually establish control in the Ohio Valley and trade along the Mississippi River. It is not known if that was the case or not, but Jefferson and Madison but the two felt strongly that it was a conspiracy by Great Britain to grab land but it was not an opinion shared by Monroe. Britain anticipated America's quest for expanding its boundaries into Canada during the Jefferson and Madison Presidencies. Britain assumed America had imperialist intensions, which was a topic often discussed in political circles by all sides. During the War of 1812, Britain immediately re-enforced it troops along the Great Lakes Region and negotiated an alliance with the regional Native American tribes. When Madison declared war in 1812, his first act of was to invade Canada; as Britain suspected and with the British build-up along the Canadian border, foiled the American advance into Canada.

The War was going badly for President Madison. The British sent an armada of ships to Maryland and British troops burned the Capital and White House. Madison removed Armstrong as Secretary of War and replaced him with Monroe who was serving as Secretary of State and his newly appointed position as Secretary of War. He later resigned as Secretary of State in 1814 and devotes his time as Secretary of War. Monroe ordered Andrew Jackson to defend against additional attacks against the US Capital and ordered 100,000 men to be drafted into military service. He established a National Bank (Second National Bank of America) to finance the war effort as well. Two months later the British consented to sit-down peace conference, which led to the Treaty of Ghent. Part of the Treaty ended the British practice of impressments of American merchant sailors and America being a free trade nation. Prior to Monroe becoming Secretary of War, there was very little leadership and a coordinated war effort. With Monroe becoming Secretary of War, America's war effort changed dramatically.

James Monroe's Presidency
(1817 – 1825)

Monroe was elected President as a Republican-Democrat in 1816. Daniel D. Tompkins, Congressman from New York, became his Vice President. Monroe skirted political protocol by appointed both Republican-Democrats and Federalist's to high positions in the Monroe government and cabinet. The Federalist Party was slowly dissolving and their influence during Monroe's Presidency would see a gradual amalgamation of Republican-Democrats and Federalist ideologies merge under Monroe's tenure as President. .He traveled along the Eastern Seaboard giving speeches, that would be called the

"Era of Good Feeling" speeches, as Jefferson called them in a letter to James Monroe, that later appeared in newspapers.

Monroe tackled three important treaties during his first few years as President. The Rush-Bagot Treaty of 1817 between the United States and Great Britain that led to the demilitarization along the Canadian border and the Great Lakes Region. The Treaty of 1818 established the current border between Canada and the United States at the 49th Parallel. The Treaty also established a joint US-British occupation of the Oregon Territory that lasted 10 years. The Russo-American Treaty of 1824 established the southernmost boundary of Alaska's Panhandle as the limit to Russia's claim to the America's Northwest along the Oregon and British Canadian west coast. .

Florida Territory

The United States made repeated attempts to purchase Florida from Spain. Monroe was Ambassador to France during the Jefferson Presidency but failed to reach a workable agreement with Spain to purchase Florida.

Times were changing with Spain. Spain's vast colonial empire once stretched from South America to Central America, of which all were now demanding independence. In addition, Spain was engaged in constant Wars in an attempt to hold on to territory. Spain became bankrupt and unable to provide a military defense of its colonies and in particular, Florida. The defense of Florida relied mostly on treaties with the Seminole Indians to protect the Florida's boundary from attacks from American settlers. By 1818, Seminole warriors frequently engaged in raids into Alabama, and Georgia. Run-a-way slaves crossed into Florida as a safe haven from the slave fugitive laws in America. The slaves were called "Black Seminoles" and join Seminole Indians in defending Florida. In retaliation, local militia from Georgia and Alabama raided villages in Florida to extract run-away slaves and in return the Seminoles attacked settlers in Georgia and Alabama who had settled on the Creek Native American land.

In 1818, Monroe became bed-stricken with fever, believed to be malaria. While bed-ridden, General Andrew Jackson claimed he sent a letter to the White House requesting permission to invade Florida. Madison, claimed he did not authorize Jackson to invade Florida, a verbal feud that lasted through their lives.

Jackson advanced his army into Pensacola, the Spanish Capital of Florida at the time. Monroe and John Quincy Adams defended Jackson's efforts publicly, but privately they considered him a loose cannon and power hungry.

In 1819, Spain and the United States signed the Adams-Onis Treaty that ceded Florida to the United States. In addition, it Spain acquiesced to all claims to the Oregon Territory, Texas and the American Southwest as part of the $5 million purchase of Florida.

The Missouri Compromise of 1820

Even during Monroe's Era of Good Feeling, slavery was never far from peoples mind. In early winter of 1819, Congress requested the residents of the Missouri Territory to formulate a Constitution and form an interim government in preparation for admission into the Union.

John Tallmadge, a Congressman from New York, submitted the Tallmadge Amendment to Congress that prohibited additional slaves from enter Missouri. In addition, the Amendment declared that all children of slaves would be free upon reaching the age of twenty-one years of age. The bill passed the House of Representative after a week of heated debates, but fell short of passage in the Senate. This single Amendment would divide Congress into to two separate groups; "restrictionist" and "anti-restrictionist" who were proslavery legislators. These two factions practiced a political ideology that divided Congress and resulted into the Civil War, 40 years later.

At stake during negotiations of the Missouri Amendment were the Louisiana Territory and the Admission of Alabama as a slave state one month earlier. In January 1920, Missouri was allowed to enter as a slave state and Maine entered the Union as a free slave state. An amendment by Jesse Thomas of Illinois excluded slavery in the Louisiana Territory north of the 36 degree 30 minute north boundary which passed Congress and signed by President Monroe.

The importance of the Missouri Compromise of 1820 was the admission of Missouri into the Union as a slave state which create an imbalance of power in Congress that would have more pro slave delegates than anti slave delegates. Prior to the compromise, there were 22 states in the Union in 1820, of which, 11 were northern free slave states and 11 southern slaves' states. With the admission of Missouri, there would be 12 slave states and 11 non slave states. To resolve the imbalance, a compromise was made in which Maine would enter the Union as a non slave state.

While the compromise resolved the issue of equal representation in Congress between pro-slave and anti- slave factions, there were still more territories that eventually would be divided into states and be admitted to the Union, all of which would require a compromise of sorts. In essence the Missouri Compromise of 1820 only stalled the looming issue of slavery for another 34 years until Kansas and Nebraska wanted admission into the Union 1850 and 1854.

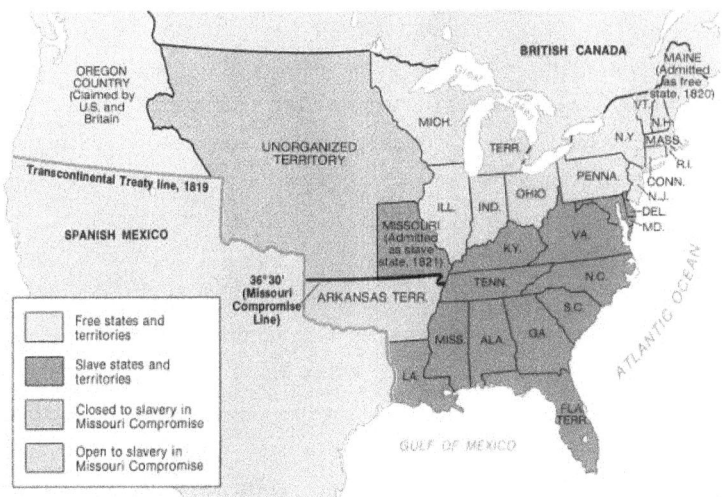

Map 11, Missouri Compromise 1820

The Panic of 1819

Two years into Monroe's Presidency, the first major depression hit America. Much of the effects of the depression began during Madison's Presidency and at the end of the War of 1812. The economic collapse was due to many economic situations colliding simultaneously together.

During the signing of the Treaty of Ghent in December of 1814 that ended the War between Britain and America; America insisted the Treaty include a break from the British mercantile system and allow America to be a free trade nation; to import and export and apply protective tariffs on goods and products it deemed necessary.

During the War, America accumulated a large war debt. Britain and Europe was unable to produce enough agricultural products to feed the general population, as a result of years fighting the Napoleonic Wars. America on the other hand, was able to supply Britain and Europe with the agricultural products it needed which created an economic boom in America, especially in the agricultural community.

However, the boom wouldn't last. In 1817, Europe began to enjoy one of their biggest bumper crops in decades and found it unnecessary to purchase agricultural products from America. India began supplying Britain with cotton, tea and tobacco much cheaper than America could supply.

Land Speculation

Since American was saddled with a huge war debt and needed to generate revenue, the one commodity the US Government had a surplus of was land. To generate revenue, the government decided to auctioned and sell public lands in the west for $2 per acre with a minimum of 160 acre parcels. The government required one-quarter of the amount as a down payment and the remaining balance to be paid in 4 equal annual payments. For most, money was in short supply, especially metallic hard currency (gold and silver). During the boom years between 1814 and 1817, the number of State Banks doubled, from 100 to over 200. Land speculators and farmers borrowed from State Banks, paper notes printed by local State Banks. The paper notes was IOU's that were used to pay the Second National Bank of America for land mortgage payments due the government.

National and State Charted Banks

The Second National Bank of America was established by James Madison in 1816 for the purpose of paying America's War debt as previously noted. It became necessary to promote a single currency system and a means to assist financing businesses and trade ventures. President Jefferson didn't extend Alexander Hamilton's First National Bank Charter when it expired in 1810, but rather passed it onto his successor, James Madison, established a second Bank of America without the regulatory controls upon the State Chartered Banks that Hamilton incorporated in the First National Bank Charter.

To open a State Charted Bank, it only required an office to do business, a printing press and paper. Hard currency was in short supply in America. State Charted Banks printed its own notes, and held the mortgage as collateral. The newly formed Second Bank of America had a loosely written charter with little government regulatory oversight. Requirements and enforcement was optional and banks could operate without metallic hard currency in their vaults to cover bad debts or a possible run on the bank. The banking system operated in which the land speculators or farmer would purchase land by going to a State Bank and mortgage the land, however the Government required a down payment in cash, however for those who didn't have cash for the down payment, State Banks accepted a first deed of trust on the land or other tangible assets. The State Bank issued a note for the down payment and sent it to the Second National Bank (Federal) as partial payment for the land. When or if the speculator made his quarterly payments to the State Bank, they would keep the down payment and issue an IOU to the Second National Bank, and if the borrower was unable to pay a quarterly payment they would issue a Second Deed of Trust on the land. Government held the first deed of trust) and held only paper and IOU's. If the Farmer or speculator defaulted on the loan, the State Bank would repossess the land. The farmer and speculator would lose the land for which they never paid a dime on. In reality the paper note was not backed by hard currency but rather an IOU notes sent to the Second National Bank (Federal Government). No currency exchanged hands, only worthless promissory notes and IOU's.

The government thought they would pass the worthless bank notes to the export traders for hard cash, however, the "House of Cards" would fall in 1818, when imports were exceeding exports and foreign governments demanded trading companies to accept only (specie) hard currency for goods, rather than the worthless notes generated by State and Federal banks which were staked to the ceiling in vaults at the Second National Bank of the United States in Philadelphia or one of its Branch Banks. When the Second National Bank Branches demanded State Banks pay in hard currency and would not accept State Bank notes after August of 1818, it caused a panic among farmers and speculators. There were eighteen branch offices of the Second Bank of the United States and if they enforced the hard currency policy on State Banks, it would cause massive bank failures throughout the South and West. The economy gradually ground to a halt by 1819 and the depression would last until 1821. .

For the land speculators and farmers who purchased land, they found the value of their land worth only 75 percent of its original value. When State banks were unable to cover their notes with hard currency, they called in their notes or foreclosed on the farmer and speculators property, thus causing the Panic of 1819.

As a result of the Panic of 1819, the general public was supportive of protective tariffs; however, it would only be a fleeting thought, when protective tariffs would cause another panic eight years later. It would be the first realization that Capitalism and economic cycles would be a reoccurring theme and that speculation using other people's money produced greed. It would be one of the primary causes of America's boom and bust cycle.

The Monroe Doctrine

On December 2, 1823, James Monroe delivered his annual message to Congress, declaring that no European powers were to colonize in the western hemisphere. In fact, it wasn't called the Monroe Doctrine until 1852. The Monroe Doctrine became a U.S. foreign policy written in 1823 by Secretary of State John Quincy Adams while serving under President James Monroe. The essence of the Monroe Doctrine was to keep European nations from colonizing or interfering with nations in the western hemisphere as acts of aggression or for colonization that would require U.S. military intervention. The Monroe Doctrine decreed that all nations in the western hemisphere were independent nations. It was among the longest standing policy declarations in American history.

The Doctrine was conceived after the conclusion of the Napoleonic Wars in 1815, when the Congress of Vienna convened and negotiated territorial disputes between France and Spain which culminated in France agreeing to restore the Spanish Monarchy in exchange for Cuba. The agreement between Spain and France alarmed Congress and President Monroe. Cuba was only 90 miles from the coast of America. Great Britain was supportive of the Monroe Doctrine and British Foreign Secretary, George Canning offered the United States a joint-venture with Great Britain to enforce the doctrine, but his suggestion was rebuffed by President Monroe. Great Britain interest in the Monroe Doctrine was not because Britain felt it fair, but rather they knew that the United States did not have the military to enforce the Doctrine. Great Britain had already established trade relations with Latin America States and established colonies in the Caribbean and South America, but wanted to curb Spain's appetite for colonization in Latin America and Spain's strict tariff laws on imports. For the British, the Monroe Doctrine would keep other nations from competing for trade in the western hemisphere.

For decades Great Britain was the only country that enforced the Monroe Doctrine, albeit for personal interest. Perhaps a defining moment in the creation of the Monroe Doctrine came two years prior when Russia claimed sovereignty over the Pacific Northwest of North America.

The "Ukase of 1821" declared that Russian, by proclamation, claimed territorial sovereignty to all rights and claims to Alaska and most of the Pacific Northwest of North America, and extending south of the Columbia River in Oregon. In the Ukase of 1821, it forbids foreign vessels from entering within 38 miles from its shores, islands, bays and inlets. The United States and Great Britain contested Russia's territorial claims and argued that Paul I of Russia had already filed and signed the "Ukase of 1799", which limited the territorial claim of Russia to Vancouver Island and Cape Scott. Great Britain asserted that Captain James Cook discovered and named Vancouver Island long before Russian explorers had ventured south from Sitka Sound, which was the Capital of Russia America at the time.

Eventually, a Russo-America Treaty led to the Anglo-Russia Convention of 1824 and 1825 declaring that Russia cedes all claims south of 55 degree North latitude, which was the southern tip of Prince of Wales Island. The only incident of a violation of the "Ukase of 1821" was the American ship Pearl, which sailed into Sitka harbor and was seized by Russia; however, after protest from the U.S. Government, it was released without incident. Eventually, the United States purchase Alaska from Russia in 1867 for 7.2 million dollars, which was negotiated by Secretary of State William H. Seward, while serving under President Andrew Johnson.

The Napoleonic Wars of 1814-15, War of 1812 and the "Ukase of 1821", increased the Monroe Doctrine's importance to America and Great Britain's interests in the Americas. It created a lifelong relationship with Great Britain and America, who had the military strength to enforce the Monroe Doctrine and other territorial claims by other European nations in Latin America.

In the early 1800's the United States, didn't have a sizeable navy capable of contesting France, Spain or Great Britain's claims for new lands. In December of 1832, Great Britain's claim to the Falkland Islands in South America found that the United States was unable to enforce the Monroe Doctrine against a powerful ally. In 1842, under President John Tyler, the United States annexed the Hawaiian Islands that were discovered by the famous British explorer, Captain James Cook, who was later killed by local Hawaiians during his last voyage of discovery while exploring and Mapping the coastal waters of Alaska in February of 1779.

While the United States was fighting the Civil War, Napoleon III invaded Mexico and installed Emperor Maximillian. The United States was unable enforce the Doctrine due to the American Civil War of the 1860's, but by 1865, the United States moved a large military forces to the borders of Texas, demanding that the French pull-out of Mexico. The French pulled-out and Emperor Maximillian was eventually executed by Mexican nationalist when they took control of Mexico from the French.

Throughout the next 75 years, the Monroe Doctrine would be tested over and over. One such event occurred in 1902, when Argentina failed to pay its debts to Great Britain, Germany and Italy. The three nations blockaded Argentina's ports and bombarded port facilities with naval artillery. The Argentine Foreign Minister appealed to President Roosevelt, claiming it was a violation of the Monroe Doctrine, however Theodore Roosevelt rejected Argentina's assertion and sent a diplomatic response stating:

"We do not guarantee any state against punishment if it misconducts itself." [1]

The interpretation of the Monroe Doctrine today is different from that of 1823. When James Monroe and John Quincy Adams drafted it in 1823, the words remained the same but the intent and purpose gradually changed to fit the circumstances of the time. For 75 years it was understood to mean that foreign colonization by Nations outside the sphere of the Western Hemisphere where not to colonize in the Western Hemisphere. By 1904, Roosevelt broadened the scope to mean military intervention. Perhaps Secretary of State John Kerry is correct in asserting that the Monroe Doctrine is no longer applicable. The Monroe Doctrine will once again be tested in 1962 when President John F. Kennedy confronted the Soviet Union for installing ballistic missiles in Cuban, known as the "Cuban Missile Crisis". The missile crisis was not about the invasion of a foreign power, but rather the security of North America and possibly other Latin American states. The author's of the Doctrine did not envision the possibility that a foreign nation may use a western nation as a military staging area. During the drafting of the Monroe Doctrine, the main concern was colonization, trade and the independence of Latin American nations.

During the election of Monroe's second term in 1820, his Vice President, Daniel D. Tompkins, once again became his Vice President. Tompkins would be the only Vice President in the 19th century to complete two full terms under the same President. During Monroe's Presidency, five states were admitted to the Union:

1. Mississippi, 1817
2. Illinois, 1818
3. Alabama, 1819
4. Maine, 1820
5. Missouri, 1821

Florida would be added as a Territory in 1819 and the Purchase of the Louisiana Territory was negotiated by Monroe as the Ambassador to France while serving under Thomas Jefferson in 1801.

Retirement and Death

James Monroe's Presidency ended on March 4, 1825. He retired in Charlottesville, Virginia at his home at Monroe Hill, which later became part of the University of Virginia campus. In 1817, during his first year as President, he sold his farm to the University of Virginia.

During his eight years as President, his life was devoted to public service and over the years, he accumulated substantial debt during his presidency. He and his wife moved to Oak Hill, Virginia until the death of his wife, Elizabeth in 1830. He moved to New York City to live with his daughter, Maria Monroe Gouverneur.

John Quincy Adams visited Monroe in April of 1831 and was surprised how his health had deteriorated. He suffered from a persistent cough, later to be diagnosed as pulmonary tuberculosis. In

April of 1831, he developed a lung infection that he would not recover from. James Monroe died on Independence Day, July 4, 1831 from heart failure and tuberculosis. He was the third President to die on July 4th, Independence Day. . His last words being:

"I regret that I should leave this world without again beholding to him"

He was referring to James Madison is closest friend. .

Monroe's Legacy

Monroe's presidency was called the Era of Good Feeling, even though shortly after becoming President, the Panic of 1819 failed to rattle the confidence of the American people. He had accomplished more than any President during his tenure as President. .

One of Monroe's greatest assets was his charm and ability to make those around him feel comfortable and important. He came across as not being a salesman or politician but a sincere and concerned humanitarian. He was easy to communicate with and had an easy going personality. He was sensitive to criticism, especially among friends and colleagues, but would not lash out to critics or be spiteful or vindictive. The Monroe Doctrine is considered his greatest legacy, but his acquisition of Florida from Spain, Texas and the Southwest and portions of the Oregon Territory can also be considered a great triumph of his leadership and ability in foreign policy and negotiation. Five States were admitted to the Union during his Presidency.

Monroe was the only person in American history to hold two cabinet positions at the same time; Secretary of State and Secretary of War (Defense). He was able to pull America out of the Panic of 1819 which was a carry-over from the heavy debt of the War of 1812 during Madison's Presidency and his effort to sell land to cover the war debt without raising taxes. The American public continued to revere Monroe as one of the great President. James Monroe is considered one of the great American Presidents. He was the last of the great founding fathers to hold the highest office in America. With his passing, it ended the era of the elegant, dignified and gentlemen colonial leaders who insisted on wearing the traditional powdered wigs with a que for which he will always be remember.

John Quincy Adams
(1767 – 1848)

"Always vote for a principle though you have to vote alone, and you can cherish the sweet reflection that your vote is never lost."
- John Quincy Adams

John Quincy Adams, the son of President John Adams America's 2nd President. John Quincy Adams became America's 6th President. He was born in Braintree, Massachusetts, now known as Quincy, Massachusetts. He was educated by private tutors from his father's law practice. His father at the time was a diplomat and Ambassador to Great Britain, Netherlands and France, in which he accompanied his father on diplomatic missions abroad and attended Leiden University in the Netherlands in 1781. He became fluent in French, Dutch and German. When he returned to America in 1783, and enrolled into Harvard College and graduated in 1787 with a Bachelors of Arts degree. Prior to entering Harvard, he was fluent in Latin and Greek and had translated Virgil, Plutarch, and Aristotle. He also translated the New Testament from Greek to English. He would earn a Masters of Arts from Harvard in 1790 and be admitted to the Massachusetts Bar in 1791.

His father, John Adams, was Vice President during Washington's administration. John Quincy met Louisa Johnson in London and they would marry several years later. She being from England would follow Adams back to America after his tenure abroad.

During his father's Presidency, he appointed John Quincy Minister to Prussia in 1797. He would return to America in 1801, when Thomas

Jefferson was elected President. Both Adams were Federalist and when Jefferson was elected President in 1801 he relieved both of them from their foreign posts. John Quincy went into private law practice in Boston, which lasted one year. He began his political career by campaigning for a seat in the U.S. Senate and elected as a Federalist. He served in the U.S. Senate until 1808 and supported the Purchase of the Louisiana Territory from France. He advocated the Embargo Act against Britain. The Embargo Act was sponsored by Jefferson's Secretary of State, James Madison, which resulted in a political and economic disaster for Jefferson, which had little effect on Britain economically but devastating effect on American trade and business.

Scholarly Endeavors

After resigning as a U.S. Senator and being alienated by the Federalist Party and the Republican-Democrat Party, he turned to the field he was most comfortable with; education. He received a professorship of Rhetoric and Oratory at Harvard College, but declined the position as President of Harvard. His tenure at Harvard College would end in 1809 when James Madison would tap his brilliance as U.S. Minister to Russia.

In 1814, John Quincy was appointed Chief negotiator for the Treaty of Ghent, between America and Great Britain. The Treaty would officially end the War of 1812. In 1815, he would later be appointed Minister to the Court of St. James's in a trade agreement with Britain and America. In 1817 James Monroe was elected President and appointed John Quincy as Secretary of State, in which he served eight years during Monroe's tenure as President. As Secretary of State, he negotiated the Rush-Bagot Treaty and the Treaty of 1818, which defined the borders of Canada-U.S. He also negotiated the Adams-Onis Treaty in which the U.S acquired Florida and the border area near Louisiana. In 1809, James Madison appointed Adams as the first Minister to Russia. Under Czar Alexander I, James Monroe appointed Adam's as his Secretary of State which he served from 1817 to 1825.

DOUGLAS G. BEAUDOIN

John Quincy Adam's Presidency
(1825 – 1829)

As the obvious successor to James Monroe, Adam's was from Massachusetts and popular in New England, but not necessarily in the South, where John Calhoun, a pro-slavery advocate dropped out early to run for Vice President. Jackson and Crawford were both from the South and popular in the west. During the voting, neither candidate would win a majority of the electoral votes, thus the election was decided on a contingent election in the House. Adams needed Henry Clay's electoral votes to win, since Clay was a member of the House and could not be considered. Clay supported Adams during the Contingent election to win the Presidency over Jackson and Crawford. Part of Adam's success was due in part to Jackson's military in subordination during his campaign in Florida, in which Monroe claimed he did not give Jackson orders to advance into Pensacola, the Capital of a Spanish territory and hanged 3 British soldiers deemed by Jackson as spies. Members of the House felt he was a "loose cannon" and an overzealous war hawk. Crawford campaigned on a platform of a weak central government and strong states rights. Both positions were not popular in Congress, thus Adam's experience and diplomacy was well established and he would have little trouble getting enough electoral votes a Congress.

The most unusual aspect of Adam's inauguration was that he was the only President to be inaugurated in the oath of office on a book of Constitutional Law, rather than the Bible. Henry Clay would become his Secretary of State and John C. Calhoun would become Vice President.

John Quincy Adams, like his father, John Adams, only served four years as President. His foreign policies were lack-luster at best and accomplished little. Most of the policy issues were resolved during his tenure as Secretary of State during the Monroe years. He opposed the annexation of Texas and later the Mexican-American War. As he promised in his inaugural speech, he carried forward a large public works project of building roads, canals and port facilities on the Mississippi river. The Chesapeake and Ohio Canal and the Cumberland Road projects opened transportation corridors between the south and west. Adams favored a gradual assimilation of Native Americans. This was to be accomplished by a series of agreements between five southern tribes, principally in Georgia and Florida. Adams rescinded the Treaty of Indian Springs, which was an agreement between the U.S. Government and the Muscogee tribe under pressure from Georgia's Governor, George Troup. Adams signed a new treaty with the Muscogee but Troup refused to sign and accept it. A third treaty with the Muscogee involved taking all of the native land from the Muscogee in Georgia. This act would culminate with the Indian Removal Act in 1829 during Andrew Jackson's first year as President. It would be the beginning of the Trail of Tears which created widespread criticism of Jackson's policies and judgment as President.

John Quincy Adam's Legacy

During the Presidential election of 1824, the campaign was among the dirtiest in American history, in which Andrew Jackson carried-out vicious attacks on his character and personality. When Jackson became President four years later, he made it a personal goal to destroy any legacy that John Quincy had established during his Presidency. John Quincy was not a Democrat, Whig or Republican-Democrat; he became an independent during his Presidency and gave no favored treatment to any particular party while serving as President. Congress gave little or no support toward getting his bills passed. Later other presidents would face the same challenges, especially when the opposing party controlled both houses, but with John Quincy and John Tyler (1841–1845), both declared they were independent, thus Congress gave no support for the President.

John Quincy Adams was not a politician, even though he was raised and taught to be a foreign diplomat as a result of his father's

Presidency, he spent most of his life as an Ambassador or Foreign Minister. Historians believe he was the most intelligent President to hold the office; however, he had few accomplishments due to his non political affiliation in Congress to get any bills passed. Even though the Washington political establishment led by Andrew Jackson, made every attempt to demonize him as an enemy of the common man, his ultimate legacy had already been established years earlier during James Monroe's Presidency. John Quincy Adams assisted in writing the Monroe Doctrine for President James Monroe, which became his greatest legacy that survives today's.

Chapter 9
Jacksonian Era

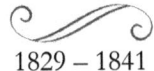

1829 – 1841

Historians consider the Jacksonian Era lasting from 1824 to 1840, which was a period that the Democrat Party dominated politics at the time. While Jackson was the first President to be elected as a Democrat, it was certainly not the same Democrat Part of today. His campaign platform embraced the concept that Jackson was: "A President of the Common Man", but in fact he was a wealthy aristocrat and strong proponent of slavery and anti-American Native and pro slavery.

Andrew Jackson
(1767 – 1845)

Andrew Jackson was perhaps one of the most controversial figures in American history, both in and out of the White House. He was born in 1767 in the Carolinas to Scottish-Irish colonist who arrived in Philadelphia in 1765. They moved to the Appalachian Mountains to a community of Scottish and Irish immigrant called Waxhaws, which lies near the border of North and South Carolina. His father would die two years later at the age of 29 from an accident on the farm. Jackson would receive his education from two local priest.

Andrew and his brother Robert served during the Revolutionary War under Colonel William Richardson Davie of the Continental Army. The two were captured by the British during the Battle of Hanging Rock in 1781. When young Andrew and his brother Robert refused to clean a British officer's boots, Jackson was slashed in the face with a broad sword, leaving a permanent scare. The two were held prisoner and contracted smallpox. They nearly died of starvation and dehydration while imprisoned. Their mother, Elizabeth was able to secure their release as they became came too ill to be use to the captures. While returning home to Waxhaws, Robert would die. Later, Elizabeth volunteered as a nurse aboard the two prison ships that were moored in Charleston Harbor; however she also became a victim of the disease and died during the cholera "outbreak" aboard the prison ships when Andrew was 14.

After the Revolutionary War, Andrew worked in a saddle-makers shop in Waxhaws for several years while completing his secondary education. He apprenticed himself to a law firm in Salisbury, North Carolina for three years and was admitted to the North Carolina bar in 1787. He received an appointment as prosecutor in North Carolina where he offended a lawyer who challenged him to a duel. The duel ended with both firing into the air.

He married Rachel Robards in Nashville, Tennessee in 1794 and engaged in a joint venture with a fellow lawyer in land speculation by acquiring Cherokee and Chickasaw Native American land grants that was protected by treaty. This could possibly explain why he was adamant about initiating the Indian Removal Act during his Presidency.

In 1796, Tennessee became a State and Jackson was elected to the U.S. House of Representatives as a Democrat-Republican. He did not seek re-election but was appointed as a Judge on the Tennessee Supreme Court in 1798. In addition, he accepted a commission as Colonel in the Tennessee militia and later promoted to Major General.

Jackson became a large plantation owner with more than 1000 acres of farm and plantation land. He owned more than 150 slaves and at one time, as many as 300. His treatment of his slaves was relatively humane for the time, even though he did whip them to increase production. Five to Ten slaves occupied a 80 square feet cabin. They often provided their own food by hunting, fishing and growing their own vegetables. Some staples such as flour, corn meal, salt and sugar were provided.

In 1806, Jackson once again engaged in yet another duel over an article published by Charles Dickinson concerning Jackson's wife. To protect his wife's honor, he challenged Dickinson to a duel. He allowed Dickinson to shoot first, while he turned sideways to limit his frontal body exposure. Jackson was shot in the Chest only inches from his heart, but remained standing, thus allowing Jackson to return fire and shot Dickinson in the Abdomen, for which he would die from his wounds two days later. Jackson survived his injury but the Doctors were unable to remove the bullet, which would cause him health problems the rest of his life.

The Battle of Horseshoe Bend

The Muskogee Native American Indians, also known as the Creek, lived along the rivers system and tributaries of present day Alabama and Georgia in small tribal villages known as confederations. With the arrival of the Anglo-American settlers, they built small towns along the river that would divided the Muskogee confederations into two separate parts; upper tribal entities along the Tallapoosa, Coosa and Alabama Rivers and the lower tribal entities along the Chattahoochee, Flint and Ocmulgee Rivers. In 1811, the Shawnee leader, Tecumseh from the Ohio River Valley, made an effort to unite the Native American Indians into a single fighting force for the purpose of creating a single native America nation. He convinced the Upper River Muskogee to join his federation along with recruiting many Cherokee, Chickasaw and the Seminole tribes from Florida.

When war broke-out in 1812 between America and Britain, Tecumseh and his confederation elected to fight alongside Britain. The British offered Tecumseh their own land and Native American Nation that straddled Canada and United States near present day north and South Dakota and upper Minnesota. There had been small skirmishes between settlers and the Upper River Muskogee for years. They were called "Red Sticks" because of the war paint they used on their faces. However, on July 27, 1813, the Mississippi Militia intercepted a small band of Red Sticks who were returning from Pensacola, Florida (Spanish Territory) with ammunition and supplies.

The Red Sticks retaliated by attacking Fort Nims one month later, killing 250 Creek Indians and white settlers. A military force of 2,500 was mobilized from Tennessee, Georgia and Mississippi territories and led by Andrew Jackson and his Tennessee militia. With a three prong attack from the Tennessee in the north and Georgia militia to the east and the Mississippi militia to the west, the three fronts advanced and forced the Red Sticks into an area called horseshoe bend on the Tallapoosa River. The Red Sticks built a log compound of 300 cabins and a 6 foot high dirt barricade that extended 400 yards across the neck of the bend. Chief Menawa of the Muskogee Red Sticks would defend the fort against the attack with his 1,000 Red Stick warriors. Jackson arrived with 3,300 militia, 500 Cherokee and 100 lower Creek warriors. He advanced head-on down the neck of the bend, while General Coffee encircle the encampment on all sides.

Jackson began the bombardment in early morning of March 14, 1814. Only one-third of the Muskogee had fire arms. At noon, Jackson launched the attack on the encampment. The battle lasted 6 hours and by early evening, 800 Red Sticks were killed. Jackson lost 49 militia and 154 wounded. Chief Menawa was found with 7 bullet wounds, and escaped down river. The Treaty of Fort Jackson ended the Creek Indian Wars. Chief Menawa survived his wounds and eventually was relocated to Oklahoma as the result of the Indian Removal Act of 1829, during Andrew Jackson's Presidency. [27]

The Creek War ended shortly after the Battle of Horseshoe Bend with the signing of a Treaty of Fort Jackson between Chief Red Eagle of the Muscogee and General Andrew Jackson. The Creek agreed to relinquish 23 million acres of land in Georgia and Alabama to the U.S. Government.

The Black Seminoles

The "Black Seminoles" played an important part in American history. The Spanish called them; "Maroon", which meant "wild or untamed". The Spanish claimed the Florida Territory when Ponce de Leon discovered it in 1513. The Spanish relied heavily on the indigenous tribes of the region to defend Florida from British and French encroachments. Eventually the indigenous people were decimated by a small pox epidemic. The Spanish encouraged run-away slaves to settle in Florida and take-up arms against invaders. The Seminoles and Creek Native Americans relied on Florida as a safe haven from military attacks from Georgia, Alabama and South Carolina. America wanted to aggressively expand it borders west and south as part of its policy of manifest destiny in an effort to acquire more land, since land speculation was a popular pursuit of making fast money. Florida was a "thorn in the side" for southern plantation owners as well, since over 1,000 slaves escaped and re-established their freedom in Spanish controlled Florida. The Spanish organized a black militia to defend St. Augustine, which infuriated the southern plantation owners. Fort Mose was the first free black settlement in North America, which was established near St. Augustine, Florida in 1738. Runaway slaves immersed themselves into the local native culture, principally the Seminoles and Creek Indians. The "Maroon" established their own villages, separate from those of the Seminoles and were completely self sufficient. The Native American's kidnapped run-away blacks as slaves, but they were treated very well as compared to the conditions they endured in on the plantations.

The Creek considered their slaves as Chattel, which was the same practice used by American slave owners as well. Children who were born into slavery became the property of the owner indefinitely, even when they moved to a free state.

The Black Seminole's relied on rice and corn as their principal food sources and the villages established large farms that fed the entire village of "Maroons". They adopted the culture and customs of the Seminoles, including their dress. In 1763, during the "Seven Years' War " with France, the British took control of the French Territory of Florida's western panhandle, in exchange for territory west of the Mississippi. Even with British control of Florida's Panhandle, it remained a sanctuary for fugitive slaves from America.

The Creek (Muscogee), Apalachicola, Calusa and other tribes merged to form a single Native group called the Seminoles. Black Seminoles helped the indigenous natives communicate with the British, since they spoke Creole English called "Gullah". The Black Seminoles enjoyed 70 years of freedom, but the Creek Indians adopted the Anglo practice of chattel slavery as well. Many Black Seminoles fled to Texas, Bermuda, Caribbean and northern Mexico as a result.

Battle of Pensacola

After the Treaty of Fort Jackson, Jackson was promoted to Major General in June of 1814. He focused his attention on Pensacola, Florida, the Spanish Capital of Florida. He accused Spain of supplying arms to the Red Sticks (Creek) which was in violation of Spanish declared neutrality. He had long since made threats of invading Florida, since slaves crossed into Florida for their freedom and he courted favor with wealthy plantation owners and governors in the south to return run-away slaves back to their owner. Jackson being a slave owner himself endorsed slavery and opposed the emancipation of slaves and had political self interest in waging war with Florida. Since he was near the border of Florida with a standing army of 2,500 men, the temptation was too great, even though it would violate Madison's direct order not to invade Florida and cause an international incident. Madison wanted to establish a friendly relationship with Spain with the hope of purchasing Florida rather than dividing the two nations.

After the destruction of Fort Negro in 1818 on the Apalachicola River, Jackson constructed Fort Gadsden where Fort Negro once stood. Monroe was unaware that Jackson was building a fort in Spanish Territory. Jackson advanced his troops toward the Indian village of Tallahassee, and burned it the ground. He continued toward the village of Miccosukee and burned to the ground also. He advanced to St. Marcos and seized the Spanish Fort, where they found Alexander George Arbuthnot, a Scottish trader from the Bahamas and two Red Stick Indians. They were captured and Jackson believed they were acting as traders for the British. Jackson believed the British were providing guns to the Black Seminoles and Muscogee. The two Red Sticks were hanged without trial. Robert Ambrister was captured and charged as a spy for the British. Ambrister and Arbuthnot stood a military trial and found guilty of aiding the Seminoles and the Spanish in an effort to incite war against the United States. They were sentenced to death. Ambrister was executed by firing squad and Arbuthnot was hung from the yard-arm of his own ship. The England and Spain were outraged with the attacks and executions, which Madison and Congress had to deal with. Jackson became a very up popular person in Washington.

Battle of New Orleans

When War broke-out in 1812, Jackson was ordered to lead his 2500 militia into New Orleans to support General Wilkinson. General Wilkinson reported directly to John Armstrong Jr., the Secretary of War under Madison. When Jackson and his militia arrived in Natchez on the Mississippi River, he was ordered not to advance toward New Orleans but to disperse the militia and send them back home. It is believed that Jackson was a "loose cannon" and any involvement would result in controversy. Jackson decided not to disperse his troops, but march his entire militia back to Tennessee as a unit, which took one month in difficult weather and terrain. Many of his men died of disease, dysentery and exhaustion en-route. The men gave Jackson the name of "Old Hickory", for his toughness and leadership. Upon his arrival in Tennessee, he would receive a hero's welcome, which would follow him into his Presidency in 1828.

Jackson was later ordered to New Orleans in December of 1814, and declared martial law in the city. Jackson recruited local residents to join in the defense of New Orleans against the imminent invasion of the British. Jackson had 5,000 regular U.S. Army troops and several thousand recruited militia from New Orleans. He recruited the pirate Jean Lafitte to help defend the harbor. On December 23, 1814, the British navy arrived under the command of Admiral Cochrane and General Edward Pakenham with 10,000 regular British soldiers. They disembarked on the east bank of the Mississippi River. The British launched a frontal attack on January 8th but failed to push back and defeat Jackson's army. General Pakenham was killed during the Battle as well as 300 of his soldiers with 1,200 wounded and 500 captured, however, neither side claimed victory. Word reached New Orleans that the Treaty of Ghent had been previously signed in December ending the War of 1812, thus the Battle of New Orleans was a battle that should not have been fought.

Even though the Battle of New Orleans was a terrible loss of human life, and since the Treaty of Ghent had already been signed months earlier, Andrew Jackson became a hero which guaranteed him the Presidency in the future.

Jackson kept New Orleans under martial law long after the British left. Even though the Battle of New Orleans was fought three months after the Treaty of Ghent, Jackson ordered the arrest of U.S. District Court Judge Dominic Hall for violating the curfew as well as a State Legislator and a Lawyer who filed a Writ of Habeas corpus against Jackson. Joshua Lewis, Louisiana State Judge also filed a writ of Habeas Corpus against Jackson for the release of the U.S. District

Court Judge, Dominic Hall. Jackson ordered the execution of six members of his militia as well. The executions were not made public until his campaign for President in 1828, where his political opponent used the ordeal in New Orleans as a political tool against Jackson which characterized him as an out-of control military dictator.

The Seminole Wars

After the Revolutionary War, Spain once again gained control of Florida. In 1790, the Treaty of New York was passed in Congress in which slave owners demanded that slaves that fled to Florida for sanctuary were to be returned to their owners. Raids were conducted into Florida to capture run-away slaves. Natives Americans and Black Seminoles moved south into the swamps of central Florida to avoid capture. Many escaped to the Bahamas with the aid from British traders. In 1816, the first Seminole war began with Andrew Jackson attacking the Negro Fort in Florida that lay on the banks of the Apalachicola River between Pensacola and Tallahassee. Up-stream at the confluence of the Flint and Apalachicola Rivers in Georgia, the U.S. Army constructed Fort Scott. For some unexplained reason, two U.S. Gunboats ventured south down the Apalachicola River into Spanish Territory without permission, into Florida's panhandle and arrived at an old abandoned British garrison, known as Fort Negro which was occupied by 324 freedmen and Creek run-away slaves.

A skirmish erupted when the sailors on the two gunboats went ashore near Fort Negro and were confronted by Maroons. (African-Americans) All but one sailor was killed. When news reached Washington of the attack, John Quincy Adams was purported to authorize Jackson to attack Fort Negro.

Several gunboats were dispatched from Fort Scott and fired several cannon volleys from into the Fort. A single incendiary canon ball hit the powder magazine and exploded, killing 274 men, women and children. Sixty would survive the blast, but only 3 escaped injury, of which, Jackson ordered their execution. The Choctaw Chief was scalped by Jackson's Creek Indian guides.

The casualties and cruelty of the Fort Negro attack created a political "fire storm" for President Monroe. Monroe maintained he gave Jackson specific orders to "terminate the conflict" in Georgia, but not to exterminate the Seminoles, Creek and the Maroon's. Monroe also maintained he didn't authorize Jackson to invade Florida. Jackson was not known for his humanitarian principals and Monroe considered him an out-of-control general; however he was not well liked by any of the past and present presidents, but the public considered him a hero for squashing the Seminole's revolt, invading Florida and the Battle of New Orleans. Monroe was reluctant to censure or remove Jackson due to his public popularity.

Andrew Jackson's Presidency
(1829 – 1837)

In 1823, Jackson re-enter politics by running for the U.S. Senate for the State of Tennessee. He would narrowly win election and the same year he run for President, but would not win the majority which was required to win the Presidency. The House of Representatives would hold a vote to determine the Presidency between, Jackson, Crawford, Henry Clay and John Quincy Adams. Clay would drop out of contention and throw his votes to Adams, who would win the electoral votes for Presidency. Adams appointed Clay as his Secretary of State after the election. Jackson called the arrangement a "corrupt bargain" and resigned his seat in the Senate and returned to his home in Tennessee, out of disgust. Jackson's personality was such that he held lifelong grudges and was considered vindictive. Unfamiliar with American politics, he began plotting for the next run for the Presidency.

Jackson once again ran for Presidency in 1828 as a Democrat. His main rival was John Quincy Adams who ran as a National Republican.

Jackson would defeat incumbent John Quincy Adams for the Presidency. His campaign focused on eliminating corruption in government, tariffs and have U.S. currency based on a gold and silver standard. Jackson was anti-banking and anti national debt advocate, which at the time appealed to the common working man. American's were still bitter over the panic of 1819, that saw the collapse of the banking system due to the lack of government regulation on banks and banks investing customers deposits on risky land speculation. The public was unaware that Jackson, himself was a land speculator which contributed to the problem that he campaigned to fix.

Jackson's wife Rachel died of a heart attack three weeks after winning the election. She was buried on Christmas Eve of 1828. Jackson blamed her death on Adams for his brutal attacks on her character during the election.

Jackson was the firsts Democrat elected President in America. During that period, the Democrat Party in 1828 was very conservative. It was much more conservative than Lincoln's Republican Party of 1861. During Jackson's inauguration on March 4, 1829, he invited the public to the White House to celebrate his inauguration, which ended in a boisterous party in the White House that raged for several days. A great deal of damage to the interior furnishings of the White House was the result. It would be the first and only public party held in the White House. For the next several years, the Petticoat Affair occupied much of Jacksons first and second year of his presidency. It would end with the termination of his entire cabinet members. Jackson appointed his own advisers who were independent from his Cabinet, whom he distrusted. The media called Jackson's advisors the "kitchen cabinet". The Kitchen Cabinet was made-up of his closest allies and friends who were completely loyal to Jackson, which he demanded. Jackson's first act as President was the Indian Removal Act in which under pressure from the Georgia Governor, wanted the Native Population completely removed from the South so that more land could be made available to grow cotton, soy bean and tobacco. As a result, land speculators, politicians and Georgia militia seized native lands for their own.

The Indian Removal Act
(The Trail of Tears)

During Thomas Jefferson's Presidency beginning in 1801, Jefferson allowed the five Native American tribes; Chckaswa, Choctaw, Muscogee Creek, Seminole and Cherokee to establish an autonomous Native American nation in the American Southeast, principally in Georgia and Alabama. Jefferson wanted the tribes to embrace an agrarian society with land ownership laws, schools to teach English and Christianity. However, when Andrew Jackson became President, he wanted to use military force to remove the five tribes west across the Mississippi River and onto land not suitable for agriculture, which had little value for homesteading. The Oklahoma Territory was considered the best choice for the relocation since it was land that settles didn't want.

The Indian Removal Act was passed into law and signed by Jackson in April of 1830. The five tribes were relocated and sent west to the Oklahoma Territory, with the exception of some of the Seminole's who resisted relocation. It resulted in the Second Seminole War in Florida. More than 3,000 Seminole's were killed during the second Seminole War that lasted 6 years. Eventually those who were caught, including the Black Seminoles, were marched west to Oklahoma.

The second Creek War began in 1835 when Jackson ordered the Creek to move west. Congressman Davy Crockett was against the Act, as well as many Northern Congressmen. Jackson maintained that it was an act of mercy, since they would not survive in a white culture anyway, but more importantly they would not survive Jackson's military attacks either. The Treaty of New Echota was signed in 1835 which involved the removal of the Cherokee known as the "Trail of Tears", in which thousands of Cherokee died during the three month of winter as they march to the Oklahoma Territory. More than 45,000 Native Americans were relocated and more than 4,000 would die during the march west.

Several court challenges made their way to the U.S. Supreme Court. Chief Justice John Marshall ruled that the Cherokee nation could occupy their land independent of state law. The Court ruled that Georgia had no jurisdiction on Native American land. Jackson violated the Supreme Court decision by stating "you have your law and I have mine" and continued to remove the tribes off their land in defiance of the Supreme Court ruling. Jackson's campaign was based on the will of the "concurrent majority", as previously discussed. Jackson's view of concurrent majority is the will of the affluent, the slave owners in which he was sympathetic. [75]

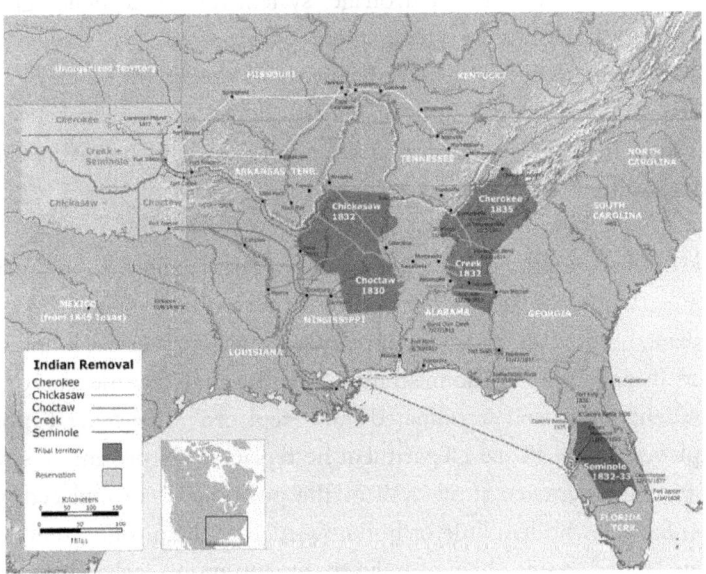

Map 12, Indian Removal Act

The concurrent majority was a proposed constitutional rule which did not take effect, which blocked any attempt of having the majority population impose a national policy upon the minority population.

Southern slave owners were concerned that the northern majority and non slave owners thus could impose laws forbidding slavery nationwide.

Jackson's Spoil System

Jackson didn't invent the Spoil System, but rather Jackson did it better than anyone else. It is also called the patronage system; however no other President abused it more than he. It would eventually be dealt with politically in 1883 with the passage of the Pendleton Act and other laws whose purpose was to protect civil servants from being fired for their political affiliation by elected officials.

Jackson operated a political spoil system better than anyone in American history. His patronage system involved building and making loyal friends by giving them positions in civil service that Jackson used to increase his influence and power over others. He placed political loyalty and obedience in his administration over anything. In reality, Jackson was a President whom the media called "King Andrew".

Jackson had a grudge and personal vendetta against John Quincy Adams, whom he felt stole the Presidency from him in 1823. To retaliate, he fired all of Adams appointees, even civil service employees hired during Adams' administration. In the first few months of his Presidency, Jackson terminated and replaced 919 federal postal employees. The Postal Department he replaced 423 postmasters with no postal experience at all. All of the positions were replaced with loyal friends who had little or no knowledge of the position they were given. As a result, like a military organization, Jackson ran the government in the same manner.

Nullification Crisis

As with other Presidents, the nullification crisis was a reoccurring theme for many presidents. In 1828, during Jackson's first year in office, Congress passed the Tariff Act of 1828, which levied a high tariff rate on southern cotton. South Carolina believed the tariff act that favored the North while punishing the southern states. South Carolina wanted to nullify the tariff act as unconstitutional and refused to abide by the tariff law. Calhoun, from South Carolina led the charge against nullification. In retaliation, Jackson introduced a bill in Congress, called the "Force Bill", which authorized military intervention to enforce the tariff acts upon any state supporting nullification as an excuse of not paying the tariff. South Carolina threatened to secede from the Union, but Jackson countered the threat with military action should it be necessary. The Tariff Act of 1828 was amended and the issue of secession and nullification by South Carolina was resolved.

Jackson's won his second term in office in 1832 with Martin Van Buren as his Vice President. He would easily win re-election over Henry Clay and John Sergeant as Clay's Vice President under the National Republican Party. Jackson vetoed a bill that extends the Second National Bank's Charter for another 10 years. He moved the federal deposits from the National Bank to the state banks and appointed his Attorney General, Roger B. Taney as his new Treasury Secretary. **(17)** Later he appointed Taney to the Supreme Court after the death of Chief Justice John Marshall. Interest rates began to rise as a result of his banking executive order. The Whig Party in Congress voted to censure Jackson for his overreach of executive power. The censure was headed by his political rival, Henry Clay who lost the election to Jackson two years earlier. Roger Taney's appointment as Secretary Treasure was rejected by the Senate and Jackson's censure would be expunged later when the Democrats assumed the majority in the Senate.

The Panic of 1837

From 1834 to 1836, the stability in Georgia and Alabama brought modest economic expansion to the south. The price of agricultural products gradually improved and for the first time in years the economy was gradually improving nationwide.

Jackson decided to issue the "specie circular" as an executive order that demanded all trade be conducted in gold and silver currency, called "specie". The United States acquired bonds from Britain to fund American infrastructure; such as roads, ports and canals in an effort to get goods to market quickly and allowed more products to be exported and available to foreign markets. It would be the first experiment in business externalism, where businesses used government to build roads, railroads, canals and ports as a third party that directly helped businesses to get their products to market. This effort would be the start of today's governmental financing of public works projects. Prior to Jackson's Presidency, Washington, Jefferson, Adams, Madison and Monroe vetoed congressional bills that introduced public funding of interstate commerce projects for the benefit of businesses rather than for public good. Washington, Jefferson and Madison believed it was a violation of the Constitution and a function of the individual States and private enterprise to build public works projects for their own community and state, since it was not specifically mentioned in the Constitution that it was a federal government responsibility.

The concept of externalization has never been tested in the Supreme Court as being constitutional or not, however, Jackson's executive order established the precedence which would go unchallenged. The Constitution made it clear that specific functions not specifically addressed in the Constitution was to be an obligation left to the sovereignty of each state and not the federal government. However, Andrew Jackson had little regard for the Constitution and in more that several occasions showed disdain for its wisdom.

In 1836, the Bank of England realized that Britain was importing more goods than they were exporting, thus causing a trade imbalance.

America's treasury expanded while Britain's treasury was shrinking due to a poor wheat harvest in Britain. As a result, Britain imported wheat from America. Bank reserves in hard currency (specie) were dwindling, and the Bank of England decided to raise the interest on loans from 3% to 5% and reduced their lending. In New York, the banks had no choice but to follow suit. The price of cotton fell by 25% in the south, causing a panic and a run on the banks.

The second cause of the panic was the result of Jackson refusing to re-charter the Second Bank of the United States in 1832. The Central Bank normally ensures that State Banks maintain a safe reserve ratio in cash in their vaults. The State Banks lacked government oversight and were free to loan-out customer's savings deposits without holding an adequate monetary reserves in the event of a run on the bank.

The final event was the real estate speculation of public lands. Andrew Jackson issued an executive order that authorized public lands in the west to be sold in gold or silver transactions only. The object was to stop or reduce speculators from purchasing cheap public land from the government on credit and resale for a substantial profit without having to front their own money. Hard currency was in short supply and few were able to purchase and pay for land on a cash basis. Banks were also in short supply since the Central Bank was dissolved, which held most of the gold and silver reserves. When the land prices began to fall, the investors and speculators weren't able to pay their bank loans with hard currency. The farmer and rancher who borrowed money from the bank were issued State Bank notes and owed more than the land was worth. The borrower was unable to pay their loan payments in hard currency. Banks in turn was unable to cover their customer's savings deposits, thus the banks foreclosed on the farmers and ranchers in an attempt to get more money to cover the run on the bank.

The panic caused 343 banks to close and 62 banks to fail. Some States weren't able to meet their bond obligations and defaulted, but by

1850, America was once again booming, after the discovery of gold in California in 1849, which added more specie in circulation. Martin Van Buren was blamed for the Panic of 1837, even though the panic began long before he took office. Much of the fault lay with the banks lack of over-sight, poor management and Jackson's monetary policy.

Jackson was the first President to have an assassination attempt on his life. As Jackson was exiting the U.S. Capital, while attending a funeral at the Capital when Richard Lawrence approached Jackson and pulled a hand gun from his pocket and pulled the trigger, but the gun misfired. He pulled another hand gun from his vest and it also misfired. Davy Crockett and several other congressmen disarmed the assassin but not before Jackson attacked Lawrence with his cane. In trial, he was declared insane, since Lawrence maintained he was King Richard III of England, however, Richard III died in 1485.

Jackson appointed six Supreme Court Justices to the U.S. Supreme Court during his tenure of eight years and admits two states to the Union, Arkansas in 1836 and Michigan in 1837. During Jackson's last days in the White House, a reporter asked him if he had any regrets while being President. Jackson replied; "he had two regrets; he was unable to shoot Henry Clay or hang John C. Calhoun" [83]

Andrew Jackson's Retirement and Death

Jackson returned to Hermitage plantation after his two terms as President. He remained active and vocal in politics. His popularity suffered drastically as a result of the panic of 1837, which continued until 1841. The panic wouldn't fully recover until 1849. Jackson directed the blame for the panic on the banks. Martin Van Buren was also blamed for the panic which cost him re-election for his second term. Andrew Jackson died at the age of 78 on June 8, 1845 of heart failure. Throughout his life he suffered from chronic headaches, abdominal pains that were partly due to the lodged musket ball in his lungs.

He was well known for his volatile temperament. He had a narcissist personality and was famous for a number of duels he fought during his lifetime. He was always accommodating and generous toward his loyal friends, but for his enemies, he was known to be vengeful, cruel, spiteful and mean-spirited. In retaliation for losing the election against John Quincy Adams, he purposely attempted to undue and undermine John Quincy Adams legacy as President. Jackson was anti civil rights and had an obvious disdain toward American Natives and African Americans. He showed little compassion or regard toward their plight, and demonstrated little regard toward their safety, health or welfare. As a life-long military general, he had little regard toward the law and the Constitution as well. [28]

Andrew Jackson's Legacy

Andrew Jackson's accomplishments before and after his Presidency will always remain controversial, and do not rise to the level of Jefferson, Franklin, Washington and many others. Even though Jackson had a flawed personality, many of his accomplishments such as negotiating 60 Native American Treaties which were eventually violated to satisfy business interest or conflicted with American's expansionism policy. His greatest legacy was not during his presidency, but rather his military career prior to becoming president. He fought in every war which opened the door to his Presidency. The Battle of New Orleans made him a hero, but few realized that the war was over 3 months before the battle. Even his military campaigns were questionable and mired in controversy and chaos. Today he is criticized for his re-settlement policy of the Native Americans in the "Trail of Tears", which resulted in the death of thousands of Native Americans in their trek to Oklahoma as well as the Seminole Wars.

He became known as the father of the "Spoil System" in which he fired more than 900 hundred federal employees and replaced them with loyal Jackson followers and family members. This action later led to the Federal Civil Service Employees Act during Rutherford Hayes's presidency, which safe guarded career civil servants from political retribution and political cronyism.

Jackson has been credited with causing the Panic of 1837; as a result of the Species Act and not extending the charter of the Second National Bank of the United States that provided oversight of State Banks and land speculation.

His externalism policy for businesses was introduced during his administration. Other presidents such as Washington, Jefferson, Madison and Monroe, feared that using public money to construct canals, roads, railroads was a violation of the constitution. Jackson was the first President that used externalism in public works projects, mostly for the benefit of businesses.

As an over view of Jackson's legacy and presidency, it can be said he was a good military leader but mostly insubordinate. His overall accomplishments during his presidency involved controversies that were surrounded in chaos and political cronyism. As for his military career, he was considered a hero by most Americans, however his most notable campaign of the Battle of New Orleans proved successful, it was a hallow victory, since the treaty of Ghant was signed before the Battle of New Orleans, for which the public was unaware. [76]

He was the first president to be brought up on charges of impeachment, but later the charges were dropped. Thomas Jefferson, Madison, Monroe and John Quincy Adams did not have a kind word about Jackson. Thomas Jefferson wrote the following in hearing of Jackson becoming President:

"I feel much alarmed at the prospect of seeing General Jackson President. He is one of the most unfit men I know of for such a place. He has had very little respect for laws and constitutions, and is, in fact, an able military chief. His passions are terrible. When I was

President of the Senate, he was Senator; and he could never speak on account of the rashness of his feelings. I have seen him attempt it repeatedly, and as often choke with rage. His passions are, no doubt, cooler now; he has been much tried since I knew him, but he is a dangerous man." "Daniel Webster's Interview with Jefferson," 1824

Martin Van Buren
(1782 – 1862)

Martin Van Buren was born in Kinderhook, New York in 1782 near Albany, New York. He was the first President not born a British subject during the British American Colonial period. His family was of Dutch ancestry and came to America in 1631. He attended local school in Kinderhook and later Kinderhook Academy and Washington Seminary. He apprenticed himself with a local law firm in Kinderhook. After six years with the Law firm he would move to New York and continue his law studies with a prominent New York law firm and admitted to the New York Bar in 1803.

Van Buren married Hannah Hoes who was his first cousin in 1807. They would have five sons together, one of which would die at birth. Martin Jr. would die in 1855 of tuberculosis. In 1819, after 12 year of marriage, Hannah died of tuberculosis and he would never remarry.

He became a member of the New York State Senate from 1813 to 1820 and serve as New York Attorney General in 1815 to 1819. In 1821 he was elected U.S. Senator from New York. He continued to be active in politics, even though he was not a polished orator. In 1829, he was elected as Governor of New York; however, five months later, Andrew Jackson would appoint him as his Secretary of State.

Van Buren was important to Jackson's bid for Presidency. To win the Presidency a candidate needed to win the majority votes from New York and Virginia, since both states had the most delegates and were the most populated states at the time. Jackson being from Tennessee and Van Buren the Governor of New York would nearly guarantee Jackson a win as Presidency in 1829. Van Buren was everything political that Jackson was not. He had charm, gracious manner and in social settings, he avoided talking politics. He selected his words carefully when speaking and avoided disclosing his political feeling.

Martin Van Buren's Presidency
(1837- 1841)

Being Andrew Jackson's Vice President may have helped him win the Presidency in 1837, but it would be a curse in his bid for a second term as President. As previously mentioned, the Panic of 1837 began during Andrew Jackson's presidency as he was leaving office and Van Buren would inherit the problems of Jackson's administration as well as the Panic of 1837, lasted until 184, the end of his presidency. He retained most of Jackson's cabinet and lower-level appointees, which was a double edge sword. Voters and Congressmen realized his intent was to continue Jackson's policies which many were becoming weary of. Van Buren blamed the panic on greedy Americans, foreign business and financial institutions. Diverting blame away from failed policies during the Jackson's presidency in which he was the key advisor to Jackson's domestic and foreign policies. Even though Jackson was no longer President, he influenced Van Buren decisions to continue his "circular monetary policy", thinking that more time was needed to see favorable results.

The Whigs wanted to re-charter the Second National Bank but Van Buren wanted to establish an independent U.S. treasury. His plan was to have gold and silver deposited and held U.S. treasury vaults in which private banks wouldn't be able to print paper currency. It wouldn't win support in Congress until 1840, but one year later in 1841 the independent treasury system would be rescinded by Congress. Van Buren continued Jackson's policy toward the Indian Removal Act of 1830, which continued with military intervention and the physically removing of Native American's from America's southeast.

The Texas annexation issue was handled differently from that proposed by Jackson. Jackson wanted to resolve the issue by using military intervention whereas Van Buren preferred using artful negotiation which accomplished much better results in the long run. The Texas annexation issue had two philosophies in America. The North feared that the South had ulterior motives in acquiring Texas as a slave territory, thus expanding slavery west of the Mississippi River. The issue of annexation of Texas was shelved during Van Buren's presidency.

The British/ Canadian border confrontation resulted into a rebellion in 1837 and 1838 over the independence of Canada from British colonization. For America, another dispute with the boundary between Maine and New Brunswick involved Van Buren to order 10,000 troops led by General Winfield Scott to settle the grievances between New Brunswick and Maine logging interests. America remained neutral in the Canadian/British Independence movement but was eager to resolve the boundary dispute between Maine and New Brunswick through arbitration and negotiation. In both situations, Van Buren's ability to resolve the boundary and annexation issues was resolved peacefully with the help of Winfield Scott. Van Buren's skill at negotiation ended with the Webster-Ashburton Treaty of 1841. Unlike Jackson, Van Buren was not a "hawk" and always approach disputes between countries to arbitration.

Van Buren and mostly Quincy Adams are best known in history for the Amistad Case. The Spanish schooner La Amistad incurred a rebellion aboard the La Amistad by Africa slaves seized in American waters. The Spanish wanted the ship and its cargo returned. A federal district judge ruled that the African's were legally free, since they were not slaves but kidnapped from Africa. He ordered them to be returned to Africa. The Van Buren Administration, representing the Government, appealed to the U.S. Supreme Court. Former President

John Quincy Adams defended the Africans with passion and reason. Quincy Adams, being a brilliant lawyer, presented a compelling argument in front of the Supreme Court Bar, which took on a great deal of public interest and support in the north. The Supreme Court ruled that the African's were free to return to Africa. It would change the public opinion in the north toward the horror of slavery and the hardships they endured, not only as slaves, but the treatment of kidnapping and transporting of slaves by to America. It also solidified Van Buren's position toward slavery as an anti abolitionist for which he would lose support in the north for his bid for a second term. .

Van Buren would appoint two Associate Supreme Court Justices during his single term as President.

Martin Van Buren's Legacy

Martin Van Buren would not be re-elected for a second term. As President in 1841, he accomplished little during his Presidency. Most historians believe his Presidency was "lack luster" and a continuation of Andrew Jackson's Presidency and historians rated him as below average as a President. His greatest accomplishment was his ability to negotiate and mediate to avoid conflict. His greatest legacy was the Webster-Ashburton Treaty that resolved issues concerning the border dispute between Maine and New Brunswick, Canada.

Chapter 10
American Expansionism Era

1841 – 1850

William Henry Harrison
(1773 – 1841)

William Henry Harrison was born in 1773 at his parents Berkeley plantation in Virginia. His family was a prominent Virginian political family in which his father, Benjamin Harrison V served as a delegate in the Continental Congress in 1774 for three years. He became one of the signers of the Declaration of Independence. His father also served in the Virginia Legislature and became the governor of Virginia in 1781 to 1784.

Harrison was home schooled until his 14th birthday at which time he attended Hampden-Sydney College. His father enrolled him into Medical School at the University of Pennsylvania; however his father would die after one year in medical school, leaving him no money to continue his education as a doctor. At the age of 17, he would enlist in the U.S. Army as an ensign and was assigned to Fort Washington. He participated in the Battle of Fallen Timbers under General Wayne's command in the Ohio frontier.

He married Anna Tuthill Symmes of North Bend, Ohio in 1795 and they would have ten children. He resigned his commission in the U.S. Military and operated a horse breeding enterprise which became successful. He would enter into politics and be elected as a Congressional delegate representing the Northwest Territory which was part of present day Ohio, eastern Michigan and the Indiana

Territory. The Indiana Territory would later become the states of Indiana, Illinois, Wisconsin and western Michigan. During Jefferson's and Madison's Presidency, Harrison was appointed Territorial Governor of the Indiana Territory in 1801. As governor, he supervised eleven treaties with Indian leaders. The treaties were designed to acquire 60 million acres of land from the Native Americans within the Indiana Territory. Some of the treaties were not popular among many of the Indian tribes.

Harrison was a staunch pro-slavery advocate. The Indiana territory requested statehood for Ohio, Indiana and Michigan. Jefferson didn't want the Northwest Territories to become slave states which became an issue between Jefferson and Harrison. Jefferson refused to admit more slave states into the union and appointed committees and assigned delegates who were anti-slavery proponents in the territory to ensure the Northwest Territories remained anti-slavery. Harrison was forced to resign as his commission as territorial governor because his authority over the region was gradually diminished by Jefferson's newly appointed committees. As governor of the Indian Territory, in 1811, he launched an attack against Chief Tecumseh of the Shawnee in Prophets Town situated on the Tippecanoe and Wabash Rivers. It would be known as the Battle of Tippecanoe. The attack made Harrison a hero and an "Indian Fighter", which later propelled himself into the White House. In 1812, with the out-break of the War with Britain, he re-enlist into the military and was given a commission as Brigadier General and constructed a fort on the Maumee River in Northwest Ohio, called Fort Meigs. He would lead his troops into the Battle of the Thames in Canada which ended in the death of Chief Tecumseh.

Harrison and Politics

After the War, he negotiated several one-sided treaties with the Native American Tribes in the Treaty of Greenville and the Treaty of Spring Wells in 1815. In 1816 he was appointed as congressmen in the U.S.

House of Representatives from Ohio. In 1819, he was elected to the Ohio State Senate and the U.S. House of Representatives in 1822 and the U.S. Senate in 1824. He would run against incumbent, Martin Van Buren in the 1840 election. Harrison was a Whig from a wealthy Virginian family, but the Whig Party stressed his gallant military career by coining the phrase "Tippecanoe and Tyler too", which became one of the most famous political slogans of all time. He would defeat Van Buren with 53% of the popular vote and arrived at his inauguration riding a horse on March 4, 1841. He was inundated with partisan patronage from the Whig Party, in which they wanted Harrison to purge all Democrats that held offices by prior Presidents. Harrison proclaimed, "So help me God, I will resign my office before I can be guilty of such an iniquity!"

On March 26th, Harrison became ill and would die nine days later. He was diagnosed with Pneumonia, however, the exact cause is not known. Harrison would be the first President to die in office, and would serve the shortest term of any U.S. President, 30 days.

William Henry Harrison's Legacy

Harrison's lasting legacies were his Native American treaties he signed while serving as Indiana Territorial Governor. He was the first sitting President to have his Photograph taken using "daguerreotype". Harrison died penniless, Congress voted his wife, Anna, a widow's pension of $25,000 plus free postage. Harrison's grandson, Benjamin Harrison was elected the 23rd President of the United States in 1889 which would be the only grandparent-grandson elected as Presidents. Harrison wasn't in office long enough to be evaluated as a President, so it is difficult to ascertain what kind of President he would ultimately become. His stance on slavery certainly didn't help his political legacy, however based on the fact that he refused to fire political opponents during his administration tells a great deal about his moral character.

DOUGLAS G. BEAUDOIN

John Tyler
(1790 – 1862)

"Let it be henceforth proclaimed to the world that man's conscience was created free; that he is no longer accountable to his fellow man for his religious opinions, being responsible therefore only to his God."

John Tyler was born in 1790 and raised in an affluent Virginia family whose ancestry dates back to William Brewster and the landing of the Pilgrims in Plymouth, Massachusetts in 1620. John Tyler was the Great Uncle of President Harry S. Truman. His father, John Senior, was a Judge and close friend and roommate of Thomas Jefferson when both served in the Virginia House of Delegates. John had had two brothers and five sisters whom he raised on the Greenway Plantation in Charles City County, Virginia.

His father paid for tutors for all of his children. John would graduate from William and Mary College in 1807. His father, John Sr. served as Governor of Virginia from 1808 to 1811. John Jr. would open a law practice in Richmond, Virginia and purchased Woodburn Plantation in 1813. His father would die in 1813 in which he would inherit his 13 slaves.

During the War of 1812, he served as a captain in the militia to protect the city of Richmond from invasion from the British. However, he never saw action during the war. For his service, he received a modest land grant in Sioux City, Iowa.

Political Career

Tyler narrowly won election into the U.S. House of Representatives in 1816 as a Republican-Democrat. He was pro-slavery and during his tenure as a Congressman, he advocated the expansion of slavery into new states and territories west of the Mississippi. Even though he disliked the thought of slavery as an institution, he didn't want to abolish slavery entirely for fear of the affects to the economy in Virginia. He would not accept a nomination for the U.S. House of Representatives in 1820 and returned to Virginia politics and elected the same year in the Virginia House of Delegates. In 1825, he was elected by the Virginia Legislature as Governor of Virginia. Upon the death of Thomas Jefferson in 1826, he would give the eloquent eulogy.

In 1827, he was elected to the U.S. Senate and was at odds with both John Quincy Adams and General Andrew Jackson, as Tyler felt they both supported a stronger Federal Government and less states rights. This was a typical political ideology ever since the drafting of the Constitution in 1787 between the northern states and the southern states. Much of the concern in the south was that the federal government was supported by the northern industrialist, who wanted to abolish slavery in the United States. Tyler's fear wasn't completely un-warranted, since the Missouri Compromised of 1820 alluded to the fact that opposition toward expanding slavery in territories created tensions between the slave states and Free states of New England.

When Andrew Jackson was elected President in 1829, Tyler's relationship became strained, however, they both agreed to extend the charter of the Second Bank of the United States. Tyler resigned from his Senate seat in 1836. He remained away from politics for the next two years but gradually re-entered Virginia Politics and elected to the Virginia House of Delegates in 1838.

John Tyler's Presidency
(1841 -1845)

During the election of 1840, two prominent politicians and a General was seeking the office of President; William Henry Harrison, Henry Clay and General Winfield Scott. Henry Clay would lose his nomination on the Whig ticket and General Scott didn't have the political support for the nomination over such powerful politicians as Henry clay and William Henry Harrison. Harrison would win the nomination as President in the Whig Party with Tyler his Vice President. He and Harrison were sworn into office on March 4, 1841. As was customary for Vice President's of the time, Tyler was not involved in Harrison's selection of his cabinet members or his appointments to key positions in government. He would serve only two hours in the Senate after the swearing-in of newly elected Senators and then returned to Williamsburg. Harrison was 68 when elected in 1841. During his campaign, he was plagued with illness which led many to think he would not complete his first term.

Harrison became ill on April 1st, just one month in office as a result of a cold that advanced into pneumonia. Tyler was notified of Harrison's illness and rushed back to Washington. Harrison died on April 4, 1841, after only one month in office. Tyler was sworn into office on the 10th of April as President of the United State at the age of 51.

The death of Harrison was the first time in American history that a President would die while in office. Confusion and debate ensued in Congress which many suggested the Vice President was to assume the duties and responsibilities as Vice President, rather than President. Tyler asserted that the Constitution clearly states that the Vice President becomes President, in the case of death or the President is unable to fulfill the office of President. He immediately insisted on being sworn in as President by Judge William Cranch in Tyler's hotel room, thus establishing the first precedent to transfer power upon the death of a President.

He kept Harrison's entire Cabinet and was informed by Daniel Webster that Harrison made policy decisions by popular vote of his cabinet. Tyler called his cabinet together gave the following speech:

"I beg your pardon, gentlemen; I am very glad to have my Cabinet such able

statesmen as you have proved yourselves to be. And I shall be pleased to avail myself of your counsel and advice. But, I can never consent to being dictated to as to what I shall or shall not do. I, as president, shall be responsible for my administration. I hope to have your hearty co-operation in carrying out its measures. So long as you see fit to do this, I shall be glad to have you with me. When you think otherwise, your resignation will be accepted. [25]

Many felt that Tyler's Presidency was not official or legal. John Quincy Adams insisted that Tyler was still the Vice President and was only acting President. Henry Clay also felt the same as Adams. Congressmen filed amendments that deleted the wording of "President" in bills and memorandums and inserted "Vice President" in its place. All attempts in Congress to force Tyler to relinquish the Presidency failed. The battle for the Presidency continued. Henry Clay lost his bid for the Presidency over Harrison and felt that Tyler would not be in line for succession, obviously for selfish reason.

In the beginning of Tyler's Presidency, he signed many bills that were sponsored and introduced by members of the Whig Party; however he vetoed the bill on the National Banking Act, which was sponsored by Henry Clay. The bill was re-worked and re-submitted and once again Tyler vetoed it. With Clay's vendetta, Tyler's Cabinet members would resign. Clay's political strategy was to force Tyler to resign and the Senate pro tempore, a Whig, would assume the Presidency. Clay's plan nearly worked except, Tyler refused to resign. In retaliation, the Whigs' expelled him from the Party. The Whig Party, as with most political parties, believed that since they nominated Harrison and Tyler on the ticket for the Whig Party, that Harrison would pass all bills presented to the President and would defer to Clay any issues important to the Whig Party. With the death of Harrison, and Tyler becoming President, Tyler didn't share the same party loyalty as Harrison or Clay. Party loyalty is everything in politics, and the Democrat Party would "blacklist" Tyler. In essence, he would become a "lame duck" president within months of assuming office.

Impeachment Proceedings

After his Cabinet members resigned, the Senate refused to confirm most of his nominees. Almost entirely out-of-spite, a battle ensued in Congress over a tariff and distribution bill that Tyler wanted to raise the tariff to cover a large projected budget deficit. Tyler vetoed the two bills over distribution of funds to states but did not address the deficit problem. The House of Representatives began impeachment proceedings against Tyler on July 10, 1842, however the first attempt to establish a nine member panel to review Tyler's conduct failed. John Quincy Adams once again appealed to Congress to begin impeachment proceedings against Tyler, but it also failed to get enough support in Congress.

Tyler's foreign and domestic policies toward expansionism were mostly successful. He expanded trade agreements with China, Germany and Great Britain. He applied the Monroe Doctrine to Hawaii when Britain showed interest in colonizing the islands.

Annexation of Texas

Tyler turned his attention on the annexation of Texas from Mexico. During the Texas Revolution of 1836, Texas declared Texas as a sovereign territory, even though Mexico didn't accept its sovereignty and considered it part of Mexico. Texas established it's on government and elected its own governor. He believed the annexation of Texas was popular in congress and the general public; he could become a serious contender for re-election in 1844.

He replaced most of his cabinet members with those who were advocates in annexing Texas. While many earlier attempts were introduced as a "rider" to funding bills, as a result of Henry Clay being a Whig and refusing to pass a single bill out of spite. His efforts continued from 1843 to the final months of his Administration in 1845. Tyler had two last ditch efforts; appoint John C. Calhoun, a Democrat in 1844 as Secretary State and avoid using the Annexation of Texas as a treaty, which required Senate approval of the Whig controlled Senate. The second option was placing the Texas annexation issue in a joint resolution of Congress where both the House and the Senate votes on the bill as a resolution. Tyler's nomination of Calhoun as Secretary of State may sway Andrew Jackson to accept Tyler into the Democrat-Republican Party and pass the Texas annexation as a Joint Resolution in the House and the Senate. Jackson wanted the Annexation of Texas, but did not what Tyler to run for a second term as President.

Calhoun was a pro slavery advocate, and needed to persuade abolitionist in Congress to vote for annexation and a possibility of war with Mexico. During the 1844 Democratic Convention in Baltimore, Maryland, the Democrats placed the Texas annexation on the party platform, since it was popular among voters. Tyler would give-up running for re-election and endorsed James K. Polk as President. Only months before the election, the House voted for annexation of Texas and the Senate won passage by only two votes. The issue of the border dispute with Mexico would be resolved during the Polk presidency.

Tyler's Retirement from Politics

Tyler fathered more children than any American President in history, with 15 from two wives. Tyler retired to his plantation in Walnut Grove and would later rename his plantation Sherwood Forest. He worked hard on his plantation and was one of the few plantation owners at the time to be successful. He rarely received visitors but he was always considered self-reliant and a hard worker.

As civil war became apparent, he became active in the Virginia Peace Conference in Washington D.C. in an effort to reach a peaceful compromise to the slavery issue. He hastily left the Conference disgusted with any hope of resolving the division between the north and the Confederate States in the south. He selected the side of pro slavery, as he had 40 slaves himself. Over the next two years, he became active in several confederate groups and signed the Ordinance of Secession. He was elected to the Confederate Congress in August of 1861 and the Confederate House of Representatives in November.

John Tyler however would die on January 18, 1862 in his room at the Ballard Hotel in Richmond, Virginia while attending the first session of the Confederate House of Representatives. Because of his role after retirement in the Confederacy, he was not honored or recognized in Washington D.C. upon his death. Jefferson Davis recognized him as a hero and draped his coffin with the Confederate flag. Tyler is buried in Richmond, Virginia, near the gravesite of James Monroe.

John Tyler's Legacy

John Tyler had a tumultuous presidency, and not necessarily the result of his own making. Historians disagree on his standing as a President. Some historians maintain he was not a good accomplished president, while others maintain he was an average and a political victim during a difficult time in American history. As for myself, I believe the later. It is however, my opinion that Tyler was a victim of circumstances beyond his control. Never before in American history had a Vice President assumed the Presidency over the sudden death of a standing President who only occupied the office for only 30 days. It divided Congress and the parties and caused political rivalry during the four years of Tyler's presidency. The Whig Party renounced him thus he became an independent President, the second since George Washington. With no political goals or aspirations from any political party he made Presidential decisions based on what he believed was right and best for the nation rather than for his political gain.

Tyler became unpopular in Congress for not stepping down as

President. He held fast to his principals and belief that the Constitution was clear that the Vice President assume the role as president in the event the President was unable to fulfill his duties. But for many Congressmen, he was to remain a Vice President and carry-out the duties as president, until a new President was elected. The issue of succession was finally resolved in 1968, when the 25th Amendment to the Constitution clarified the order of succession of the Vice President and would vindicate Tyler's assertion. While his annexation of Texas was to be his primary legacy, his greatest legacy was establishing the precedent of succession of the Vice President, which would be tested many times before the 25th Amendment became an Amendment to the Constitution.

During his Presidency, he accomplished a great deal toward establishing treaties and trade agreements with Great Britain, China and Germany, even though he didn't have the full support from either parties in Congress. He is known as the President with no party. Much of his legacy was tarnished due to his support of the Confederacy after leaving office and his position on state sovereignty which was not popular with previous presidents. Tyler made a concerted effort to mediate a compromise between both sides to avoid secession of the Southern states. He was a political outsider who became President under unusual circumstances. I consider John Tyler a good President for what he was able to accomplish under a vindictive congress who was more interested in achieving failure than creating success.

James K. Polk
(1795 – 1849)

"One great object of the Constitution was to restrain majorities from oppressing minorities or encroaching upon their just rights." James K. Polk

James Polk was born in a log cabin in Pineville, North Carolina in 1795. He is the eldest of ten siblings of Samuel Polk, his father who was a slave holder, farmer, and surveyor of Scottish and Irish descent.

When James was eight years old, he and his family would move to Duck River, Tennessee. He was home schooled by his mother and later attend Zion Church Academy. In 1816 he was admitted to the University of North Carolina as a sophomore and later graduated and studied law under Felix Grundy, a well known and respected Lawyer. He would be elected as a clerk for the Tennessee State Senate from 1819 to 1822. He was elected to the Tennessee State Legislature in 1823. In 1825 he was elected to the U.S. House of Representatives at the age of 29 and re-elected in 1827. He became a supporter and friend to Andrew Jackson and became a Jacksonian Democrat. He became Speaker of the House in 1835 and supported the "gag rule", which was to quiet any debate pertaining to slavery in the House. Polk would not seek re-election to the House and resigned as Speaker in 1839 to run for Governor of Tennessee.

James Polk's Presidency
(1845 -1849)

Polk didn't seek the Democrat nomination for President; in fact he never attended the convention. When he learned of his nomination, he accepted it under the condition that he would only run for one term. In the 1844 election between Polk and Henry Clay, a Whig, he won the election by 50% of the popular vote and 170 Electoral College votes. Polk's Vice President was Senator George Dallas of Pennsylvania. Polk's victory shocked everyone. He was well known in political circles but the general populous knew little about him before the election. He would get the southern vote, except for his home states of Tennessee and North Carolina. Even though being from a southern state, he would win New York and Pennsylvania, partly because of his Vice President, George Dallas.

Polk wanted to create a diverse cabinet based on a political division rather than a geographical in balance, since slavery had become the main issue at the time. He chose James Buchanan, a Democrat from Pennsylvania as his Secretary of State and Robert Walker of Mississippi as his Attorney General. The famous Historian, George Bancroft would be nominated as Secretary of the Navy, and would later write a biography about James Polk and other historical books about American history. In all, Polk selected 3 cabinet members from 3 slave states and 3 from free slavery states. Before Polk assumed office on March 4, 1845, President Tyler and James Polk would initiate the annexation of Texas, which was one of Polk's campaign promises, along with the acquisition of the Oregon Territory. However, during his Presidency he accomplished much more than he expected by acquiring California as well.

Polk would be the youngest American President to take office at the time and the only Speaker of the House to become President.

His established a set of goals he wanted to accomplish in the four years of his presidency. An n Independent Treasury System topped his list.

1. Reduce Tariffs.
2. Acquire the Oregon Territory.
3. Acquire California and New Mexico from Mexico
4. And the acquisition of Texas, which was already in the works under Tyler's Presidency.

The Treaty of 1818

Polk didn't concern himself about slavery, but rather focused on his policy of manifest destiny. His first order of business was the Oregon Country and the Treaty of 1818 between the United States and Great Britain, which established a joint occupation of the Oregon Country for a period of 10 years between the two countries.

The Treaty of 1818 established the Canadian-American boundary at the 49th parallel north, called the Columbia District by Britain. It allowed free passage and fishing rights to both countries. The treaty was relatively casual and mutually accepted by both parties. Years later the agreement produced a conflict between America and Britain concerning the encroachment of the Canadian Hudson Bay Company establishing forts in the Oregon Territory along the Oregon coast, Puget Sound, Columbia River and as far east as Idaho. In would later be resolved peacefully.

The Mexican-American War

President John Tyler was able to pass a bill in Congress to annex Texas two months before leaving office. What remained to be resolved were the boundary disputes with Mexico. In July of 1845, in Austin, Texas ratified the Annexation of Texas and Polk signed the annex declaration and Texas became the 28th State to enter the Union. Mexico continued not to acknowledge Texas's independence.

Polk's effort to grant Texas Statehood was an effort to grab land from Mexico which would include California should a war follow. He sent John Slidell to Mexico City to negotiate a settlement to purchase California and a border dispute along the Rio Grande River, but negotiations failed to materialize and Slidell returned to Washington. Polk asked Congress to declare war on Mexico, which they eventually did.

Polk sent 50 thousand troops into Texas in an effort to get Mexico to negotiate a peace settlement. When that effort failed, Polk ordered John C. Freemont into California to neutralize the Mexican garrison in Sonoma and Monterrey, while Stephen Kearny invaded New Mexico and took control of Santa Fe and the border area along the Rio Grande and the Baja of Mexico.

Polk ordered the landing of troops at Port of Veracruz, in the Gulf of Mexico under the command of U.S. General Winfield Scott. Zackary

Taylor was engaged in the battle of Monterrey thus defeating Ampudia's forces. Polk ordered Taylor to remain in Monterey however he disobeyed orders and marched south toward Baja California.

In August of 1847, General Winfield Scott defeated Santa Anna in the Battles of Contreras and Churubusco which placed him in a position to advance toward Mexico City. Santa Anna requested a truce with General Scott and Polk sent a negotiator, Nicholas Trist to Mexico to negotiate a truce with Santa Anna, but negotiations failed and Scott advanced into Mexico City and captured the capital. As negotiations ground to a halt, Polk ordered Trist and General Scott back to Washington, while American troops remained in Northern Mexico and California, waiting for a treaty.

Treaty of Guadalupe Hidalgo

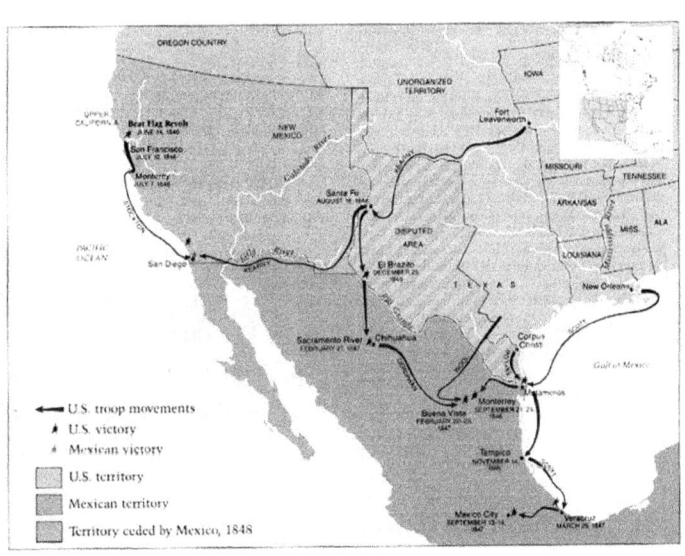

Map 13, Mexican-American War

In September of 1847, Santa Anna was replaced as President of Mexico by Manuel de la Pena. Trist was once again sent to negotiate with Mexico President Pena in the town of Guadalupe Hidalgo, north of Mexico City. On February 2, 1848, the Treaty of Guadalupe Hidalgo was signed by delegates and sent to Polk and Congress for acceptance. As part of the Treaty, America would receive 600,000 square miles of territory. California, Nevada, Utah, Arizona, parts of New Mexico, Colorado and Wyoming. In addition, Mexico acknowledged the annexation of Texas and the southern border separated by the Rio Grande River.

Mexico received $15 million, for Mexican's residing in America, they became American citizens. It was also agreed that all churches, which were mostly Catholic, were allowed to remain. The present day boundaries of America's southern border were established by the Treaty of Guadalupe Hidalgo.

The Wilmot Proviso

The Wilmot Proviso was a proposed law that would not allow slavery to expand into new states admitted into the Union or territories acquired during the Mexican War.

Pennsylvania Congressman David Wilmot attached a rider to a $2 million appropriation bill for the purpose of funding the cost of the Mexican War Treaty. The Wilmot's rider was called the Wilmot Proviso. Once the treaty with Mexico was signed, American territorial lands would expand American boundaries by 600,000 square miles. At issue was how territories and states would be formed as slave states and free slave states. Wilmot and other northern Congressmen were strong opponents to slavery however, Polk was a southerner with more than 40 slaves and several plantations, although he disliked the idea of slavery on moral grounds, he wanted slavery for economic reasons, as did most southern plantation owners.

With Wilmot attaching a rider to the appropriations bill, Wilmot was in a good position to stop slavery from expanding west into new territories west of the Mississippi. Wilmot was not the original author of the Slavery Proviso. The Northwest Ordinance of 1787 included similar language. Wilmot was not the only Congressman who advocated the Proviso, many northern Congressmen also wanted to stop the spread of slavery as well.

When the appropriations bill was presented to the Senate, it failed to get the votes for passage, since the Senate was controlled by Southern delegates. The Proviso would once again appear on the floor of the House and failed to pass the Senate. The voting followed along regional lines; North versus South, rather than political party lines, Whigs versus Democrats.

While the Wilmot Proviso failed numerous times in Congress and was never enacted into law, it would set the stage for the divisional and regional separation in America. The Compromise of 1850 would soon follow, which delayed the inevitable civil war for ten years. Because of the Wilmot Proviso, it raised the consciousness of the southern delegates and plantation owners that northern abolitionist were going to make every effort to thwart the expansion of slavery in the new territories in the west.

Polk kept his word and refuses to run for a second term in Office. One of his last acts as President was to sign a bill that created a new department, the Department of the Interior. He was skeptical about creating a department that managed public lands, thinking it was taking away states rights, but signed the bill anyway. During his Presidency he would admit three states into the Union;

1. Texas, 1845
2. Iowa, 1846
3. Wisconsin, 1848

Polk would leave the White House on March 4, 1849 and travel on a goodwill tour to New Orleans, Louisiana where he contracted cholera.

He would die at his plantation, "Polk Place" in Nashville, Tennessee on June 15, 1849, three months after leaving office.

James K. Polk's Legacy

Perhaps without exaggeration, James Polk accomplished more in four years than any President in American history. He changed the map of the United States to include a nation that expanded its boundaries from the Atlantic to the Pacific. He was among the strongest of presidents and showed uncompromising leadership and drive Even though he was reluctant to create the Department of the Interior to manage public lands, he could find nothing in the Constitution that forbid it. He is criticized for his strong arm tactics used during the Mexican War, but he placed America's manifest destiny ahead of everything. He defined the duties of the Chief Executive and Commander in Chief of the military and maintained complete oversight of his cabinet and military leaders. He is considered the 12th highest rated Presidents in American history by the C-span poll of historians. [58]

Daniel Webster
(1782 - 1852)

"If we work upon marble, it will perish; if we work upon brass, time will effaceit; if we rear temples, they crumble to dust; but if we work on men's immortal minds, if we impress on them with high principals, the just fear of God and love for their fellow-men, we engrave on those tablets something which no time can efface, and which will brighten and brighten to all eternity." Daniel Webster

Daniel Webster was born in Salisbury, New Hampshire in 1782. He was raised in a large family of nine siblings. His parents, Abigail and Ebenezer Webster owned a small farm in Salisbury. He attended a preparatory school, Phillips Exeter Academy and after which attended

Dartmouth College. After graduation he apprenticed himself to a lawyer in Salisbury, Thomas W. Thompson and admitted to the bar in 1805. He worked as a school teacher to raise money for his brother who was attending college to be a lawyer.

He became active in politics and the Federalist Party during Jefferson's and Madison's Presidency. He prepared a speech at the Washington Benevolent Society condemning the war of 1812 and Madison's embargo against Britain. He was elected to the U.S. House of Representatives in 1812 in which he served until 1817, after which he opened a law practice and became among the most famous Constitutional lawyers at the time. He argued 223 cases before the U.S. Supreme Court and won 50 percent of his cases. I won't belabor the reader with detail, but he may have been one of the most accomplished lawyers on Constitutional law in American history.

He was elected to the U. S. House of Representatives again from 1823 to 1827 and elected to the U. S. Senate from 1827 to 1841. He severed as the U.S. Secretary of State under three Presidents; .William H. Harrison and John Tyler from 1841 to 1843 and Millard Fillmore from 1850 to 1852.

During his second term in the Senate he opposed the annexation of Texas and the Mexican-American War. He felt that America was "teetering" on a delicate balance between slave states and non-slave states, yet supported the Missouri Compromise of 1850 which included the Fugitive Slave Law, which was not popular in the Northern States, especially Massachusetts for which he represented. He would give one of his most powerful and moving speeches in an effort to clarify his acceptance of the Compromise of 1850 and the Fugitive Slave Law by giving the "Seventh of March Speech" which was not well received by the abolitionist and the northern states. He became so unpopular in New England he would resign his Massachusetts Senate seat in 1850. Millard Fillmore would assume the Presidency after the death of President Taylor in July of 1850.

Fillmore appointed Daniel Webster as his Secretary of State.

Webster continued to speak-out openly for the Compromise of 1850 and the Fugitive Slave Laws while serving as Secretary of State. Jury Nullification was used in the north to acquit those who violated the Fugitive Slave Laws. Webster insisted that the law be enforced which only alienated Webster more. He would be passed over in the Whig Party for a second time as a result, which effectively ended his political career. Not to be discouraged, Webster campaigned again in 1852 as a Whig for the President. He would come in third in a field of three and failed once more to get a nomination.

Daniel Webster's Death

Daniel Webster would die in October of 1852 at his home in Marshfield, Massachusetts. He had fallen from his horse and suffered a severe head injury. He had cirrhosis of the liver which complicated any hope of recovery. His last words were; "I still live."

Daniel Webster's Legacy

Webster's brilliance as an orator and legal scholar has never been questioned, however, his moral values as a Lawyer was often called into question. He was always in heavy debt and solicited money from business men to pay for his drinking and over indulgence at parties. He lived an opulent life style and owed almost everyone money. He had ambitions to become President; however he was not favored by the political parties because of his outspoken nature and lack of moral character. His moral behavior and his demeanor would distance him from other politicians and political parties. He was offered the Vice Presidency on the ticket with William Henry Harrison in 1841, but Webster turned down the offer, claiming that he was worthy of being the President and not a Vice President. Harrison would die 30 days after being elected and John Tyler, his Vice President, became President. That would have been the closest Webster would have become President, but his vanity would take the opportunity away. Webster was known to be arrogant and at times mean spirited. He felt he was superior to his peers. While his accomplishments as a lawyer, orator and constitutional scholar would give him popularity, fame and notoriety while he was alive, history has not been kind to his legacy.

Zachary Taylor
(1784 – 1850)

"The power given by the Constitution to the Executive to interpose his veto is a high conservative power; but in my opinion it should never be exercised except in cases of clear violation of the Constitution, or manifest haste and want of due consideration by Congress." Zackary Taylor

Zachary Taylor was born in 1784 on his family's plantation in Orange County, Virginia. He was a direct descendant of William Brewster who was the leader of the Pilgrim colonist that arrived on the Mayflower and landed at Plymouth, Massachusetts. His fourth cousin was James Madison, the fourth President of the United States. His father, Richard Taylor served as a colonel during the American Revolution.

His family migrated west from Virginia and established a farm in Louisville, Kentucky. They expanded the farm into a 10,000 acre plantation with 26 slaves. Zachary spent little time toward his education and especially his grammar and writing skills and decided on a military career which best suited him. In 1808, he enlisted into the U.S. Army and was assigned to New Orleans. Two years later he met and married Margaret Mackall Smith in Louisville. They would have six children together, however two would die in infancy and one died at the age of 21 of malaria.

Taylor's Military Career
(1808 to 1848)

Taylor's military career lasted from 1808 to 1848. He fought in the War of 1812 against the British in the Siege of Fort Harrison and the Black Hawk War during the second Seminole Indian War and the Battle of Lake Okeechobee. Taylor became famous during the Mexican-American War with several successful battles in California and in Northern Mexico with the battles of Palo Alto, Resaca de la Palma, Monterrey and Buena Vista. When he arrived in New Orleans, he received a hero's welcome.

Taylor's Political Career
(1848 to 1850)

With his overwhelming popularity in the Mexican-American War, the Whig Party wanted Taylor to run for Presidential. Taylor disliked political parties and wanted to run as an independent, since he felt strongly in a central banking system and thought it foolish to discuss expanding slavery west of the Mississippi River. He opposed the secession of states, protective tariffs and government funding of internal improvement in public works projects.

Taylor felt strongly that presidential power to veto bills should only be exercised on bills that violated the Constitution. He also felt it was in poor judgment to have the President interfere in bills before Congress. Taylor became the presidential candidate in the Whig party in which his running mate for Vice President was Millard Fillmore. The Whig Party dissolved after Fillmore's presidency and most members joined the newly formed Republican Party under Presidential candidate, John C. Freemont of New York, during the election of Franklin Pierce as President in 1853.

Zachary Taylor's Presidency
(1849 – 1850)

He was not a polished politician and would not follow the Whig platform during his Presidency. His first order of business was to appoint the first Secretary of the Interior. During his inaugural address on March 4th, he made it clear he would follow Washington's lead in avoiding "entangled alliances" with other countries. During the first summer of his presidency, he toured the Northeast and gave speeches in an effort to acquaint himself with the region and the people who elected him. He attended Dolley Madison's funeral and gave the eulogy in which he referred to Dolley Madison as the "First Lady". It would be a term used throughout history in referring to the President's wife.

The Mexican Cession was a major issue during the first year of his presidency. Even though he was from Kentucky and a slave owner, the south believed they could count on him to tip the balance of power in government toward expanding slavery into new American territories and states in the west. The North believed his forty years as a top general in the Union Army and being the most famous General since Washington would help abolitionist from expanding slavery west. Taylor was opposed to the concept of slavery. As with Washington, Jefferson and Madison who also opposed slavery. He avoided the issue of slavery throughout his campaign, so both sides weren't sure of his political position until after being elected President, since slavery was a volatile issue during campaigns at the time.

Under a stroke of political genius or luck as it maybe, the California gold rush of 1849 saw an explosion in the California population. Most believed the California Territory should include Utah as well, but Taylor wanted California and New Mexico to become two separate States rather than a single territory after Mexico's land cession. He promoted a bill in Congress for California's Statehood, which include a portion of Utah and New Mexico. California submitted a State Constitution that included a provision allowing California to be a free State and Congress approved its Statehood, but rejected New Mexico's claim to Statehood as a result of Texas' claiming a portion of New Mexico, which had to be resolved before statehood could be granted. The Utah Territory had been settled by the Church of the

Ladder Day Saints who drew-up their own territorial boundaries; however Congress rejected their boundary claim. When California became a State in 1849, it created an up-roar in the south among southern Democrats who openly accused Taylor as a Southern traitor. With California becoming a State, it gave the Northern States an edge in Congressional delegates over the southern delegates. In February of 1850, southern leaders openly announced that they would secede from the Union and Taylor immediately took action by informing them:

"......taken in rebellion against the Union, he would hang.......with less reluctance than he had hanged deserter and spies in Mexico."

For the southern leaders upon receiving Taylor's ultimatum, they knew that Taylor did not make idle threats.

The Compromise of 1850 was before Congress for consideration. Congress was unable to get the Compromised passed during his tenure as President. During the election of 1849, Taylor kept his command of the Western Division until January of 1849. When selecting his cabinet, he refused to appoint any Democrat's or Whig's to his cabinet.

Zachary Taylor was warm and comfortable in conversation with others, but at times out-spoken. He was shy when meeting people for the first time. He chose his words carefully before speaking as to not offend anyone. He was always gracious and a perfect gentlemen at social occasions and was admired by the women for his sincerity and gracious hospitality and manners. His one flaw was his manner of dress. Taylor was best known for mixing military attire with civilian clothes for comfort. His clothes were not neatly pressed as would be expected of a Major General with 40 years of military service. He was 5 feet 8 inches tall, wore reading glasses and walked with one arm behind his back. He was well liked and respected by all his men and under his command and was considered a great leader.

Zachary Taylor's Death

Taylor attended a 4th of July celebration at the Washington Monument where he and his cabinet members consumed large amounts of Cherries and milk. Over the next few days his condition worsened. The Doctor's believed it to be Chorlera Morbus, an intestinal infection. Several of his cabinet members who attended also became ill with similar symptoms. On July 9, 1850, Zachary Taylor died at the age of 65. It was never established medically what type of illness Zachary Taylor died from. During his funeral procession through the Streets of Washington, more than 10,000 mourners lined the streets. He is buried in the Zachary Taylor National Cemetery, Louisville, Kentucky.

Zachary Taylor's Legacy

Taylor was the last President to own slaves while in office. Even though he was a slave owner, he was steadfast in curtailing the spread of slavery west of the Mississippi River. While Taylor was only in office for 16 months, most historians failed to rate him well as a President, however his accomplishments and patriotism in battle and service to America shouldn't be overlooked. His goal while in office was to resolve the issue of slavery, but died before he was able to accomplish his final goal. He had served the nation for 40 years as a great military General with campaigns during the War of 1812 and the Mexican-American Wars.

After Taylor's death in the summer of 1850, Millard Fillmore became President. Taylor's last act as President was the Clayton-Bulwer Treaty in which he negotiated an agreement with Britain to acquire land in Nicaragua for a possible site for a Canal through Central America, connecting the Atlantic to the Pacific Oceans as a trade route. Britain was actively acquiring land for a canal and America wanted a joint effort with Britain for the construction. The canal would not be constructed until Theodore Roosevelt's Presidency, but today's

Panama Canal would have its origins during Zachary Taylor' Administration, nearly 60 years before the actual construction. In the 16 months of his Presidency, he accomplished a great deal. He supported the principals of separation between the executive and legislative branch of government, held America together when southern states wanted to secede from the Union and was a visionary that helped America realize its manifest destiny. I consider him among one of the more important Presidents in American history.

Chapter 11
Prelude to Civil War

1850 – 1861

The pretext to the America Civil War began as early as 1776, when the founding fathers of the U.S. Constitution failed to address the issue of slavery in the document. It was assumed that the Constitution allowed slavery because it existed prior to the signing of the Constitution in 1787. Even Abraham Lincoln acknowledged the constitutional legality of slavery in the south, but disagreed that slavery was a constitutional right to be expanded into new territories and states. Tensions began to manifest itself decades before Abraham Lincoln became the 16th President in 1861. Dissension and distrust between regional boundaries dividing the north and south which began as early as 1828, when congress passed the Tariff Act of 1828. The northern States levied tariffs on southern cotton imports bound to northern textile mills in New England. The tariff rates excluded imports from Britain, which infuriated Southern plantation owners and southern politicians. The South had few industrial plants to process cotton into yarn and clothing and grain mills for wheat and soy beans, in which the south depended on for processing. The system made the northern industrial states wealthy while the Southern economy remained stagnant. The South had no desire to industrialize, since they labor to do the work for them. In the north, it was the opposite, they industrialized out of necessity and cut labor cost and improve production through the use of machinery.

The tariff act started sectionalism between the agrarian South and the industrial North. In addition to the unfair tariff structure, slavery became the overriding issue that further exacerbated the sectionalism. Rhode Island became the first state to abolish slavery shortly after the signing of the Constitution in 1787, which gradually spread throughout the New England States. It would become a political issue since the Southern States didn't have the Congressional representation to change the law. As new states were added, the northern States acquired more and more electoral delegates. By 1840, America had 15 northern states and 11 southern states and of the 11 southern States, most of the population consisted of African-American slaves (40%) who were only counted as 1/5 toward apportionment. The northern States had 181 electoral votes, whereas the South's 111. It would require 148 electoral votes to win the Presidency. The south no longer had the voting power to elect a southern President or a quorum to pass a bill.

The Missouri Compromise of 1820 became a factor that slowed down the push to add more slave states but didn't eliminate the tensions between the north and south. The Dred Scott decision in 1857 created the final rift between pro slavery and anti-slavery factions and dashed away any hope for a solution and compromise between the two sides.

The American Civil War began in 1861; however few history books mentions the 24 year period prior to the start of the civil war. Eight Presidents were elected president but only remained in office for an average of 3 years each. Several died in office and the remainder would serve a single term. Of the 6 who served a single term, historians rated their Presidency as the worst or at the bottom of the rating scale. There is a perfect explanation for this as I will discuss later in the chapter. While Presidential ratings are seldom an accurate measure of a person's life long accomplishments, even though some Presidents were sympathetic to the south, yet had only modest influence in the final outcome of finding a solution.

Political Parties such as the Whig Party gradually lost support of the voters. New political parties began to immerge and run for President. Part of the problem was the pending collapse of the Whig party while the Democrat Party began to fractionalize into the northern Democrats and Bourbon Democrats in the South. With the exception of Martin Van Buren and the Depression of 1837, it became a major factor that cost Van Buren the re-election for his second term. The other seven Presidents were caught in a political "whirlpool" between political factions, abolitionist from the North, Free Spoiler's and Southern pro-slavery advocates. If they openly supported abolition, they would lose the southern vote; if they supported slavery, they would lose the northern vote. It became a delicate balance for the south but not nearly as much for the north. A pro-slavery advocate needed most of the southern delegates and at least 1/2 of the northern delegates to carry a presidential election.

During the 24 year period from 1837 to 1861, the President was helpless to institute programs and policy without the support of a unified majority in Congress. Congress was in tight control of four dominate congressmen, Calhoun, Clay, Webster and Douglas.

Millard Fillmore
(1800 – 1874)

Millard Fillmore was born in poverty and raised in a long cabin in Locke, New York in 1800. He had only limited schooling and at the age of 15, he apprenticed himself as a cloth maker. At the age of 17 he left his apprenticeship and enrolled in New Hope Academy where he married Abigail Powers in 1826.

In 1819, he got a job as a clerk for a local judge and apprenticed himself for 4 years which led to his admittance to the New York Bar in 1823. Over the years, he became part of the New York State Assembly and the U.S. House of Representatives. He joined the Whig Party and held various prestigious positions in New York as Comptroller and chief financial officer.

The Whig Party recruited Fillmore as Zackary Taylor's Vice President in 1849. Fillmore was opposed slavery as was Taylor.

Compromise of 1850

In January of 1850, Senator Henry Clay gave a speech in the Senate proposing a division of the Union into Free States and Slave States. Henry Clay was a prominent Whig in Congress while Stephan Douglas a Democrat from Illinois and elected to assist Clays' bill for passage in Congress by creating several small rider bills. Clay was unable to debate the merits of his bill in the Senate because of poor health and Stephan Douglas took up the cause for passage. The bills contained five elements;

1. California would be admitted to the Union as a Free State.
2. Utah and New Mexico Territories would decide by popular vote if they wanted to be a Slave State or Free State.
3. Texas would cede land to New Mexico, Colorado, Kansas, Oklahoma and Wyoming for a payment of 10 million dollars to pay its debts.
4. The Fugitive Slave Act was strengthened.
5. Slave trade was abolished in Washington DC but not slavery.

The bill had heavy opposition from the Northern Whig's and Southern Democrat's as well, thus passage required a compromise and political maneuvering. President Zachery Taylor hadn't made clear of his position toward the Fugitive Slave Act which was part of the bill, but was strongly opposed to slavery for new territories and states. However, he would die in July and Vice President Millard Fillmore became President and was forced to accept the Compromise of 1850.

The bill passed both house of Congress in September of 1850. The opposing congressmen were from the South and passage of the bill only served to postpone the inevitable between Slave States and Free slave States. Civil war was averted for a decade which allowed the

Northern States to become more industrialized and more populated than the south. Railroads were constructed in the North to carry passengers and goods west to coal fields and iron mills. The south used slave labor to work the fields thus found it unnecessary to industrialize, which was a situation that would eventually cost them the Civil War.

The Fugitive Slave Law

The Fugitive Slave Law was the 4th Statute in the Compromise of 1850. It strengthened the original Fugitive Slave Act of 1793. The law required all judicial officials in all free slave states and territories to return runaway and escaped slaves to the owner of origin. US Marshals failing to return runaway slaves were liable for a $1,000 fine. Slaves were not allowed a jury trial or testify on their own behalf. Anyone aiding a runaway slave was liable for a $1,000 fine also. The law was so egregious that even George Washington's 300 slaves he freed upon his death could not escape the law and were forced back into slavery. It set off bounty hunt for northern freemen to collect a bounty for capturing slaves who worked in the north and were freed by former owners.

He also did nothing to abolish the owner from severe punishment of runaway slaves and those who were granted freedom by the slave owners. Fillmore's signing of the Fugitive Slave Act tarnish his Presidency and any hopes for a second term. He would lose popular support in the Northeast as a result. In the north they were defiant of the law and sheltered hundreds of Freemen.

Fillmore was known to be a slow and deliberate speaker and did well in small groups and one-on-one conversations, but in large audiences his speeches failed to connect with the audience. The audience felt he was too unemotional and perhaps expressionless in his presentation, which made his speeches boring and ineffective.

Millard Fillmore's Legacy

Fillmore was President for only three years; however, his greatest accomplishment while president was sending Mathew Perry to Japan and opening up relations with Japan. The Compromise of 1850 delayed the Civil War but it was repealed three years later with the passage of the Kansas-Nebraska Act of 1854. Up to this point in history, no single President wanted to deal with the issue of slavery during their Presidency, with perhaps Zachary Taylor. Fillmore failed to get nominated by the Whig Party as a presidential candidate for a second term, partly due to his signing of the Fugitive Slaves Laws that ruined any chance for a nomination. Fillmore was very active in the No Nothing Party, whose platform was based on political conspiracies and deep state theories and anti immigration and anti Catholics. When he lost the election as the New York Governor, he believed his loss was the result of the immigrant Catholics. Millard Fillmore retired from politics after suffering a divesting defeat for President in 1855 as a candidate in the No Nothing Party. He was critical of Abraham Lincoln and his predecessor, James Buchanan. He felt that Buchanan should have taken immediate action in 1860 when South Carolina seceded from the Union. His legacy has always been tarnished over his criticism of other Presidents and his disdain for Catholics and Immigrants in general. He gravitated toward fringe party politics throughout his political career and those that embraced conspiracy theories. Millard Fillmore died from the effects of a stroke in Buffalo, New York in 1874.

Franklin Pierce

(1804 – 1869)

Franklin Pierce was born in Hillsboro, New Hampshire in 1804. He served as the 14th President from 1853 to 1857. He was one of the forgotten Presidents in American History. Much was due to the Civil War and Abraham Lincoln, who over-shadowed his accomplishments during his Presidency.

He was not expected to become a Democratic candidate, but during the Democratic Convention in 1852, 40 names were considered. Most of the prospective candidates were disqualified until Franklin Pierce's name appeared. He was popular and out-going and a devout family man. Well educated; attended Bowdoin College and Northampton Law School. He was a member of the U.S. House of Representatives and a war hero and served in the U.S. Army as a Brigadier General during the Mexican American War. He was wounded in battle and ordered his men to lash him into the saddle of his horse so he could lead his men into a Charge during the Battle of Churubusco. He would eventually collapse due to the pain, but his heroism earned him the respect of his men and his commanding officer, General Winfield Scott.

He received criticism from others who claimed he was a coward and not a hero, and that his injuries were due to carelessness rather than heroism. He would live with the stigma of cowardice for the rest of his life. After his death in 1869, Ulysses S. Grant published his memoirs and settles the issue of his dedication and military service;

"Whatever General Pierces' qualifications may have been for the Presidency, he was a gentleman and a man of courage? I was not a supporter of him politically, but I knew him more intimately than I did any other of the volunteer generals."
[26]

Franklin would marry Jane Means Appleton in 1834 and they would have three children. One would die at infancy while the other two would die at four years old of typhus. Benjamin was killed at the age of 11 while Pierce and his wife were en-route to Washington. The train they were riding in derailed and killed young Benjamin Pierce, just two month before his inauguration. His wife, Jane was constantly ill and suffered from tuberculosis and bouts of depression and psychological issues.

DOUGLAS G. BEAUDOIN

Franklin Pierce's Presidency
(1853 – 1857)

Pierce would narrowly win the election in 1853 over his former commanding general during the Mexican-American War, Winfield Scott, who was a Whig. His cabinet consisted of a well rounded mix of different parties; Whigs, Free-soiler's, Democrats and Independents. His Vice President, William Rufus King would die of tuberculosis after one month in office. The Constitution was silent on the issue of appointing another Vice President thus the Senate President Pro tempore, David Atchison of Missouri would be the next successor to the Presidency should something happen to Pierce.

His most notable accomplishment during his presidency was the Gadsden Purchase in 1853. The Gadsden Purchase added part of northern Mexico to America which later became known as Arizona and New Mexico. He repealed part of the Compromise of 1850 that added Kansas and Nebraska as territories under the Kansas-Nebraska Act of 1854.

The Kansas-Nebraska Act of 1854 was drafted by Senator Steven A. Douglas of Illinois for the purpose of opening-up the mid-western territories; Kansas and Nebraska, which was known as America's heartland and notable for its wheat and corn crops. The Transcontinental Railroad had been on the drawing board since the early 1840's, which was designed to traverse the mid-western plains, known as the "Grain Belt" with a terminus in Chicago. It transported passengers as well as wheat, corn, barley and cattle to market and made connecting routes west and east from Chicago. The railroad was built by private interests and financed by the government through public land grants, which was supported politically by Douglas who had real estate holdings near Chicago and along the proposed railroad corridors west toward Omaha, Nebraska, the starting point of the transcontinental railroad.

When the Kansas-Nebraska Bill entered the Senate committee on Territories, Stephan Douglas became chairman and he aggressively pushed the Bill for passage. One obstacle for passage was Senator David Atchison of Missouri, who was the Senate President Pro tempore and wheeled a lot of influence in the Senate. Atchison said he would only support the Bill if Slavery was allowed in Nebraska. Under the Missouri Compromise of 1850, slavery was prohibited and since the Nebraska territory was never part of the Louisiana Purchase, and not deemed a free state or slave state. All of the Southern Senators voted to table the Bill rather allow Kansas and Nebraska to become free slave states.

In January of 1854, Douglas introduced a modified version of the Nebraska Bill that extended the Nebraska Territory boundary from Kansas to the Canadian border. The territory would later be divided into states. (North and South Dakota, Idaho, Colorado, Wyoming) The remaining territory became the State of Nebraska, (Statehood in 1867). Douglas included a provision that allowed slavery to be determined by "popular sovereignty", in which each state voted to determine their status as a slave state or free slave state.

Douglas's proposal was a brilliant attempt to encourage passage of the Kansas-Nebraska Act and defer any debates on the issue of Free State and slave state. The Northern States were opposed to the Bill, while the Southern States press congressional delegates for passage. For more than 4 months the debate raged in Congress until its final passage came on May 30, 1854. As a result of the Act, the Compromise of 1820 would be repealed except the provision allowing Missouri statehood as a slave state. The Missouri Compromise of 1850 would be appealed to allow the Kansas and Nebraska Territories to determine their destiny by "popular sovereignty" (public vote) to determine if they are to be a slave state or a free slave state.

Bleeding Kansas

DOUGLAS G. BEAUDOIN

As a result of the "popular sovereignty" provision in the Kansas-Nebraska Act, Kansas requested to be admitted into the Union. However, in accordance to the Kansas-Nebraska Act, an election had to be held to determine if it were to be admitted to the Union as a free slave state or a slave state. The territorial capital was Lecompton and the unofficial territorial legislature was in Topeka. With news of Kansas having territorial elections, settlers poured across the border from Missouri and as far east as New England for the purpose of voting for or against Kansas becoming a slave state. Violence erupted after anti-slavery radical, John Brown and his sons murdered five pro-slavery squatters with a broadsword. Kansas was in a state of civil war. President Pierce order federal troops into Kansas and dispersed the anti-slavery legislature. When ballots were tallied, the pro-slavery faction won, however not without claims of voter fraud and ballot "stuffing". Congress refused to certify the election and Kansas was not admitted into the Union.

Pierce wanted to make government more efficient by implementing a civil service system with the hope of eliminating crony capitalism. Thirty years later, the Pendleton Act would be passed in which selective service examinations would become law and civil service employees could not legally be remove service. He would expand the duties of the Attorney General's Office by selecting Federal Judgeships and District Attorney's.

Pierce reformed the Treasury Department and appointed Treasury Secretary James Guthrie to lead the reformation of the Department. During the Whig Administration, private banks were not legally authorized to withhold government funds such as taxes and tariffs. Guthrie was able to secure the funds from private banks but was not successful in prosecuting officials for corruption and fraud.

Pierces' Secretary of War, Jefferson Davis made plans to survey and construct railroads for national security. He expanded the size of the U.S. Capital and Constructed the Washington Monument. Behind the scenes of diplomacy, three U.S. Diplomats stationed in Europe proposed the purchase of Cuba from Spain for $120 million. The Secretary of State, William Macy, prepared the Ostend Manifesto that advocated the military take-over of Cuba from Spain if Spain refused their offer to purchase, however Spain refused. Part of the plan was to annex Cuba as a slave state which would give the south more territory and more delegates in Congress. The southern democrats campaigned on the premise that the acquisition of Cuba was part of America's policy of manifest destiny; however the Northern States viewed it as a political maneuver to grab slave territory to gain a political advantage in Congress. The effort to acquire Cuba from Spain failed to materialize until the Spanish American War under Theodore Roosevelt in 1903.

During the 1856 Democrat Convention, Pierce didn't get nominated for a second term as President. James Buchanan became the Democratic nominee and ultimately President after defeating John C. Freemont of California under the first Republican ticket. On March 4, 1857, Franklin Pierce and his cabinet left the White House. It would be the first and only time in American history that the entire Cabinet members would serve the entire four years under a single President. Buchanan entered the White House and replaced all of Pierces' cabinet members.

He would retire to Concord, New Hampshire, but remained politically active by giving speeches against Civil War and his disdain for the new Republican Party. He remained friends with Jefferson Davis and visited him often after the war while he was in prison at Fort Monroe in Virginia. The Media in the North criticized Pierce as a southern traitor and sympathizer. Upon Lincoln's assignation, he refused to lower the flag half mast in Lincoln's honor.

His Wife, Jane would die of tuberculosis in Andover, Massachusetts in 1863. After his wife's death, his drinking became worse and he suffered from advanced cirrhosis of the liver. He was a lifelong friend of Nathaniel Hawthorn, where both attended Bowdoin College together. On October 8, 1869, Franklin Pierce would die in the presence of his caretaker.

President Grant declared a day of national mourning in honor of Franklin Pierce. He would be interred next to his wife and two sons in Concord, New Hampshire.

After Franklin Pierces' death, he was nearly forgotten in history. Historians consider Pierces' Presidency a failure, which I respectively disagree or at least in part. He was blamed for the Kansas-Nebraska Act, which was in fact the "brain child" of Stephen Douglas who designed and pushed the act through Congress; however he did sign the bill into law.

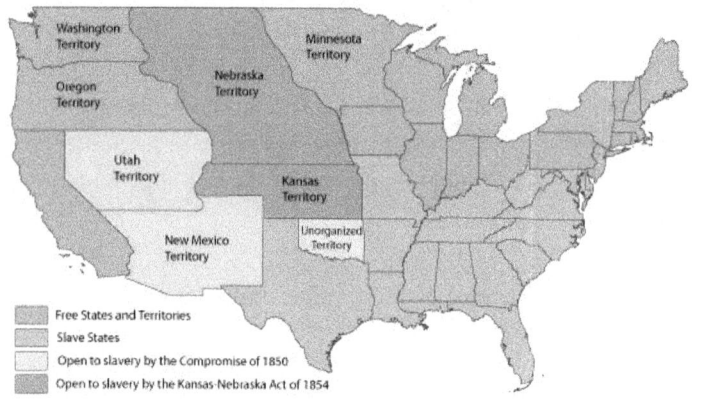

He is also criticized for the collapse of the Democrat Party for the next seventy years, but in fact, James Buchanan preceded him as a Democrat President, so I doubt there is any substance to the claim. With Lincoln becoming President, it would over-shadow other presidencies prior to the Civil War. At this point in American history and even prior to 1820, a compromise didn't appear to be an option acceptable to either side. Civil War at some point was the only viable option. Zackary Taylor and Andrew Jackson both suggested military action in the event of secession by the south but Peirce was sympathetic to the southern cause. Peirce's accomplishments were well established prior to becoming president. During his Presidency; he reformed the Treasury Department, increased military pay and retirement, established a selective service examination system for competitive employment in government and targeted government corruption. He expanded the duties and function of the U.S. Attorney's office and the Department of Justice, thus allowing them to oversee and recommend appointments of Federal Judges and District Attorney's. He negotiated a trade agreement with Canada and Japan and signed the Guano Islands Act which was an act that selected a random group of Islands in the Pacific as claimed territories of the United States.

The act reads:

"Whenever any citizen of the United States discovers a deposit of guano on any island, rock, or key, not within the lawful jurisdiction of any other Government, and not occupied by the citizens of any other Government, and takes peaceable possession thereof, and occupies the same, such island, rock, or key may, at the discretion of the President, be considered as appertaining to the United States. "
-First section of Guano Islands Act-

He constructed the Washington Monument and expanded the U.S. Capital and Signed the Gadsden Purchase. He served in the U.S. House of Representatives and became a General in the Mexican-American War. Franklin Pierce may not have been a notable President at the time, but he was a devoted President who accomplished a great deal in his four years in office as well as his distinguished military service. Like so many Presidents during the period of resolving the slavery issue, he became a victim of the times.

Stephen A. Douglas
(1813 – 1861)

Stephen A. Douglas was born in 1813 in Brandon, Vermont. His father was a physician and a graduated of Middlebury College. He would die suddenly when Stephen was only a few months old. Douglas was educated in local schools and as a teenager apprenticed himself as a cabinet maker. He attended Canandaigua Academy in upstate New York in 1830.

He taught school while working for a local law firm. He later became close friends with Henry B. Payne who was also studying law. In 1833, he and Payne moved to Cleveland, Ohio and later to Winchester, Illinois where the two opened a school and charged $3 per student per year as tutors. He eventually settled in Jacksonville, Illinois and was admitted into the Illinois Bar. In 1834, he was appointed State Attorney of Morgan County, Illinois for a two year term and joined the Democrat party in the interim and elected to the Illinois House of Representatives. He served as Illinois Secretary of State and Associate Justice of the Illinois Supreme Court in 1841. In 1843 Douglas was elected to the U.S. House of Representative for Illinois and the U.S. Senate in 1846.

In 1847 he married Martha Martin of North Carolina. Martha's father died one year later and she would inherit his father's 2,500 acre cotton plantation and 100 slaves on the Pearl River in Mississippi. He hired a manager to tend the plantation.

Douglas was an advocate for the Compromise of 1850 and supported Henry Clay's political position on the Compromise. Clay being a Whig and Douglas a Democrat, the two worked together to debate the issue in Congress for passage. During the 1852 Presidential election, the Democrat Party considered Douglas their best hope for winning the Presidency, but because of "back door" politics, Franklin Pierce was named the Democrats choice as the Presidential candidate. Douglas would win his re-election to the U.S. Senate in 1853. Douglas was pro railroad expansionist and secured through Congress land grants for funding the Illinois Central railroad that was to link with other railroad systems in the South and North.

Kansas-Nebraska Act of 1854

During the Missouri Compromise of 1820, slavery was prohibited beyond the 36 degree – 30 minute compromise line. The Compromise of 1850 further affirmed the Compromise line of 1820. Douglas being a slave owner himself, and a real estate speculator who owned large tracts of land near Chicago and in Mississippi, he maintained a close alliance with the railroad industry, and saw an opportunity to make his Chicago real estate more valuable if the railroad was built near his land. Southern congressmen accepted a proposal of a central railroad route into Chicago if slavery was allowed in the new territories. Douglas accepted the agreement and allowed the Territories to choose to be a slave state when applying for Statehood, known as "Popular Sovereignty". Douglas' popularity in the North suffered as a result of his decision to support the Southern interest and more importantly his ties with the railroad. The media in the north was ruthless toward "doughface" Douglas as they called him. Douglas countered the criticism by claiming he resolved the slavery issue in America by allowing each state to choose their destiny when it came to slavery. He felt certain it would avoid future conflicts between the north and the south.

In 1856, Douglas made an effort to secure the Democratic nomination for President. He used the ploy of avoiding the slavery issues altogether and practiced middle of the road campaign politics, in an effort to garner support for the South and the North. The Whig Party collapsed in 1854 over the Kansas-Nebraska Act, and Douglas hoped to gain support from the old Whig Party members. Lincoln gave three separate speeches criticizing Douglas for his position during the

Kansas-Nebraska debates, and his position toward "popular sovereignty". He would once again loose the Democratic nomination for President to James Buchanan in November of 1856.

The Dred Scott Supreme Court decision had a devastating consequence for Douglas when the Supreme Court ruled that neither Congress nor the Territorial Legislature could prohibit slavery in any territory. The Supreme Court decision nullifies portions of the Compromise of 1850 and renders much of the Kansas-Nebraska Act void. It also called into question the validity of the "popular sovereignty" argument that Douglas was using to justify his decision to support slavery beyond the Mississippi River boundary.

Douglas and James Buchanan became bitter enemies over the Kansas-Nebraska Act, which restored much of Douglas' popularity in the north. His Senate seat was up for re-election in 1859 in Illinois, which was a free state, thus he needed support to win re-election. His republican challenger was Abraham Lincoln, who was running on the Republican ticket and a staunch anti-slavery proponent.

Lincoln-Douglas Debates

Douglas was financially backed by the Illinois Central Railroad. His relationship with the railroad involved congressional support for railroad land grants to finance railroad construction. Douglas was able to pass a rider onto bills in Congress that favored the Illinois Central Railroad. In return, the railroad provided Douglas a private campaign train to travel and campaign throughout Illinois. Lincoln didn't have the political backing as Douglas had, even though as a lawyer, he represented the railroad in legal matters and avoided conflicts of interest. When Douglas gave a campaign speech in a town; two days later Lincoln arrived on horseback to rebut the issues Douglas gave in his speech days earlier. It would serve to Lincoln's advantage, since he had time to carefully craft a response to Douglas's campaign speeches without Douglas' rebuttal. Douglas caught on to his tactic and wanted a level playing field, thus agreed to a debate Lincoln on a series of seven debates held jointly. These seven appearances were called the Lincoln-Douglas Debates. While I won't belabor the reader with extraneous detail of the debates, the most important issue was slavery. Douglas was a proponent of popular sovereignty, thus allowing the citizens in the territory or state to decide if they wanted slavery or not by popular vote.

Lincoln's position was that the Federal Government was the only mediator of slavery, since the issue of slavery involved all states, and therefore, slavery became a national issue protected by the Constitution. The other issue was the wording in the Constitution "...all men are created equal". Douglas maintained that the Constitution only referred to whites and not blacks when it stated that "all men are created equal". Lincoln's rebuttal was: the Constitution did not make a distinction between race, color or creed when drafting the phrase that all people are equal under the law. Douglas was a competent public speaker, but was no match against the logic and eloquence of Abraham Lincoln. At the conclusion of the debates, Douglas won his re-election to Congress; however, the debates give Lincoln notoriety and popular acceptance in the Northern States.

Douglas ran for President in 1860 as a Democrat, against his rival Republican, Abraham Lincoln. During his campaign, Douglas broke a cardinal rules for presidential campaigning at the time; "never campaigned directly for President". It was considered undignified and un-presidential for a presidential candidate to campaign directly. People viewed it as being a "snake-oil salesman" who traveled from town to town begging for votes. At the time, they were called "Parachute Candidates". Douglas felt he had little chance to garner enough support in the North, and concentrated his campaign efforts in the south where Bourbon Democratic support was strongest. Even though Douglas was opposed to secession, he was crafty enough to skirt around the issue of slavery by proclaiming that a vote for Lincoln was a vote for secession. Douglas was a slave owner himself but gave his Mississippi plantation and slaves to his children after his wife's death in 1858. It was hoped that this act would lend credence to his impartiality toward slavery. The northern media was quick to uncover the deception and portray him as another "slick" politician and "fence sitter".

His efforts to win the Presidency failed and Abraham Lincoln was elected President in November of 1860 and inaugurated on March 4, 1861. Lincoln and Douglas both stood on the podium during his inauguration while Douglas held Lincoln's "stove pipe" hat during his inaugural address. On June 3, 1861, just 3 months later, Douglas died in Chicago from typhoid fever.

James Buchanan
(1791 – 1868)

James Buchanan was born in a log cabin in Cove Gap, Pennsylvania in 1791. His parents were of Ulster Scottish decent, having emigrated from Ireland in 1783. His father, James Buchanan Sr. became a prosperous merchant and real estate investor in Mercersburg, Pennsylvania. He attended Dickinson Collage in Carlisle, Pennsylvania in 1807 and graduated with honors in 1809. We would understudy law with James Hopkins in Lancaster and be admitted to the Pennsylvania Bar in 1812. He had never married and remained a bachelor his entire life. Buchanan served as a private in the 1st Brigade, 4th Division in the Pennsylvania Militia and served in the defense of Baltimore. He was the only President to serve in the military that didn't serve as an officer.

He began his political career in 1814, when he was elected to the Pennsylvania House of Representatives and served from1814 to 1816 as a Federalist. He supported a national bank, federally funded public works projects, high tariffs, slavery was an issue to be resolved by the states, an anti-abolitionist, pro states rights and a vocal critic of the War of 1812. In 1820 Buchanan was elected to the U.S. House of

Representatives as a Republican-Federalist and became a staunch supporter of Democrat, Andrew Jackson. When Jackson became President in 1832, he appointed Buchanan as U.S. Ambassador to Russia where he served for 18 months and returned to his home in Pennsylvania. In 1834, Buchanan was appointed by the State Legislature to assume a vacant seat in the U.S. Senate. He would win re-election in 1836 and again in 1842. Under the Polk administration he served as Secretary of State and Ambassador to the United Kingdom in 1852 under Franklin Pierce's Presidency.

James Buchanan's Presidency
(1857 – 1861)

During the 1856 Democratic National Convention, delegates listed their party platform that aligned with Buchanan's political ideology and as a result, he was selected as the party's choice for the Democratic Party nominee for President. During the Presidential election against John C. Freemont, who was the Radical Republican nominee, Buchanan won every southern slave state and five Free states with 174 electoral votes to Freemont's 114 votes. He would be the first and only President elected from Pennsylvania. Buchanan's success was due to his political position as a pro slavery, pro south and pro Fugitive Slave Laws advocate.

During his Inauguration on March 4, 1857, Buchanan outlined specifically his position as serving only a single term office and his position toward slavery.

1. The U.S. Government should not encourage or discourage slavery and allow States to decide by popular sovereignty.
2. The Federal slave code, known as the Fugitive Slave Law should be enforced in federal territories.
3. The pending Supreme Court Case, Dred Scott V. Sanford would permanently settle the all issues of slavery. (Buchanan knew the outcome of the case before it was issued)

Buchanan's cabinet choices included 4 from the North and 5 from the southern states. He kept several Pierce's appointees but removed all those who were from the north and those who had ties to Pierce and Stephan Douglas. His cabinet was selected based on their loyalty toward Buchanan and those who would not question his decisions and authority. His Vice President, Breckinridge, would serve a minor role in his administration. He often held secret and private meetings with his loyalist and excluded cabinet members in meetings. It was felt that Buchanan wanted complete control of his cabinet with little input from his staff and Vice President. He was among the most secretive of Presidents and trusted only a few within his inner circle.

The Dred Scott Case

Dred Scott and his wife belonged to Doctor John Emerson, who had bought them from Peter Blow in St. Louis, Missouri. When Dr. Emerson died, Dred Scott and his wife filed a law suit against Mrs. Emerson, the widow of Dr. Emerson, where Dred Scott requested their freedom; however Scott would lose his case in Missouri State Court. Mrs. Emerson left the Scott's with her brother, John Sanford, a New York resident; Scott sued in Federal Court claiming he was a Missouri resident. Scott once again lost his case and appealed to the U.S. Supreme Court.

President Buchanan was not an innocent by-stander in the Dred Scott decision. While the case was being considered in the Supreme Court, Buchanan needed Southern support for his possible reelection bid. In doing so, Buchanan openly advocated slavery. As a result of his pro slavery stance during his election, he carried all of the southern states and won the Presidency. Buchanan had a political interest in having the Supreme Court rule against Dred Scott. He knew that all five southern Supreme Court justices would rule against Dred Scott, but he needed one of the four northern anti slavery judges to rule against Dred Scott as well, so as to give the appearance that the decision was non partisan and not solely based on racial and southern bias by the Southern Justices.

Buchanan contacted Supreme Court Justice Robert Cooper Grier and asked him to join the southern majority opinion against Dred Scott. Buchanan thought once the decision was handed down against Dred Scott, it would forever resolve the issue of the Free State and the free territorial issue. During his administration, he did not want to deal with the issue of slavery during tenure as President, so he thought. When the Supreme Court issued its decision against Dred Scott in 1857, Court was forced to declare the Compromise of 1820 unconstitutional, thus justifying their Supreme Court decision against Dred Scott.

It would later be revealed that Chief Justice Roger B. Taney had told James Buchanan in advance of the decision during his inauguration. The northern states denounced the decision, which began the succession of the southern States. Historians believe the Dred Scott decision created a sectional division within the Supreme Court and the country, but perhaps not as much as some historians claim. It would propel Abraham Lincoln into the Presidency who was known for his anti-slavery position. The Dred Scott decision affirmed that the anti-slavery north could not depend solely on the Judicial Branch to render an impartial decision toward slavery, since the Supreme Court had already demonstrated its partiality. The north needed a strong anti-slavery president to counteract the bias within the Judicial System that began with the appointment of Roger B. Taney by Andrew Jackson who was a southern slave owner and southern sympathizer.

The Panic of 1857

During the summer of 1857, nearly 1,400 state banks and 5,000 businesses closed their doors as the economy began to slow down in the northern states. The south experienced little effect of the Panic. Buchanan's policy of economic recovery was "reform not relief". He encouraged banks not to accept federal or state bonds and restricted the credit level of banks. The economy gradually improved.

In 1858, Buchanan was still actively involved in the Kansas battle over the Lecompton Constitution in an effort to get congress to accept it and allow Kansas admission to the Union as a slave state. He was unable to get congress to accept the Kansas's Constitution. It wouldn't be until January of 1861 that Kansas was admitted to the Union as a free state. Two other states were admitted into the Union during his Presidency; Minnesota, May 1858 and Oregon, February 1859.

Prelude to Civil War

It was of little secret that Buchanan placated the south, since he received full support from the southern states during his election four years earlier, but with the election of 1860 approaching, the Democrat Party began to fracture between the Democrats of the north and those of the south, commonly known as the Bourbon Democrats. It would become a relatively easy victory for the Republican Party and Abraham Lincoln of Illinois to win the Electoral College, since there were four political parties running for President and the most popular being the Democrat party which was divided by regional and secular divisions.

It was rumored, that should Lincoln win the election, seven southern states were prepared to secede from the union. General Winfield Scott mentioned this fact to Buchanan and wanted him to fortify Fort Sumter in South Carolina before Lincoln takes office, however rather than building a military defense; he scaled back the federal army to a Skelton militia for the protection of the capital and federal property. Buchanan opposed secession from the Union, but contributed little to prevent it. He wasted little time to cast blame on the northern states for not allowing slavery to expand to new states and territories. His effort to resolve the issue of secession was to introduce an amendment that would reaffirm slavery and the fugitive slave laws and the right of states to decide slavery by "popular sovereignty". The suggestion of popular sovereignty by voting inflamed the situation further in the north. In the southern states, he was criticized for declaring that the south didn't have the right to secede. Buchanan was now despised by both the north and the south. When Lincoln was elected President in November of 1860, South Carolina, declared its secession from the Union in late December of 1860. Buchanan hastily made efforts to reach a compromise with South Carolina without success.

To add "fuel" to the controversy, Secretary of War, John B. Floyd was involved in an embezzlement scandal and was asked to resign, but upon leaving office, he transferred firearms belonging to the federal armory at Harpers Ferry to the southern confederates. One month later, six more southern states seceded. In a last ditch effort months before Lincoln takes office in March, Buchanan appealed to Lincoln to call a national referendum to resolve the issue, allowing slavery in territories and new states, however Lincoln without hesitation refused his recommendation.

Civil War erupted two months before Buchanan's term ended. He retired in "Wheatland" near Lancaster, Pennsylvania. Over the next few years while the Civil War raged, he vigorously defended his position, since most felt he started the Civil War. Even though he personally didn't start the Civil War, he certainly made little effort to avoid it or any attempt to unify the nation, which is one of lasting legacies of most president's. He received hate mail and was criticized frequently in the newspapers for his role in not stopping South Carolina from secession, as did Jackson and Taylor had years earlier. Buchanan did not have a pleasant retirement. He was ridiculed and condemned by the north and the south. He received death threats and remained sheltered in his estate at Wheatland. Buchanan would catch a cold and die of respiratory failure in 1868 at the age of 77.

James Buchanan's Legacy

When James Buchanan took office, he told a friend he wanted a legacy equal to or greater than George Washington. In the course of his four years as President, he is considered by historians as the worst President in American history by both conservative and liberal evaluators.

Perhaps critics are judging Buchanan too harshly in blaming him for the Civil War, even though he did little to show leadership and only made modest attempts to unify a nation.

Civil War was brewing as a result of the Tariff Act of 1828 under Andrew Jackson's Presidency. Secession would once again be raised during Zachary Taylor's administration in 1850. In 1854, during Franklin Peirce's administration, the Kansas-Nebraska Act temporarily delayed the issue of slavery and secession. Buchanan's approach was to placate the south and as a result became a victim of the times and perhaps a scapegoat for the war. He was too much of a politician to find a solution and demonstrated distrusted even among his closest advisors. He wanted to appeal to north and the south simultaneously which was an impossible goal at the time. In doing so, he selected his cabinet that was also divided by regional loyalties that created administrative chaos throughout his tenure as President.

Buchanan was a complex person. He disliked slavery yet he aligned himself with the pro-slavery south and fringe factions who appeared to dictate domestic policy. He was from the north, yet showed extreme partiality to the South. Rather than appearing to be neutral on the issue and devoting his time in office to find a solution, he chose the political route. During the election, the north believed he would be sympathetic toward northern issues and the south believed he was a "dough face" who was sympathetic toward the south. In the end, he would lose the support of both sides.

Buchanan is the only Bachelor to occupy the White House. Most historians believe he was homosexual. He had an intimate relationship with Franklin Peirce's Vice President, William Rufus King. The two lived together for 10 years until 1853, when King became ill and died of tuberculosis. Letters between the two were discovered that suggest they had a long lasting romance with each other. Andrew Jackson made derogatory comments about Buchanan and King concerning their personal relationship, which became well known in political circles in Washington but kept secret from the public for nearly 150 years.

Buchanan was never considered charismatic and a good public speaker. He kept to himself much of the time. Newspapers ridiculed him about his failure to make decisions and openly called him a "Doughface", which made him unpopular. Buchanan tried very hard to mediate a resolution near the end of his tenure; however his half hearted efforts would fail. His administration was known to be corrupt and many in his administration aligned themselves with southern sympathies, rather than making an effort to unify the nation. Like other Presidents of the period, prior to the Civil War, they became victims as well. The solution to the problem was not about political compromise, but rather realizing that his goal should have been uniting to factions without prejudice. It will be a common error that many presidents will make in future as well.

General Winfield Scott
(1786 – 1866)

"My politics are of a practical kind - the integrity of the country, the supremacy of the Federal government, an honorable peace, or none at all."
   -Winfield Scott

Perhaps one of the most difficult decisions while writing this book is where to place General Winfield Scott chronologically in the book. The reason being, General Scott served under every President from

Thomas Jefferson to Abraham Lincoln, 14 in all, and a military service that spanned 53 years, of which, 47 as General and 20 years as Commanding General of the Army and served in three major wars. It is only fitting that he be considered as one of America's great legends and leading Generals.

Winfield Scott was born in 1786, to William Scott and Ann Mason in Petersburg, Virginia. He was educated by tutors and in local schools. In 1805 he attended the College of William and Mary but left to study law under the noted attorney David Robinson. He was admitted to the Virginia Bar in 1807. After which he enlisted in the Virginia militia as a corporal. His military career began when he interview for a commission as captain in the light artillery when he was 22 years of age. He was given orders to report to General James Wilkinson who was involved in the Aaron Burr conspiracy during Jefferson's presidency. Scott and Wilkinson would clash and become bitter enemies throughout both of their careers. Scott would be convicted in a court-martial in 1810 for conduct unfitting an officer for making disrespectful comments about General Wilkinson and for not keeping accurate financial records for $50 missing while serving as a recruiter. He would be re-instated a year later and became involved in a duel over the incident by a medical officer and a close friend of General Wilkinson; however neither was seriously injured in the duel.

He was involved in the War of 1812 where he was captured by the British during the Battle of Queenstown Heights in Canada while serving as a lieutenant colonel in an Artillery Regiment in July of 1812. The British executed 13 Irish-Americans prisoners as traitor to Britain and released Scott in a prisoner exchange. Scott would be wounded in the Battle of Fort George in 1813 and remained out of action for the duration of the War.

The Indian Wars of 1832

President Jackson and Van Buren ignored the Supreme Court ruling of Worcester v. Georgia, which allowed the Cherokee Nation their own sovereignty over Native American lands in Georgia. In 1838, Scott was ordered to enforce the Treaty of Ne Echota, which included the removal of the Cherokee Indians from the Southeast and relocate them to Oklahoma. Scott wanted to use only the regular army in the removal of the Cherokee's off native lands rather use Georgia or militia. It was well established that local militia from Georgia and Alabama claimed the Cherokee lands as their own after removing them off their land, however before the regular army arrived in Georgia, 4,000 Georgia militia arrived and a militia land grab ensued. John Quincy opposed the relocation of Native Americans, claiming it was nothing more than an attempt by southern politicians to grab free land. Scott ordered the militia to exercise proper treatment and avoid harsh and cruel treatment of the Native Americans. The first 3,000 Cherokees left Georgia and Tennessee by steamboat, but looting and pillage by the militia and steamboat employees was pervasive. Cherokee Chief John Ross appealed to Washington to allow the Cherokee to travel unarmed and without supervision by militia and the regular army to Oklahoma. Government contractors, steamboat owners who profited from the removal plan objected, since the Native American's traveled overland and didn't use steamship travel. Jackson, no longer President, demanded that Scott be replaced, and Cherokee Chief Ross be executed. Van Buren allowed the plan to proceed as planned. Scott rounded-up the Cherokee and placed them in stockades, waiting for their relocation. More than 4,000 Cherokee would die while in stockades before beginning the trek to Oklahoma. Thousands died during the "Trail of Tears" to Oklahoma as a result of the heat in summer. Scott allowed the march to end until fall when the weather was more favorable.

Private John G. Burnett wrote:

"Future generations will read and condemn the act and I do hope posterity will remember that private soldiers like myself, and like the four Cherokees who were forced by General Scott to shoot an Indian Chief and his children,

and to execute the orders of our superiors. We had no choice in the matter." **[91]**

Scott became Commanding General of the Army in 1841, during the Mexican-American War. James Polk was President and he and Scott did not get along well. Scott and Zachary Taylor would begin the campaign of the Rio Grande in which Taylor was placed in charge while Scott landed his forces south in Veracruz in March of 1847. Scott's staff officer was Robert. E. Lee and his Mexican opponent was Antonio Santa Anna. After numerous battles inland, Scott advance toward Mexico City in which Santa Anna surrender in the fall of 1847. When the Duke of Wellington, learned of Scotts success in taking Mexico City, he proclaim Scott the "greatest living general" **[92]** As a side note, The Duke of Willington fought at the Battle of Waterloo, defeating Napoleon Bonaparte's Army on 18 June 1815..

Scott was a Whig, and in 1840, he ran for President against William Henry Harrison and Senator Henry Clay. He would not win the election and came in third. In 1848, he once again ran as a Whig against Henry Clay, Daniel Webster and General Zachary Taylor. Taylor would win the election. His political career was short lived. Scott was anti-slavery and would lose the southern vote and had made many political enemies in Washington.

When Abraham Lincoln became President in 1861, he appointed Scott as Commanding General of the Union Army. His health was not good. He had gained more than 300 pounds and many questioned his fitness to command in the field. Scott would turn down Lincoln's appointment and suggested Robert E. Lee, however Lee declined. Scott remained as the Commanding General until Lincoln could find a replacement, George B. McClellan. Scott's retired in November of 1861.

He retired and lived the rest of his life at the U.S. Military Academy at

West Point, New York where he taught. He would see the end of the Civil War in 1865 and the Union victory. He died on May 29, 1866 and was buried at the West Point Cemetery, where his monument remains today.

Winfield Scott's Legacy

Fanny Crosby wrote of his passing:

"Gentle manner did not indicate a hero of so many battles; yet there was strength beneath the exterior appearance and a heart of iron within his breast. But from him I learned that the warrior only it is, who can fully appreciate the blessing of peace..." **[93]**

As with many great American generals, Winfield Scott disliked war and was a firm believer in peaceful negotiation to resolve differences. He had many successes in negotiating peace before military intervention; such was the case with the British over the boundary dispute with Canada in Maine and New Hampshire, which diverted another war with Britain. During the Mexican-American campaign and the siege of Mexico City, he made numerous attempts for Santa Anna to negotiate peace a settlement prior to his invasion. It was a lesson well learned by may subsequent generals in history such as U.S Grant and Zachary Taylor who also preferred negotiation over war, but when called to duty, they gave their all.

DOUGLAS G. BEAUDOIN

Chapter 12
The American Civil War

1861 -1865

As a summary of events previously mentioned, the road to Civil War began over basically two overriding issues pointed out previously, but State's Rights became the underlying cause that encompassed slavery and the right of the states to choose secession and the will to have slavery expand in to new states and territories. The issue of slavery in the Deep South was never at issue, as it was deemed Constitutional at the time. Tariffs levied on cotton by the northern states was also an issue in the 1820's, but it could be negotiated by repealing the tariff laws, however the expansion of slavery in new territories and states through manifest destiny was the major issue that resulted in the Civil War. The southern states believed they had the legal right to secede from the union, while the Federal government claimed the opposite. The Constitution is silent on the issue of secession; however, it was discussed and debated during the drafting of the Articles of the Constitution in 1787. Slavery was also discussed and debated behind closed doors rather than on the floor of the Constitutional Convention, as not to exacerbate a sensitive and delicate issue during the Convention for fear that a Constitution would not be accepted by the Southern contingent which was needed for ratification of the Constitution. As it were, some delegates refused to sign the Constitution and "walked-out" of the Convention over the issue of State's Rights that was part and parcel to the eventual slavery issue.

George Mason of Virginia perceived that slavery would become an issue at some point in history when he gave a speech during the Virginia House of Delegates:

"Every master of slaves is born a petty tyrant. They bring the judgment of heaven on a country. As nations cannot be rewarded or punished in the next world, they must be in this. By an inevitable chain of causes and effects, providence punishes national sins by national calamities."

He also made his views known about slavery when he said;

"As much as I value a union of all the states, I would not admit the southern states into the union, unless they agreed to the discontinuance of this disgraceful trade (slavery), because it would bring weakness and not strength to the union."

It was presumed that many believed the issue of slavery would eventually be addressed by the individual states; therefore, it would become a state's rights issue. Abraham Lincoln acknowledged that slavery was not a violation of the Constitution; however, he and other scholars believed secession by states was not allowed under the Constitution, or at least in directly.

Two months prior to Abraham Lincoln's inauguration on March 4, 1861, seven southern states seceded from the Union. Negotiations were stalled between President Buchanan and the Southern Confederate States concerning secession. Any compromise between the two, would involve allowing slavery to expand into all States and U.S. Territories by "popular sovereignty". The political experiment of popular sovereignty in Kansas failed miserably and claims of ballot "stuffing" and election fraud on both sides sparked riots that became known as "Bleeding Kansas". The Federal Government was reluctant to use "popular Sovereignty" as a method of determining the will of the people, since most were not actually residents of Kansas when they voted. Most fled across the border from neighboring Missouri, which was a slave state, to unbalance the voting in their favor.

Abolitionists from New England traveled great distances to upend the balance of voting in Kansas by both abolitionist and pro slavery advocates. For the South, the Confederate States gave up all hope of a compromise. Kansas and Nebraska became non-slave states in the end. For the north, nothing short of abolishing slavery in the territories and the newly admitted states became their ultimate goal and the Confederate States feared that should their efforts fail to expand slavery into other states and territories, it would be a matter of time before Congress would have a majority in support by the radical Republicans whose tenant was complete abolition and the enactment of laws and Constitutional Amendment in abolishing slavery would soon follow. The Kansas-Nebraska Act of 1854 was an example of what was to be expected in the future, and their assumption was correct. Civil War between slave states and Free states became the only option for the southern states.

When Buchanan became President, the south considered him a "doughface" and sympathetic to the south and its slavery issue. However, with Lincoln being elected in November and taking office in March, the southern states knew Lincoln's position toward slavery during the Lincoln-Douglas debates two years earlier. The south was certain Lincoln wanted to abolish slavery in America which was not entirely true. South Carolina wasted little time to secede from the Union in late December, and the remainder of the southern states followed one month later, just prior to Lincoln taking office on March 4, 1861.

No single person or President was responsible for the Civil War. The battle lines had long been drawn between the North and the South decades before 1861. Two previous Presidents; Andrew Jackson and Zackary Taylor were confronted the threat of secession decades before the Civil War and both threatened to use military force. The Compromises of 1820 and 1850 only delayed the inevitable.

Clarissa (Clara) Harlowe Barton
(1821 – 1912)

"The Angle of the Battlefield"

Clarissa Harlowe Barton was born in North Oxford, Massachusetts in 1821. Even though she followed many directions in her early years, she would be known most for her humanitarian work and especially here work as a nurse during the American Civil War. Nursing did not require a formal nursing education in those days. It was a self taught desire to provided humanitarian aid to those who were in desperate need. She acquires her teaching certificate in 1839 at the age of 17 but later resigned from teaching children in 1852 and moved to Washington D.C. to work as a clerk in the U.S. Patent Office. When the Civil War broke-out in 1861, the Massachusetts regiment arrived in Washington D.C. at the train station, where she greeted and gave them food, medical care and humanitarian support. Other women also volunteered to help and soon she had a small army of volunteers providing aid to Union soldiers. Barton would write letters to families of the wounded and provide books and reading material while convalescing.

In 1862, she and her legion of volunteers were granted permission to go to the front lines and administer medical aid to the wounded. After the Battle of Bull Run, Barton placed an ad in the newspaper for supplies to help fallen soldiers. The response was over whelming and Barton and her legion of nurses and humanitarians appeared at the Battles of Cedar Mountain, Second Bull Run, Antietam, Cold Harbor, Petersburg and Fredericksburg to name only a few. During the Battle of Antietam, among the bloodiest battle of the war, Barton ran out of bandages and used corn husk and other cloth to stop the bleeding. On the battlefield she was known as the "Angle of the Battlefield" and "The American Nightingale".

It is not known how many lives Sara Barton and her legion of nurses may have saved, perhaps hundreds or even thousands. After the War, here humanitarian duties were not over. Thousands of Union and Confederate families pleaded to the U.S. Government to locate or acknowledge missing loved ones who fought in the war. She wrote Lincoln asking permission search and write letters to the bereaved family of missing loved ones, and Lincoln gave her permission. Clara and her legion of followers began looking for missing soldiers. Barton and her assistants wrote 41,855 replies and helped locate twenty-two thousand missing men. She helped bury 13,000 men who died in Andersonville Prison Camp in Georgia as well. Over the next four years, she would bury another 20,000 union soldiers. Years later, Congress appropriated $15,000 for her project. Her work on missing and buried soldiers would end in 1868.

She would meet Fredrick Douglas and Susan B. Anthony and would have a lifelong friendship with both. While visiting Switzerland, she was approached and offered to open a branch of the "Red Cross" in America. She continued her work as American Red Cross Chairman until her 84th birthday in 1904. In 1907 at her home in Glen Echo, Maryland, Clara Barton would die at the age of 90 in April of 1912. [63]

Fredrick Douglass
(1818 – 1895)

"Education means emancipation. It means light and liberty. It means the uplifting of the soul of man into the glorious light of truth, the light by which men can only be made free."

Fredrick Augustus Washington Bailey was born a slave in 1818 in Tuckahoe, Maryland. Later in life he would change his name to Fredrick Douglass. His mother, Harriet Bailey, was a slave working on a Plantation in Talbot County, Maryland. It is believed that Douglass was the son of the white plantation owner but that has not been confirmed. When Douglass was 10, his mother died and he was sent to live with his Grandmother, who was also a slave housekeeper for Hugh Auld of Baltimore. Douglass' Grandmother raised him and the Masters wife, Sophia Auld, taught him English and reading, which was illegal at the time. Along with his perseverance for education, be became self taught. In 1833, he was sent to work as a slave for Edward Covey, in which Douglass was routinely beaten and whipped.

He organized a plan to escape slavery and was caught and sent to prison. He would escape from prison and travel to Philadelphia and later New York.

He would marry Anna while in New York who had helped him escape and they would have five children together. After 44 years of marriage, Anna would die in 1882. At the age of 23, he would meet abolitionist David Ruggles in New York and he began his life as an abolitionist. Douglass was an eloquent speaker and traveled throughout the northern States giving passionate speeches about the evils of slavery. In 1845, Douglass wrote his first Autobiography, "Narrative of the Life of Fredrick Douglass, an American Slave". In 1855, he wrote a second book, "My Bondage and My Freedom". Both books were well received and inspired many in the north to join the abolitionist cause. However, during speaking engagements, he was often beaten by mobs and assaulted.

He went on a lecture tour to the British Isle in 1845 where he spent 2 years. He was still considered a run-away slave and if caught he would once again lose his freedom. It was at this point in his life he changed his name to Fredric Douglass and with the help of donations while in Britain, he would raise 500 pounds to purchase his freedom when he returned to America.

When he returned to America, he frequently was invited to speak at women suffrage meetings and became an avid supporter of women suffrage. Douglass never advocate violence with violence and believed the Constitution held the key to the abolition of slavery in America. He spoke of a 15th Amendment to the Constitution that someday would emancipate African-Americans from the bondage of slavery. His speeches did not go unheard. A lawyer from Illinois also took up the cause of emancipation which in 1861 would put him in office as President of the United States. In his July 5, 1852 speech, Douglass lamented:

"Fellow-citizens! there is no matter in respect to which, the people of the North have allowed themselves to be so ruinously imposed upon, as that of the pro-slavery character of the Constitution. In that instrument I hold there is no warrant, license, nor sanction of the hateful thing; but, interpreted as it ought to be interpreted, the constitution is a glorious liberty document." **[89]**

Although his speeches were often well received in the north, but not necessarily in the south and at times he would be "booed" by younger African-American's who wanted a more confrontational approach to change. He would meet abolitionist John Brown who wanted radical change and armed rebellion to end slavery, but Douglass disapproved of his approach. When Douglass read of Lincoln's Emancipation Proclamation in 1863, he wrote:

"….we were watching …. By the dim light of the stars for the dawn of a new day … we were longing for the answer to the agonizing prayers of centuries."

In 1865, the 14th and 15th Amendment to the Constitution was ratified, and Douglass wrote;

"Mr. Lincoln was not only a great President, but a great man – too great to be small in anything. In his company I was never in any way reminded of my humble origin, or of my unpopular color." **[90]**

After the death of Anna, he re-marries a white feminist, Helen Pitts who being 20 year younger than he. He would visit Europe once more in his later years. During the Civil War, Douglass became a consultant to Abraham Lincoln and during the reconstruction period from 1866 to 1877 he continued his fight for civil rights during Grants Administration and advocated and supported the women's rights movement. He was appointed U.S. Minister and Consul General to Haiti from 1889 to 1891. In 1895 he would die of a stroke in Washington D.C. **[88]**

Abraham Lincoln
(1809 – 1865)

"This country, with its institutions, belongs to the people who inhabit it. Whenever they shall grow weary of the existing government, they can exercise their constitutional right of amending it, or exercise their revolutionary right to overthrow it." - Abraham Lincoln

Abraham Lincoln was born in a log cabin in Hodgenville, Kentucky in 1809. He was the second child of three children of Thomas and Nancy Hanks Lincoln of Sinking Springs Farm, Kentucky. One child would die at infancy; only Sarah and Abraham would survive to adulthood.

The Lincoln's were descendants of Samuel Lincoln of Hingham, Norfolk, England, who migrated to America in 1638. Over the years the Lincoln family would move and purchase or lease farm land in Kentucky. He acquired 230 acres of land and title that ended in a legal dispute over ownership. The Lincoln family would sell the remaining land they owned and move to the Indiana Territory in 1816 when Abraham was only 7 and his sister, Sarah was 9 years old.

Thomas Lincoln, Abraham's father, worked odd jobs to make a living in Hurricane Township, Indiana Territory. He acquired 80 acres in Little Pigeon Creek, Spencer County, Indiana. He also worked as a cabinet maker and a carpenter and continued to maintain his farm in Little Pigeon Creek. Thomas became a respected member of the community and an active member of the Separate Baptist Church. In 1818, his mother Nancy would die when Abraham was only 9 years old. Thomas would remarry one year later to Sally Bush Johnston from Elizabethtown, Kentucky. His sister Sarah would die in 1828 while giving birth.

Frontier life was difficult, and Abraham was self taught and educated. Abraham disliked frontier life and did very little to help with the daily chores around the farm. He devoted most of his time writing and reading and many believed he did so to avoid work. He gets odd jobs outside the home and gave his father his earnings. In 1830, Thomas and the entire extended family moved to Illinois, near the town of Decatur and later to Coles County Illinois. Lincoln would leave his family and get a job in New Salem, Illinois.

While in New Salem, he would Marry Mary Todd in 1841. Mary was the daughter of a wealthy plantation owner in Lexington, Kentucky. Mary's father was a slave owner and slave trader. Abraham and Mary would move to Springfield, Illinois. They would have four children together; only Robert Todd Lincoln would survive until adulthood and have a family of his own.

Lincoln's Political Career

Lincoln was admitted to the Illinois bar in 1836. He practiced law under John T. Stuart, Mary Todd's cousin and later partnered with Stephan T. Logan from 1841 to 1844. He opened his own law practice in 1844. In 1835, he ran and won four terms in the Illinois House of Representatives as a Whig. During his term in the Illinois Legislature, Lincoln voiced his opinion openly about abolishing slavery and allowing African-American's to return as free-men to Liberia, Africa for which many originally came. He and Henry Clay shared much of the same political ideology toward slavery.

Lincoln ran for the U.S. House of Representatives in 1846 and served only one term. During his brief tenure, he spoke against the Mexican-American War being waged by President James K. Polk and supported the Wilmot Proviso that abolishes slavery in any territory acquired from Mexico during the Mexican-American War.

Lincoln became strongly opposed to the Mexican-American War that he challenged President Polk in a Resolution in Congress to show the exact spot where the first American blood was shed on American soil, which ultimately started the Mexican-American War. **(20)** Lincoln's resolution became known as the "spot resolution" in which congress, the president and his constituents in Illinois would ignore his pleas. His popularity among politicians and voters would suffer as a result.

Most considered America's invasion of Mexico justified and patriotic rather than criticizing the legality and morality of the invasion. The South wanted Texas as a slave state and the north wanted California as an anti slavery state. Both sides were in a 'rush' to acquire as much land as slave states and as anti-slave states as possible before all the available land was gone.

Lincoln served only one term in the U.S. Legislature and gave his support to Zackary Taylor, a Whig candidate, for President in 1848. Taylor would win the Presidency but died only sixteen months while in office. His Vice President, Millard Fillmore became the 13th President of the United States in 1850 and served only one term in office

Lincoln returned to his law practice in Springfield, Illinois shortly after the election of Zackary Taylor in 1849. His law practice dealt mainly with interstate commerce issues but later he accepted all types of cases, including criminal and contract law. He appeared before the Illinois Supreme Court in 175 cases. The Illinois Central Railroad retained Lincoln as one of their company lawyers, which lasted ten years under a retainer from the railroad. Company executives gave him the nickname "Honest Abe". **[30]**

In 1849, Lincoln received a patent for a floatation device for boats and barges so they wouldn't run aground" during low tide. He would be the first and only president to receive a patent. Jefferson was well known as an inventor but never acquired a patent for any of his inventions.

The Kansas-Nebraska Act was passed in May of 1854. Lincoln

favored mediation over confrontation, since the Act was a potential political "fire storm". After the Act passed, Lincoln gave a speech in Peoria, Illinois in which he openly declared his strong opposition toward slavery;

"…..declared indifference, but as I must think, a covert real zeal for the spread of slavery. I cannot but hate it. I hate it because of the monstrous injustice of slavery itself. I hate it because it deprives our republican example of its just influence in the world…" [31]

In 1854 he enters into politics as a result of the Kansas-Nebraska Act in May of 1854. He ran for the U.S. Senate and did not win and made an effort to run as a Vice Presidential candidate as a Republican in the same year but lost his bid to Republican, John C. Freemont. Lincoln was active during the first Republican Convention, giving speeches concerning anti-slavery issues which later propelled him as the leading Republican during the next presidential election in 1860.

Lincoln felt strongly that sectional-regional differences between the North and the South could be mediated successfully. He believed slavery was protected under the Constitution, however, he did not agree that States had a right to secede from the Union or participate in the nullification of Federal Laws. He believed the Federal government had a legal right to determine if a state or territory was to be a slave hold or not. Even though a compromised was possible, the nullification issue and the right to succession remained a major obstacle that neither side would compromise on. The last major issue became the Fugitive Slave Act of 1850, in which many in the North refused to honor and return run-away slaves to their owners. The issue of slavery was not just an issue of law, but also an issue of moral conscience and belief, which could never be mediated or compromised.

When the Supreme Court ruled on the Dred Scott Case in March of 1857, the Northern States were outraged over the decision. Lincoln denounced the decision publicly by declaring;

"...The authors of the Declaration of Independence never intended to say all were equal in color, size, intellect, moral developments, or social capacity, but they did consider 'all men created equal-equal in certain inalienable rights, among which are life, liberty, and the pursuit of happiness' ". Ref: *Lincoln-Douglas Debates, Cooper Union Speech* **[32]**

Presidential Election of 1860

By the end of Buchanan's Presidency, it became clear that Buchanan would not be re-elected to a second term in office. Buchanan's effort to mediate a last minute effort to reach a compromise between the North and the South was futile. The campaign between Douglas, a Democrat, and Lincoln, a Republican, would become the biggest political battle over a single issue in American History.

Illinois held the first local Republican State Convention in Decatur on May 9th of 1860. Lincoln was nominated as Illinois' choice for President. The Republican National Convention was held in Chicago on May 18, 1860. Lincoln would be nominated as the Republican Presidential candidate and Hannibal Hamlin of Maine nominated as his Vice Presidential running mate.

The Republican platform centered around the party being a moderate voice on the slavery issues, protective tariffs, support for the defunct Whig party programs and the federally financing of public works projects. Lincoln believed that America would not become engage in a civil war over slavery and believed a compromise was possible to divert a military confrontation over the slavery issue.

During Lincoln's campaign for President, he never gave campaign speeches. The act of campaigning by a presidential candidate was not an acceptable practice at the time. Lincoln knew he had little chance of winning electoral votes in the South, thus concentrated on the northern and western states and as a result, decisively won the election with 180 electoral votes over his opponents with 123. He also won the popular vote as well. He would only win 2 counties out of the

996 counties in the South.

The Confederate States of America

As soon as the election returns were made public and Lincoln was the victor, the South began to organize an effort for secession from the Union. South Carolina became the first State to secede. Buchanan was still President and Lincoln wouldn't be inaugurated until March 4, 1861. By late January, six more states seceded from the union The South began to make plans to select a President for the Confederate States of America. During the Confederate Constitutional Convention in Montgomery, Alabama on February 9, 1861, two prominent nominees were selected as possible Presidents; Jefferson Davis of Mississippi and Robert Toombs of Georgia. The committee selected Davis as President and Alexander H. Stephens as his Vice President. Davis was selected over Toombs because of his West Point military training and his tenure in the U.S. Congress. During deliberations for President, Davis voiced his desire to be the Commander and Chief of the Confederate Army which he preferred over being President. However, when the telegram arrived notifying him that he was selected as the Confederate President; he was somewhat disappointed, since he preferred being the Commander and Chief of the Confederate Forces. This side note in history would have devastating results in history as Jefferson Davis would operated the Confederate Presidency as a military "Pentagon" and neglect the running of the government for which he was pointed.

Stephens as Vice President of the Confederacy would only play a minor role in government, since Davis and Stephens were in a constant state of feuding among themselves. Davis appointed General Beauregard to Command Confederate troops in Charleston, South Carolina in preparation the siege of Fort Sumter. Robert Toombs was appointed Secretary of State and Leroy Pope Walker of Alabama his Secretary of War, however, Walker would resign after 3 months when Davis insisted he take over the War Department and make all decisions. Among one of the major problems within the Confederate Government was the constant turn-over of Davis' Cabinet, which demoralized the affluent and government legislators. Davis became relatively unpopular throughout the Civil War among the populous and especially among the affluent and wealthy.

Financing the Confederacy

Christopher Memminger was appointed Secretary Treasurer of the Confederate States of America in 1861. The Confederacy was in financial trouble from the first days of secession. They only had $27 million in specie in reserve. They began selling government bonds worth $150 million for financing the War effort, however in doing so; hard currency was used as security against the loans. To pay the bonds, the Confederate Congress passed a 10% war tax on property and agricultural produce, but had little means to enforce collection, and was not able to meet its bond obligation, thus creditors were reluctant to loan money to the Confederacy. The Confederate States was unable to keep up with the "ballooning" war debt as well. They needed to borrow more money from foreign banks but the banks were cautious about loaning money to the Confederacy for fear that it would cause a rife between the United States and cause a possible war.

The Embargo and Blockade

When South Carolina seceded from the Union in December of 1860, it actively began seeking a coalition with other southern slave states. The main message was to convince other southern states they could win the war with the aid of Britain and possibly France coming to their aid.

The Northeast was the industrial backbone of America with enough capital to sustain a war for a much longer period of time than the south. They also had a large and growing pool of eligible recruits to draw from, for which many were immigrants from Europe. The north could manufacture ships, guns and canons in mass quantities, whereas, the South depended on importing large quantities of arms and ammunitions from abroad, primarily Britain. For the success of the Confederacy's, Britain had to be drawn into the war. Cotton was the bait they were going to use to do it.

In April of 1861, Lincoln announced a blockade of all shipping in and out of the South, but prior to implementing the blockade (June), the South devised a plan to draw Britain into the war by placing an embargo on cotton exports several months prior to the blockade by the Union. This tactical error immediately stopped the Confederacy's cash flow but Britain did not take the bait, since they were already importing cotton from their colony in India for a much lower price. When the blockade was finally implemented by June, ten confederate seaports were shut down and lay idle for the remainder of the war.

Britain's investors saw a financial opportunity by building and converting old British Naval ships to sell to the North and establish a much more impenetrable blockade for the south to export cotton to France, thus France was forced to buy cotton from Britain. They were also supplying refurbished ships designed as blockade runners for the Confederacy at the same time. British ships owned and operated by British investors, flying the Confederacy flag, were captured and goods and war materials confiscated by Union ships were sold. British sailors were freed so as to not inflame Great Britain or France. It wasn't long before the investors realized they were making little or no money on their investment and curtailed much of the blockade running and left it to the Confederacy.

The Confederate Government and State Treasuries began printed more and more confederate paper currency throughout the war, which resulted in fueling inflation. Riots broke-out in 1863 in Richmond over food shortages and high inflation. By 1864, inflation in the south jumped a staggering 600%. Davis fired his Treasury Secretary, Memminger in July of 1864 and replaced him with George Trenholm of South Carolina. Trenholm entered the treasury with a monumental national debt of $700 million, but could do nothing to fix the present financial situation of the Confederacy. England and France refused to get involved in trade with the South since their currency was worthless. Many Confederate leaders believed that Britain and France would come to aid of the Confederacy, since the south once provided 75% of Europe's cotton and fabric. The South failed to realize that France and Great Britain had previously realized ten years before that civil war was imminent in America. Britain and France both began establishing large cotton plantations in their colonies in India, Africa, and Indonesia and Egypt, thus when the Civil War broke-out; Europe was not dependant of southern cotton and tobacco any longer. In addition, the Union blockade around the southern coastline depriving the south of vital war materials.

Abraham Lincoln's Presidency
(1861- 1865)

Buchanan told President Elect Lincoln that seven states were planning to secede from the Union before his March 4, 1861 inauguration. The border states of Delaware, Maryland, Virginia, North Carolina, Tennessee, Kentucky, Missouri and Arkansas were yet undecided. Maryland, Delaware, Missouri and Kentucky were slave states but, opposed to secession. The State of Virginia would be divided, in which West Virginia was granted statehood in 1863. Of the 40 thousand eligible recruits in West Virginia, half joined the Union army Soldiers and the remainder joined the Confederacy.

Failed Compromises

Buchanan presented a compromise plan to the Confederacy with the hope that the south would choose mediation over secession and war. The Crittenden Compromise extended the Missouri Compromise line of 1820, thus creating two territories, one of which being a slave territory the other a free slave territory. Lincoln rejected the plan unconditionally, however he did support the proposed Corwin Amendment that passed Congress and was waiting for ratification by the states. Lincoln was not inaugurated when the Corwin Amendment passed Congress. The Amendment proposed that states already slave states could remain so without government interference. However, any new states or territories would be slave free. Not one Southern State accepted the Corwin Amendment and the Southern States would not ratify the Amendment. The only option for Lincoln was Civil War.

Lincoln was inaugurated on March 4, 1861, even though there was a failed assassination attempt on his life prior to his inauguration, he continued with the inauguration without incident. Seven Confederate States had already prepared for War in 1860 and later added another 4 states to the Confederacy. As previously mentioned, some of Buchanan's cabinet members were sympathetic to the southern cause including Buchanan himself, who was considered a dough-face throughout his Presidency. Union weapons were being smuggled into the South months before the siege of Fort Sumner in South Carolina.
Lincoln was adamant about not allowing any of the Border States to become part of the Confederacy; however, he especially was concerned about Maryland and Kentucky. Washington D.C. was nearly surrounded by the State of Maryland, thus having Maryland as a border state was essential in the protection of the Capital. Kentucky was another key tactical state that protected the Northern industrial states of Pennsylvania and New York and provided a transportation corridor to the two large navigable river systems that flowed into the south. Maryland presented a much larger problem for Lincoln; the Maryland Legislature voted to remain in the Union, however they stipulated that Union troops could not have access to railroads, bridges and transportation corridors for the purpose of mobilizing Union troops against the South. In essence, Maryland would remain in the Union, but would not become an active participant in the war.

Rioting broke-out in Baltimore that led to the burning of the bridges in and around Maryland. Lincoln responded by declaring martial law and suspending "habeas corpus" in Maryland. Union troops were sent into Maryland and Washington D.C. to maintain law and order that resulted in the arrest of one-third of the members in the Maryland Legislature who were sympathetic to the southern cause. Many of the State legislators were imprisoned for the duration of the war without trial. Chief Justice Roger Taney declared the act unconstitutional, however, Lincoln ignored his ruling since Congress was in recess and he declared the issue a state of emergency which stated in the Constitution that the President could suspend "habeas corpus" during acts of insurrection and war, thus Lincoln had established legal standing his decision.

Kentucky declared itself neutral from the beginning of the threat of secession. In September of 1861, Confederate troops invaded Kentucky with the primary goal of swaying and recruiting rural residents to join the confederacy. Rallies and local meetings were held throughout rural Kentucky as a recruitment tool for the Confederacy. When the Southern sympathizers appointed their own governor, Union troops marched into Kentucky and took control of the State Legislature and forced the confederate sympathizers to flee into exile. More than 20,000 of the estimated 43,000 eligible recruits would join the Confederacy, while the remainder would join the Union Amy. This footnote in history is important. Many rural communities were made-up of extended families, most of which were related to each other in one way or another. The war would split entire families over political ideology, which made the war especially sad and cruel. It was not uncommon to see brothers or cousins fighting on opposite sides on the same battle fields, especially for those from the Border States such as Kentucky.

Conscription and the Draft

During the first year (1861) of the Civil War, volunteers and recruitment levels were high, but beginning in the second year of the war, the Confederacy resorted to conscription (draft) to meet their recruitment goals. The Union soon followed. The Union had an advantage over the Confederacy when it came to volunteerism. Foreign born immigrants were more eager to volunteer between the ages of 18 to 35. Since the North was the industrial center of America, Irish and German immigrants poured into New York and settled throughout New England. More than 300,000 immigrants volunteered in the Union Army during the war. But even with the influx of immigrant volunteers, it was not enough to maintain a 1 million man army on both sides, since the attrition rate during the war was extremely high.

Conscription and Draft was very unpopular on both sides. In 1863, a riot broke-out in New York City over the signing-up of Irish Immigrants in the New York Democrat Party in exchange for their U.S. citizenship. More than 160,000 Irish Immigrants signed up as Democrats in exchange they were to receive U.S. Citizenship, only to find that they were now eligible for the draft. However, the draft system at the time allowed for paid substitutes and only 50,000 Irish immigrants served in the military. This illustration serves as an example of the lengths both sides went to in order to recruit more men to fight in the war. In the North, over 100,000 would flee into Canada to avoid the draft and nearly 300,000 deserted. The numbers weren't much better in the South. It is estimated that 10% of Confederate Army deserted, but most deserted as a result of family problems or death in the family, and most would return to duty after resolving the family issues.

The North offered enlistment bonuses for signing-up. Some signed-up for the bonus and traveled to another recruiting station in another county using an alias and sign-up again for a second or third bonus. Over the course of the war, 141 were captured and executed for sign-up under fraud pretense.

As the War continued into the third year and the casualty rate increase exponentially, both sides became desperate in their recruiting efforts. In 1863, and after Lincoln's declaration of the Emancipation Proclamation in January of 1863, a new approach to recruitment was used in the North. Each state was required to meet a particular quota for recruitment. States offered higher cash bonuses for Whites but allowed them to substitute their service until June of 1864. Blacks in the North were eagerly recruited, but were offered less wages and a modest bonus than those of the whites. When the North began to recruit Blacks, the Confederacy declared that if Black's were caught, they would be hanged as traitors. Surprisingly, it had little effect on Black enlistment and entire black regiments were formed.

At the beginning of the Civil War in the spring of 1861, most European nations considered the American Civil War as an amateur and unprofessional military attempt to engage in a conflict. However, British historian John Keegan's assessment claimed that the Union and the Confederacy armies individually out-matched the Russian, Prussian and French armies at the time; however he left out the British. [33]

The Union Military Command

Civil War began with the siege of Fort Sumner in South Carolina on April 12, 1861 with the Confederate firing canon volleys on the Fort. During the siege, the Union Army had 1080 commissioned officers; some were regulars and some were militia volunteers. In addition the Union had only 15,000 regular enlisted soldiers in the U.S. Army. During the beginning of the war, 142 commissioned officers resigned and accepted commissions in the Confederate Army. There would be 4 Commanding General of the United States Army; Winfield Scott, George B. McClellan, Henry Halleck and Ulysses S. Grant. There were two Secretaries' of War; Simon Cameron and Edwin M. Stanton who would replace Cameron in 1862.

Union Military Strategy

During the siege of Fort Sumner, President Lincoln convened his military staff in Washington to work on a military strategy for the war. General Winfield Scott was selected as his first Commanding General of the U.S. Army, but he was old and only accepted the position until Lincoln could find a replacement. In late 1861, Major General George B. McClellan was selected as Scott's replacement.

The Union's basic military strategy for the Civil War was not to take territory but to defeat the enemy through attrition. Lincoln believed the key to winning the war quickly was to take the Confederate Capital of Richmond, Virginia, however with the Battle of Bull Run; this strategy was abandoned early in the war when the Union Army would be defeat in both attempts to advance on Richmond. The Union Army decided that the war was going to take years rather than months and elected to take an offensive position, forcing the Confederate Army into a defensive posture. In addition, as a result of the naval blockade of the south, it disrupted trade, which caused serious financial problems for the Confederacy and slowly starved the south into defeat. The first strategy after the failure to take Richmond was to divide the South in half, separating it north and south and not allowing the Confederacy to use the Mississippi River drainage as a means of resupply. This would be accomplished during the Vicksburg Campaign of January of 1863 under the command of General U.S. Grant. Grant laid siege on the town of Vicksburg until its eventual surrender by Confederate General Pemberton on July 4, 1863. From that point on, U.S. Grant was known as "Unconditional Surrender Grant". As a result of the Battle of Vicksburg, the South was denied accesses to the Mississippi transportation corridor.

Confederate Military Strategy

The Confederate military strategy was in stark contrast to that of the Union's. Jefferson Davis' focused on defeating the naval blockade along the coast and the inland water ways of the Mississippi transportation corridor failed. Davis' overland strategy was based on

George Washington's tactic of "trading space for time", with the hope that Britain or France would intervene and come to the Confederate's aid. This strategy was speculative at best, and would fail to materialize. The designers of the "stalled" strategy tactic failed to realize the effects of engaging the army in 29 campaigns, 76 battles and 310 military engagements that culminated in a high number of casualties that depended on knowing which battles were worth winning and which battles were not worth fighting. The Confederate Army had 592,000 in conscription, but of the total, 490,000 were casualties during the entire war. In contrast, the Union Army had 1.5 million in conscription and 597,000 casualties, with another 2.4 million eligible and held in reserve, but did not served. [35]

Davis advocated a defensive battle plan from the beginning, but like Lincoln in the North, public and political pressure forced Davis, as well as Lincoln, to change their strategy from a defensive to an offensive strategy as the war expanded. The media and public perceived that the South could win the war by engaging aggressively with the Union Army and take Washington D.C. The Confederate Army demonstrated in the Battle of Bull Run and the Seven Day Battles in 1862 that the Confederate Army could defeat a much larger Union Army. Southerner's believed in an idealistic view that Southern tradition of waiting for the enemy to attack was cowardly and actively pushed for a more aggressive stance. They wanted Davis to attack the northern States and force the Union Army into a defensive posture and eventually they would sue for peace.

The Civil War (1861-1865)

I purposely avoided going into great detail about the actual battles during the four years of the Civil War, but rather focused on the individual participants who were actively involved, either militarily or politically. Abraham Lincoln and the Civil War is perhaps the most written period in American History and for those interested I suggest reading The Personal Memoirs of Ulysses S. Grant, 1884, which is still available in bookstores and online.

Lincoln immediately called upon the northern States to enlist 75,000 volunteers to help defend Washington D.C., as riots and insurrection erupted in Maryland against the Union. It wasn't until the fall of Fort Sumner that Lincoln believed a compromised couldn't be reached with the South. With the fall of Fort Sumner, the Union immediately began recruiting men and acquiring war materials in preparation for an extended war. For the Confederacy, they began preparing for war as early as December of 1860, if not earlier. They recruited and built a substantial Confederate Army by the time Fort Sumner was under siege.

Shortly after the fall of Fort Sumner, public pressure forced Lincoln to order General Irvin McDowell to advance toward Richmond in an effort to take the Capital of the Confederacy. He was met by Confederate Generals; Joseph Johnston and Beauregard at Bull Run Creek, both were highly competent. There would be two different attempts at Bull Run Creek to defeat the Confederate Army and both attempts would fail in 1861

Lincoln ordered General George McClellan to once again take Richmond during the Seven Days Battle of July of 1862, but was driven back by General Robert E. Lee. After a series of small battles, the Confederate Army forced McClellan's Army of the Potomac to retreat. The Union suffered 16,000 casualties and the South 20,000.
Lincoln appointed General George McClellan in late 1861 after Winfield Scott retired as Commander of the Army. McClellan was 35 years old, and a graduate of West Point with a degree in civil engineering. He served briefly during the Mexican-American War after graduating from West Point, but had little battlefield combat experience. In civilian life, he became the Vice President of the Illinois-Ohio Central Railroad. As an executive for the railroad, he hired Lincoln as one of the railroad's company lawyers. When the Civil War became imminent in 1860, McClellan volunteered in the

Union Army, even though his loyalties favored southern sympathies and pro slavery. He elected to serve in the Union Army for political gain, but was against secession of the states.

McClellan was a Democrat, but Lincoln was known to appoint many from a cross section of society including different political parties. During Lincoln's second term he insisted on having a southerner serve as a Vice President. Lincoln appointed McClellan as Commander-in-Chief of the Union Army upon Winfield Scott's retirement. However, it became apparent to Lincoln that he was a poor military leader, but was well liked by his men. His defeat at the Battle of Bull Run and the series of Battles during the Seven Day Campaign and Peninsula Campaign would spell doom for McClellan. McClellan openly mocked Lincoln in the company of others and refused to establish a battle plan when asked by the President or the Secretary of War. He was brought up on charges on two different occasions for insubordination and dereliction of duty for leaving the battle field and not appointing a successor. McClellan wrote a letter to Lincoln after being sent to Harrison's landing to put down an up-rising over slavery, which culminated in the removal of McClellan as Commander-in-Chief of the Army in March of 1862. General Henry Halleck was assigned as his replacement several months later. The McClellan's letter infuriated Congressional Republican's and Lincoln's Cabinet. Most demanded that McClellan be discharged from military service. Lincoln however, kept McClellan in charge of the defense of Washington D.C. McClellan's insubordination and poor military judgment and his indecisiveness to go into battle continued throughout his service in the civil War, however, he did win a few battles in the process.

During the first ten months of the Civil War, the Union suffered numerous defeats and heavy casualties. The General's in the Union Army were not as organized or as disciplined as Robert E. Lee, General Beauregard and Longstreet.

The Confederate generals often anticipate Union Army's field movements, their strength and skill level before going into battle. Part of the problem could be traced to General Halleck and McClellan's indecisiveness. He felt he should not go into battle unless his troop strength was at least 2 or 3:1. Lincoln wanted him to immediately confront Lee's invading force before it gathered reinforcements and hold a firm line protecting Washington until reinforcements arrived, but during the first Battle of Bull Run his troop turned tail and ran for Washington.

On April 6, 1862, General Grant sat in front of his tent having breakfast at Pittsburg Landing, Tennessee with his 70,000 troops, when gun fire echoed through camp. The Battle of Shiloh had begun. Grant thought General Johnston's Confederate force was retreating, but in fact Johnston was repositioning his army to attack the Union Army the following morning. General Robert E. Lee would follow with 40,000 Confederate soldiers. The battle became brutal with huge losses on both sides, but Grant was able to get an advantage over Lee when Union General Buell arrived the following morning with 18,000 Union troops. The Confederate troops under the command of General Beauregard retreated. The casualties rates on both sides were staggering; 13,000 Union casualties versus 10,000 Confederates casualties. General Albert Johnston of the Confederacy was killed in battle, which was a big loss for the Confederacy, since he was one of the best Generals the Confederate Army had at the time. However, the overall out-come of the battle was neither a decisive victory nor loss for both sides. It did teach Grant not to assume the movement of the enemy indicates that it is retreating, assume it is positioning itself for an attack.

McClellan had marginal success in the second Battle of Bull Run in August of 1862, but failed to capitalize on Lee's retreat by chasing Lee's Army all the way to Richmond, the capital of the Confederacy. Once again Lincoln was disappointed with McClellan's military judgment for not taking advantage of fortunate situation.
In September of 1862, the second bloodiest battle of the war occurred

in Antietam, Maryland. Lee advanced his troops near Washington D.C. and was met by McClellan's large Union Army. With each side claiming 11,000 killed, Lee's reinforcements didn't arrive as planned and Lee withdrew from the Battle field. Even though 22,000 were killed in the Battle of Antietam, neither side gained an advantage as a result of the heavy losses.

The Emancipation Proclamation

Lincoln was eager to declare the Emancipation of Proclamation for the abolishment of slavery early during the course of the civil war. However, it could only be accomplished by Presidential executive order as a war time strategy imposed upon the belligerents. The primary reason was to use his Presidential war powers granted to the president under the Constitution to suppress rebellion within the United States. His authority only pertained to the rebellion within the confederate states however and Lincoln didn't need a vote from Congress or a Constitutional Amendment to implement the war time policy. Executive orders only apply as long as his presidential predecessor doesn't void the executive order. Lincoln wanted to use the Emancipation of Proclamation as a tool to force the Confederacy to stop the war and restore the status quo of the Confederacy prior to secession by the southern states. He issued a deadline of January 1, 1862 for a response; however no response was received by the deadline from any of the Confederate States.
Copperheads were a common term used at the time for Democrats who wanted stop the war entirely and create two divided unions. It was gaining popularity during the darkest days of the war, but after success at Gettysburg in 1963, Lincoln felt that the war was turning in the Union's favor and there was no need to entertain the idea proposed by the "copperheads".

The Emancipation Proclamation changed the entire goal and purpose of the Civil War, or at least part of it. Lincoln's original goal was to keep the Union together at all cost. When the States began to secede and his compromises to allow slavery to continue in the south failed, war was imminent. With the Emancipation Proclamation in the fall of 1862, Lincoln wanted to use his executive presidential powers to force the Southern states to rejoin the Union and maintain their status quo toward slavery. Once the executive order went into effect on January 1, 1863, the focus shifted from a single goal to several goals; 1) unification of the Union and 2) the abolishment of slavery.

Lincoln was well aware that England and France had long since abolished slavery. He did not want Great Britain or France to get involved in the Civil War. On several occasions during the Civil War, Lincoln threatened England with war when they violated their own neutrality treaty by supplying the Confederacy with weapons. With the Union taking a firm stand on abolishing slavery, it was doubtful Britain or France would become involved directly in fighting a war in support of slavery. Great Britain and France remained neutral as a result throughout the Civil War. The Southern States seceded from the Union predicated that Britain and France would enter the war in support of the Confederacy, however without foreign military support, it was almost certain that the Confederacy could sustain a long and protracted campaign.

Under the terms of the executive order #95, failure to accept the terms of the executive order to dissolve the Confederacy by January 1st, the Emancipation of all slaves within the rebellion of the Confederacy (10 states) was to take place under executive order, except those states that were not in rebellion or were occupied by Union forces as of the last day of 1862. The executive order only pertained to the ten states that were engaged in rebellion against the Union and not the Border States that were slave states.

- North and South Carolina
- Georgia
- Mississippi
- Louisiana

- Alabama
- Texas
- Florida
- Virginia
- Tennessee
- Arkansas

For the States that were not part of the rebellion or occupied by Union forces as of 1862, yet were slave states (Border States); Kentucky, Maryland, Delaware, Missouri, lower Louisiana and West Virginia, which were not part of the Emancipation Proclamation decree, known as executive order #95. However, the thirteenth Amendment to the Constitution would be ratified on December 6, 1865, ended slavery in the United States. The Confederate States rejoining the Union after seceding from the Union were required to amend their state constitution banning slavery, which became a requirement of all states in the United States after the Thirteenth Amendment.

Even though the ten southern states did not accept the Emancipation Proclamation, however, it did have a positive effect in the north and the states that were already under Union control. More than 20,000 to 75,000 slaves were immediately freed. As Union forces advanced deep into the South, Union Armies freed thousands of slaves. By 1865, 3.9 million slaves were free.
By mid 1863, Union General Order 143 authorized the formation of the United States Colored Troops. By the end of the War, 200,000 African-Americans would serve in the Union Army and Navy. [35]

The idea of having African-American troops fighting as part of the Union Army raised outrage in the south. Robert E. Lee was especially concerned that the Union Army would begin recruiting African-American's into the Army, whereas in the South the Confederate recruitment efforts stalled with little hope of acquiring more recruits to continue fighting the war. He believed the Emancipation Proclamation was a Union ploy to increase it ranks using African-Americans as a tool to fight against South. However, it wasn't Lincoln's intension at all, since the North already had twice the military force as the Confederates. By the end of 1862, the Union Army enjoyed numerous victories until the Battle of Fredericksburg in December of 1862 where Robert E. Lee would defeat General Burnside who had a much large army. Congress would begin to consider removing Lincoln as the Commander and Chief of the military, which didn't materialize, since it would require an amendment to the Constitution.

Naval Warfare

Even though the land campaign wasn't going well for the Union during the first few years of the war however, the Union's blockade of the south, called the "Anaconda Plan" was slowly affecting the southern economy. The full effect of the naval blockade wouldn't be fully realized for one or two years after its inception, but it would eventually have devastating effect on the outcome of the war. Lincoln initiated the naval blockade almost immediately upon the attack of Fort Sumner, even though the Union only had 40 active ships to cover a 2,500 miles of coastline and inland waterways. The Union had another 50 ships but was not battle ready. Lincoln purchased old war ships from England and began a naval ship building program in New England By the end of the war, the U.S. Navy had 600 ships and 80 iron clad gun boats, in contrast to the Confederate Navies 33 ships at the beginning of the war, but only 14 were sea worthy. By the end of the war, the Confederate Navy had 101 ships of which, 40 were iron clad gun boats. The Confederate goal was to break the naval blockade and conduct commercial privateer raids on the high seas to acquire and seize cargo and destroy goods bound to the ports in the North. Both the Union and Confederate navies began building iron clad gun boats in late 1861 and early 1862. In March of 1862, five U.S. Navy ships lay anchored off Hampton Roads, Virginia. The first

Confederate iron clad ship, the *Merrimack,* was constructed from an old sunken U.S. ship and clad with 4 inches of iron plates. It approached the five U.S. Naval ships and immediately sank two ships. The following day, it attacked the third ship, but was met with the Union's own iron clad ship, the *Monitor.* The two iron clad boats engaged in a naval gun battle. The *Monitor* had a single advantage over the *Merrimack,* it's main cannon was mounted on a rotating gun turret, and would need not be broad side to the enemy ship when it fired.. The commander of the Merrimack became badly wounded and the *Merrimack* badly damaged and was forced to retreat back to port. It would usher in a new era in U.S. Naval history, where wooden war ships would be rendered useless in battle.

The *Merrimack* would be repaired and renamed the *Virginia* the U.S. Navy constructed 50 prototypes of the *Monitor* during the Civil War and put them into service.

The Confederacy depended on raiding Northern merchant ships as a means of reducing the size of the Northern Merchant fleet. The Confederate ship "Alabama" was built in Liverpool, England for the Confederate States of America. It would be constructed in complete secrecy in 1862, since Britain's neutrality forbid them to build ships for military purposes. Upon completion, the Alabama sailed to the Azores to have the guns mounted and military materials loaded. The ship's crew was mostly recruited from Liverpool, England. The Alabama was a coal fired steam sloop made entirely of wood. The ship never docked in America, but remained on the high seas as a privateer merchant raiding ship for cargo destined to the United States. In the two years at high sea, the Alabama captured or sunk more than 60 ships for their prizes. Her fate would eventually be sealed when she arrived at the French port of Cherbourg for dry docking. While in dry dock, the USS Kearsarge blocked the harbor entrance, waiting for the CSS Alabama to leave port. After 3 days in dry dock, the Alabama left port and engaged the USS Kearsarge into a naval battle. The Alabama fired more than 300 volleys at the Kearsarge and only managed to damage the rudder; however, the Kearsarge accurately fired 150 volleys at the Alabama thus sinking her. The Captain and Crew were rescued by a passing ship. When the Captain learned that the USS Kearsarge had installed chain armor around the starboard and port sides and covered it with a thin planking to conceal the chain armor, the Captain of the Alabama said he would have never engaged. However, the Captain of the Alabama had little choice other than abandon the Alabama while in dry dock. The "Anaconda Plan" of blockading the southern ports only had modest success. Prior to the Civil War, more than 20,000 foreign merchant ships arrived at ports in the south, however as a result of the blockade; the s number fell to 8,500 during the war.

At the beginning of the war, the Union merchant fleet numbered 5,000 ships, but with the construction of twenty Confederate commerce raiders that patrolled the Atlantic and Pacific Oceans, only 2,500 merchant ships survived by war's end..

David Glasgow. Farragut
(1801- 1870)

David G. Farragut was a flag officer in the U.S. Navy and commanded a blockade squadron in the Gulf of Mexico. Louisiana and New Orleans were within his naval jurisdiction. New Orleans was a major sea port for the Confederacy, which lay at the mouth of the Mississippi River. It was also the largest city in the Gulf Coast region. Further north on the banks of the Mississippi River, lay the Confederate Forts of Jackson and St. Philip whose purpose was to protect commerce up and down the Mississippi River and the Port of New Orleans. Farragut engaged in several naval battles in the Gulf of Mexico against the Confederate Navy and eventually gains naval superiority in the Gulf Coast region. In April of 1862, Farragut attacked Fort Jackson and Fort St. Philip with a barrage of naval bombardment that lasted for 12 days. Both forts were reduced to rubble and fell in the hands of Farragut's expeditionary force. New

Orleans was remained unprotected as a result of the fall of Fort Jackson. Farragut ordered the expeditionary force of 5,000 marines to invade New Orleans and take control of the Port and the city. Lincoln was impressed with Farragut's leadership and self-reliance and determination that he promoted Farragut as the first Naval Admiral in American history.

By January of 1863, the U.S. Navy controlled most of the Mississippi River and its tributaries, which allowed General Ulysses S. Grant to lay siege on Vicksburg, Mississippi, thus dividing the South into two halves; east and west. The Union's iron clad gun boats greatly outnumbered the Confederates iron clad boats by 1863. The U.S. Navy continued to patrol the inland waterways to secure dominance of the major inland transportation corridors in the South, in preparation for an overland invasion from the north by the Union Army in 1864 by General William T. Sherman in his march to the sea. [35]

The Gettysburg Address

There were five known drafts of the Gettysburg Address, all of which was written by Abraham Lincoln while on the train from Washington D.C. to the Gettysburg Battle Field and Cemetery on November 19, 1863. Lincoln wasn't feeling well at the time but gave the address after anyway. It was later learned he had a mild case of small pox. The first phrase in the address begins with "Four score and seven years ago" which relates to the 87 years earlier of the signing of the Declaration of Independence. One score represents 20 years.

" Four score and seven years ago our fathers brought forth on this continent a new nation, conceived in Liberty, and dedicated to the proposition that all men are created equal.

Now we are engaged in a great civil war, testing whether that nation or any nation so conceived and so dedicated, can long endure. We are met on a great battle-field of that war. We have come to dedicate a portion of that field, as a final resting place for those who here gave their lives that that nation might live. It is altogether fitting and proper that we should do this.

But, in a larger sense, we can not dedicate—we can not consecrate—we can not hallow—this ground. The brave men, living and dead, who struggled here, have consecrated it, far above our poor power to add or detract. The world will little note, nor long remember what we say here, but it can never forget what they did here. It is for us the living, rather, to be dedicated here to the unfinished work which they who fought here have thus far so nobly advanced. It is rather for us to be here dedicated to the great task remaining before us—that from these honored dead we take increased devotion to that cause for which they gave the last full measure of devotion—that we here highly resolve that these dead shall not have died in vain—that this nation, under God, shall have a new birth of freedom—and that government of the people, by the people, for the people, shall not perish from the earth."
Abraham Lincoln November 19, 1863

The media scavenged the notes of Lincoln's speech, which lasted only 2 minutes, and published his address in all the newspapers in the north and west. It gave inspiration and purpose to the Civil War which helped the recruitment effort and re-enforced the Unions resolve for victory. The British claimed that Lincoln's Emancipation Proclamation was a reckless political attempt that could not be enforced, however, in retrospect, it would later be considered among the most important documents aside from the Declaration of Independence in American history. Lincoln was given a gift to inspire, which is perhaps his greatest legacy of all.

With the victory at Gettysburg, Lincoln was not pleased with General Meade for not pursuing Lee as he retreated from the battle field. Lincoln thought Meade allowed perfect chance to crush Lee's army pass.

U.S. Grant - Commander-in-Chief of the Army

Lincoln once again wanted to make a change in command toward the end of the war. He felt his other leading generals were not aggressive enough to stop General Lee from attacking and taking the initiative. Lincoln was impressed with U.S. Grant, also known as "Unconditional Surrender Grant", ever since his victory at Vicksburg and Shiloh. He wanted Grant to replace McClellan from the start, but was reported as saying, "I can't spare this man. He fights." **[38]** Grant also believed that African-America volunteers could be a valuable fighting force in an offensive drive into the South. **[39]**

With Lincoln's second term one year away, McClellan had already decided to run against Lincoln for the Presidency in November of 1864. Lincoln wanted an assurance from Grant that he was not running for President before appointing him as General of the Army, which he expressed he had no desire. On March 9, 1864, Grant was confirmed as Commander-in-Chief of the U.S. Army and promoted to Lieutenant General in which he became the second Lieutenant General since George Washington.

In May of 1864, Grant went on the offensive into the South in an effort to destroy crops, railroads and bridges and military outpost in an effort to destroy the South's means to go on the offensive in the north. He engaged in the Overland Campaign that included the Battle of the Wilderness, Cold Harbor and Spotsylvania, all of which incurred heavy losses on both sides and were considered inconclusive. Lee was unable to replenish men he lost during the Overland Campaign which allowed General Sherman to advance and burn a 60 mile wide swath south toward Atlanta and toward the shores of the Atlantic Ocean. General Sheridan advanced south to destroy infrastructure, which would divide the South into four sections. Fighting was confined mostly in Virginia with only small confined clashes near the Border States.

Confederate General Jubal Early made several assaults on Washington D.C. but Sheridan arrived to defend any further attacks. Meetings were held between William Seward and Confederate Vice President

Stephens at Hampton Roads, Virginia to end the fighting but no agreement was made. Richmond would fall to Union forces and General Lee and Grant would have the final Battle of the War at Five Forks in which Grant encircled Lee's Army and the town of Petersburg. Lee would surrender at the Courthouse of Appomattox on April 9, 1865. General Robert E. Lee offered Grant his Battle Sword, but General Grant refused to take it. The America Civil war was over, or so it seems.

Lincoln's Assassination

While the Civil War was over, for some it was not. Such was the case with John Wilkes Booth. On April 14, 1865 Booth would proceed with a plan to assassinate President Lincoln, U.S. Grant, Vice President Johnson and Secretary William H. Seward. Each of his co-conspirators was assigned the task of assassinating each of the officials. His original plan was to kidnap the President in exchange for the release of Confederate prisoners held in jail, but when Lincoln announced plans for Blacks to vote, he decided on assassination as a plan.

Grant and Lincoln were to attend the Ford Theater in Washington on the evening of April 14, 1865, however, Grant decided to visit family rather than attend the theater with Lincoln. William Seward and Vice President Johnson were at home. At 10:13 pm Booth entered Lincoln's Theater box and discharged his pistol to the back of Lincoln's head and jumped onto the stage and fled out the back entrance of the Theater. Simultaneously as pre-arranged, his co-conspirators entered William Seward's home while he was sleeping and attacked him with a knife. Vice President Johnson was not attacked since the co-conspirator had second thoughts. Lincoln would die of his wound at 7:22 am on April 15, 1865. Booth was on the run for 12 days and found hiding in a barn in Virginia, 70 miles from Washington. After refusing to surrender, Booth was shot by Sergeant Boston Corbett on April 26th.

William Seward received numerous deep cuts to his face, body and arms, but survived. However, he remained grotesquely scared. He continued as Secretary of State under President Johnson, even though he did not get along with him. President Johnson was sworn in as President at 10:00 am April 15, 1865.

Abraham Lincoln's Legacy

There is perhaps, no other person in American history that embodies the spirit of the American legacy and a sincere dedication to preserve a nation more than Abraham Lincoln. His legacy was not about tax cuts or food stamps, unemployment or a bull market, but rather the sincere effort of holding a nation together when 14 states wanted to secede. It was about a civil war that was tearing a nation apart over slavery and states' rights. It was about the Emancipation of slaves in America. Abraham Lincoln, like those who fought in the Civil War, gave the ultimate sacrifice, their life. While the scares and the practice of racism still exist in America, it continues to inspire hope for those that one day all people will be treated equal as it was intended when the Constitution was written 232 years ago and encouraged by Lincoln and Grant. [76]

Years after Lincoln's death, the south remained bitter over the outcome of the war and the Emancipation Proclamation. Just a few years later after his death, the Thirteenth Amendment to the Constitution was ratified making slavery illegal and became the law of the land.

Section 1. *Neither slavery nor involuntary servitude, except as a punishment for crime whereof the party shall have been duly convicted, shall exist within the United States, or any place subject to their jurisdiction.*

In the south, photos of Jefferson Davis and Robert E. Lee hung in most homes. In the North, Abraham Lincoln's photo was displayed. Even though unification of the North and South became the law, it was not the law in the hearts of many in the south. Lincoln did not live long enough to ensure that his vision of unity and the Emancipation was carried out as he envisioned. It would take another 150 years before progress was made toward his goal. In 2009, 146 year later, the first Black President was elected, so Lincoln's legacy continues 153 years later. The London Times declared: "Together with Washington, Lincoln occupies a pinnacle to which no third person is likely to attain"

Lincoln was compassionate toward the hardships and grief of others because he had endured so much in his personal life as well. When Lincoln learned of a mother who had lost five of her son's in the Civil War, he wrote her the following letter of solace:

"I pray that our Heavenly Father may assuage the anguish of your bereavement, and leave you only the cherished memory of the loved and lost, and the solemn pride that must be yours to have laid so costly a sacrifice upon the altar of freedom"

Jefferson Davis
(1808 – 1889)

Jefferson Finis Davis was born in 1808 in the town of Fairview, Kentucky. His father, Samuel Davis was of Welsh decent and fought in the Revolutionary War. After the war, Samuel married Jane Cook in which they would have 10 children. Jefferson would be the youngest of the 10 siblings. His father died in 1824 and his older brother, Joseph Davis, who was 24 years his senior, would raise and educate Jefferson. Joseph was a wealthy plantation owner in both Mississippi and Louisiana. Because of Joseph's wealth and political influence, he was able to get Jefferson an appointment into West Point Military Academy. After graduation, he served six year in the U.S. Army as a Lieutenant. He also served from 1846 to 1848 during the Mexican-American War as a colonel.

After the Mexican-American War, Joseph gave Davis the Brier Field Plantation; twenty miles from Vicksburg, Mississippi. It was part of the Hurricane Plantation owned by his brother. Brier Field encompassed 1,000 acres and had 74 slaves working the fields. It was a profitable plantation; however, Davis would not visit the plantation while serving as President of the Confederacy.

After the Mexican-American war in 1848, He was considered a war hero in the South. Governor Brown of Mississippi appointed him to fill the vacant position as U.S. Senator from Mississippi. President Franklin Pierce appointed Jefferson Davis as Secretary of War in 1853. After President Buchanan became elected President in 1857, he was elected to the U.S. Senate in 1857.

Davis strongly opposed of the idea of secession of the states, however, he felt they had a legal right to do so as did Abraham Lincoln, but Lincoln felt that secession required a vote by all states rather than a random act of defiance over a particular tax or law by the federal government. When Abraham Lincoln was elected President in 1860, seven southern states seceded from the Union by late January of 1861. Jefferson Davis resigned from his Senate seat and returned to Mississippi.

Davis sent a telegraph message to Governor John Pettus, requesting that he be considered for service in defense of his home state of Mississippi. Governor Pettus gave him a commission as Major General of the Mississippi regiment. Several months later the Confederate Constitutional Convention was held in Montgomery, Alabama and Jefferson Davis was nominated as President and Alexander H. Stephens as Vice President. The relationship between Davis and his Vice President was tumultuous at best. The two engaged in frequent disagreements.

With the bombardment of Fort Sumter in South Carolina by the Confederate Army and the subsequent fall of the Fort to the

Confederate Army, it would mark the beginning of the American Civil War.

Jefferson Davis was the only President of the Confederate States of America. He served from February 18, 1861 to the May 5, 1865. Twenty days earlier, on April 14th, President Lincoln would be assassinated at the Ford Theater in Washington DC. A $100,000 reward for the capture of Jefferson Davis was offered by the government shortly after President Andrew Johnson was inaugurated. He was captured with his wife, Varina on May 10th in Irwinville, Georgia. Before his capture, his wife placed a women's overcoat on him and a black shawl that covered his head, so as to conceal his identity while waiting for the train to Cedar Key, Florida. Davis was shackled and sent to Fort Monroe in Virginia awaiting trial for treason. After two years in prison, he would be released on a $100,000 bail that was posted by prominent businessmen and women in the South. Davis and his wife moved to Montreal, Canada to await trial. On Christmas day 1868, Andrew Johnson issued a pardon and amnesty for the crime of treason against Jefferson Davis and all others who were directly or indirectly involved in the insurrection. However, Robert E. Lee and Davis would be stripped of their U.S. citizenship. Davis' citizenship would be restored 113 years later by President Jimmy Carter in 1978.

Davis remained in the sidelines during the reconstruction efforts in the South and continued to remain enormously popular among southerners and was asked to preside over Robert E. Lee's funeral in 1870.

His Brier Field Plantation remained in litigation after the Civil War, but he would eventually gain title to the plantation in 1881 after a State Supreme Court issued a final judgment in his favor. The issue of Secession being constitutional was resolved in the U.S. Supreme Court Case of Texas v. White in 1869, in which the court ruled that Secession was unconstitutional, which laid to rest the issue of secession.

While returning from New Orleans to Brier Field, Davis caught a cold that turned into bronchitis. His condition worsened over the next few months and he would die on December 6, 1889. His funeral was the largest in the South at the time. He was interred in Richmond, Virginia.

Jefferson Davis' legacy as the Confederate President over-shadowed his accomplishments as a military leader and graduate of the U.S. Military Academy at West Point, New York. He became an American hero during the Mexican-American War which was instrumental in his election to Congress as a Senator from Mississippi. A wide consensus among historians revealed that Davis was considered domineering and inflexible. He was not known for delegating authority but best known for his micro management style of leadership. He refused to appoint a General-in-Chief of the Confederate Army as Lincoln did, claiming he was in a better position of directing military operations from Richmond that his Generals. He was not popular with the Southern elite and many claimed he was out of touch with the overall population. Davis believed that Negroes were inferior to whites and slavery was the economic future for America and in particular the south. He seldom gave public speeches and often neglected domestic affairs. Davis believed his primary duties as President was to manage military affairs, rather than recruit foreign support for trade and diplomatic posturing. Even as a military leader, he made numerous battle field tactical errors that ultimately seal the fate for the Confederacy. [29]

It is interesting to note, as a U.S. Senator from Mississippi, he openly criticized the South's efforts toward secession. He advocated that the South couldn't possibly win a war with the Northern industrial states, either militarily or financially. Most foreign countries refused to loan money to the Confederacy and their economy was directly tied to the northern industrial states prior to the war. It was his devotion to duty and loyalty over practicality and common sense that forced him to throw caution to the wind and accept the position as the Confederate President. More than likely his sense of obligation and personal belief toward slavery would ultimately sway his decision to join the Confederacy.

Jefferson Davis is a study in leadership. Not all military leaders make good Presidents nor do they make good military leaders. It is a delicate balance between leadership humility and self confidence that makes some leaders stand-out among all others. Robert E. Lee was the senior officer in the Confederacy, however, unlike Lincoln; Davis refused to appoint a Commander-in- Chief of the Army until January 28, 1865, just three months before the surrender of the Confederate Army at Appomattox Court House on April 9, 1865. In contrast, Abraham Lincoln had minimal military experience, but had the strength of leadership and self confidence to be flexible in his decisions and open to opinions. He would select several Generals as his Commander-in-Chief but replaced them when they suffered humiliating defeats in battle by a less formidable foe. In the latter part of the war, Lincoln appointed Ulysses S. Grant as his Commander–in–Chief in the spring of 1964, just one year before the surrender of Robert E. Lee at Appomattox Court House in April of 1865.

Robert E. Lee
(1807 – 1870)

Robert Edward Lee was born at the Stratford Hall Plantation, Virginia in 1807. His father was Major General Henry Lee II, fondly known as "Light Horse Harry" who at the time was Governor of Virginia. His mother was Anne Carter who was raised on the Shirley Plantation, which was reported as being the most lavish plantation in Virginia. The Lee's were of English heritage and his great grandfather immigrated to America in the mid 1600's. Henry Lee would spend one year in debtor's prison in 1809 as a result of several poor investments he made. In 1812, Henry Lee was injured during a riot in

THE AMERICAN LEGACY

Baltimore and move to the West Indies, leaving his family behind. He never returned to America and would die when Robert was eleven. A relative of the Lee's, William Fitzhugh took in the Lee family. When Robert was 18, Fitzhugh applied for an appointment for Robert to the United States Military Academy at West Point, New York and was accepted in 1825. His field of study was engineering. He would graduate in 1829, second in his class. One month later his mother would die.

Lee was assigned to assist in the building of Fort Pulaski on Cockspur Island, Georgia. He was later assigned to Fort Monroe in Virginia. While stationed at Fort Monroe, he met childhood friend Mary Custis. They would marry in June of 1831, and have seven children together of which two would die of typhoid and tuberculosis. The oldest child, George Washington Custis Lee was born in 1832 and would become Major General in the Confederate Army. He would die of natural causes in 1913. William Henry Fitzhugh Lee was born in 1837 and would be commissioned as a Major General in the Confederate Army as well. He would die of natural causes in 1891. His Last son, Robert Edward Lee Jr. was born in 1843 and would be commissioned as a Captain in the Confederate Army. He would die of natural causes in 1914.

The Custis family was a very affluent family in Virginia if not in the entire United States. George Washington married Martha Custis who was Mary Custis' great granddaughter, and the step granddaughter of George Washington. Mary was the daughter of George Washington Parke Custis, George Washington's step grandson. Robert E. Lee was the great-great- great grandson of William Randolph. The Lee was well connected in Virginia, from George Washington to the Randolph family.

Lee participated in the Mexican-America War from 1846 to 1848 as an aide to General Winfield Scott. During the Battle of Veracruz to Mexico City he provided reconnaissance for Scott which became help for Scott in his invasion of Mexico City. He was promoted to Major after the Battle of Cerro Gordo. It was during the Mexican-American War that Lee and Grant would meet for the first time.

After the war in February of 1848, he was assigned to Fort Carroll in Baltimore. In 1852, he was appointed as Superintendent of the U.S. Military Academy at West Point which lasted until 1855. His son, George Washington Custis Lee graduated from West Point in 1854 while serving as Superintendent.
In 1857, his father-in-law, George Washington Parke Custis died living Lee as the executor. The Custis estate was very large with hundreds of slave. The plantation was in heavy debt he was unable to find anyone to manage the plantation. He took a two year leave of absence from the military to manage the estate. The New York Daily Tribune reported that Lee whipped and flogged three slaves, one of which was a woman for being a run-away. It was not clear if Lee actually whipped the women or not, but his reputation as a gentlemen damaged his legacy and the honor of the Custis Family. His slaves would be emancipated in accordance to the Will in 1862.
John Brown

John Brown was a radical abolitionist born and raised in Connecticut. He had a following of 21 likeminded people who believed strongly in abolishing slavery in North America. Brown and his two sons travel around New England preaching their message on the evils of Slavery. Brown and his group followers seized the federal armory at Harpers Ferry and took about twenty hostages in the process. His motive was to create insurrection among the local slave population to openly rebel against slavery. President James Buchanan gave the order to Lee to surpass the uprising. After two days of confrontation, Lee captured John Brown and his hostages. Some of his group was killed including both of Brown's son's. He would go on trial and be sentenced to hang.

THE AMERICAN LEGACY

The Civil War (April 1861 to March 1865)

Under each participant of the Civil War, I have listed some of the campaigns and battles they were active in. Robert E. Lee was the commander of the Army of the Virginia for much of the war, while Grant was commander of the Army of the Ohio and Tennessee, but later commanded the Army of the Potomac and General of the Union Army.

Lee was pro-slavery, even though he did not discuss his views openly, especially while serving the military. He believed that blacks were inferior and that separation of the races was an accepted standard. He also felt that blacks didn't have the intellectual capacity to vote. He voted for candidates that were pro slavery advocates, however, he strongly believed that while serving in the military, it was his duty to be apolitical. It is also widely accepted that he was good to his slaves and treated them with respect.

He was born and raised as a Virginian aristocrat, even though his family fell upon hard times, his marriage to Mary Custis elevated his status as southern gentlemen. His firmness toward slaves would test his legacy while he was an alive and long after his death. He was a military man, and it was well established that he was well disciplined and with exceptional demeanor.

When South Carolina seceded from the Union in December of 1860, Lee was opposed to cession in the beginning; however, he resigned his commission in the United States Army on April 20, 1861. When General Winfield Scott heard that Lee resigned his commission, Scott was forlorn. Robert E. Lee would become the only general of the Confederate Army, even though it was only one month before his surrender at Appomattox. **[61]**

DOUGLAS G. BEAUDOIN

First Battle of Bull Run
(July 1861)

The first battle of the Civil War started near the Manassas Junction, about 25 miles south of Washington D.C. There were several battles at Manassas Junction, which were called Bull Run 1 and Bull Run 2 by the Union and Manassas 1 and 2 by the Confederates. When it became obvious that the two armies would collide at Bull Run Creek and Manassas Junction, many from Washington D.C. would take picnic lunches and travel to the rolling hills surrounding Bull Run Creek to watch the Battle. It would be hot summer day in July when General Irvin McDowell and 28,400 Union Volunteers would advance toward Manassas Junction, Virginia on July 16, 1861. General Beauregard was camped near the Junction with 20,000 Confederate troops. Beauregard had already sent for re-enforcements from General Johnston who commanded a force of 11,000 from the Shenandoah Valley east of Manassas Junction.

Lincoln wanted General McDowell to attack Beauregard's army on July 1st, but McDowell procrastinated and wanted to do additional training of his troops before going into battle. McDowell's Army of 35,000 wouldn't leave Washington D.C. until the 16th of July, which infuriated Lincoln. Because of the two week delay, General Beauregard was able to move another 11,000 troops toward Manassas and have additional re-enforcements available on demand. McDowell's army would engage the enemy on July 21 with 10,000 union soldiers, driving the confederates toward Henry House Hill. The on-lookers and picnic observers lounging on the hill sides believed that the Union Army was going to pull-off and easy victory, but didn't realize that Beauregard was holding back 18,000 of his main force and attacked McDowell's Union army at Bull Run Creek, led by General Thomas Jackson from Johnston's Shenandoah Valley Command. The Union Army fled over the hills where the picnic goes and loungers were watching the battle from the nearby hill top and soon realized that they were soon to become part of the battle of Bull Run when

Confederate troops with bayonets began charging fleeing union troops over the hill, thus sending picnic and on-lookers fleeing with the Yankee troops in chaos.

The Confederate Army failed to seize the opportunity to charge fleeing Union soldiers from the battlefield, which potentially could have destroyed McDowell's entire Army. Lincoln soon replaced McDowell with George B. McClellan; in which Lincoln soon discovered that he had replaced one mediocre General with another less than mediocre General.

Near the end of the Battle of Bull Run, the Confederate Army numbered 30,800 after re-enforcements arrived, thus tipping the balance of the war in favor of the Confederate Army. The Union Army suffered 2,600 casualties while the Confederate Army suffered 2,000. Most of the casualties were captured soldiers, since both sides recorded 400 killed, the remainder were injured during the battle itself and it was not known with certainty how many died from wounds inflicted during the battle days later.

Second Battle of Bull Run
(August 1862)

The second Battle of Bull Run occurred in late August of 1862 at the same location as the first Battle one year earlier. Lincoln appointed General Henry Halleck to replace General George B. McClelland as the Commander in Chief of the Union Armies in July of 1862. Halleck recalled the Army of the Potomac to Washington and created the Army of Virginia as part of the Army of the Potomac. The idea was to combine the two armies for an eventual campaign to launch against Richmond, the Capital of the Confederacy. John Pope was given the command of the Army of Virginia.

Robert E. Lee learned of the plan to join the two armies in the north for an offensive attack on Richmond and decided to attack General

Pope's Army before he could join McClellan's Army of the Potomac. Lee divided his army in half, giving General Thomas Jackson (Stonewall Jackson) half (24,000). Jackson's marched his Army to Manassas Junction for the purpose of destroying the Union's supply warehouse and retreat in the dense forest and hills around Bull Run Creek. Pope arrived at Manassas Junction in late August and believed that Jackson's Army would retreat rather than fight, but in fact Jackson was waiting for General Longstreet's Army. General McClellan refused to send troops to re-enforce Pope's Army because McClellan needed them to protect Washington D.C., since Manassas Junction was only 25 miles from Washington D.C. During the evening of August 29th, Pope's scouts reported that several brigades were moving and changing battlefield positions. Pope immediately believed they were in the process of retreating when in fact they were repositioning themselves for an early morning attack. Pope sent a message to Halleck and Lincoln declaring a victory and that they were preparing to attack the retreating army. The following morning Jackson and Longstreet ordered the attack on Pope's position, causing him and his army to make a hasty retreat toward Washington. This was perhaps the most humiliating defeat and military miscalculation of the Civil War.

When news arrived of the second battle of Bull Run and the second loss, what followed was a barge of accusation of who was responsible for the loss. Secretary of War, Stanton wanted McClellan dismissed. Lincoln had lost all faith in his Generals and wanted to reorganize his entire military leadership. General Pope lost 15,000 men while the Confederates lost 9,000, Pope was reassigned to the Department of the Northwest, completely out of sight and completely out of mind. General McClellan would join the Army of the Potomac and the Army of the Virginia and advance toward Antietam to block Lee's army from advancing into the north.

The Battle of Antietam
(September 1862)

The Battle of Antietam began on September 22, 1862. McClellan's army of 54,000 engaged Lee's Army of 30,600 near the town of Sharpsburg, Maryland. Lee's plan was to move the war from northern Virginia into the North, since much of northern Virginia carried the brunt of the Civil War. With Lee's victory at the Battle of the Second Bull Run, he was apparently over confident that his army could not be stopped. The main objective of the second Battle of Bull Run was not fully realized. Lee's Army under the command of Stonewall Jackson and Johnston did not pursue and destroy Pope's Army and only delayed Pope from uniting with McClellan's Army of the Potomac. As Lee's Army continued north into Maryland, the two northern armies united to form an army twice the size of Lee's Northern Army of Virginia. During McClellan's Peninsula Campaign to take Richmond, it ended in McClellan's retreating and Lee's victory. Lincoln was certain that McClellan's loses was due to the Union's lack of clear leadership and no definitive war strategy to counter Lee's aggressive military style.

Lee's plan, called the "Maryland Campaign", also known as Special Order 191, was to divide his army and each unit would attack; Boonsboro, Hagerstown and Harper's Ferry and Martinsburg. Lee's army was camped at Frederick, Maryland but after Lee divided his army into units, a messenger delivering the battle plan via horseback dropped the plan along a roadway, which was wrapped around three cigars. When Union troops arrived in Frederick, the message was found and delivered to General McClellan. McClellan immediately set-out to foil Lee's plans. When Lee found that his message and battle plans were missing, he immediately attempted to gather his divided army together. Near Sharpsburg, General Hill and Longstreet's army was intercepted by McClellan's army. Lee wanted to retreat back to Virginia but learned that Stonewall Jackson was victorious in taking Harper's Ferry and decided to continue with his plan. The two armies would meet near Antietam Creek. Within 8 hours of battle, 15,000 casualties covered over a 30 acre cornfield. The battle continued as the body count increased every hour. After 12 hours of fighting and as darkness closed in, 23,000 casualties laid dead or wounded in the fields. The following morning, Lee began to collect his wounded and began the exodus south into Virginia, while McClellan looked on. President Lincoln was infuriated that McClellan did not take advantage once again of Lee's retreat, which certainly could have ended the war earlier. McClellan had a 2 to 1 advantage and could have forced Lee to surrender his entire army. McClellan would be removed from command on November 5, 1862 as a result. The victory of Antietam would give Lincoln the victory he needed to announce his Emancipation Proclamation on September 22, 1862.

General Lee, "stonewall" Jackson and Longstreet were humbled by the defeat at Antietam, even though the Confederacy didn't call it a defeat, but rather an inconclusive battle with little damaging effect on the outcome of the war. Even though the Battle of Antietam had little military strategic value, President Lincoln began his search for a replacement for McClellan.

The Battle of Antietam would be a turning point of the war. General Grant was having success in the west, Lee was turned back from moving the war into the north and Lincoln's Emancipation Proclamation was viewed in the North as a success.

For the Confederacy, the hope that France and Great Britain would come to their aid was dashed, and the brutality of war was realized when Alexander Gardner's photographs of battlefield carnage was seen by everyone, which made the war visible and horrible rather than just a news brief of battles won and lost on both sides.

The Battle of Chancellorsville and Gettysburg
(April 1863) and (July 1863)

These two battles of the Civil War changed the tactic and strategy of the war. For the Union Army it would change the overall command. In January of 1863, shortly after Lincoln's Emancipation Proclamation, Grant, with the help of David Farragut's naval assault on Vicksburg, Mississippi which divide the Confederacy East and West. General Hooker advanced his army of 130,000 to Chancellorsville, Virginia in April of 1863. General Lee's scouts reported Hooker's movements and Lee decided to go on the offensive. General Stonewall Jackson began attacking Union Armies left flank as a maneuver to weaken and drive through the Union line. The battle raged for 6 days which resulted in a decisive victory for the Lee. The Union Army suffered 17,000 casualties against Lee's 13,000. Jefferson Davis was insistent on having his Confederate Army push north into Union territory. Davis rationalized that if they moved the battles north it would force Lincoln to sue for peace. It was a desperate measure and a risky military tactic at best, since moving much of his confederate forces north to fight battles would also leave Richmond and the south vulnerable for a Union invasion.

The Union's military strength was twice that of the South, thus a casualty loss of 15,000 troops would only be a 10% casualty rate, but a 15,000 casualty loss for the Confederate army would equate to a 20% casualty rate. Statistically speaking, the Union Army had a reserve force of 2.5 million and could easily replenish losses sustained; however in contrast, the Confederate Army only had 5,800 men in reserve and would suffer a loss of half of their fighting force in the first two years of the war. Even though Lee enjoyed a victory at Chancellorsville, a 21% casualty loss even with a victory was unsustainable for any period of time.

Lincoln in turn wanted his generals to advance toward Richmond and take the capital. Robert E. Lee was hesitant to extend his army into

Pennsylvania, thus leaving Richmond and the South vulnerable to attack should he sustain heavy losses and unable to return to defend Richmond. But he also realized that his 75,000 men advancing north toward Harrisburg and Philadelphia could cause Lincoln to consider an armistice. General Hooker began his pursuit but was relieved by General Meade. Hooker wanted to change assignments and threatened to resign if he was not given a command at Harper's Ferry. Needless to say, Halleck accepted his resignation. The two armies clashed at Gettysburg, Pennsylvania on July 1, 1863. The battle lasted three days when 12,500 Confederates, known as "Pickett's Charge" rushed the Union's front lines in a desperate move to take control of the battle field, but his charge was repelled. Only 3 of Pickett's brigades were used during the attack the remainders of the 12,000 troops were provided by General Longstreet's Army. The logistics of the Charge was not well throughout.

The distance from Picket's line to the Union line at Cemetery Ridge was about 1,000 to 1,400 yards up hill. In a full charge it would take 15 minutes at to cover the distance. Of the 12,000 who charged, only 100 men were able to reach the Union line on Cemetery Ridge. According to Longstreet's report in 1886, he reported that there were 7,300 Confederate casualties during Pickett's charge, which lasted less than 30 minutes. With cannon fire and reloading every 12 seconds, Pickett's men were slaughtered by the time they reached the fence. It would be the turning point in the Battle of Gettysburg and it forced Lee's army to retreat the following day to Virginia in a rain storm of thunder and lightning.

The Battle of Gettysburg was the most costly battle in American history, with more than 51,000 casualties in three days of fighting. More American casualties in the Battle of Gettysburg than in the Revolutionary War, War of 1812 and the Mexican-American War combined.

Upon Lee's return to Virginia, he was bewildered at the loss at

Gettysburg and the loss of 21,000 men in a single battle. The Union could afford the loss but the South could not. He offered his resignation to Jefferson Davis, but Davis refused to accept it.

For Robert E. Lee, there were other battles to win and lose before the war ended at Appomattox Court House in April of 1865, but he would face a different opponent on the battlefield when Lincoln appointed a General he once met during the Mexican-American War sixteen years earlier. Unlike other Union General at the time, Grant was aggressive for which the soldiers nicknamed him "Never Surrender Grant", and yet as cunning on the battlefield as Lee.

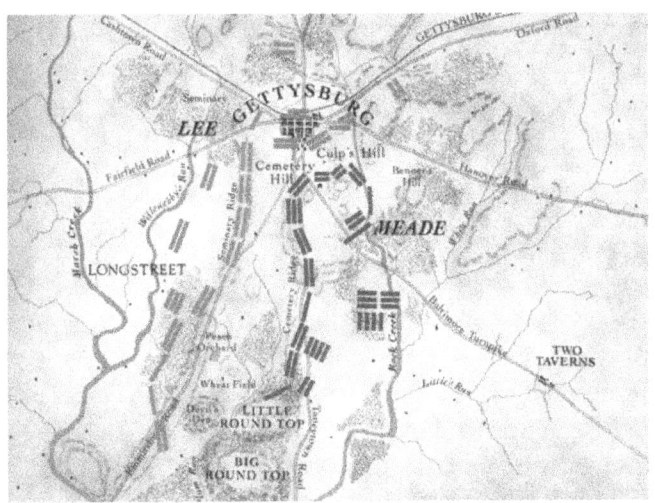

Map 15, Battle of Gettysburg, July 1863

Ulysses S. Grant
(1822 – 1885)

"Although a soldier by profession, I have never felt any sort of fondness for war, and I have never advocated it, except as a means of peace."   - Ulysses S. Grant

Hirm Ulysses Grant was born in Point Pleasant, Ohio in 1822. His ancestors arrived in the Massachusetts Bay Colony in 1630. The

Grant's eventually settled in Pennsylvania where his father, Jesse Root Grant was born. Jesse became a Whig supporter early in his youth and a staunch abolitionist.

He and his family moved to Point Pleasant, Ohio in 1820 and Jesse would marry Hannah Grant (Simpson) in 1821. Jesse was a successful tanner and merchant in Ohio. They would have six children with Hirm Ulysses being the eldest. His other two brothers continued in their father's footsteps as tanners, however, Ulysses disliked the slaughter house and would have little interest in the family business.

The Grant family was active in the local Methodist Church, however, Ulysses remained non denominational throughout most of his entire life. It is said that he preferred to pray privately and not publicly. Ulysses preferred working with horses and his father gave him the job of driving a freight wagon for his father's business.

U.S. Military Academy, West Point
(1839- 1843)

The Grant's family was not wealthy but middle class; however, his father began Ulysses' formal education when he was five years old. He attended Maryville Seminary and the John Rankin's Academy in his early years. When he was 16 years old, his father wrote to the U.S. Senator in Ohio and requested admission to the U.S. Military Academy at West Point. Ulysses was accepted and began his first year 1839. During his application process for enrollment, Ulysses wrote his name as: "Ulysses S. Grant". It was never made clear why he elected to drop the name of Hirm and add a middle initial of "S". Other cadets called him "Uncle Sam" or just plain Sam.

His skill as a horseman at West Point became legendary. He held the high jump record at West Point which he held for 25 years. It was obvious that the Calvary was going to be his military field. He would graduate from West Point in July of 1843 in the middle of his class.

His closest friends at West Point were James Longstreet and Fredrick Tracy Dent. Grant wasn't a model cadet; in fact during his four years at West Point he had accumulated 250 demerits. In contrast, Robert E. Lee had none. Most of his infractions were minor, mostly for being late for muster or sleeping in. Grant wrote, "….. There is much to dislike (military and West Point), but more to like." After graduation, he decided not to make the military a career, but became a school teacher; however he first complete his military obligation of 4 years of service as part of his West Point education. He was not assigned to the Cavalry as he hoped, but to the 4th Infantry Regiment as a quartermaster.

While stationed at Jefferson Barracks, Missouri, he often visited Fredrick Dent's family who lived near the Fort. He met and courted Dent's sister, Julia and they would marry four years later in 1848. They would have four children together; Fredrick, Ulysses Jr., Ellen, and Jesse. Since starting a family, Grant decided to remain in the U.S. Army since it was a steady job and income.

During James K. Polk's presidency, (1845 to 1849), the Mexican-American war broke-out in 1846. General Winfield Scott was in charge of the U.S. Forces against Mexico. Grant assigned Zachary Taylor to a command in Louisiana, but Taylor's command was ordered to Texas to engage in the Battle of Palo Alto. Grant was given the command of leading a cavalry charge during the Battle of Resaca de la Palma and Monterrey. His unit would be assigned to General Winfield Scott who was in the process of marching his army into Mexico City. They would meet stiff resistance in the Battle of Molino del Rey and Chapultepec near Mexico City. For bravery, he received a field promoted to captain. The Mexican-American War ended in September of 1847, at which time he was reassigned to the Vancouver Barracks in the Oregon Territory and in January of 1854 he was reassigned to Fort Humbolt in northern California.

Grant had been away from his wife and family for nearly two years and he and his commanding officer at Fort Humbolt, Colonel Buchanan, did not get along well. He began drinking heavily out of boredom and from missing his family. He often arrived at muster late and inebriated. At one point, General McClellan arrived at the fort and noticed Grant being under the influence. McClellan would always remember Captain Grant as a "drunk".

Grant resigned his commission in July of 1854, while at Fort Humboldt, however not because of his alleged drinking but, according to Grant, because he missed his family. Colonel Buchanan did not report the incident of his drinking, but gave a favorable departing evaluation. His drinking problem never appeared in his service record; however, it never escaped the attention of General George McClellan.

After leaving the Army at the age of 32, immediately returned to Covington, Kentucky and later moved to St. Louis, Missouri with his family and farmed on his brother-in-laws land, only earning $50 per month. He was given a slave by Julia's father to help with the farming but the land was poor and Julia's father gave them a farm in which he built a rustic cabin on. When the Panic of 1857 struck America, Grant pawned his gold watch for $50 to pay for Christmas. He would rent out his farm and move to Julia's father's estate but after suffering a serious bout of malaria, he decided he was not a farmer and quit farming altogether. The slave he was given years earlier, he freed him. He would move to St. Louis and became a partner in Julia's cousin's real estate company, but the business would be dissolved a year later. In 1860, he and his family returned to Galena and began work in his father's successful tannery and leather goods business.

For 7 years of being a civilian, he and his family encountered poverty and failed enterprises in business and farming. His only lifeline was his family and Julia's family. With the attack on Fort Sumter in April 12, 1861, Lincoln called for 75,000 volunteers. Recruitment centers were opened throughout the north. Grant was selected to be in charge of the recruitment in the town of Galena. In Springfield,

Governor Yates offered him a commission in the 21st Illinois Volunteer Infantry Regiment. Major General George McClellan refused to acknowledge Grant's correspondence for a commission in the Union Army; however he was promoted to Brigadier General of the Illinois Volunteer Infantry.

The Union upper ranks in the Regular U.S. Army were in a constant state of chaos with "back-stabbing", jealousy and gossiping. Rumors circulated about Grants drinking problem while he was stationed at Fort Humbolt, however, John C. Freemont would give Grant a commission as Major General and assigned him to command regiment in Cairo, Illinois, which lay on the banks of the Mississippi River. Freemont heard of Grant's earlier drinking problem, but dismissed them as petty jealousy and believed Grant demonstrated an "Iron Will" that other Generals wanting the position did not possess the characteristics that John C. Freemont saw in Grant.

Battle of Fort Henry and Fort Donelson
(November 1861)

During the first 10 months of the War, The Union Army suffered defeat after defeat by the Confederate Army. Winfield Scott retired only 3 months after being appointed as General-in-Chief of the U.S. Army and Lincoln appointed General George McClellan as General-in-Chief because of his War-Winning Strategy paper he submitted to Lincoln. In addition, he was appointed General of the Army of the Potomac. Lincoln was eager for a series of wins that would give the Union Army a slight edge in the War. The Union built a military force of 200,000 in the Army of the Potomac, Lincoln instructed McClellan that the standing army of the Potomac under McClellan's command was costing $600,000 per day but had yet engaged the enemy. McClellan continued to draft plans for an invasion of Richmond, which encountered multiple delay. General Johnson of the Confederate Army defending Richmond knew of McClellan's propensity of not acting unless conditions and man power was suitable for the task, which allowed Johnson time to reinforce his positions around Richmond. [44]

While the invasion of Richmond was stalled time after time by McClellan, Grant had devised a plan to take control of the inland waterways of the Mississippi River and its tributaries. In doing so, the Confederacy would be split from east and west and the Union forces could cripple the Confederacy's ability to supply troops by way of the river system, thus slowly strangling the Confederacy into surrender.

McClellan was in command of the Army of the Potomac while General Halleck was in command of the Army of the West, Missouri Department. Both Generals disliked Grant, not as much as his drinking habits, but his liaise affair attitude toward his superiors and the lack of military discipline and organization which greatly annoyed Halleck and McClellan. When Grant requested a meeting with General Halleck to discuss his plan for taking Fort Henry and Fort Donelson on the Mississippi, Halleck rebuffed Grant rudely and dismissed him before he could discuss his plan. A week later, he got a message ordering Grant to advance toward Fort Henry.

Halleck and McClellan both were West Point graduates; however, they lacked field experience. McClellan saw some action in the Mexican-American War, but spent a month or more in the hospital with dysentery. Both of their military experience consisted of text book battlefield strategy and theory as taught in class at West Point. Halleck wrote a book on Battle Field Strategy and spent time in Europe learning and writing about other views on military strategy, but their knowledge was mostly confined to library scholarly education. Both Halleck and McClellan were businessmen; banking, law, real estate and in the railroad industry, prior to being appointed to top commands under Lincoln. Halleck's temperament was demanding and intolerant of those who lacked procedural perfection and bureaucratic organizational skills. Halleck's primary role was administrative duties such as logistics and military politics. He was masterful at organizing troop movement and supplies, however beyond that, Halleck, was indecisive if the enemy showed unpredictable that didn't fit within his neatly organized world of predictability. When Lincoln appointed Halleck as General-in-Chief of the U.S. Army, he once said, "Halleck was little more than a first rate clerked".

In November of 1861, Grant, along with General John McClernand landed 2,500 men near the town of Belmont, Missouri. Grant was re-enforced by General McPherson who had 25,000 men and all would advance toward Fort Henry. In addition, Naval Commander Foote and his armada of gunboats would rendezvous up river. Grant easily took Fort Henry and advanced toward Fort Donelson. However, Fort Donelson had a military strength equal to Grant's army and was in a perfect position to repel any frontal attacks by Union forces. After a several days of battle with mounting union casualties, Grant refused to give-up and instructed his field commanders to intensify the pressure on the fort, find a weak spot in their defense. Grant sent a message to Confederate Commander Floyd to surrender, but he refused, since Floyd realized he had the upper hand in the battle and siege. Grant continued the siege until eventually Commander Floyd could no longer hold on. He conceded defeat. From that day on he would be known as "**Unconditional Surrender Grant**". Floyd would surrender his entire army of 12,000 to Grant.

Lincoln and the North were elated to find that Grant had won two battles simultaneously and controlled a major portion of the Cumberland and Tennessee Rivers. Before the Battles, Grant was little known, however with his success, he became a hero. When a picture of Grant appeared in the northern news papers with a cigar in his mouth, people sent him hundred of cigars in the mail. His success at Fort Donelson and Fort Henry was welcomed news.

General Halleck was furious with Grant and sent a telegram to McClellan accusing Grant as being "negligent and inefficient". Halleck sent another telegram claiming he had not heard from Grant in more than a week and assumed that he had resumed his bad habits of drinking. Lincoln was becoming weary of the petty feuding of his top generals and decided to promote Grant to Major General.

Grant's Alleged Drinking Problem

When he applied for a commission in the U.S. Army at the beginning of the Civil War in 1861, General McClellan refused to give him a commission, in fact refused to even respond to his correspondence. Rumors of his drinking circulated among the officers in Washington, which would ruin any chances for a field commission in the regular army. Governor Richard Yates of Ohio appointed Grant to the Ohio Militia in Springfield, Ohio as a recruiter and trainer. Grant wanted a field command in the regular army and once again made a request to General George B. McClellan but was ignored. Much of the rumors of Grant's drinking problem were greatly exaggerated. He never drank during battles and would only drink occasionally during periods of boredom and being away from home for long periods of time. His wife, Julia, did not approve of drinking and it was well documented that he did not drink at home or in her presence. Abraham Lincoln dismissed the constant rants of Grant's drinking as idle gossip and professional jealously among the Generals. During the entire Civil War, Generals McClernand, McClellan and Halleck wasted little time pointing out Grant's failings to Lincoln. Newspaper reports described Grant as arriving on the battle field wearing a private soldiers jacket with his general insignia crudely sewn on the shoulder and wearing muddy boots and a farmer's hat. Grant dressed for comfort as did Zachary Taylor which fueled disdain in the upper command. While his military appearance drew constant criticism from his superiors, Lincoln must have admired him for not being just another "Tin Soldier from West Point".

The Battle of Shiloh
(April 1862)

Halleck relieved Grant from the field, but Secretary of War, Stanton and President Lincoln demanded that Halleck reinstate Grant. Grant took command of 45,000 troops against the Confederates 40,000. They converged near the town of Corinth. Grant telegraphed Halleck that he wanted to attack the Confederates at Corinth, but Halleck wanted Grant to wait until General Buell's army arrived with a division of 25,000 men. While Grant waited, the Confederates took the initiative and attacked Grants force, obviously realizing that Grant was waiting for re-enforcements. Both General Halleck and McClellan were overly cautious in battle and both shared the same battle strategy of waiting. General Albert Johnston of the Confederate Army was shot during the battle leaving General Beauregard in command of the Confederate forces at Shiloh.

One of Grants main front lines held several attacks but eventually collapsed and allowed the Confederate Army to push into Grants held position. Grant was able to regroup and reform his line and hold off any further attack before nightfall. The battle at Shiloh appeared to be lost for Grant. That evening during a cold heavy down pour of rain and sitting around a campfire, General McPherson ask Grant if he was going to retreat in the morning, Grant replied, *"Retreat?, no. I propose to attack them at daylight and whip them."* The following morning, true to his word, with Buell's 18,000 fresh troops arriving, Grant attacked and drove the Confederate army into a retreat, thus winning the battle of Shiloh.

The Battle of Shiloh was among the most costly and one of the most strategically important battles of the Civil War. With the Unions 23,746 casualties, the north once again considered Grant a hero; however, it was short lived. The newspapers began to report the casualty rate and rumors circulated accusing him of being back on the bottle. While there was will proof or evidence in such rumor, Lincoln considered it professional jealousy and the rumors were being leaked to the media.

Halleck relieved him of his field command and replaced him with General George Henry Thomas. Halleck himself would take command of 120,000 men and marched to Corinth on May 30th, but half of his command would be given back to Grant and Halleck would once again reinstate Grant as a field commander. It is not certain why Halleck had a change of mind, however, I suspect that the Battle of Corinth would be his first and only field engagement, and he lacked the self confidence in going alone on the battlefield. Halleck more than likely received pressure from Secretary of War Stanton and President Lincoln, who had little faith in Halleck's ability as a field commander.

The Vicksburg Campaign
(May 1863)

With Grant's previous victories and control of the inland waterways, the last big obstacle was take control of the entire Mississippi River drainage. The fort at Vicksburg had to be taken in order to completely divide the South in half from north and south. There had been two previous attempts to take Vicksburg but both failed. Grant would be promoted to Command the District of Tennessee, which covered most of the Southwest. After Lincoln's Emancipation Proclamation, Grant ordered former slaves freed and an option to join the U.S. Army, in which they were given food, clothing and wages. Grants Tennessee command had only 40,000 troops, however, Sherman was ordered to march toward Vicksburg, and however, his army got cut-off by Confederate General John Pemberton. McClernand was able to reach Sherman's Army and took command of both his and Sherman's Army. They would capture Fort Hindman while en-route toward Vicksburg.

Grant's relationship with General McClernand became strained over several events. Captain Kountz was placed in charge of river transportation and was a good friend of General McClernand whom Kountz reported to. When the newspaper began printing stories about Captain Kountz and possible corruption, Grant arrested him, but never filed formal charges against him.

Kountz was also close friends of General McClellan and General Helleck in retaliation against Grant, Kountz made allegations concerning Grants' drinking. McClernand supported Kountz and Grant decided to adjourn a meeting to explain the reason Kountz was arrested, however, it didn't satisfy McClernand or McClellan. It would later be uncovered that McClernand was writing Lincoln often about Grant's drinking and other short coming and boasted to others of his personal connection with Lincoln, which forced Grant to distance himself, professionally, from McClernand. Lincoln was being bombarded with accusations of Grant's drinking from all three men, Lincoln casually responded, "I wish some of you would tell me the brand of whiskey that Grant drinks. I would like to send a barrel of it to my other generals." [47] [48]

Lincoln was becoming wary of the in-house gossip and criticism over Grant's drinking and battlefield tactics. Lincoln viewed the criticism as jealousy, while Grant rarely responded to such criticism. Grant didn't have the personality of constantly needing approval and acceptance from his superiors.

McClernand was known to be politically driven and a braggart, in contrast, Grant was unassuming and humble and non confrontational. Their two personalities would clash. Grant, however had a great deal of respect for William T. Sherman and even though Sherman was McClernand's junior, Grant selected Sherman over McClernand as his second in command on the battlefield, which only fueled resentment between the two. . [45]

On January 29, 1863, Grant's army fought their way through the swamps along the western flood plains of the Mississippi River, hoping to find an area in which to stage an attack from. On the east side was high banks which made it impossible to mount an attack. Admiral David Porter's gunboats arrived but were unable to get close enough to the bluffs at Vicksburg without being sunk by the canons overlooking the river. Pemberton's Confederate Army occupied Champion Hill outside Vicksburg, blocking any advance from the east toward Vicksburg. Vicksburg's location on the high bluffs overlooking the Mississippi River made it difficult for naval bombardment from the river. Vicksburg was a perfect defensive position with only an inland frontal attack possible, yet blocked by Pemberton's army on Champion Hill. Grant's Army marched southeast of Vicksburg toward Jackson, Mississippi (the Capital of Mississippi) to connect with McClernand and Sherman's army. Jackson, Mississippi fall to the Union Army on May 14, 1863 and Grant would march his army toward Champion Hill to confront Pemberton which blocked his only avenue to take Vicksburg. Pemberton's army was dug-in at Champion Hill, but after fierce fighting, Grant was able to overpower Pemberton's army and force his main body to retreat to Vicksburg and leaving 7,000 troops at the bridge crossing the Big Black River to slow Grants advance and allowing his main force to safely get to Vicksburg. When arriving at Vicksburg and after a frontal attack which was easily repelled, Grant began his seven week siege of the City and the Fort.

During the seven week siege, Grant would occasionally drink in the evening while waiting, but not to any excess as others have reported. Pemberton eventually surrendered Vicksburg to Grant on July 4, 1863, as many were starving and illness began to take their toll on the civilian population.

Secretary of War, Edwin Stanton requested Grant to take Command of the Army of the Potomac, but he sent a letter to Stanton and respectfully declined the appointment, since he did not know the Virginia country side well enough and that his knowledge of the Tennessee District would be of better use for the Union. Stanton consented and promoted him to Major General of the Regular Army in the newly formed Division of the Mississippi, which included Ohio, Tennessee and the Cumberland region. After the Chattanooga Campaign which opened the possibility of a Union invasion of Georgia, Lincoln promoted Grant to lieutenant general, with the full command of all Union Armies and he would answer only to the President. Halleck was appointed to a desk job as Army Chief of Staff, which put him out of the War as a commanding general of leading troops into battle. McClellan had been out of favor with Lincoln from the first day he was appointed General of the Army. He was in the process of campaigning for President against Lincoln's in his second term in 1884.

Grant immediately engages in the Chattanooga Campaign, which involved the Battle of Chickamauga, Missionary Ridge and Lookout Mountain. Grant gives the Mississippi Command to Sherman and he and General Meade would occupy an office near Washington. **(22)**

Grant proposed to Lincoln and Stanton a plan to finally cripple the Confederate Army. He wanted to carry-out 5 separate coordinated attacks simultaneously against the Confederate Army so they could not reinforce or resupply each other during the battles. Grant knew that Lee did not have enough recruits to replace those lost in battle, so driving Robert E. Lee's Army south would leave Richmond vulnerable to attack by Grant from the north and Meade and Butler's Armies from the South. Richmond would be defenseless with three Armies attacking from two sides, since Lee did not have a large enough army to defend two armies.

Grant's next campaign was the Overland Campaign which involved a series of battles of terrible consequences on both sides. In the battle of the Wilderness alone, Grant's Army suffered 17,666 casualties to the Confederates 11,125. In Spotsylvania the battle lasted 13 days with 18,399 union casualties to 13,421 confederates. At Cold Harbor, the Union suffered 52,788 casualties to Lee's 32,907. The newspapers were calling Grant "The Butcher" by sending union troops into slaughter. Grant ordered Sheridan to the Shenandoah Valley and told Sheridan to "follow the enemy to their death". Lee's army was now confined to an area around Richmond in an effort to hold on to the

Capital at all cost. Grant's Army slowly squeezes Lee's army tighter and tighter while Sheridan's army keeping confederate General Mosby's Cavalry from attacking from the west. With the capture of Richmond and defeating Lee's Army in the bloodiest combination of battles, Sherman convinced Grant and Lincoln to march south into Georgia and take Atlanta, the last Confederate strong hold and push his army to the port of Savannah.

Sherman raze a 60 mile swath south and headed east through Atlanta, and to Savannah on December 22, 1864. Grant severed the Confederate States from East to West during the battles of Vicksburg and took Richmond while Sherman march south into Atlanta and to the port of Savanna, Georgia. With the exception of a military command in Florida, Lee's major force was confined to defending Richmond.

The fall of Richmond
(April 1865)

When Grant arrived at Cold Harbor, east of Richmond and a major railroad hub, Lee's Army was already dug in. Grant led an assault on Lee's Army but it was repelled. He engaged in one assault after another in which the casualty rate increased proportionately. Grant would later claim that he regretted having to wage an assault on Cold Harbor, which he admitted was one of his military tactical mistakes of the Civil War. But as the siege of Cold Bay continued with no hope of defeating Lee's Army, Grant slipped away undetected and moved his army south toward Petersburg, another railroad hub south into Richmond. Lee still in Cold Harbor, left Petersburg unprotected. Grant moved within only a few miles from Richmond. His failed battle at Cold Harbor helped the Union Army hold Lee's army at Cold Harbor, thus allowing Grant a perfect opportunity to take Richmond. Grant was now able to launch mortars into Lee's over extended armies around Richmond. In Nashville, Tennessee, Hood's Confederate Army was defeated. Sherman's March to the Sea was successful, and

Grant was in a perfect position to advance on Richmond. Lee moved to Petersburg to confront Grant. As skirmishes continued through the winter of 1864-65, President Lincoln easily won reelection in November. In April 1, 1865, residents of Richmond began to flee Richmond. Jefferson Davis had already fled to Georgia with plans to board a train to Florida with his family.

Jefferson Davis' last act as Confederate President was to make Robert E. Lee the General of the Army of the Confederate States of America. During the entire Civil War, Jefferson Davis refused to appoint a Commanding General of the Army, and left that position open for himself. The reason for appointing Lee as the Commanding General allowed Davis to flee and not be available to negotiate a surrender which would surely lead to his arrest. On April 3, 1865, Richmond fell to Union forces and among the first union troops to enter the city was Grant's all Black 5th Massachusetts Cavalry. Lincoln would arrive in Richmond the following day and go to Jefferson Davis' office and sat in his chair, a symbolic gesture that the war was finally over.

On April 9, 1865, at Appomattox Court House, General Robert E. Lee and General Ulysses S. Grant would sign the letter of Unconditional Surrender. Lee offered Grant his battle sword as was customary in surrender, but Grant refused to accept it. Grant gives Lee's men their amnesty and horses as long as they didn't take-up arms against the Union. Lee accepted the terms of the Surrender. Further south in Georgia, William T. Sherman offered the same terms of surrender to General Johnson's Army. The Civil War was over. [46]

The Political Aftermath of War

Lincoln and his wife attended the performance at the Ford Theater in Washington D.C. During the second act, Lincoln was fatally shot in the back of the head by John Wilkes Booth, a performer at the Ford

Theater. Vice President Andrew Johnson was sworn in as the 17th President. During Abraham Lincoln's funeral, Grant wept and later said, *"Lincoln was the greatest man I have ever known."*

After the war, Grant remained Commanding General of the Army. He was placed in charge of enforcing the Reconstruction efforts in the South under President Johnson. In July of 1866, Congress appointed Grant as a four star general. He would hold the position until his election as President in 1869. His successor was William T. Sherman.

Grants relationship with Johnson started out fine, but soon deteriorated as Johnson's reconstruction ideas drifted further away from those of Grant's and those of the radical Republicans in Congress. It soon became obvious that the issue of slavery remained much the same as before the Civil War. Johnson vetoed the Civil Rights Act of 1866 and wanted the immediate return of the Southern States into the union without any concession toward improving African American's civil rights. Congress passed the Reconstruction Act which divided the South into five military districts. In addition, it protected Grant from being terminated by Johnson. Congress also passed the Command of the Army Act, which prevented his removal or relocation of Grant. In August of 1867, Johnson suspended Secretary of War, Edwin Stanton, who supported the Congressional Reconstruction Act. Johnson appointed Grant as his acting Secretary; however Congress voted to reinstate Stanton as Secretary under the Tenure of Office Act that Johnson violated, Grant resigned his position as to not undercut Stanton's re-instatement. Johnson was impeached by the House, but was acquitted by one vote in the Senate.

William H. Seward
(1801 – 1872)

William Seward was appointed by Abraham Lincoln as Secretary of State in March of 1861. He had a great deal of political experience and connections in New York when he was Governor from 1839 to 1842 and served in the U.S. Senate from 1849 to 1861. He was born in Auburn, New York, where his parents owned a large farm with slaves. He attended Union College in Schenectady, New York and graduated in 1820. He apprenticed himself with a law firm for two years and admitted to the New York Bar in 1822. He married his former classmate, Frances Mill in 1824 and they would have three children. He opened a law practice in Auburn and became restless and decided to go into politics.

Seward's Politics

He became friends with a local and well connected, politically, newspaper publisher named; Thurlow Weed in 1824. Weed convinced Seward to join his political party, the Anti-Masonic Party. The Party opposed the principals of the Freemasonry party. In 1830, the Anti-Masonic Party merged with the Whig Party and later the Republican Party. Weed was instrumental in convincing Seward to fun for New York Governor 1839; he would be successful with the help of Mr. Weed and his connections. After serving as Governor, he returned to Auburn, New York and re-opened his law practice. Over time, he defended many freemen against the Fugitive Slave Laws. His popularity as a defense attorney and protecting the rights of slaves and freeman earned him a notable reputation. His political support grew which attracted the attention of Abraham Lincoln who was also a Whig prior to the formation of the Republican Party in 1854.

In 1849, a New York's Senate seats became available and Seward applied for the position. At this time in history, U.S. Congressmen were appointed by State Legislatures. The Legislators reluctantly appointed Seward, even though they felt his anti-slavery position might needed to be shelved for the time being, since slavery was a "powder keg" politically. He agreed to the terms and was appointed U.S. Senator to New York.

During the Buchanan's president's message to Congress in December of 1857, Buchanan wanted Congress to admit Kansas as a slave State in keeping with the Kansas Lecompton Constitution, which Buchanan wanted Congress to pass. Serious debates began between the Southern Democrats and the Northern Republicans on the floor of Congress. The Dred Scott Case of 1856 by the U.S. Supreme Court didn't allow Federal or State Governments to ban slavery in new territories. (As previously discussed) Seward became vocal toward Buchanan's arrogance and accused Buchanan and Chief Justice Roger Taney of collusion and conspiring to alter the Supreme Court Case in favor of the South. Taney later said if Seward was re-elected in 1860, he would not administer the oath of office. Buchanan reportedly said he would deny Seward access to the White House. Seward gave the following speech on the floor of Congress;

"The interest of the white races demands the ultimate emancipation of all men. Whether that consummation shall be allowed to take effect, with needful and wise precautions against sudden change and disaster, or be hurried on by violence, is all that remains for you to decide." [82]

Seward gained nationwide support for a possible nomination as the Republican candidate for President in the 1860. The Southern Democrats became concerned; since they didn't have a popular candidate that could bridge the voters in the North and their pro-slavery proponents in the south. The one option was having multiple parties running for President simultaneously, thus diluting the Republican vote. The south offered John Breckinridge and John Bell from Tennessee as candidates. Seward was certain that he would become the Republican nominee for President, when the convention convened in Chicago, Illinois; so Seward remained in Auburn, New York and didn't attend the convention. The Southern Democrats waged a media blitz against Seward, claiming he instigated the slave insurrection that ended in the execution of John Brown. Seward had little time to prepare a rebuttal and defense against the allegations, since he just returned from an eight month tour of Europe. It would influence the delegate's decision as to his electability and they decided to select Lincoln as the Republican candidate instead.

Seward as Secretary of State
(1861 – 1869)

William Seward was devastated over loosing the nomination for President. He felt he was due the Presidency because of his tenure and experience. After Lincoln's inauguration in March of 1861, he met with Seward and he offered Seward the Secretary of State position in which he refused, but later accepted.

Perhaps the most important accomplishment Seward made was during the Civil War. His efforts in keeping Britain and France out of the war were critical to the success of the Union. The Confederacy relied heavily on support from either France or Britain in supporting the Confederacy cause. It became the enticement offered to other confederate states to secede and join the Confederacy. In 1862, after the blockade of the south, Union ships intercepted a British mail ship that had two Confederate diplomats aboard, James Mason and John Slidell. The Union ship allowed the British ship to pass, however they detained and held the two Confederate diplomats. Britain demanded the immediate release of the diplomats. Britain moved 11,000 troops to the Canadian border for a possible attack. Lincoln released the diplomats and defused the situation between the U.S. and Britain. From then on, Seward entered into talks with both Britain and France and made efforts to convinced them not to aid the Confederacy, however they never gave a commitment until Lincoln's Emancipation Proclamation in 1862. He convinced the Prime Minister of Britain not to sell two new war ships currently being built as blockade runners to the Confederate Navy. After 1862, Britain continued to supply Confederate ships on the high seas, with materials and food bound for the south; however most of the war materials were captured and confiscated by the Union navy.

Seward was opposed to Lincoln declaring the Emancipation

DOUGLAS G. BEAUDOIN

Proclamation in 1862, but Lincoln's timing was well thought out and designed for political effect. As a result of Lincoln's timing, the Confederacy lost their support from Britain and France and both countries declare the Confederacy a "Belligerent". France and Britain were anti-slavery nations and the Lincoln's Emancipation Proclamation coincided with their policy toward slavery and they thought in being political suicide in their nations to give aid to a pro-slavery state. It was at this point in Seward's life that he realized that Lincoln was an exceptional person and a gifted politician with a remarkable insight on human behavior.

Seward's relationship with Lincoln gradually improved over time. Seward always harbored ill feeling that he was a much more qualified person to be President. However, Lincoln could sense the animosity, but over time he won Seward's respect and admiration.

Lincoln and Seward's Assassination Attempt

During Lincoln's assassination attempt, Vice President, Andrew Johnson and Secretary of State, William Seward was also targets to the assassination attempt. John Wilkes Booth was to assassinate Lincoln and Lewis Powell was to assassinate William Seward, lastly George Atzerodt was to assassinate Andrew Johnson. David Harold guided Powell to Seward's home, since he knew the streets of Washington D.C. well. However, when Harold heard the commotion in the Seward home, he fled, leaving Powell's horse tied to a tree.

John Wilkes Booth fatally shot Abraham Lincoln at 10:30 pm in Ford's Theater on April 14, 1865, while Lewis Powell entered Seward's home under the auspices of delivering medicine to Seward who was convalescing in bed after an a carriage accident days earlier. The accident left Seward with a broken leg and other serious injuries and was bedridden. Seward's son, Fredrick, stopped Powell at the top of the stairs and demanded that take the medication to Seward but Powell pulled out a hand gun and attempted to shoot Fredrick, but the gun misfired, and Powell beat Fredrick over the head with his cane. Powell raced into Seward's room where his daughter, Fanny sat at Seward's bedside. Powell jumped on top of Seward and began stabbing him 5 times about the face and neck. George Robinson, a soldier assigned to protect Seward, jumped on Powell, which forced him to flee out the front door. As a result of the scuffle, Robinson would be stabbed in the chest, but would survive his injuries.

When police arrived at Seward's home, it was thought that Seward was dead, but of the five who were attacked by Powell, all survived their wounds, including William Seward. Powell was captured at Mary Surratt's boarding house three days later, along with coconspirators, George Atzerodt, David Harold and Mary Surratt and of course, Lewis Powell. The four would be executed by hanging on July 7, 1865. John Wilkes Booth was tracked down by U.S. Soldiers and killed at the Garrett's tobacco farm in Port Royal, Virginia.

Andrew Johnson was sworn in as President the following day (April 15, 1865) and William Seward, even though badly injured from the carriage accident and being stabbed 5 times, managed to survive. Seward would continue as Johnson's Secretary of State until the election of Ulysses S. Grant in 1869.

His relationship with Johnson was guarded, unlike his relationship with Lincoln at first. Johnson created his own political core group he confided in and most always excluded Seward. There were constant confrontations between the Legislative and Executive Branches of government. Johnson would veto 28 bills while in office and 15 were over ridden in Congress. Congress filed impeachment against Johnson but the effort failed by one vote in the Senate.

The Purchase of Alaska
(1867)

While Seward was a Senator, he opposed the Gadsden Purchase, which involved a small sliver of land near the borders of Arizona and New Mexico in 1854. Buchanan wanted desperately to purchase Cuba from Spain, but for reasons and purpose of extending slavery. Seward had voiced and interest in acquiring Greenland and Iceland in the northern arctic but Congress had little interest. He made an attempt to acquire the Dominican Republic and the Danish West Indies, known today as the U.S. Virgin Islands. When he presented his proposal to Congress it was rejected.

When Russia expressed an interest in selling Alaska, Seward immediately entered into negotiations and a price. He would close the sale of Alaska on March 30, 1867 for $7.2 million which increased the size of the United States by one-fifth and 586,000 square miles.

Seward retired from politics after Grant became President. He would first go on a worldwide tour that lasted two years. He visited Sitka, Alaska and the Pacific Northwest as well. He visited China, Japan, India and Europe and returned in 1871 to his home in Auburn, New York.

On the morning of October of 1872, while working at his desk, he began to have trouble breathing. His condition became worse by evening and a doctor was summoned. By evening someone ask Seward if he had any final words and he said, "Love one another" and died shortly after. [85]

Seward's Legacy

Most historians agree that next to John Quincy Adams, William H. Seward was perhaps the second most accomplished Secretary of State in American history. His purchase of Alaska guaranteed his legacy forever and increased the size of America by 20 percent and doubled the U.S. coastline. Most historians claim his ability to negotiate a deal with Britain and France from coming to the aid of the Confederacy was his greatest accomplishment and perhaps rightly so.

He had a great relationship with Lincoln and the two always had a sincere admiration for each other. One day Seward walked into the Lincoln's office and saw Lincoln sitting near the fireplace blackening his boots, Seward replied to Lincoln, "In Washington, we do not blacken our own boots", Lincoln replied, "Indeed, then whose boots do you blacken, Mr. Secretary." [84]

After the death of Abraham Lincoln, a group of people stood in front of Seward's home. Seeing the group assemble, Seward went outdoors and gave the following brief speech;

"The election has placed our President beyond the pale of human envy or human harm, as he is above the pale of ambition. Henceforth all men will come to see him as you and I have seen him – a true, loyal, patient, patriotic, and benevolent man. Abraham Lincoln will take his place with Washington and Franklin and Jefferson and Adams and Jackson, among the benefactors of the country and of the human race." [5]

DOUGLAS G. BEAUDOIN

Chapter 13
Reconstruction Period

1865 -1877

After the Civil War and the assassination of President Lincoln on April 15, 1865, Andrew Johnson was sworn in as the 17th President of the United States and reconstruction after the Civil War in the South was became the major topic for the next decade. The Mid-term elections saw radical Republicans dominate both houses in Congress, thus efforts to move reconstruction forward lead to bitter disagreements between the Legislative and Executive Branches of government. Johnson's plan for reconstruction involved the pardoning of southerners who were active during the confederacy. He allowed confederate states to re-enter the union with only 10% of the population giving their oath of allegiance to the United States and allowed the states to form their state governments without laws banning slavery or reform the southern slave laws. Needless to say, very little was accomplished toward reconstruction of the south during Johnson's administration. Much of Johnson's tenure in the White House was mired in Legislative and Executive Branch feuding.

Of major concern in Congress was the speed in which the Southern States passed laws that limited the freedom of former black slaves, which was the major impetus behind the civil war in the first place. Johnson did nothing to discourage compliance to the Emancipation of slavery in America, but rather remained indecisive and non-committal.

The result of the lack of leadership in the White House, allowed the use of Government troops to be stationed throughout the South and in major towns and cities after the Civil War. Congress was controlled by the Radical Republicans. **(23)** They wanted to disassemble the white power structure in the South by passing a bill that instituted the "Freeman's Bureau" in March of 1865. Its purpose was an agency that protected the former slaves and granted freedom under the Emancipation Proclamation and provided assistance in finding employment, housing and health care for African American's. However, Johnson vetoed the bill as well as other bills pertaining to the emancipation of former slaves. During the election of 1866, more Radical Republicans were elected in Congress. The Reconstruction Act of 1866 was passed and the South was divided into five military districts. As part of the Reconstruction Act, the Fourteenth Amendment was introduced to the Southern States to rejoin the Union upon the ratification of the Amendment. Johnson, being true to form, vetoed the Bill, but Congress over-rode Johnson's veto and it became law. See Appendix A, Fourteenth Amendment.

The Rise of the Ku Klux Klan and the White Supremacist

The KKK first appeared in Pulaski, Tennessee in May 1866. It was organized by former Confederate soldiers. The Grand Wizard was General Nathan Forest of the Confederate Army. It spread to Nashville, Tennessee the following year and during the first two year, they wore mask, but later used white sheets with white cardboard hats to hide their identity.

The Klan had completely altered the politics in Georgia, South Carolina and Tennessee from 1868 to 1870. The KKK was one of many white supremacy groups in the south at the time. White Brotherhood, the Men of Justice, the Constitutional Union Guards and the Knights of the White Camelia, were just a few that operated throughout the south with support of the community. With the 13th Amendment making slavery illegal in the United States and the Fourteenth Amendment granting citizenship to all who were born in the United States with equal protection of all immigrants and freed

Blacks it did little to curb the violence against African American's. With new laws protecting the oppressed, a surge in recruitment of white supremacist groups in the south soon followed. Black men were not allowed to vote until the 15th Amendment was ratified in 1870, but even though they had the right to vote, very few did out of fear of retribution by the hate groups.

The 15th Amendment did little to change the voting situation in the South. Southern States levied poll taxes, literacy tests and other methods to discourage Black men from voting. By 1870 and with the passage of the 15th Amendment, the KKK and the Southern White Supremacist had instilled fear among the African-America population which created America apartheid of its own and a policy of segregation and political and economic discrimination against the African-American population which lasted for the next 100 years, until Civil Rights Act of 1964.

With the Ku Klux Klan Act of 1871 and the passage of the 15th Amendment under President Grant's administration, it gave Grant the authority to intervene in the south and suspend the writ of habeas corpus in southern counties where racial disorder was most frequent. Most of the KKK went underground and would only surface at night to terrorize Blacks and supporters of Black freedom. The KKK would once again reappear in 1915 after President Woodrow Wilson passed the Constitutional Amendment that both black and white women could vote. It would once again resurface after World War II and in particular in the 1950's. **[43]**

Andrew Johnson
(1865 – 1869)

Andrew Johnson was born Raleigh, North Carolina. His family was poor farming family and Andrew didn't attend school so he could work on the farm, which at that time was not uncommon. He apprenticed himself as a tailor at the age of 12 and run away from home at the age of 16 to settle in Greenville, Tennessee to open a successful tailor shop. He married Eliza McCardle who home schooled him. They would have five children.

Since he was raised in a poor family and had no formal education, he became politically active and gave local speeches to the rural farmers about the wealthy land owners who controlled most of the land and businesses in the area. His popularity with local residents and small merchants in rural Tennessee grew and as a result he was elected mayor of Greenville and later became Tennessee's democratic U.S. Senator. During the Civil War in 1862, Lincoln appointed him as military governor of Tennessee. In 1864, Lincoln chose Johnson as his Vice Presidential running mate, since he was a southern democrat, loyal to the Union, anti secessionist and a slave owner; which helped Lincoln's second term election.

When Andrew Johnson became the Democrat President, he refused to retaliate against the south for the war, which infuriated the Radical Republican faction in Congress who gained control of Congress during the midterm elections. The Republican far right gained the majority in both houses, which precipitated the impeachment of Johnson for not applying retribution and allowing states to resume the status quo in the south. Congress brought impeachment charges against Johnson but the Senate failed to remove him from office by a single vote. Even though impeachment for removal from office failed, he continued his effort not to support the reconstruction or basic civil rights the Radical Republicans in Congress wanted. Much of the criticism of his presidency was his laissez-faire attitude toward punishing the leaders of the Confederacy and allowing the southern states to continue down the same path that led to the civil war to begin with.

His pardoning of Jefferson Davis and other Confederate leaders certainly didn't help his popularity in Congress or the general public in the northern states. The Thirteenth Amendment was ratified during his tenure as President, even though Presidents don't play an active role in Constitutional Amendments nor do they have veto power. The Thirteenth Amendment reads:

"Neither slavery nor involuntary servitude, except as a punishment for crime whereof the party shall have been duly convicted, shall exist within the United States, or any place subject to their jurisdiction" and two, "Congress shall have power to enforce this article by appropriate legislation"

I am relatively certain Andrew Johnson would have vetoed the Thirteenth Amendment if he had the Constitutional authority to do. My reasoning being; he vetoed the Civil Rights Act of 1866; however it was overridden by both Houses. During his Presidency, Johnson initiated 21 regular vetoes and 8 pocket vetoes; however 15 were overridden by Congress. His purchase of Alaska remains his only true legacy; however, William H. Seward is credited with the purchase and negotiated the terms with Russia.

Much of Johnson's unpopularity was of his own making. His refused to take advice from his own cabinet and Congress on issues concerning reconstruction and making an honest effort toward bringing both the North and the South together as a unified nation. His administration was filled with chaos between the Executive and Legislative branches of government with 52 percent of vetoes being overridden. He was defiant toward laws being passed by Congress and believed as President he had the final word. He was obstinate toward those who wanted to curtail the rising popularity of white supremacy groups that wanted to keep African American's in the same social status as before the Civil War. It became immediately clear that Johnson wanted to placate southern interest or at least cave in to southern interests toward reconstruction. Southern enclaves wanted to continue apartheid in the South. Grant was to take charge of reconstruction effort, but their relationship became strained as a result differing solutions to reconstruction.

Grant's Presidency (1869 – 1877)

Gant's Republican nomination was to be expected and at the Republican Convention in Chicago in 1868. He won unanimously as the Republican presidential nominee. For the Democrats, Johnson was not considered at all, thus Horatio Seymour, the former governor of New York would be nominated as the Democratic nominee for President. The Democrat platform focused on allowing the Southern States to immediately join the Union and be given amnesty for all past political offenses. The Republican platform on the other hand, wanted "equal civil and political rights to all", amnesty for most, but more importantly for the civil rights of African Americans. The Democrats would lose the election by 300 popular votes, while Grant was able to collect an additional 500 Black votes which made the difference in the election. However, he would receive 214 electoral votes against Seymour's 80.

On March 4, 1869, Ulysses S. Grant was sworn in as the 18th President of the United State. At 46 years old, he would be the youngest president to occupy the office, to-date. Andrew Johnson did not attend his inauguration as was usually customary. Grant's primary focus for his first term in office was:

- Ratification of the Fifteenth Amendment to the Constitution which prohibits using race as a basis for qualification for voting.

- Reconstruction of the South and eliminate sectional and racial divisions of its citizens.

- The proper treatment of Native Americans and their citizenship.

His policy on reconstruction was his highest priority. President Johnson resisted every effort of the Radical Republican Congress to implement change to the old system long held in the south.

The Radical Republicans

Lincoln was not a Radical Republican; however, Grant was, since he had been a Whig most of his life. The Radical's believed Lincoln was too "soft" or lenient toward the South and the Confederacy during the reconstruction era. The Radical's controlled the Senate Joint Committee on Reconstruction, which passed the Wade-Davis Bill in the Senate in 1864, but was vetoed by Lincoln. The bill purposed that southerner's take an oath of loyalty to the United States and those who supported the Confederacy were not allowed to vote in Southern elections. Lincoln preferred his "ten percent plan" which involved three points toward reconciliation and amnesty:

1. A Presidential pardon and amnesty be given to rebels who vowed an oath of loyalty to the United States and its laws toward slavery. This amnesty did not apply to confederate government officials or military officers.
2. Only 10 percent of the State voters swore their allegiance to the United States, thus the right to form a state government was granted.
3. States could create policies in dealing with freed African Americans, as long as they were not subject to bondage as in slavery.

Much of Johnson's efforts toward reconstruction appeared to be Laissez-faire toward reconciliation between the issues of slavery in the south and the Radical Republican's position toward the punishment of the Confederacy. Johnson vetoed 21 bills passed by Congress during his 3 year 11 month in office. Fifteen bills were over-ridden by Congress. The most important bills over-ridden were the Reconstruction Acts and the Enforcement Acts which dealt with a vast variety of laws such as prohibiting Confederate officers from holding office, allowing Black men to vote and election laws.

The Radical Republican's pushed for civil rights for freed slaves relentlessly, however Johnson was opposed to most every law introduced by the Radical Republicans. The Civil Rights Act of 1866 was vetoed by Johnson but over-ridden by Congress. The Act gave citizenship to African American's born in the United States, and made it illegal to discriminate against on the basis of color or race, thus protected by Federal Law rather than indifferent state laws at the time. The Fourteenth Amendment to the Constitution and the Equal Protection Clause became the law in 1868.

The Radicals were opposed to the Ku Klux Klan and other white supremacist groups growing in popularity in the south after the war. While Grant generally sided with the Radical Republicans, he also was not a hardliner on all issues regarding Radical Republican issues. The Liberal Republicans begin to split the Republican Party during Grant's second term in 1872. When the depression of 1873 and 1874 swept the nation, the Democrats were able to take advantage of the situation and voters replaced most of the Radical Republicans with Democrats. The Radical Republicans were never able to regain power in Congress again.

The Scalawags and Carpetbaggers

"Scalawags" was a derogatory term used to describe a radical and moderate faction of the Republican Party by conservative southern white Republicans. The term "carpetbagger" refers to freed Blacks and white opportunist from the North who moved into the south during the reconstruction period for the purpose of exploiting and taking advantage of a situation as a result of someone else's hardship and back luck. The name came from the type of luggage they carried, that resembled a heavy carpet sewn into a bag with two large handles.

Shortly after the War, and near the end of Johnson's Presidency, most of the once lavish plantations were abandoned during the war and fields left unplowed for years, and later reclaimed by their owners after the war. However, many remained unclaimed, perhaps because of death in a family or financial hardships and possible bankruptcy, which became common after the war. The Carpetbagger's from the north came from all walks of life. Some were lawyers, bankers, retail businessmen, snake oil salesmen and real estate speculators; all were trying to make a quick fortune at the expense of others hardship. They bought or leased plantations and large parcels of land and opened banks, built stores and opened newspapers. By 1870, the Northerner's controlled 21 percent of the railroads in the South and by 1890; they controlled 88 percent of the railroads. After the War, the United States divided the south into 5 military districts and many carpetbagger's became interim mayors and governors appointed in key positions by the Radical Republicans Party that dominated Washington politics at the time. As reconstruction continued, many from the south were not eligible to vote or become part of the southern political process, since many failed or refused to take the oath of allegiance to the United States, in fact only 10 percent would. As a result, much of the political structure remained in the hands of a few and the remainder in the hands of the carpetbagger turned southerner.

Of course along with the influx of the Carpetbagger came the influx of federal reconstruction money and corruption soon followed. During the Mississippi Constitutional Convention in 1868, 70 delegates were selected to attend the Convention for drafting a new state constitution, however, only four were residents of the South and only two served in the Confederate Army. While this was an extreme case, it wasn't altogether uncommon in southern politics during the early period of reconstruction. Grant wanted to unify the United States as a homogenous people even though they had extreme contrasting political ideologies, whereas, Johnson enjoyed the separation geographically and racially. It would lead to an attempt of having him impeached by the radical Republican faction of government but failed by one vote in the Senate to have him removed from office.

Grant appointed long time friend William T. Sherman as Commander in-Chief of the United States Army. To show his impartiality, he selected several confederate leaders to positions in government. He appointed three associate Justices and one Chief Justice to the Supreme Court, but found that two of the Justices most often voted against Grant's reconstruction laws passed by Congress. One of which was Grant's own Ohio nominee as Supreme Court Justice, Morrison Waite. Waite was Chief Justice from 1874 to 1888 and often took sides with States concerning crimes against Blacks by the Ku Klux Klan and other racial hate groups. The Fifteenth Amendment to the Constitution was ratified by the States in February of 1870. Grant stepped up his attacks against the KKK and white supremacist groups in the Deep South. He viewed reconstruction in the south as including federal enforcement of civil rights and voter intimidation as part and parcel to his reconstruction effort. Georgia would be the last confederate State to reinstate black legislators and adopt the new amendment granting equal rights to all citizens. With Georgia being the last confederate state to accept and adopt the federally mandated amendments to their constitution, it only fueled the racism felt by the KKK. Grant proposed the Klu Klux Klan Act in the spring of 1871, which was passed by Congress. He ordered federal troops into the south to assist federal marshals to enforce the act and to arrest Klansmen that violated the civil rights of Black's and sometimes white as well. As the U.S. Marshals captured and incarcerated Klansmen, local sheriffs and local courts would release them. Grant then suspended Habeas Corpus for Klansmen and treated them as racial terrorist, which was consistent with the Constitution. Its purpose was to keep Klansmen incarcerated long enough to conduct an investigation and determine if they violated federal law in regards to an individual's civil rights and civil liberties.

Grant's U.S. Attorney General, Amos T. Akerman, would issue 3,000 indictments during Grant's first term in office, and received 600 convictions for the worst cases. Much of the effort and most of the crimes were in Georgia. During this time, more than 2,000 Klansmen fled Georgia. As a result of Grant's attack against the KKK, Black voters registered and voted in record numbers. Several controversial Supreme Court cases restricted Grant toward enforcing civil rights violations, in which the Supreme Court maintained that capital crimes were judicial issues left for the States to adjudicate and not the federal government. [48]

Southern Redeemers

The "Redeemers" were a coalition of southern whites with political ideology of Pro business, states' rights and the return of slavery in the South. They were a faction of the Democrat Party, known as the Bourbon Democrats whose purpose was to remove the "Radical Republicans" that were freedmen, Carpetbaggers and scalawags and anyone else who supported civil rights and Grant's reconstruction program. The Redeemers came into power in the south in the early 1870's when Grant moved the military into the south to enforce civil rights and suppress the KKK and other white supremacist groups engaged in violent attacks against Black Americans in Georgia, Louisiana, North Carolina and Mississippi. White supremacist groups such as the White League in Louisiana and the Red Shirts in Mississippi and North Carolina were essentially a paramilitary organization similar to the KKK and were considered a terrorist group.

In 1874, the White League in Louisiana descended on Coushatta, Louisiana and removed six Republican's from office. They were told to leave the state, however, the event turned into a massacre when the White League killed the Republicans and a dozen witnesses. In the Battle of Liberty Place in New Orleans, police battle with the White League and occupied the Capital and armory. They physically removed the Governor from office. Grant sent U.S. Troops into

Louisiana to quell the uprising. During the Colfax Massacre in 1873, the White League kills more than 100 Black Republicans. Eventually the "Redeemers" took control of the political machine in the southern states by removing northern Radical Republicans, both White and Black from elected state and local positions of government.

The Redeemer's believed all Radical Republican's were corrupt and their primary goal was to drain the south of their finances and resources and move on. They wanted to continue with the status quo of declaring that slavery was a state rights issue and not a federal issue. The Redeemers established a political ideology that addressed seven basic political principals:

- A system based on a white majority and white rule
- Lower taxes
- pro-business
- Reduce public debt
- Cut government spending
- Reduce support for public education
- Reduce support for welfare institutions

After, Grant left office, the Redeemers would take-over the southern legislatures and implement voter registration rules that discriminated against Blacks from voting which lead to "Disfranchising" in the 1890's. Disfranchising will be discussed in volume II, "The American Legacy" and the resurgence of the KKK and other hate groups after Grant left office in 1877.

The reconstruction period ended 1877 with Georgia being the last former confederate state to accept the federal mandate that granted civil rights to Black Americans and allowing them to vote and participate in local and state elections, however, it was a veiled attempt to placate the federal government and only became a veiled attempt toward civil rights. As long as Grant was in the White House, the

Redeemers were willing to wait until a more laissez-faire administration moved into the White House, similar to Andrew Johnson or James Buchanan's administrations that were sympathetic toward the south's view of racial inequality and the separation of races.

Grant's reconstruction policies were controlled by the Federal Government which administered reconstruction and enforced voter's civil rights. To enforce both, Grant moved troops into the cities and small towns throughout the south to oversee the enforcement and compliance. The Southern States and local governments had little control over how reconstruction money was spent and who occupied political office. During the reconstruction period many Black Americans occupied state legislatures and local boards. The Redeemers wanted federal troops out of the South. After Georgia acquiesced to the demands of the Federal Government in 1872, to revise their State Constitution and agree not to take-up arms against the Government, Grant reluctantly gradually pulled Federal troops out of the South. Within a few years after Grant's reconstruction plan, Southern Democrats reestablished the same sociopolitical system that existed prior to the Civil War. Vagrancy laws and laws that made it illegal to not to have a job that only applied to Black American's which became common in the South as a means to control the situation.

Grant considered running for a third term in 1877. It wasn't until 1954 by Constitutional Amendment that presidents were to serve two terms as President. Grant feared that his effort to bring about Civil Rights would last indefinitely unless the next incoming president continued to enforced years his efforts to bring racial bigotry to an end. Grant's efforts to neutralize the KKK and other hate groups forced them to go underground until his administration was over. His premonition was correct; it would once again emerge in the early 1900's with greater vengeance.

Panic of 1873

From 1868 to 1873, America enjoyed a boom period in America, especially for the railroad industry with the addition of 33,000 miles of new track laid. To expand, the railroad industry, capital and land was needed to build a railroad infrastructure that need land corridors, docks and warehouses. The Federal government issued land grants and subsides to the railroad companies in which banks and investment firms could borrow against as collateral and sale. Jay Cooke & Company was the largest investment banker in America at the time. They were responsible for selling the bonds that financed the Civil War for the Union. During the early part of the civil war, Congress investigated Jay Cooke & Company for price manipulation. The Governor of Canada was also involved in a bribery and kick-back scandal orchestrated by Jay Cooke & Company which led to the resignation of the Canadian Governor... Even with all of the scandals involving Jay Cooke & Company, the Secretary of Treasury, Salmon Chase need Jay Cooke to market government bonds in order to finance the Civil War, so Cooke's indiscretions were overlooked.

Europe began to have financial problems in 1871 and 1873 as Austria and the Ottoman Empire, began to slide into a depression, soon followed by France and Germany. Europe abandoned the silver monetary system and went on the gold standard, as did America when Congress passed the Coinage Act of 1873. With the tightening of currency, Great Britain raised the interest rate on loans to 8%. Business in America couldn't borrow money cheaply to complete projects already started. The final death blow came in September of 1873, when Jay Cooke & Company over valued its capital assets to get loans to build the Pacific Northern Railroad and guaranteed millions of dollars in bonds to construct the transcontinental Northern Pacific Railway from Duluth to the West Coast, and Jay Cooke & Company would be forced to file bankruptcy. Canadian Pacific bought the Northern Pacific Railway for pennies on the dollar. The investors who owned Jay Cooke Bonds, lost their investment As a result, 18.000

businesses failed, 55 of the nation's railroads would also fail and 60 would file for bankruptcy. Unemployment rose to 8.5%. In America, the Panic of 1873 would last for 6 years, but in Europe it lasted for nearly 10 years. Grant would leave office in March of 1877, just as the economy began to improve. Incoming President Rutherford D. Hayes continued to battle economic problems in the timber industry and massive railroad strikes that were the after effects of the Panic of 1873.

Scandals in the Grant Administration

Grant remained popular during his eight years in office, however, the 1873 depression and corruption and scandals that plagued his administration became his legacy, which he was unable to reverse. While few believed that Grant was not directly involved in any of events, it would still leave a black mark on his legacy. Three major scandals immerged during his tenure; one such scandal involved a dummy railroad construction company set-up by a congressmen and stock investor that received 20 million dollars from the Government to build 600 miles of railroad, but never built it. The Vice President, Colfax and House Speaker Garfield were also connected to receiving possible bribes to drop charges against them. The second scandal involved Grant's Brother-in-law and a co-conspirator in manipulating gold futures. The third was the Whiskey Ring in which the federal government levied heavy taxes on whiskey to help pay for war and reconstruction costs. Many Whiskey distillers bribed Department of Treasury Officials to issue them tax stamps at a fraction of the price. When caught in the act, more than 100 were convicted.

The Compromise of 1877

The Compromise of 1877 involved the November election of 1876, between Republican Rutherford B. Hayes and Democrat Samuel J. Tilden. At issue during the election were the irregularities of three southern states which would decide the close election of the Presidency. Grant commissioned a legislative Electoral Commission to decide the issue and Rutherford B. Hayes as the next President to secede Grant. To keep the peace in the south Grant pulled all the troops out of south except two for two states, ending the reconstruction period. As a result of this compromise Hayes was elected President and the south would not be over-seen by federal troops. The five points of the Compromise were:

1. The removal of all military forces from the former confederate states

2. The appointment of at least one southern Democrat to Hayes' Cabinet

3. Construction of another transcontinental railroad that connects with the Texas and Pacific railroad route in the South.

4. Legislation to industrialize the south.

5. The right to deal with blacks without northern interference.

As a result of the Compromise of 1877, it was mutually agreed by both the Republican and Southern Democrat parties that Hayes become President and the Federal Government's involvement in continuing its mission toward enforcement of Civil Rights for Black Americans be put on hold.

Grant's Retirement

When Grant left the Presidency he gave a Farwell address to Congress in which he apologized for the eight years he served as President and the mistakes he made and his lack of political prowess to deal effectively as President.

Presidential pensions up-until President Eisenhower's tenure, were non-existent. Eisenhower, Hoover and Truman would receive a $25,000 pension, but before that period, most Presidents retired from the White House either penniless or were wealthy when entering office. So was the case with Ulysses S. Grant. President Rutherford B. Hayes encouraged Grant and his family to travel on a diplomatic tour of the world to foster good relations with other countries. He returned from his world tour on September 20, 1879. Grant made a half-hearted attempt to run for a third term as the Republican nominee but lost the nomination to James A. Garfield.

Grant was nearly broke after his world tour in 1879. His son, Ulysses Jr. (Buck) opened a Wall Street brokerage firm with Ferdinand Ward. President Grant saw how well the business was doing and invested $100,000 and became a partner in 1883. Ward and a banker named James D. Fish were paying investors high interest rates to build-up the business using the company's securities on loans. It was in affect a Ponzi scheme. Ward new the company was going into bankruptcy unless there was an infusion of outside capital. Grant went to William Henry Vanderbilt who gave Grant a personal loan for $150,000, to keep the company going, unaware that the company securities were already pledged. The Company would file bankruptcy and Fish and Ward were convicted of fraud in 1885 and served nearly seven years in prison. Grant was broke and in the summer of 1884 he complained of a sore throat and in October and diagnosed with throat cancer. He was in heavy debt with no job or pension. Congress passed a law that would restore his military pension and survivor benefits to his wife Julia. His home in New York was given to him by several wealthy patrons before leaving office.

Mark twain was among the most famous and influential people in America at the time and owned a publishing house in New York. Realizing that Grant was penniless and suffering from cancer, he encouraged Grant to write his memoirs. His two volume set of memoirs sold 300,000 copies which earned Julia $450,000. Grant completed Volume II of his memoirs 4 days before his death. Mark

Twain called Grant's memoirs "The Personal Memoirs of Ulysses S. Grant" a literary masterpiece.

On July 23, 1885 at 8:00am, Ulysses S. Grant died at the age of 63, at his Mount McGregor cottage in New York, surrounded by family. President Grover Cleveland ordered a thirty-day nationwide period of morning. The funeral train traveled to West Point and New York City where his body was laid to rest at a temporary tomb and twelve years later in Grant's Tomb, which is the largest mausoleum in North America. Grants funeral included General Sherman, Sheridan, Confederate Generals, Buckner, Johnston, Admiral Porter and Senator Logan and two Presidents, Hayes and Arthur along with more than 1.5 million people attended Grants funeral procession.

U.S. Grant's Legacy

"My failures have been errors of judgment, not of intent."
-U.S. Grant

While many considered Grant's Presidency lack-luster and riddled with scandal, many have neglected the many achievements he was able to accomplish in one of the most difficult times in American history. He is considered among the top American Generals in U.S. history and as President, he carried forward Lincoln's vision of emancipation of Black American's which is sadly overlooked. He pressed the south for civil rights and forced hate groups and white supremacist underground, so that Black Americans could vote and run for political office. However, after Grant left office in 1877, the south resumed the same course of racial division and the persecution that was not tolerated during Grant's Presidency.

Grant is one of those men in American history that has remained the subject of conversation. Few doubt his sincerity, moral character and self discipline. Historians are taking a second look at Grant and his accomplishments and legacy. His policy toward Civil Rights and enforcement of Emancipation may have over shadowed his greatness as one of America's greatest Generals and humanitarian.

Chapter 14
The American Frontier

1840 – 1877

In 1845, John L. O'Sullivan was the first known person to use the phrase, "Manifest Destiny" to describe America's right to claim new territory in North America. It was understood that America's boundaries would expand all the way to the Pacific Ocean, north to the Canadian border and South to the Mexican border and beyond. America's first interest into expanding its boundaries began in 1801 when President Thomas Jefferson began negotiations with Spain to acquire Florida, however, being unsuccessful. During Madison's and Monroe's Presidencies, America purchased Florida from Spain and the Louisiana Territory from France. America's quest to acquire Canada failed during the War of 1812. . Thomas Jefferson was the first President to aggressively send expeditions west for the purpose of mapping and exploring the vast territory west of the Mississippi River. The Lewis and Clark expedition being one of six he commissioned during his Presidency.

By the time John L. O'Sullivan gave his speech concerning the movement of acquiring new territories and America's thirst for expansion had dribble to a few remaining territories that need to be resolved with Britain in the Oregon Territory, the Southwest that was being fought in the Mexican American War. The one big prize remaining was Alaska, which became an American possession in 1867 under Andrew Johnson's Presidency.

DOUGLAS G. BEAUDOIN

The Oregon Territory

America's Pacific Northwest; Oregon, Washington and Idaho, known as the Oregon Territory was a region mutually agreed upon by Britain and the United States as a territory jointly managed by both countries and were allowed to construct forts and trading post for the purpose of conducting trade until a permanent agreement on ownership could be established between the two countries. The Hudson Bay Company, a British Company in Canada, built a dozen trading post and forts in the Pacific Northwest for the purpose of traded furs with the local Natives and resident trappers. John Jacob Astor opened his own fur trading company; the American Fur Company in 1808 and its subsidiary, the Pacific Fur Company in 1810. Astor sent Wilson Price Hunt to the mouth of the Columbia River to construct Fort Astor, later renamed Fort Astoria. The Hudson Bay Company of Canada constructed Fort Vancouver which served as its main headquarters for America on the Columbia River and the confluence of the Willamette River, known today as Vancouver, Washington.

The Northwest Company was a French Canadian company that relied on Coureur des bais (2) to trap and trade with the local native tribes for furs. (24) They established a trading post near the confluence of the Columbia and Snake Rivers and claimed the region as British Territory. The fort was named Fort Nez Perce today known as Walla Walla, Washington. The Hudson Bay Company controlled most of the fur trade in the Oregon Territory until 1840. They openly discouraged settlement in the Pacific Northwest for fear that it would ruin the fur trade.

Footnote (2): Coureur des bais were French Canadian woodsmen, able to survive in the harshest conditions. They were fluent in local Native language and loners who traded fur with the Natives. They would sell their furs to the Northwest Company, which was owned by French Canadian's. They established a reputation of being the toughest trappers and woodsmen in

THE AMERICAN LEGACY

North America.

The British Government intervened and merged both companies as the new Hudson Bay Company. In 1821, The Northwest Company and the Hudson Bay Company entered into an armed conflict with each other over rival trapping territory.

John McLaughlin was the manager of the Hudson Bay Company for the Oregon Territory in Fort Vancouver. Contrary to company policy, he provided food and medical care to settlers who arrived by wagon train until they were able to get established in the Willamette Valley in Oregon. In 1957, the State of Oregon recognize John McLaughlin as the "Father of Oregon" In 1846, the Oregon Treaty was signed between Britain and the United States which established the border between Canada and United States at the 49th Parallel. The Hudson Bay Company vacated its Forts and trading posts in the Pacific Northwest and moved its headquarters to Victoria Island in British Columbia. John McLaughlin refused to move and remained in Oregon until his death in Oregon City in 1857.

John Jacob Astor was a German immigrant who arrived in New York in 1784. While working in his brothers butcher shop in New York, he meet a trappers who had returned from the west, which inspired him to open his own fur businesses. He purchased furs from the local Natives and sold them in London. He eventually expand his business west into the Great Lakes region and later into the Oregon Territory where he built Fort Astoria at the mouth of the Columbia River. During the War of 1812, his company; American Fur Company, purchased tons of Turkish Opium and sold it in Canton, China during the British-Chinese opium wars. Later he traded and distributed opium in London. The opium trade made Astor very wealthy and he began purchasing real estate in Manhattan, which at the time was sparsely populated. He liquidated his fur businesses and other ventures in 1830 and purchased large real estate holdings in New York. By the time of his death in 1848, he was the wealthiest man in America and the first multi millionaire.

General William Ashley and Colonel Andrew Henry started the Rocky Mountain Fur Company in 1822. They posted ads in the St. Louis Gazette and Public Advertiser wanting fur trappers that craved adventure and the outdoors. More than 150 answered his ad, even though many were too young and had little knowledge or experience in trapping. Of those who answered Ashley's ad were Jedediah Smith, Etienne Provost, Jim Bridger, Thomas Fitzpatrick and Hugh Glass. The Rocky Mountain Fur Company's competitor was John Jacob Astor who owned the American Fur Company that opened for business in 1808. The company filed for bankruptcy in 1842 and closed its doors in 1847. The Rocky Mountain Fur Company closed for business in 1834. These fur trading companies would meet their doom around 1840, when people in Europe demanded silk and cotton for hats and clothing and the appeal for furs were not as fashionable as they once were. The beaver and fur bearing animals were being greatly diminished as a result of over trapping. During the peak, more than 500 trappers occupied Idaho region alone, by 1840, only 50 remained. The trading posts and forts were revitalized with the influx of settlers traveling the Oregon Trail beginning in 1834.

Jim Bridger
(1804 – 1881)

James Felix Bridger was born in 1804 in Richmond, Virginia. His father was an innkeeper in Richmond and in 1812; the Bridger family moved to St. Louis, Missouri but shortly after arriving, both his parents die when he was 13 years of age. Jim did not receive education and could not read or write. He worked as an apprentice blacksmith for a short while but in March of 1822, at the age of 18, he heard that the Rocky Mountain Fur Company (William Henry Ashley) need men for a trapping expedition in the upper Missouri River and he applied and was accepted.

In 1823, while on an expedition along the Missouri River, Ashley's expedition was attacked by Arikara warriors. Fifteen men in the expedition were killed. The trapping expedition traveled to the Grand River in South Dakota when a fellow trapper, Hugh Glass was attacked by a sow grizzly with two cubs. He was badly mauled and laid unconscious when Ashley's men found him. Ashley instructed Bridger and Fitzgerald to stay with him until he died and bury him. The remainder of the party continued toward Montana. The following day a scouting party of Arikara was spotted by Bridger and Fitzgerald decided to leave Glass there to die. Bridger and Fitzgerald rendezvoused with Ashley's party days later and told Ashley that Glass had died and was buried. Glass woke from unconsciousness days later and managed to walk and find Bridger and Fitzgerald near the Bighorn River. Glass forgave both men and elected not take revenge.

In 1850, while guiding the Stansbury Expedition, Bridger found an easier route through the Rocky Mountains than the South Pass, which shortened the Oregon Trail by 61 miles. It would be named the Bridger Pass and would be the route for the Union Pacific Railroad and present day Interstate Highway 80. He led many more expeditions over the years and served as an Army scout during the Sioux and Cheyenne wars of 1865 and 1868. The Sioux Treaty of 1868 at Fort Laramie would bring peace among the Sioux and Cheyenne in exchange the United States give them the Black Hill of the Dakota's as their own land and reservation, or at least until gold was discovered in the Black Hills which would lead to the Battle of Little Bighorn in 1876 which is discussed later.

Jim Bridger died on his farm in Kansas City, Missouri on July 17, 1881, at the age of 77. [50]

The Early American West
(1804 – 1877)

The exploration of the American west began when Thomas Jefferson sent expeditions west to explore and map the western frontiers of

America. It started with small groups of explorers looking for routes into the wilderness and making assessments about the demeanor and population of the American Natives. They were to map mineral deposits and transportation corridors west into regions yet to be explored. Lewis and Clark being the most notable of the overland explorers reached the shores of the Pacific Ocean via an overland route through numerous mountain ranges, rivers and hostile territory occupied by American Indians. Soon to follow were the trappers, miners, mountain men and frontiersmen looking for adventure and solitude. Lastly, the settlers, farmers and homesteaders moved west for fresh start in life and free land.

Once the wilderness was tamed, the western railroad industrialist, cattlemen, ranchers, business men, bankers, saloon owner, hotel owners, prostitutes, gamblers and gunslingers soon followed. This last group was made popular by the dime novels that were popular in the large cities of the east. There were some notable characters worthy of mentioning that had contributed a great deal to America's manifest destiny, such as the railroad tycoons, miners and prospectors.

Joseph Nicollet
(1786 – 1843)

Jean-Nicolas Nicollet was a French geographer, astronomer and mathematician who mapped the Upper Mississippi and Missouri Rivers in 1835. Born in France and immigrated to America in 1832. He arrived in St. Louis to begin his expedition to map the Upper Mississippi River. At the completion of his first expedition in 1837 the U.S. Army commissioned him to map the Missouri River and correct errors found in Zebulon Pikes map as well. John C. Freemont was assigned to Nicollet's expedition. The third and final expedition included botanist Charles Geyer, Freemont recorded and mapped the upper Missouri River Valley. Upon his return to Washington D.C. to report his findings, he would die of an extended illness in 1843.

Nicollet's maps were among the first in the world to use hachuring and the first maps of the region to use Native American names for geological features. Hachuring is a series of short parallel lines drawn on a map to indicate topographic relief. In U.S. Grant's Personal Memoirs, he used hachuring to depict topographic relief of military battle positions.

John C. Fremont
(1813 – 1890)

Fremont was perhaps among the most controversial figures in American history. Born in Savannah, Georgia he became an anti-slavery advocate throughout his life. Prior to the Civil War, Freemont was the first radical Republican nominee to run for President, but was defeated by James Buchanan in the election of 1856. Lincoln would defeat Buchanan four years later, being the first Republican President.

He served honorably during the Mexican-American War and Civil War but was charged in a military court martial for insubordination over a feud over becoming the Military Governor of California, obviously believing he should be Governor of California.

President Polk later commutes his sentence and reinstates him into the Military, but he elected to resign his commission in 1862 and return to New York. During the Civil War, Lincoln relieve him of his command as Brigadier General of the Western Department for his emancipation edict, in which Freemont ordered Union troops to seize property from those in the border and Confederate states as hostile to the Union. Lincoln wanted Freemont to rescind his orders, so as not to inflame an already tense situation between the Border States and the northern states. Lincoln gave assurances that the Border States could keep their slaves as long as they didn't rebel against the North. Fremont's edict undermined Lincoln's agreement with the non hostile border states.

DOUGLAS G. BEAUDOIN

Freemont's Expedition's

To turn the clock back prior to the Civil War, Freemont had learned a great deal from Nicollet's methods of mapping and turning his expeditions into a scientific as well as geographic expedition. Because of Freemont's confrontational demeanor, unlike Nicollet, who won the respect and honor to the Native American's he encountered, Freemont's attitude toward the Native American's were more confrontational. Perhaps in some situation it was justified, but most often not.

Upon the death of Nicollet in 1843, Senator Lewis Linn and his father-in-law, Benton, wanted Freemont to become Nicollet's successor and send an expedition to the Oregon Territory as a scientific and mapping expedition in the summer of 1842. He was to explore the Wind River, Rocky Mountains, the South Pass of the Rocky Mountains and the Oregon Trail to its terminus on the Pacific Ocean. He hired Kit Carson and Fitzgerald as his guides during most of his five expeditions. The first expedition lasted five months and was considered a success. He and his wife Jesse Fremont would write; "Report of the Exploring Expedition of the Rocky Mountains (1843), which was published in most of the newspapers in America. Freemont was well known as a self promoter and used the media extensively for his self promotion. Today it is called "Branding" his name. It would help him to get patrons to finance his expeditions, and slowly became a lucrative business for Freemont.

Freemont wasted little time to begin his second expedition in the summer of 1843. This expedition was to map the last portion of the Oregon Trail and find alternate routes to the South Pass through the Rocky Mountains. With a well financed expedition and 40 men, he acquired 12 pound howitzer cannon in St. Louis which raised concerns as to Freemont's motives for the expedition. Questions rose as to if it were a military operation or a scientific expedition for which investors placed their trust. In any event, he would once again hire

Kit Carson as his guide.

Freemont's second expedition of 1843 to 1844 was much more ambitious than all of the other expeditions. Once completing the journey to the Cascade Mountains of Oregon and Washington he paralleled the south along the Cascade Range to California's Sierra Nevada Mountains and discovered Lake Tahoe and named the pass after Kit Carson. He led his expedition to Sacramento, California and Sutter's Fort and returned over the Sierra Range into the Great Basin and Salt Lake and to the terminus of the expedition in St. Louis.

He and wife, Jesse published his second report of expedition and made 10,000 copies to be sold to those heading west. In 1845, the Mexican-American war was imminent and he led his third expedition of 60 armed military men on a scouting expedition financed by the War Department. With 60 armed men and Kit Carson as their guide, the expedition crossed the Great Basin and Salt Lake and into the Yosemite Valley of California in 1845. They arrived in Sacramento where the local settlers claimed that a band of Wintu Indians were camped nearby. Freemont led the attack on the Wintu Camp killing nearly all. As the Wintu fled, Freemont's men pursued until there were no survivors. Some who were present at the massacre stated that about 200 or more were killed. Kit Carson later said, "It was a perfect butchery".

The Klamath Indians were getting reports of Freemont's advance toward Klamath Lake and were making preparation for their defense. When Freemont's army arrived at Klamath Lake and made camp, during the night of May 9, 1846, a band of 20 Klamath Indians attacked Fremont's camp, killing 3 of his men. On May 12th, Freemont and Carson attacked the Klamath village, killing 14 villagers, only to find later that those in village were not involved in the attack. He would be criticized for his error in judgment

John C. Freemont became the Military Governor of California in

January of 1847, but was removed from office two months later. President Hayes appointed him Governor of Arizona in 1878, but he never took-up residence in Arizona and was asked to step-down. Much of Kit Carson's notoriety in the dime book novels about Kit Carson was due to Freemont and his use of media to promote his expeditions and his own legacy and notoriety. At one time he was very wealthy, but he invested heavily in the Union Pacific Railroad and lost most of his money during the Panic of 1873 and the collapse and bankruptcy of many of the railroads. He would die in 1890 at the age of 77 in New York City.

Christopher Houston Carson
(1809 – 1868)

Christopher Houston Carson (Kit Carson) was born in Richmond, Kentucky in 1809. He would leave home when he was 16 and work as a trapper in the Rocky Mountains and the American Southwest. In 1842 to 1848 he guide for John C. Fremont on four expeditions in the Great Basin of Utah and Nevada, California and Oregon.

Kit Carson became famous for the dime novels written about him as a fierce Indian fighter and guide while on Freemont's expeditions. The dime novels were sold and circulated about his adventures as a frontier hero. John C. Fremont told editors about his guide, Kit Carson years before, which prompted a writers to begin an exaggerated series about his exploits fighting Indians. Readers imagined Carson as 6 foot 5 inches tall, 230 pound man who could fight ten men at once.. Carson himself was quiet, humble and not boastful. In 1847, General William Tecumseh Sherman met Carson in Monterey, California and was surprised to see a man weighing 140 pounds, only 5 feet 5 inches tall, reddish hair, freckles, blue eyes, clean shaven and soft spoken. In fact, of all of the men portrayed in the western dime store novels, Kit Carson's portrayal of a tough Indian fighter and guide was mostly accurate, Freemont was engaged in three known massacres of the Wintu and Klamath Indians, where it was reported that Freemont ordered his men to kill men, women and children in raids. It is my impression that Carson was embarrassed about talking about his exploits. It wasn't until 1848 that Carson noticed a dime store book that portrayed him while visiting a Native village. He repudiated the accuracy of the book and perhaps all of the dime store books written about him.

He served in the Union Army during the Mexican-American War and the Civil War, and spent the remainder of his later life in Colorado and New Mexico where he died in 1868 in Fort Lyon, Colorado of an aneurysm at the age of 58. Carson City, Nevada and Carson Pass was named after Kit Carson. [51]

James Butler Hickok
(1837 – 1876)

James Butler Hickok was born in Homer, Illinois in 1837. He moved to Leavenworth, Kansas when he was 18 and would meet a 12 year old boy named William Cody, later be known as Buffalo Bill. Hickok had many jobs over his short lifetime; drover, wagon master, scout, lawman, gunfighter, gambler and actor/showman. Like Carson, his fame was the result of the popular dime novels. He had only shot six or seven men in gunfights. In 1860, he was driving a freight team from Independence, Missouri to Santa Fe, New Mexico, when he saw a sow bear with two cubs were blocking the road. He got off the wagon and shot the bear in the head. The bullet lanced of the skull and she charged. He would kill the bear with his knife but he was badly mauled. He was hospitalized for four months with a crushed chest, broken shoulder and arm.

He was elected City Marshal of Hays, Kansas in September of 1869. His first month on the job he killed two men. Ten months later he would kill one man and wound another and would be fired. His next law enforcement job was Marshal of Abilene, Kansas in 1871. Six months later he would get into a gun fight and kill Phil Coe and accidently kill his own deputy. He was also fired from his job as a result. In 1876, Hickok was diagnosed having glaucoma. He had other minor health problems as well, but he was aware that he would go blind in a few years. While playing poker at Nuttal & Mann's Saloon in Deadwood, Dakota Territory, and Jack McCall approached Hickok from behind and shot him in the head at point blank range. Hickok was only 39 years old. McCall would hang for the shooting of Wild Bill Hickok. [49]

The Oregon Trail
(1834 – 1868)

As previously mentioned, in 1803, President Thomas Jefferson commissioned Meriwether Lewis and William Clark to find a route from the Mississippi River to the Pacific Ocean.

Their westerly route crossed the Rocky Mountains into the prairies of Kansas and Nebraska to the Snake River along the Oregon and Idaho border and followed along the Columbia River to the Pacific Ocean, near the town of present day Astoria. They found that the straight route west was much too difficult for wagons and decided to return to Kansas City traveling the Columbia River north into Montana heading east over the Grand Tetons to the head waters of the Missouri River. The northern route passed through the Blackfoot Tribal Indian lands of Montana, who were known to be hostile to trespassers. Over the next thirty years, mostly fur traders and trappers used the route that Lewis and Clark mapped. Most trappers, miners and adventurer are traveled by horse or on foot. Lewis and Clark drew detailed maps of both routes; however it wasn't until 1859 that the Mullan Trail would connect the Missouri River and Columbia River in a much more direct route through Wyoming, the Grand Tetons, and the Snake River and down the Columbia River to Fort Astoria at the mouth of the Columbia River.

Jedidiah Smith located the South Pass over the Rocky Mountains in

1824 which became the dominant route used for wagon trains traveling west. The length of the Oregon Trail was 2,170 brutal miles east and west by wagon train from Independence, Missouri to Oregon City in the Willamette Valley.

It would take about 200 days to make the trip by wagon train. For nearly 40 years it was primarily used by mountain men and trappers, but until the transcontinental railroad was built in 1869, trail transportation gradually diminished. The Oregon Trail was only active for 25 years as a wagons trail. Jedidah Smith and Jim Bridger became part owner Astor's American Fur Company in 1830, but Smith would be killed by Comanche Indians in 1831 while exploring in New Mexico. Approximately 3,000 trappers and explorers traveled west from 1810 to 1840. Once the furs trapping declined and became unprofitable, many remained in the mountains and became mountain men, prospectors and Buffalo hunters and gamblers. Others became Army Indian guides and Frontier and Wagon train guides that began around 1839 and lasted until the Civil War in 1861.

In May of 1839, the first wagon train left Peoria, Illinois with eighteen men whose goal was to colonize the Oregon Territory, only nine eventually arrived in Oregon, the rest would settle in Idaho and western Washington. It would be the first wagon train to travel the Oregon Trail. In September of 1840, Robert Newell and Joseph Meek and their families arrived in Walla Walla (Washington) which was the first party to open the Oregon Trail west of the Snake River and down the Columbia River.

The following year, Bartleson-Bidwell's party arrived in the Willamette Valley in Oregon. In 1843, the "Great Oregon Trail Migration" began with as many as 1,000 men and women in 120 wagons traveled west on the Oregon Trail. The wagon train was called the "cow column".

More than 268,000 headed west via wagon train or horse for the next 20 years until railroads replaced them after the Civil War and during the reconstruction period of 1865 to 1877. Gold was discovered at Sutter's Mill in California in 1849 which contributed to more than 200,000 migrants heading west over the Sierra Nevada Mountains in California. The Civil War ended most of the overland travel for the next 5 years, however it resume after the Civil War, but the rate of migration was only a trickle.

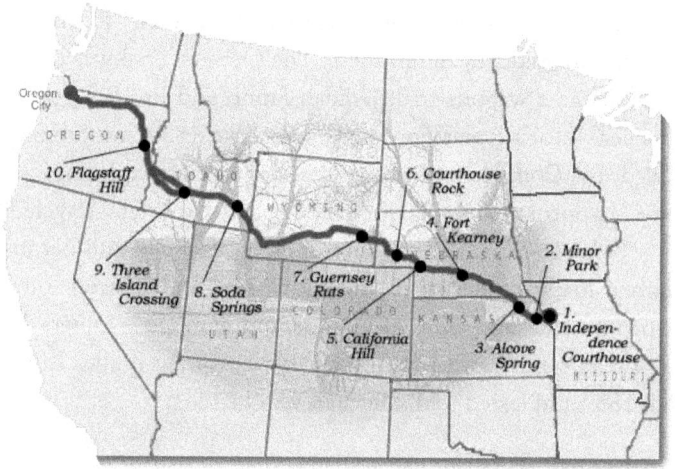

Map 21, Oregon Trail

There were Forts along the route, but only three were operated as military forts, the remainder were trading posts designed for protection from Indian attacks and trading furs for supplies. Fort Laramie, Wyoming and Fort Kearney in Nebraska had long been established as military forts. Others Forts were later built after the Civil War, primarily as a result of the American Indian Wars which accelerated during the Civil War in the American Southwest. The major along the trail were operated by Fur Trading Companies; Fort Astoria, Fort Vancouver, Fort Walla Walla (called Fort Nez Perce) and Fort Hall in Idaho and Fort Bridger near the Sierra Nevada's, which played an important part during the wagon trains heading west.

Fort Hall was situated near the junction of the Oregon Trail and a side route south toward California and over the Sierra Nevada Mountains.

The Pony Express Route started at St. Joseph, Missouri and ended in San Francisco after much of the western trail routes were established

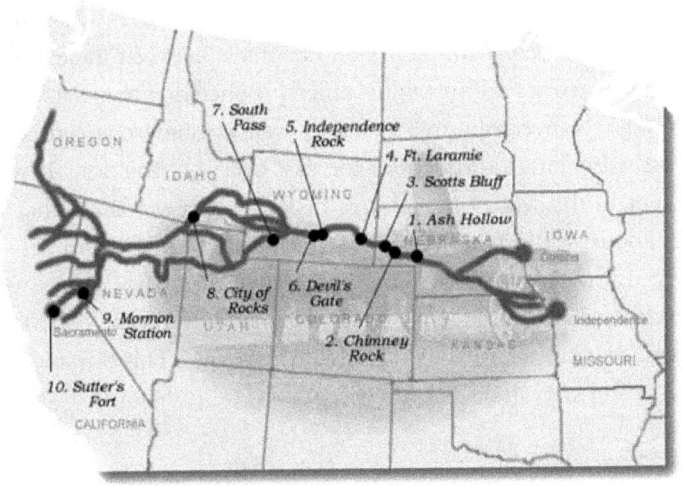

Map 22, California Trail

Kit Carson served as a guide for the Army and John Freemont, but guided mostly along the Santa Fe and California trail system. Jim Bridger was an interpreter for the Fort Laramie Treaty of 1851 and an Indian guide for Government survey parties and expeditions. Since many of the explorers of old were fluent in the various Indian languages, they were in high demand as guides for the Army and the Wagon Trains heading west.

As the population in the West exploded and gold was discovered in California in 1849 and the Dakota Territory, the need for trains traveling from coast to coast became a parent, however it would bring a different type of adventurer west, the rancher, cowboy and gambler. [74]

DOUGLAS G. BEAUDOIN

The American Indian Wars
(West of the Mississippi)

Ever since the first Anglo Europeans landed in the North America, there have been constant battles and conflicts between the indigenous tribes of America and the white settlers. Ponce de Leon was killed by the Calusa Native tribe in Florida as well as numerous settlers who established colonies throughout the east coast of America. It was no different in the west, only later in history. It is estimated that there were about 40 Indian wars for which the U.S. Government was involved in after the Civil War. The Native American Tribes wanted an independent nation with their own land. About 19,000 white settlers were killed and 30,000 Native Americans. This doesn't include diseases and starvation.

Surprisingly, Indian raids west of the Mississippi began with the encroachment of trappers, miners and settlers, including wagon trains along the trail system west of the Mississippi River from 1804 to 1838. Most direct confrontations involved the theft of horses and food and supplies during the night. It wasn't uncommon for the Native Americans to follow the wagon trains hoping find an opportunity to steal a horse or two. Many begged for tobacco, ammunition and food, especially the Snake Indians along the Idaho and Oregon border. Most wagon masters accommodated their requests as to avoid exacerbating a conflict. There were some documented raids and massacres on both sides however; diaries of those traveling the trails claimed most didn't see any Native American Indians during their trip. Wagon trains traveled in large caravans which deterred small raiding parties from attacking.

Most of the Indian wars were the result of the U.S. Government forcing tribes onto reservations, violation of treaties by both sides, and encroachment by settlers onto Native lands designated by treaty. With dozens or hundreds of different tribal entities in America, each had their own leader or Chief. It was difficult to negotiate with so many tribes and leaders. Specific bands or war parties emerged who refused to accept the terms and conditions of any treaty entered into by their appointed Chief of the tribe or by the U.S. Government.

Most of the conflicts occurred along the border of Mexico. Arizona engaged in 310 battles with over 4,340 Native Americans, soldiers and civilians killed.

Native America Reservations

As was customary at the time, many white settlers who traveled the Oregon Trail or Santa Fe Trail maintained accurate journals and diaries. The same was true for many of the trappers and guides. During the Civil War, the Indian Wars increased, mostly in the southwest due partly as a result of settlers moving into Texas after the Mexican-American War. Land was cheap in Texas and the Southwest, with large parcels of land was available for cattle ranches just for staking. This region of America was mostly hot an arid and not suitable as agricultural land, but ideal for cattle, cotton and corn. The Apache and Comanche of the desert southwest increased their raids on ranches while stealing horses and cattle, knowing that law enforcement by the U.S. Military was nonexistent due to the Civil War. Ranchers established militia's and in Texas, the Texas Rangers. Gold was found in the Black Hills of the Dakota's and the Fort Laramie Treaty of 1851 was not enforced. The same situation occurred in Oregon, Idaho and California during the Snake Wars. The Treaty of Fort Laramie in 1851 between the U.S. Government and the Sioux, Cheyenne, Arapahos and the Crow, created tribal zones that allowed the construction of roads and trading posts on tribal land. The same agreement was offered along the Santa Fe Trail as well for safe passage of wagon trains by the Apache, Comanche and Navajo. However, in Utah, the Mormon migration established trails and settlements on land without the federal government acquiring legal ownership from the Ute Native American tribe. In 1849, the Ute and the U.S. Government entered into a Peace Treaty. Abraham Lincoln would establish the

Uintah Reservation in 1865, which remains today's.

One of the Provisions in the Fort Laramie Treaty gave the tribal entities a ten year annual monetary compensation for damages done to tribal lands by those traveling through the tribal reservation. In some cases, Native American's were given the option of not moving onto reservation land if they accepted 640 acres of land in exchange for leaving the tribal lands and not accepting food or other compensations. They were to pledge to honor Federal and State Laws. While the terms and conditions seem fair, it opened the door to unscrupulous speculators, politicians and carpet baggers who took advantage of the less sophisticated victims. In Mississippi, fraudulent land claims reached 3,800,000 acres, in which speculators swindled land from the American Natives and leaving most homeless. It is one reason the Seminole's resisted moving to the reservation in Oklahoma with little option other than relocation.

Thomas Jefferson was the first President to establish Native American's right to from independent Nations for the indigenous Native tribe which shielded them from State laws. He established the Creek and Seminole nation for the purpose of stabilizing peace in the American Southeast, principally in Georgia, Alabama and Florida. Jefferson's plan for an independent Indian Nation ended with Jackson's Indian Removal Act of 1830, which lead to the Trail of Tears as previously mentioned. The Bureau of Indian Affairs was established in March of 1824, under James Monroe's Presidency. Politicians in Washington had long held the position that the United States had an obligation to negotiate treaties with Native Americans, as if they were a foreign entity and the land rightly belonged to the indigenes tribes. Jackson disagreed, and refused to enter into treaties with American Natives, but rather instituted policies to force compliance to State and Federal Law. While many at the time believed they understood the Native American's and their way of life, however in reality, they had little cultural knowledge of the Native American's life and culture. The concept of reservations was a failure to the Native tribes who were nomadic, such as those in the west and mid-west who moved from summer ranges to winter ranges and followed the migration of game. Reservations did not accommodate the nomadic lifestyle. With the depletion of the wildlife, especially the plains buffalo and the inability to migrate, it caused widespread starvation. The indigenous tribes of the mid-west were not farmers, but hunter and gatherers. The reservations allocated to Native American's were not suitable for agriculture and had little value for industry, mining or forest land. To solve the problem, the U.S. Government supplied food through agents working for the Bureau of Indian Affairs. Widespread corruption became common and much of the food never reached the reservation or was spoiled in transit. About 60 percent of Native American's do not live on reservations today. [73]

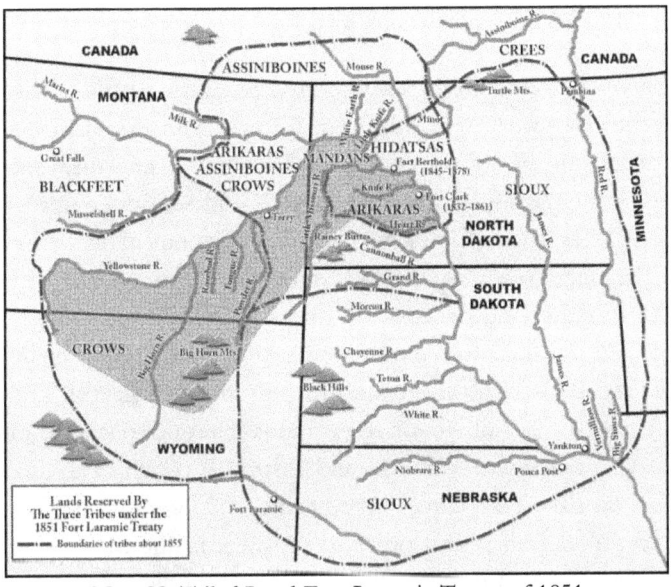

Map 22, Tribal Land Fort Laramie Treaty of 1851

Chief Sitting Bull
(1831 – 1890)

Over 50% of the Indian battles took place in Arizona, Texas and New

Mexico from 1864 to 1890. In 1877, Chief Joseph of the Nez Perce in Eastern Oregon, Washington and Idaho refused to be relocated to the reservation. The 200 warriors battled 2,000 U.S. soldiers over an area that extended 1,200 miles to the Canadian border in Montana. They were eventually captured in the battle of Bear Paw in 1877. While the Nez Perce were engaged in their own battle 1876, Colonel Custer was defeated in the Battle of Little Big Horn in Montana by Sitting Bull and Crazy Horse. Sitting Bull and his son, "Crow Foot", were killed in 1890, over a gun battle with reservation police. The Federal Agent, James McLaughlin, ordered Sitting Bull's arrest under the suspicion that he was planning to leave the Reservation with a group of Indian Cloud Dancers. [71] [53]

Chief Red Cloud
(1822 – 1890)

Although Chief Red Cloud was not involved in the Battle of Little Big Horn, he and several delegates went to meet with President Grant to help defuse the tensions in the Dakota Territory over settlers squatting on reservation land and hunting game. Gold was discovered in the Black Hills and Red Cloud wanted the Government to enforce the Fort Laramie Treaty of 1851. Grant offered the Oglala Lakota's $25,000 for the land occupied by the settlers and squatters, but the Lakota refused the offer. Red Cloud would devote the remainder of his life try to enforce the Treaties forced upon the Lakota Tribe. In his life time, he would see the reservations that once occupied most of the Dakota's, western Montana and eastern Wyoming be reduced to an area the size of a county in the Dakota's. Upon his death in 1909, the New York Times and other newspapers in the east praised Red Cloud for efforts to negotiate peace without conflict. Red Cloud was the most photographed Native American in American history. The Pine Ridge Reservation in the Dakota's is Red Clouds lasting legacy for his people and his final resting place.

One of his famous quotes:

"They made us many promises, more than I can remember. But they kept but one -- They promised to take our land ... and they took it."

The last major armed conflict with Native Americans was Wounded Knee Massacre in 1890 in the Dakota's. The 7th Cavalry set-out to disarm a Sioux in the reservation, which led to massacre of 150 Sioux men, women and children. [72]

The American Railroad Empire

Perhaps out of a course of necessity, during the Civil War of the 1860's, are the railroads miles that doubled. The U.S. Government offered generous incentives to Companies to construct railroads from the mid-west to San Francisco and as a result of the gold rush in California and the silver mines in Nevada, large land grants were issued to railroads to expand routes west which helped finance construction projects. As a result, small towns in the mid-west were connected in a network that allowed farmers to ship cattle and grain east and west to markets. The Northern Pacific would connect to Seattle in 1883. The Atchison & Topeka would extend its line to Santa Fe in 1880. The Southern Pacific of the San Joaquin Valley of California headed west and connected to El Paso, Texas in 1882. Time zones were established in 1876 as a result of the transcendental railway system. In addition, the gauge size of railroad tracks were standardized, which allowed trains to connect to a network of connecting cities throughout America. Other changes to the trains were made which made them safer and more comfortable for transporting passengers. The Central Overland California and Pikes Peak Express Company began pony express service using a 125 pound rider and small quarter horses that followed the Oregon Trail and connected to the Mormon Trail route to Sacramento and San Francisco in April of 1860. They advertised express mail service in 10 days from Kansas to San Francisco. Along the route, 186 stations were placed 10 mile apart to exchange horses. The company purchased 400 horses for the express service and stabled them along the route. While the pony express service was successful logistic wise, it was not profitable after railroad service replaced express mail service and they lost the Postal Service contract. Pony express service only lasted one year, from 1860 to 1861. Wells Fargo Stage Company acquired the pony express logo in 1866. Towns sprang-up throughout the mid-west as a result of the land grant given to the railroads. [73]

Cornelius Vanderbilt
(1794 – 1877)

Vanderbilt was born in Staten Island, New York in 1794. At the age of 11, he purchased a small shallow draft boat for $100 and opened a ferry service when he was 16. Father and younger brother were partners and it was agreed that he received half of the profits from the ferry service between Staten Island and Manhattan Island. At the age of 19, he married his first cousin, Sophia and had 13 children. He would later captain a steamship owned by Thomas Gibbons, between New Jersey and New York while continuing to operate his ferry system with his brother.

When gold was discovered in California in 1849, he commanded a steamship from the East Coast to San Francisco. By 1853, he bought out his competitors in the Steamship business in New England and controlled a monopoly in steamship trade to California.

Vanderbilt wasn't content controlling the Steamship trade; he purchased the New York and Harlem Railroad in 1863. The New York and Hrlem Railroad was considered a "white elephant" that drained money and showed little profit for the cost and effort, however, he was able to make it profitable after one year. He acquired the Erie Railroad, Central Railroad of New Jersey and Hartford and New Haven as well. He connected the railroads by building the Manhattan Station on 26th Street in New York City. He later acquired the New York Central, Hudson River Railroad and Lake Shore and Michigan Southern Railway in 1869. That same year he built the Grand Central Depot on 42nd Street in Manhattan.

By 1869, Vanderbilt had a monopoly over steamship trade to the West Coast and most of the ferry and steamship trade in New England. In addition, he had a monopoly of the railroads in the region. He purchased large amounts of real estate in Manhattan and Staten Island. Vanderbilt became the wealthiest man in the world by 1870. He was an active philanthropist, giving millions to churches in New York and the Vanderbilt University in Nashville, Tennessee. Although his family was active members of the Episcopal Church, he remained a member of the Moravian Church his entire life.

Cornelius Vanderbilt died at the age of 82 on January 4, 1877 in New York after being confined to bed for eight months. Even after giving millions to charities, he had a net worth of $100 million, equivalent to 147 billion dollars today. He gave $2 million to each of his children except William who received $100 million and his entire business ventures to manage. [70]

DOUGLAS G. BEAUDOIN

Epilogue

Volume I of "American Legacy" covers 385 years of American history from the arrival of Columbus to President Grant's tenure as President in 1877. Volume II continues another 141 years beginning with Rutherford B. Hayes' Presidency to President Trump's presidential victory in 2016. American Legacy continues through history with the Spanish American War, World War I and II, the Great Depression, Korean and Vietnam Wars and may more events that redirected and reshaped America's domestic and national policies.

The Civil Rights movement of 1964 would once again raise the issue of separate yet equal, segregation and civil rights. Vietnam War would divide the nation along political lines and America's role as a globally leader which would questioned during the Iran Contra Affair and the secret and clandestine wars in Laos, Cambodia and Central America. Political parties were once again altering political ideology in an effort to gain a political advantage over the other. Even though the events have changed, history has repeated itself over and over with only a change in circumstances and a different foreign policy.

In volume 1, I discussed the numerous panics, depressions and recessions that threaten our capitalist system and often leaving America in constant flux of boom and bust. In addition, the issue of a Central Bank became a hotly debated issue throughout history until 1913 when the Federal Reserve Bank was established under President Wilson's presidency. However, it didn't resolve the boom and bust periods, it only extended the periods between each event.

Volume II continues to explore the legacies of those who have contributed to society in different ways from those of the past. It once was relatively uncomplicated but yet very complicated. During the early years of America, issues were just as emotional as they are today other than the issue of slavery. In early American history, a single individual could effect change by discovering new territories, discovering new oceans and inventing new products. By the late 20th and 21st centuries, fewer and fewer individuals established that type of a lasting legacy. Advancement in cyber technology didn't replace Alexander Graham Bell's telephone phone but rather improved upon an existing idea. By the late 20th century, America became part of a global trading community that promoted the exchange of new ideas and technology for profit.

The issue over media is here to stay; the constitution guaranties it. It becomes the only life line between a bureaucracy in crisis and the public's desire to know. Benjamin Franklin used his newspaper to discredit Washington and his presidency in 1789.

The issue of immigration has been an ongoing issue since President John Adams signed the first **Alien and Sedition Acts in July of 1798.** However, later be nullified. Nearly every president since and passed instituted some form of legislation addressing immigration. As with most everything in history, it repeats itself. Immigration laws are particularly important in American history since America was founded on the principals of immigration and the workforce it provided to advance industrialization and agriculture for a better society. The delicate balance lies between what is moral, politically and constitutionally legal and the intellect to know the difference. The Statue of Liberty in New York harbor eloquently declares the principals that built America in poetic style:

"Give me your tired, your poor your huddled masses yearning to breathe free, The wretched refuse of your teeming shore, Send these, the homeless, tempest-tost to me, I lift my lamp beside the golden door!" - **By Emma Lazarus**

DOUGLAS G. BEAUDOIN

APPENDIX A

THE ARCTICLES AND AMENDMENTS
TO THE CONSTITUTION

Article I - The Legislative Branch

<u>Article I, Section 1</u>
Establishes the <u>legislature</u> -- Congress -- as the first of the three branches of government

<u>Article I, Section 2</u>
Defines the <u>House of Representatives</u>

<u>Article I, Section 3</u>
Defines the <u>Senate</u>

<u>Article I, Section 4</u>
Defines how members of Congress are to be elected, and how often Congress must meet

<u>Article I, Section 5</u>
Establishes procedural rules of Congress

<u>Article I, Section 6</u>
Establishes that members of Congress will be paid for their service, that members cannot be detained while traveling to and from meetings of Congress, and that members can hold no other elective office while serving in Congress

<u>Article I, Section 7</u>
Defines the legislative process -- <u>how bills become laws</u>

<u>Article I, Section 8</u>
Defines the <u>powers of Congress</u>

<u>Article I, Section 9</u>
Defines the legal limitations on Congress' powers

Article I, Section 10
Defines specific powers denied to the states

Article II -- The Executive Branch

Article II, Section 1

Establishes the offices of the President and Vice President, establishes the Electoral College

Article II, Section 2
Defines the powers of the President and establishes the President's Cabinet

Article II, Section 3
Defines miscellaneous duties of the President

Article II, Section 4
Addresses the removal from office of the President by impeachment

Article III -- The Judicial Branch

Article III, Section 1

Establishes the Supreme Court and defines the terms of service of all U.S. federal judges

Article III, Section 2
Defines the jurisdiction of the Supreme Court and lower federal courts, and guarantees trial by jury in criminal courts

Article III, Section 3
Defines the crime of treason

Article IV -- Concerning the States

Article IV, Section 1

Requires that each state must respect the laws of all other states

Article IV, Section 2
Ensures that citizens of each state will be treated fairly and equally in all states, and requires the interstate extradition of criminals

Article IV, Section 3
Defines how new states may be incorporated as part of the United States, and defines the control of federally-owned lands

Article IV, Section 4
Ensures each state a "Republican form of Government" (functioning as a representative democracy), and protection against invasion

Article V - Amendment Process

Defines the method of amending the Constitution

Article VI - Legal Status of the Constitution

Defines the Constitution as the supreme law of the United States

Article VII - Signatures

Amendments

The first 10 amendments are the Bill of Rights.

1st Amendment
Ensures the five basic freedoms: freedom of religion, freedom of speech, freedom of the press, freedom to assemble and freedom to petition the government to remedy ("redress") grievances

2nd Amendment
Ensures the right to own firearms (defined by the Supreme Court as an individual right) a well organized militia

3rd Amendment
Ensures private citizens that they cannot be forced to house U.S

.soldiers during peace

4th Amendment
Protects against police searches or seizures without a warrant issued by a court and based on probable cause

5th Amendment
Establishes the rights of citizens accused of crimes

6th Amendment
Establishes the rights of citizens in regard to trials and juries

7th Amendment
Guarantees the right to trial by jury in federal civil court cases

8th Amendment
Protects against "cruel and unusual" criminal punishments and extraordinarily large fines

9th Amendment
States that just because a right is not specifically listed in the Constitution, does not mean that right should not be respected

10th Amendment
States that powers not granted to the federal government are granted either to the states or the people (the basis of federalism)

11th Amendment
Clarifies the jurisdiction of the Supreme Court

12th Amendment
Redefines how the Electoral College chooses the President and Vice President

13th Amendment
Abolishes slavery in all states

14th Amendment
Guarantees citizens of all states rights on both the state and federal level

DOUGLAS G. BEAUDOIN

<u>15th Amendment</u>
Prohibits the use of race as a qualification to vote

<u>16th Amendment</u>
Authorizes the collection of income taxes

<u>17th Amendment</u>
Specifies that U.S. Senators will be elected by the people, rather than the state legislatures

<u>18th Amendment</u>
Prohibited the sale or manufacture of alcoholic beverages in the U.S. (Prohibition)

<u>19th Amendment</u>
Prohibited the use of gender as a qualification to vote (Women's Suffrage)

<u>20th Amendment</u>
Creates new starting dates for sessions of Congress, addresses the death of Presidents before they are sworn in

<u>21st Amendment</u>
Repealed the 18th Amendment

<u>22nd Amendment</u>
Limits to two the number of 4-year terms a President can serve.

<u>23rd Amendment</u>
Grants the District of Columbia three electors in the <u>Electoral College</u>

<u>24th Amendment</u>
Prohibits the charging of a tax (Poll Tax) in order to vote in federal elections

<u>25th Amendment</u>
Further clarifies the process of <u>presidential succession</u>

<u>26th Amendment</u>
Grants 18-year olds the right to vote

<u>27th Amendment</u>
Establishes that laws raising the pay of members of Congress cannot take effect until after an election

References

[1] Young, Alfred F (1999) The Shoemaker and the Tea Party, Boston Press ISBN 0-8070-5405-4 pg. 116
[2] Thomas R. Eddlem (2206) Author of the Preamble, lipdigital. US embassy.gov retrieved 9-11-2016
[3] Mount, S. (2010). Constitutional topic: due process. Retrieved February 23, 2011 from http://www.usconstitution.net/consttop_duep.html
[4] Gaines, James R. *(2007).* For Liberty and Glory: Washington, La Fayette, and Their Revolutions. *W.W. Norton & Co.* ISBN 978-0-393-06138-3.
[5] John M. Taylor, *William Henry Seward: Lincoln's Right Hand*, p. 234.
[6] Smithsonian Magazine, "Myths of the American Revolution," Jan. 2010, John Ferling, retrieved 9/2016
[7] McNamara, Robert. "John Quincy Adams: Significant Facts and Brief Biography." Thought Co. https://www.thoughtco.com/john-quincy-adams-significant-facts-1773433 (accessed April 6, 2018).
[9] Wikipedia, Charles Wilson Peale, Friedrich Wilhelm von Steuben, retrieved 9/2016
[10] Leepson, Marc (2011). Lafayette: Lessons in Leadership From the Idealist General. *Palgrave Macmillan.* ISBN 978-0-230-10504-1 pg 176
[11] "Alexander Hamilton's Final Version of the Report on the Subject of Manufactures" 12/5/1791 Article, "What is Mercantilism" by Martin Kelly, retrieved 9/22/2016, http://founders.archives.gov

[12] Handy, Robert, T "A History of the Churches in U.S. and Canada", New York, Oxford University Press, 1977
[13] A History of the United States, by Charles A. Goodrich, 1857
[20] Wikipedia, James Madison, "Father of the Constitution" retrieved 10/2/2017, William Pierce
[21] *Hutchinson, William T.; et al., eds. (1962).* "The Papers of James Madison". *University of Chicago Press.* Retrieved February 16, 2017.
[22] "Iowa's Redistricting Process: An Example of the Right Way to Draw Legislative". *Centrists.Org. 22 July 2004. Archived from* the original *on 7 November 2009.* Retrieved 5 August 2009. Retrived Wikipedia, 9/4/17
[23] *Jewett, James C. (1908). "The United States Congress of 1817 and Some of its Celebrities". Pg. 143 The William and Mary Quarterly.* **17** *(2): 139.* ISSN 0043-5597. JSTOR 1916057. doi:10.2307/1916057.
[24] Rafuse, Ethan S. (June 12, 2006). *"John C. Calhoun: He Started the Civil War".* Historynet. *Retrieved May 1, 2016. Wikipedia John C. Calhoun Retreived Oct. 10, 2017*
[25] Chitwood, Oliver Perry (1964) [Orig. 1939, Appleton-Century]. John Tyler, Champion of the Old South. Russell & Russell. *OCLC 424864. Page 270*
[26] Grant, Ulysses S. *(1892) [1885].* Personal Memoirs of U. S. Grant. *1. C. L. Webster. pp. 146–147.* Wikipedia, retrieved Nov. 15, 2017
[27] Ove Jensen, Horseshoe Bend National Military Park.
[28] DeGregorio, William A. "The Complete Book of U.S. Presidents, 7th ed. Fort Lee: Barricade Books, 2009

[29] "Jefferson Davis, American" by William Cooper
[30] Philosophical Library (2010). "The Wisdom of Abraham Lincoln". Open Road Media. p. 1828. ISBN *1-4532-0281-1*.

[31] Basler, Roy P., ed. (1953). pg. 255 "The Collected Works of Abraham Lincoln". **5**. Rutgers University Press.
[32] Jaffa, Harry V. (2000). A New Birth of Freedom: Abraham Lincoln and the Coming of the Civil War. PP 247-248 Rowman & Littlefield. ISBN 0-8476-9952-8.
[33] Keegan, John (2009). "The American Civil War: A Military" Pg. 57, History. New York: Alfred A. Knopf. ISBN 978-0-307-26343-8.
[34] "Civil War Casualties." HistoryNet. Accessed January 13, 2018. http://www.historynet.com/civil-war-casualties.
[35] "10 Facts: Civil War Navies." Civil War Trust. Accessed January 14, 2018. https://www.civilwar.org/learn/articles/10-facts-civil-war-navies.
[36] "Emancipation Proclamation." Wikipedia. January 13, 2018. Accessed January 17, 2018. https://en.wikipedia.org/wiki/Emancipation_Proclamation.
[37] "Battle of Gettysburg." Wikipedia. January 11, 2018. Accessed January 18, 2018. https://en.wikipedia.org/wiki/Battle_of_Gettysburg.
[38] *Thomas, Benjamin P.* (2008) pg 315. Abraham Lincoln: A Biography. Southern Illinois University. *ISBN 978-0-8093-2887-1*.
[39] Nevins, Ordeal of the Union (. *Nevins, Allan (1947–71). Ordeal of the Union;* Vol. IV), pp. 6–178 *vol. Scribner's*. ISBN 978-0-684-10416-4.
[40] (john@spartacus-educational.com), John Simkin. Spartacus Educational. Accessed January 22, 2018. http://spartacus-educational.com/USAkkk.htm.
[41] "Carpetbagger." Wikipedia. January 12, 2018. Accessed January 22, 2018. https://simple.wikipedia.org/wiki/Carpetbagger.
[42] "Reconstruction (1865–1877)." SparkNotes. Accessed January 25, 2018. http://www.sparknotes.com/history/american/reconstruction/.
[43] "Ku Klux Klan." Wikipedia. January 24, 2018. Accessed January 25, 2018. https://en.wikipedia.org/wiki/Ku_Klux_Klan.
[44] "McClellan's War-Winning Strategy." HistoryNet. November 01, 2017. Accessed January 28, 2018. http://www.historynet.com/mcclellans-war-winning-strategy.htm.
[45] "Tag Archives: John McClernand." Emerging Civil War. Chick, Sean M. Accessed January 30, 2018. https://emergingcivilwar.com/tag/john-mcclernand/.
[46] "Ulysses S. Grant." Wikipedia. January 28, 2018. Accessed January 30, 2018. https://en.wikipedia.org/wiki/Ulysses_S._Grant.
[47] "Ulysses S. Grant, a drunken fighting machine from American history." Lords of the Drinks. March 26, 2015.] Bumbar, Micky. Accessed January 30, 2018. https://lordsofthedrinks.com/2015/01/26/ulysses-s-grant-a-drunken-fighting-machine-from-american-history/.
[48] "Ulysses S. Grant." Wikipedia. January 21, 2018. Accessed January 22, 2018. https://en.wikipedia.org/wiki/Ulysses_S._Grant.
[49] "Wild Bill Hickok." Wikipedia. February 18, 2018. Accessed February 21, 2018. https://en.wikipedia.org/wiki/Wild_Bill_Hickok.
[50] "Jim Bridger." Wikipedia. February 18, 2018. Accessed February 21, 2018. https://en.wikipedia.org/wiki/Jim_Bridger.
[51] "Kit Carson." Wikipedia. February 18, 2018. Accessed February 21, 2018. https://en.wikipedia.org/wiki/Kit_Carson.

[52] "Oregon Trail." Wikipedia. February 18, 2018. Accessed February 21, 2018. https://en.wikipedia.org/wiki/Oregon_Trail.
[53] "George Armstrong Custer." Wikipedia. February 20, 2018. Accessed February 21, 2018. https://en.wikipedia.org/wiki/George_Armstrong_Custer.
[54] "Sitting Bull." Wikipedia. February 18, 2018. Accessed February 21, 2018. https://en.wikipedia.org/wiki/Sitting_Bull.
[55] "Abraham Lincoln." Wikipedia. December 29, 2017. Accessed December 29, 2017. https://en.wikipedia.org/wiki/Abraham_Lincoln.
[56] "Christopher Columbus." Wikipedia. December 27, 2017. Accessed December 29, 2017. https://en.wikipedia.org/wiki/Christopher_Columbus.
[57] "George Washington." Wikipedia. December 29, 2017. Accessed December 29, 2017. https://en.wikipedia.org/wiki/George_Washington.
[58] "James K. Polk." Wikipedia. December 28, 2017. Accessed December 29, 2017. https://ast.wikipedia.org/wiki/James_K._Polk.
[59] "James Otis, Jr." Wikipedia. November 27, 2017. Accessed December 29, 2017. https://en.wikipedia.org/wiki/James_Otis,_Jr.
[60] "Juan Ponce de León." Wikipedia. December 29, 2017. Accessed December 29, 2017. https://en.wikipedia.org/wiki/Juan_Ponce_de_Le%C3%B3n.
[61] "Robert E. Lee." Wikipedia. January 20, 2018. Accessed January 22, 2018. https://en.wikipedia.org/wiki/Robert_E._Lee.
[62] "Ulysses S. Grant's Lifelong Struggle With Alcohol." HistoryNet. August 05, 2016. Accessed January 22, 2018. http://www.historynet.com/ulysses-s-grants-lifelong-struggle-with-alcohol.htm.
[63] "Clara Barton." Wikipedia. February 23, 2018. Accessed February 25, 2018. https://en.wikipedia.org/wiki/Clara_Barton.
[64] "What Was the Dominion of New England?" History of Massachusetts. January 14, 2018. Accessed February 28, 2018. http://historyofmassachusetts.org/what-was-the-dominion-of-new-england/. Rebecca Beatrice Brooks January 11, 2016
[65] "Province of New Hampshire." Wikipedia. February 22, 2018. Accessed February 28, 2018. https://en.wikipedia.org/wiki/Province_of_New_Hampshire.
[66] "Providence, Rhode Island." Wikipedia. February 25, 2018. Accessed February 28, 2018. https://en.wikipedia.org/wiki/Providence,_Rhode_Island.
[67] "Connecticut Colony." Wikipedia. February 25, 2018. Accessed February 28, 2018. https://en.wikipedia.org/wiki/Connecticut_Colony.
[68] Coffman, Steve (2012). *Words of the Founding Fathers*. North Carolina: McFarland. p. 184. *ISBN 978-0-7864-5862-2*.
[69] "John Marshall." Wikipedia. February 27, 2018. Accessed March 01, 2018. https://en.wikipedia.org/wiki/John_Marshall.
[70] "Cornelius Vanderbilt." Wikipedia. March 16, 2018. Accessed March 23, 2018. https://en.wikipedia.org/wiki/Cornelius_Vanderbilt.
[71] "Sitting Bull." Wikipedia. March 17, 2018. Accessed March 23, 2018. https://en.wikipedia.org/wiki/Sitting_Bull.
[72] "Red Cloud." Wikipedia. March 16, 2018. Accessed March 23, 2018. https://en.wikipedia.org/wiki/Red_Cloud.
[73] "Indian Reservation." Wikipedia. March 18, 2018. Accessed March 23, 2018. https://en.wikipedia.org/wiki/Indian_reservation.
[74] "Oregon Trail." Wikipedia. March 21, 2018. Accessed March 23, 2018. https://en.wikipedia.org/wiki/Oregon_Trail.
[75] "Indian Removal Act." Wikipedia. March 16, 2018. Accessed March 23, 2018.

https://en.wikipedia.org/wiki/Indian_Removal_Act.
[76] "Andrew Jackson." Wikipedia. March 18, 2018. Accessed March 23, 2018. https://en.wikipedia.org/wiki/Andrew_Jackson.
[76] "Abraham Lincoln." Wikipedia. December 29, 2017. Accessed December 29, 2017. https://en.wikipedia.org/wiki/Abraham_Lincoln.
[77] blank
[78] "George Washington." Wikipedia. December 29, 2017. Accessed December 29, 2017. https://en.wikipedia.org/wiki/George_Washington.
[79] "James Otis, Jr." Wikipedia. November 27, 2017. Accessed December 29, 2017. https://en.wikipedia.org/wiki/James_Otis,_Jr.
[80] The Inauguration of George Washington, 1789. Accessed March 24, 2018. http://www.eyewitnesstohistory.com/washingtoninaug.htm.
[81] "Was Manhattan Really Bought for $24?" Mental Floss. October 02, 2012. Accessed March 28, 2018. http://mentalfloss.com/article/12657/was-manhattan-really-bought-24.
[82] Stegmaier, Mark J. (September 1985). *"Intensifying the Sectional Conflict: William Seward versus James Hammond in the Lecompton Debate of 1858"*. Pg 205-205, Civil War History. Kent State University Press. **31** (3): 197–221. *doi:10.1353/cwh.1985.0038.*
[83] Remini, Robert V. (1984). Andrew Jackson and the Course of American Democracy, Pg 218-219. 1833–1845. New York: Harper & Row Publishers, Inc. *ISBN 0-8018-5913-1.*
[84] Taylor, John M. (1991). William Henry Seward: Lincoln's Right Hand. Pg 188-189 Washington, DC: Brassey's. ISBN 978-1-57488-119-6.
[85] "William H. Seward." Wikipedia. April 03, 2018. Accessed April 04, 2018. https://en.wikipedia.org/wiki/William_H._Seward.
[86] Ambrose, Stephen E. *(1996).* Undaunted Courage: Meriwether Lewis, Thomas Jefferson, and the Opening of the American West..pg. 94 *Simon and Schuster, New York. p. 511.* ISBN 9780684811079.
[87] "Sacagawea." Wikipedia. April 09, 2018. Accessed April 11, 2018. https://en.wikipedia.org/wiki/Sacagawea.
[88] Petting, Tejvan, "Biography of Fredrick Douglass", Oxford, UK, 23 January 2014 www.biographyonline.net
[89] Frederick Douglass, Narrative of the Life of Frederick Douglass, An American Slave, *p. 126.*
[90] Fredrick Douglass, "The Life and times of Fredrick Douglass (1892), Part 2, Chapter 12: Hope of a Nation.
[91] Cherokee Nation official website Archived October 9, 2008, at the Wayback Machine. John Burnett's Story of the Trail of Tears
[92] Johnson, Timothy D., *Winfield Scott* (Lawrence, Kansas: University of Kansas Press, 1998), 1.
[93] Fanny J. Crosby: An Autobiography (Peabody, Massachusetts: Hendrickson Publishers Marketing, 2013 printing), p. 88, ISBN 978-1-59856-281-1.
[94] Leepson, Marc (2011). Lafayette: Lessons in Leadership From the Idealist General. Pg.172 Palgrave Macmillan. ISBN 978-0-230-10504-1.
[95] http://www.duhc.org/page/the-hidden-history-of, retrieved May6, 2018 Democracy Unlimited

[96] http://reclaimdemocracy.org/corporate-accountability-history-corporations-us/ retrieved May 7, 2018

[1-1] "Christopher Columbus." Wikipedia. December 27, 2017. Accessed December 29, 2017.
https://en.wikipedia.org/wiki/Christopher_Columbus.

[1-2] "Juan Ponce de León." Wikipedia. December 29, 2017. Accessed December 29, 2017.
https://en.wikipedia.org/wiki/Juan_Ponce_de_Leon

[1-3] "Roanoke Colony." Wikipedia. December 27, 2017. Accessed December 30, 2017.
https://en.wikipedia.org/wiki/Roanoke_Colony.

[1-4] "Plymouth Colony." Wikipedia. December 27, 2017. Accessed December 30, 2017.
https://en.wikipedia.org/wiki/Plymouth_Colony.

[1-5] "Puritan migration to New England (1620–1640)." Wikipedia. December 19, 2017. Accessed December 30, 2017.
https://en.wikipedia.org/wiki/Puritan_migration_to_New_England_(1620%E2%80%931640).

[1-6] "William Penn." Wikipedia. December 28, 2017. Accessed December 30, 2017.
https://en.wikipedia.org/wiki/William_Penn.

[1-7] "American colonies." Wikipedia. December 14, 2017. Accessed December 30, 2017.
https://en.wikipedia.org/wiki/American_colonies.

ABOUT THE AUTHOR

Douglas G. Beaudoin is an avid follower of American history. Born in Portland, Oregon in 1946, his family moved to Alaska to homestead in 1961. He served four years in the U.S. Navy from 1966 to 1970. He attended the University of Alaska in the 1970's and retired from Alaska State Service in 2000. He currently devotes much of his retirement writing books about Alaska, Asian and American history.

www.ingramcontent.com/pod-product-compliance
Lightning Source LLC
Chambersburg PA
CBHW071643090426
42738CB00009B/1412